MW01703369

PRENTICE HALL

RCT for NEW YORK STATE Science Review

O R D E R

Send orders to:

PRENTICE HALL SCHOOL DIVISION
CUSTOMER SERVICE CENTER
4350 Equity Drive
P.O. Box 2649
Columbus, OH 43216 *OR*

CALL TOLL-FREE: 1-800-848-9500 (8:00 AM–4:30 PM)

- Orders processed with your call. Please include the ISBN number on the back cover when ordering.
- **Your price includes all shipping and handling.**
- Prentice Hall also publishes science textbooks for the middle and junior high school, as well as high school textbooks and *Brief Reviews* that help you meet the requirements of the New York State Regents in: • Earth Science • Biology • Chemistry • Physics

PRENTICE HALL

RCT for NEW YORK STATE Science Review

SECOND EDITION

Carl M. Raab

Assistant Principal—Science Supervision
Fort Hamilton High School
Brooklyn, New York

David R. Kiefer

Assistant Principal—Physical Science
Midwood High School at Brooklyn College
Brooklyn, New York

Needham, Massachusetts • Prentice Hall • Englewood Cliffs, New Jersey

Credits

Editorial Development Roland E. Boucher, Lois B. Arnold
Marketing Direction Arthur C. Germano, Michael Buckley
Director of Production David Graham
Production Buyer Jo-Ann Connolly
Senior Copy Editor Virginia Shine
Design Direction L. Christopher Valente
Senior Designer Jack Pollard
Manufacturing Buyer Valerie Rhoades

Cover Design: Richard Hannus, Betty Fiora
Contributing Writer: David Marshak

Lab Safety table on page 144 adapted from *Science Safety* by permission of the Board of Education of the City of New York.

PRENTICE HALL
A Division of Simon & Schuster
Needham Heights, Massachusetts 02194
Englewood Cliffs, New Jersey 07632

ISBN 0-13-753823-5

Printed in the United States of America
1 2 3 4 5 6 7 8 99 98 97 96 95 94 93 92

ABOUT THIS BOOK

RCT Science Review for New York State provides a thorough review of the 7th, 8th, and 9th grade science programs and intensive preparation for the Regents Competency Test in Science. The Regents Competency Test in Science is a survey test of the core process skills and core understandings contained in the ten blocks of the science syllabus for middle and junior high schools. Students are expected to pass the Regents Competency Test in Science in order to receive a high school diploma.

The following features of this book will be of particular interest to teachers and students.

1. Clear, concise explanations of the understandings, vocabulary, and science concepts required by the ten blocks of the middle/junior high syllabus for grades 7, 8, and 9. Life, earth, and physical science topics are covered equally. Many applications and examples are presented to clarify and reinforce learning.

2. Organization closely following the syllabus. Numbers in parentheses following each heading correlate sections of the text to the core understandings and process skills.

3. Emphasis on essential vocabulary. Important vocabulary terms are printed in **bold type** and clearly defined in the glossary.

4. An abundance of illustrations. Numerous drawings, charts, graphs, and tables supplement the text, each designed to help students visualize the concepts and understand the vocabulary.

5. A convenient arrangement of text and sample questions. Short sections of text are followed by RCT-type questions, testing knowledge (recall and recognition), comprehension, application, and the process skills. In all, there are more than 400 sample questions.

6. Features highlighting Science (process) Skills and Issues in Science, Technology, and Society. Each chapter contains one or more of these features.

7. A separate chapter on Science (process) Skills. This chapter further reinforces the 23 process skills that form the 7th, 8th, and 9th grade syllabus, with emphasis on the core skills that will be tested on the RCT in Science.

8. A section entitled "RCT Test-Taking Strategies." This section focuses on strategies for answering various types of questions and studying for the test.

9. Four complete tests. Practice Test 1, which has 60 questions, contains both answers and an explanation why the answer is correct. Practice Test 2, which has 60 questions, and Practice Tests 3 and 4, which have 70 questions each, do not contain answers in the text. Answers for these tests are provided in a separate answer key for teachers.

Contents

7 Energy and Motion

8 The Chemistry of Matter

9 Energy: Sources and Issues

10 Science, Technology, and Society

11 Science Skills

RCT Test-Taking Strategies

CHAPTER 1 Living Systems: Organisms

I. CHARACTERISTICS OF LIVING THINGS

1. Living Things and the Environment *(A1)*

All living things live in a set of surroundings, or **environment**. Some examples of different types of environments include an ocean, a lake, a tropical forest, a desert, and the soil. An organism's environment includes all the living and nonliving things in the surroundings that affect the way the organism lives and acts. The amount of water, the temperature, the amount of light, and the kinds of other living things available for food are examples of these environmental conditions.

Organisms (living things) depend upon the environment for survival. They take in food and oxygen from their environment and release waste products. Their survival involves a continuous exchange of materials with the environment in which they live.

Organisms carry on life activities in their environment. Table 1 lists some of the important life activities and their functions. If an organism stops these activities it becomes sick or dies.

Table 1 Life Activities

Activity	Function
Ingestion	Taking in food
Breathing	Taking in oxygen; releasing carbon dioxide
Digestion	Preparing food for use by cells
Transport	Distributing food and oxygen to all the cells
Cellular respiration	Releasing energy from food
Excretion	Producing and eliminating wastes
Regulation	Responding to changes in the environment
Reproduction	Producing more of one's own kind

2. Living Things Need Food *(A2, A16)*

All organisms need food to live. Some organisms, such as green plants, make their own food. Other organisms, such as animals, cannot make their own food and must obtain it from their environment. Green plants continually make and provide food for themselves as well as for animals.

Food provides energy for living things. The energy contained in food is used by organisms to carry on their life activities. Food also provides the materials needed for growth and repair.

The substances in food that provide energy and the materials for growth and repair are called **nutrients.** All foods contain one or more of the following nutrients: *carbohydrates, fats, proteins, minerals,* and *vitamins*.

Carbohydrates include *sugars* and *starch*. Carbohydrates are used by organisms for energy. Excess amounts of carbohydrates are changed to and stored as fat. Like carbohydrates, fats are used for energy. Before they can be used for energy, however, fats must first be changed back into sugars. Proteins in food are broken down into amino acids, which are used to build or repair the parts of living things.

Minerals are needed for normal growth and repair. Calcium and phosphorus are minerals needed for the formation of bones and teeth. Iron is needed for the production of red blood cells to carry oxygen to all the parts of the body. Vitamins are needed in very small amounts. They help living things use the other nutrients properly.

Science Skill

OBSERVING

A scientist closely observed a goldfish in an aquarium tank for 15 minutes. Then she listed the factors she observed that indicated that the goldfish was alive.

1. Make a list of some of the factors that you think appeared on the scientist's list.
2. Based on your own observations of some living things, describe how they are dependent on their environment.

3. Green Plants Make the Food *(A3)*

Green plants make food in a process called **photosynthesis**. Photosynthesis takes place in the leaves of the green plants. To carry on photosynthesis green plants need light energy, carbon dioxide, and water.

The light energy needed for photosynthesis comes from the sun. Sunlight is absorbed by **chlorophyll**, a green pigment found in leaves. The water needed for photosynthesis is absorbed by the green plant from the soil through the roots. Once absorbed by the roots, the water is carried through the plant stem to the leaves. The carbon dioxide needed for photosynthesis comes from the atmosphere. It enters the plant through tiny openings located on the underside of the leaves (Figure 1–1).

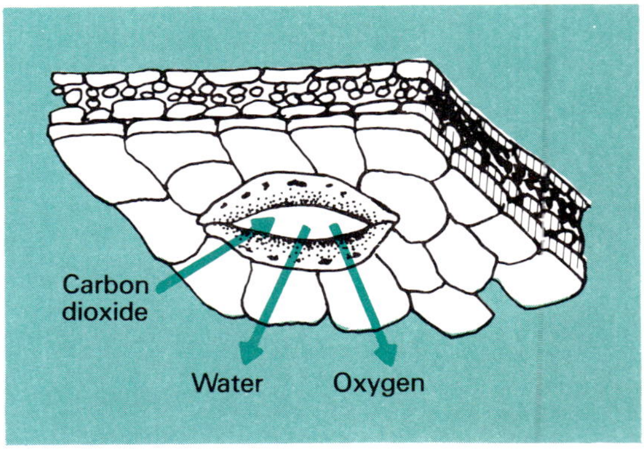

Figure 1–1. Gases pass in and out through tiny openings on the underside of the leaf.

In the leaves, in the presence of light energy, carbon dioxide and water combine during photosynthesis to produce food and oxygen (Figure 1–2). The food and oxygen made by the green plants are used by other green plants or by animals.

Figure 1–2. The process of photosynthesis.

Carbon Dioxide + Water + Sunlight $\xrightarrow{\text{Chlorophyll}}$ Sugar + Oxygen + Water

$$CO_2 + H_2O + \text{Light Energy} \xrightarrow{\text{Chlorophyll}} C_6H_{12}O_6 + O_2\uparrow + H_2O$$

4. Living Things Combine Food and Oxygen *(A4)*

All living things require energy to carry on their life functions. The food made available by the photosynthetic activities of the green plants provides this energy.

The food is processed and then distributed to all the cells. In the cells, energy is released from the food. This release of energy from food takes place during the process of **cellular respiration**. In cellular respiration the food combines with oxygen, and energy is released. Carbon dioxide and water are produced during cellular respiration as waste products (Figure 1–3).

To carry on cellular respiration, oxygen is required. Living things take in oxygen when they breathe. The oxygen is distributed to all the cells and then used during cellular respiration. Carbon dioxide and water, the waste products of cellular respiration, are returned to the environment during breathing.

5. Living Things Need Water *(A6)*

All living things contain water—in fact, they are 65%–95% water. Living

Figure 1–3. Cellular respiration.

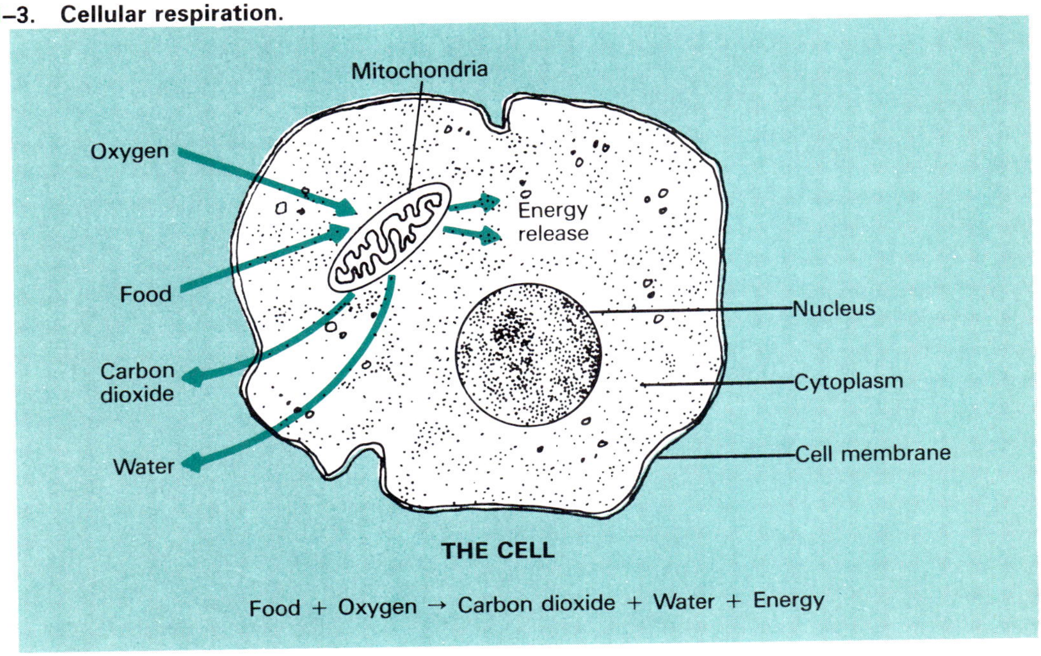

things constantly exchange water with the environment. (Fresh water is taken in and waste water is removed). Without this exchange of water living things die.

Water is needed in cells to dissolve materials. Only dissolved materials can be used in cells for energy and for growth and repair.

Water is needed by green plants for photosynthesis. Water combines with carbon dioxide during photosynthesis, and food and oxygen are produced.

Without water animals and plants become dehydrated. They are no longer able to carry on the chemical reactions essential for life.

INTERPRETING DATA

A scientist planted three identical tomato seedlings in flowerpots labeled 1, 2, and 3. Each pot contained the same amount and type of soil. The three planted seedlings were placed on the same window ledge to ensure that they were all kept at the same temperature and received equal amounts of sunlight.

Each time the seedlings were watered, pot 2 received twice as much water as pot 1. Pot 3 received three times as much water as pot 1.

At the end of each week the heights of the plants were measured and recorded in a data table. From the data, a graph was constructed. The graph shows the effect of varying amounts of water on tomato plant growth.

Data Table

Time	Height		
	Pot 1	**Pot 2**	**Pot 3**
1 week	1/2 cm	1/2 cm	3/4 cm
2 weeks	1 cm	1-1/4 cm	1-3/8 cm
3 weeks	1-1/2 cm	1-3/4 cm	2 cm

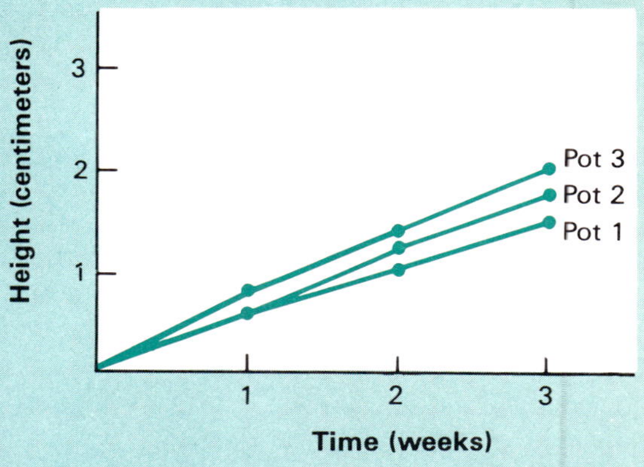

1. What environmental factors were kept constant in this experiment?
2. What environmental factors were varied in this experiment?
3. From the data shown in the data table and on the graph, what relationships exist between the amount of water and the rate of growth of tomato seedlings?
4. Suppose a fourth seedling were added, but that pot 4 received only half as much water as pot 1. How would you expect the rate of growth of this fourth seedling to compare with the rate of growth of the other seedlings? Why?

6. Living Things Respond to Stimuli *(A7)*

A change in the environment that causes an organism to react is called a **stimulus**. The reaction to a stimulus is known as the **response**. For example, if a person touches a hot stove (the stimulus), the reaction is pulling the hand away (the response). Table 2 lists some other examples of stimuli and responses in humans.

Table 2 Human Stimuli and Responses

Stimulus	Response
Unexpected loud noise	Jumping
Tiny object in eye	Blinking
Smell of food	Flowing saliva
High temperature	Sweating
Dust in nose	Sneezing

It is important for living things to be able to detect and respond to changes in their environment. This ability to respond enables living things to protect themselves, to avoid dangers, and to obtain what they need to survive.

7. Some Living Things Withstand Extreme Changes in the Environment *(A8)*

In some places the environment is very harsh and severe. In the desert, for example, it may be dry for many months. In other places on Earth the winters are very cold. In spite of these conditions, some living things manage to survive.

To survive in cold climates some living things, such as bears, may *hibernate*, or remain inactive during the winter. Other living things *migrate*—they move to another location to avoid the cold. For example, many kinds of birds migrate to warmer climates when winter comes.

In the desert, plants and animals survive by storing water. When the water shortage is severe some desert plants become *dormant*, or inactive. For example, to avoid long periods without water desert plants may turn to seed. The seeds grow once water returns.

Hibernation, migration, and dormancy are methods used by organisms to survive severe environmental changes.

8. Living Things Adjust to Their Environment *(A10)*

Living things must adjust for survival in the environment in which they live. They evolve with certain structures or patterns of behavior necessary for living in their surroundings. For example, a duck has webbed feet for swimming, a hawk has wings for flying, and a fish has gills for breathing under water. These structures are known as **adaptations**. Each living thing represents a collection of adaptations that fit it for survival in its **habitat**, the environment in which it lives. Figure 1-4 shows some organisms and their adaptations for survival.

9. Living Things Are Adapted for Survival *(A11)*

Living things are adapted for survival in particular environments. For example, to survive in the Arctic living things must be able to withstand very cold temperatures and lots of snow. The arctic hare thrives in the Arctic because it has a thick coat to survive the cold and its white fur matches the snow, making it less easily seen and eaten by its enemies.

To survive in the desert living things must be able to withstand high daytime

A B C

Figure 1–4. (A) The giraffe's long neck is an adaptation that allows it to feed on tree leaves. (B) The webbing of the frog's foot is an adaptation for swimming. (C) The hummingbird's long beak enables it to obtain nectar from flowers.

temperatures and water shortages. Cactus plants, for example, have adaptations that enable them to live in the desert. They have water-storing stems and spiny leaves that prevent water loss by evaporation. Desert animals adapt to their environment by storing water. Some desert animals become dormant during periods of drought or intense daytime heat. Some desert animals are sand-colored and blend into their desert surroundings, making them less visible to their enemies.

To survive life in aquatic environments, water-dwelling organisms may have a number of adaptations. Some water animals have gills to remove the oxygen dis-

Science Skill

DESCRIBING OBSERVATIONS

Each kind of organism is adapted for survival in its natural environment. Study the illustrations below, which show three different organisms. For each organism, name one adaptation and describe how it adapts the organism for survival.

Owl Pelican Duck

solved in water. Many water animals have fins for swimming and water-repellent scales. Some air-breathing aquatic animals, such as frogs and ducks, are adapted for swimming by having webs of skin between their toes.

Many plants and animals are adapted for life in the soil. The roots anchor plants in the soil and assist in the absorption of water. Worms have tiny grasping structures which, together with their muscles, enable them to move through the soil.

Birds and insects are adapted for survival in the air. Birds have hollow air-filled bones that make them light. Their feathers give their wings a large surface area for flight. Insects have light bodies with air tubes. Many insects are also equipped with wings for flight.

10. Living Things Reproduce

(A9, A17, A18)

Living things grow larger as they get older. Eventually they die. Yet there are always new generations to replace them. New generations come about as a result of a life process called **reproduction**. During reproduction, living things make more of their own kind. To put it another way, living things come from other living things. Humans produce new humans, wolves produce new wolves, and bean plants produce new bean plants.

Reproduction may be asexual or sexual. During **asexual reproduction** a new individual, or *offspring*, forms from a single parent. Offspring produced asexually are usually identical to the parent. Figure 1–5 shows three types of asexual reproduction.

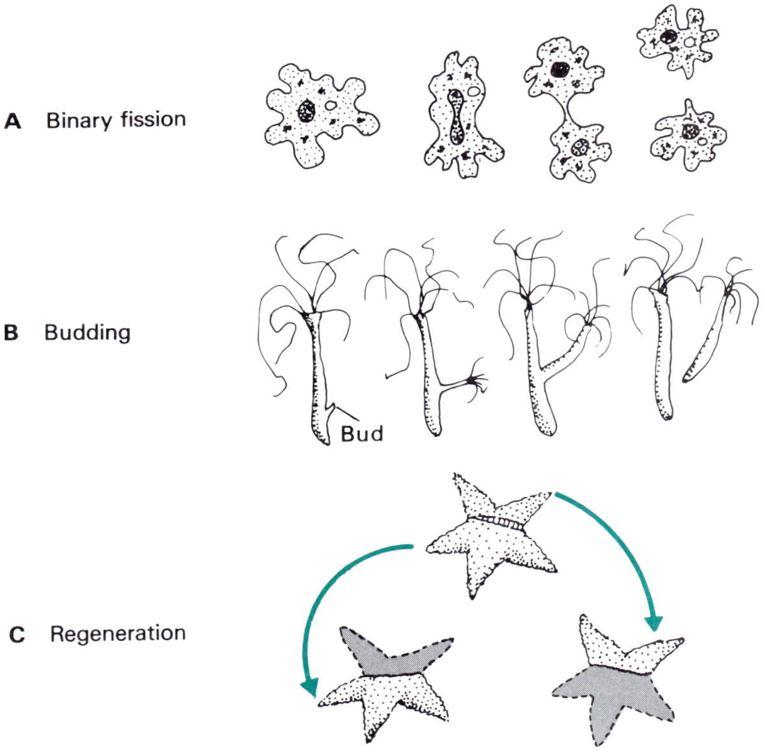

Figure 1–5. Asexual reproduction. (A) Binary fission in *Ameba*. (B) Budding in *Hydra*. (C) Regeneration in starfish.

Two parents are required for reproduction of most higher plants and animals. Reproduction that requires two parents is known as **sexual reproduction**. During sexual reproduction a sperm cell from the male parent unites with an egg from the female parent in a process called *fertilization* (Figure 1–6). The fertilized egg develops into a new individual.

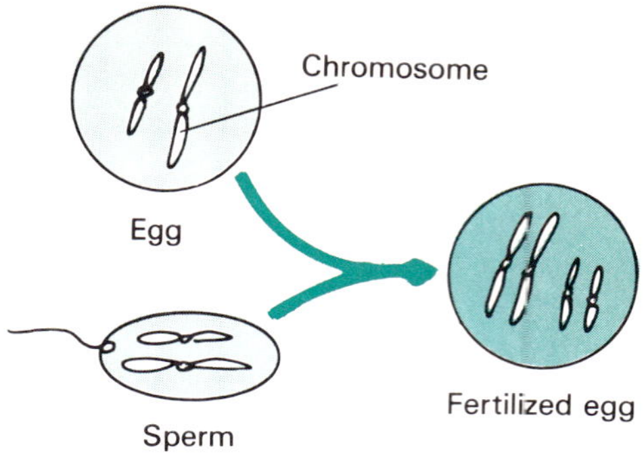

Figure 1–6. Fertilization.

The *life cycle* of an organism is the series of changes it goes through in its own development and in reproducing more of its own kind. Figure 1–7 shows the stages in the life cycle of a frog. Frog eggs are deposited by females in pond water in early spring. Sperm are also deposited in the pond by the males. The sperm swim to and fertilize nearby eggs. The fertilized eggs develop into tadpoles with gills and finlike tails. Eventually a jaw and legs develop. Then the gills and tail disappear and the adult frog is formed. As a result of life cycles such as this one, new generations of living things are produced.

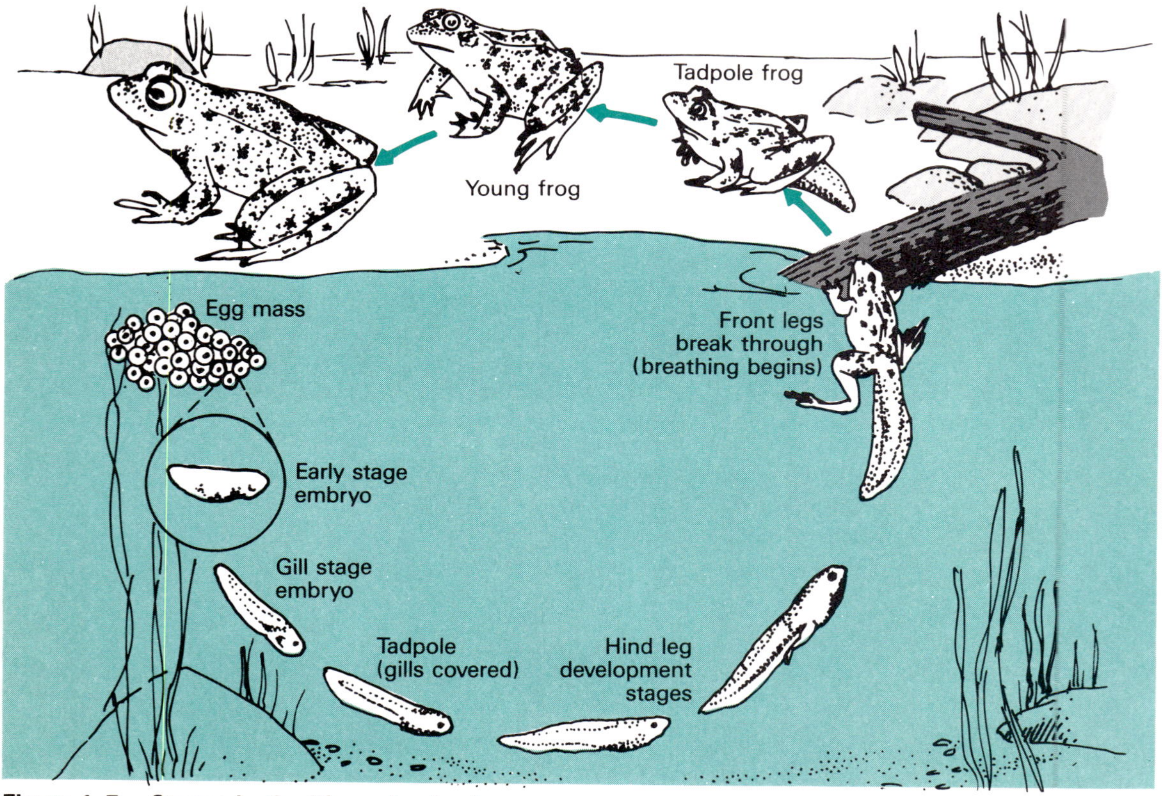

Figure 1–7. Stages in the life cycle of a frog.

Sample Questions

1. Which nutrient serves as a source of energy for living things?
(1) minerals (3) water
(2) vitamins (4) carbohydrates

2. Green plants are necessary for the survival of all living things because they
(1) release light energy
(2) produce food
(3) manufacture waste products
(4) bend toward the sunlight

3. Which of the following represents the word formula for photosynthesis?
(1) starch → many glucose molecules
(2) glucose + oxygen → carbon dioxide + water + energy
(3) carbon dioxide + water → glucose + oxygen
(4) fats → sugar molecules

4–5. Base your answers to questions 4 and 5 on the diagram below, which shows the three main parts of a plant.

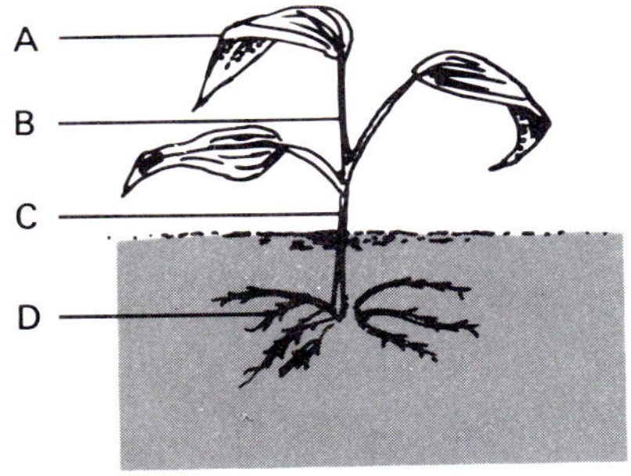

4. Most carbon dioxide enters the plant through
(1) A (2) B (3) C (4) D

5. Most photosynthesis occurs in part
(1) A (2) B (3) C (4) D

6. Which waste products are produced as a result of cellular respiration?
(1) glucose and starch
(2) water and carbon dioxide
(3) oxygen and carbon dioxide
(4) protein and fat

7. Which life activity is linked with carrying food and oxygen to all the cells?
(1) digestion (3) excretion
(2) breathing (4) transport

8–9. Base your answers to questions 8 and 9 on the graph below, which shows the effects of different-colored light on the rate of photosynthesis.

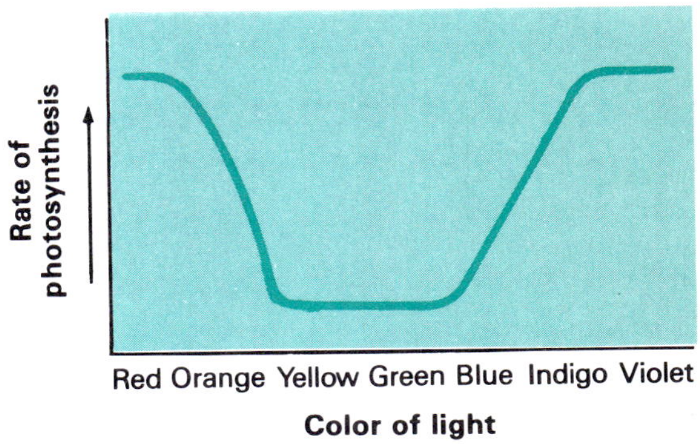

8. In which colors of light does photosynthesis occur best?
(1) green and yellow
(2) red and violet
(3) orange and yellow
(4) green and blue

9. A plant would probably grow the slowest under what color of light?
(1) red (3) green
(2) violet (4) blue

10. A biologist discovered a new plant with spiny leaves and a water-storing stem. Based on this description, one can conclude that this plant probably lives in a(n)
(1) ocean
(2) desert
(3) lake
(4) stream

11. When water is scarce, some plants turn to seed. This method of survival is called
(1) dormancy
(2) expectancy
(3) stagnation
(4) respiration

12. New generations come about as a result of a life process called
(1) respiration
(2) regulation
(3) reproduction
(4) reconstruction

13. All of the following are adaptations that help birds survive in the air *except*
(1) lightweight bones
(2) water-repellent feathers
(3) broad, flat wings
(4) internal air tubes

14. Which organism is properly matched to an activity?
(1) A whale breathes through its gills.
(2) A desert plant stores water.
(3) A fish breathes through its lungs.
(4) A hawk swims with webbed feet.

15. An example of an organism that reproduces asexually is the
(1) fish
(2) frog
(3) starfish
(4) reptile

II. LIVING THINGS DEPEND UPON THE ENVIRONMENT

1. *Interdependence of Living Things* *(A12)*

Organisms exist in an environment that consists of living and nonliving things. Listed below are some nonliving things in the environment.

Nonliving Things in the Environment

Type of soil
Temperature range
Amount of sunlight
Amount and kinds of minerals
Supply of gases

This environment of the living and nonliving things is referred to as an **ecosystem**. Living things interact with other living things and nonliving things in the ecosystem. For example, green plants require carbon dioxide, water, and sunlight to make food. Animals, in turn, eat the plants. Dead organisms are decomposed and recycle minerals back to the soil for use by the green plants.

2. *Green Plants: The Producers* *(A5)*

All organisms need energy for their life activities. This energy comes from food. Food energy enters the ecosystem when green plants capture light energy during photosynthesis. Some of this energy is used by the plants themselves and some is stored. The energy of the stored food is transferred to animals when they eat the plants.

For an ecosystem to be maintained there must be a flow of energy between organisms. The pathways of food through the organisms of an ecosystem are represented by **food chains**.

A food chain involves the transfer of energy from green plants through a series of organisms, with repeated stages of eating and being eaten. An example is grass eaten by a cow eaten by a human (Figure 1–8).

All food chains begin with green plants. Green plants are the **producers** in the food chain. During photosynthesis, green plants change the sun's energy into chemical energy stored as foods. Therefore energy in foods is supplied initially to the food chain by the activities of green plants.

Figure 1–8. A simple food chain.

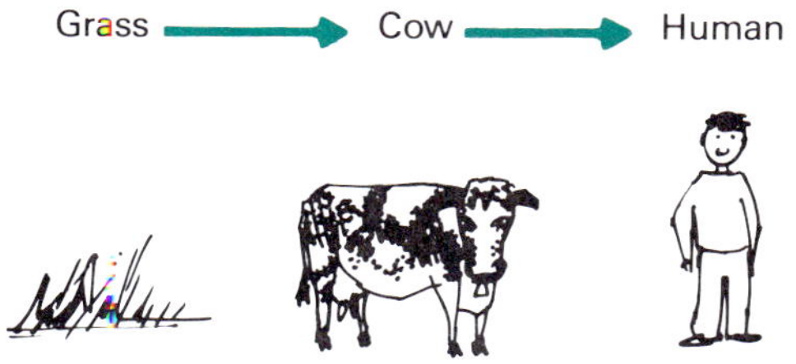

3. Animals: The Consumers *(A15)*

All of the animals in an ecosystem are **consumers**. They obtain chemical energy from the food they eat. Animals that feed on green plants are called *primary consumers*. Animals that feed on primary consumers are called *secondary consumers*.

4. The Decomposers *(A13, A14)*

All living and nonliving things are composed of the same materials. When organisms die they eventually return to the soil, where they are acted on by decomposers. **Decomposers** break down the remains of dead organisms and organic wastes. Examples of decomposers include some bacteria and all fungi. Decomposers return minerals in the remains of plants and animals to the soil, where the minerals are reused by green plants to produce food.

5. Living Things Interact in a Community *(A19)*

All the populations of living things interacting in any given area form a natural **community**. For example, all the populations in a pond (frogs, dragonflies, water striders, cattails, pond lilies, trout, etc.) make up a pond community. All the living things in the ocean (flounders, starfish, shrimp, seaweed, clams, oysters, etc.) make up an ocean community. All the living things in the soil (earthworms, bacteria, slugs, grass, etc.) make up a soil community.

Living things live together in a community and interact with each other. For example, living things use other living things for their food. Starfish eat oysters and clams. Frogs eat insects in the pond. Snakes eat the mice in a field. Organisms such as some bacteria and fungi feed upon and decompose the wastes of living and dead organisms. Plants make food and provide oxygen in every natural community.

6. Balance Within the Ecosystem *(A21)*

Members of the community live side by side in the ecosystem. Each kind of organism occupies a specific place in the ecosystem called its *habitat*. The habitat supplies the organism with all its needs.

One habitat may be shared by several organisms. For example, green plants grow in the soil, where earthworms live also. Seagulls live together with oysters and clams along the seashore. Fish and frogs share the pond with dragonflies, water striders, and cattails. Organisms sharing the same habitat depend upon each other in many ways. Seagulls eat the shellfish found along the shore. Earthworms feed on decayed plants in the soil.

The dependency or interaction of living things on other living things and nonliving things in the habitat establishes a balance in the ecosystem. In the process of eating and being eaten, for example, populations are balanced or kept in check. Gases in the atmosphere are kept constant as green plants give off oxygen, which animals use, and as animals give off carbon dioxide, which green plants use. In the process of decomposition, some bacteria and fungi recycle the mineral content in the soil. The natural balance in an ecosystem results from the interaction of community members and between community members and the nonliving environment.

Figure 1–9 shows some interactions in a balanced aquarium, a kind of miniature community. How many interactions can you identify? How does this illustrate the balance present in an ecosystem?

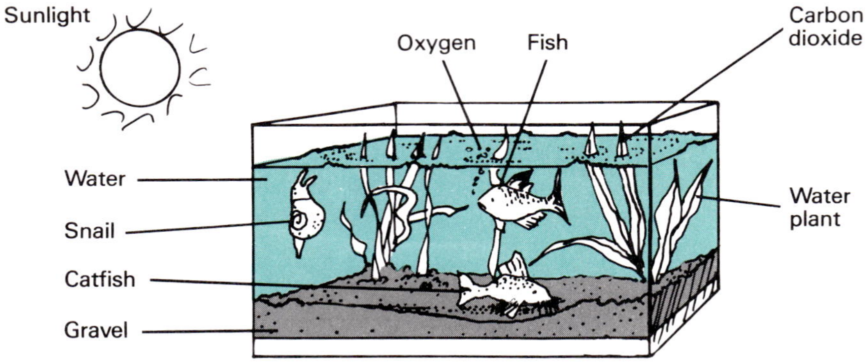

Figure 1–9. Interactions in a balanced aquarium.

Sample Questions

1. Living things interact with other living things for survival. Which of the following examples illustrates this?
(1) Green plants require sunlight to make food.
(2) Vertebrates require calcium to make bones and teeth.
(3) Animals use plants for food.
(4) Animals require water for their life functions.

2. Which of the following represents an ecosystem?
(1) a population of field mice
(2) water in a pond
(3) all the living and nonliving things in a lake
(4) all the living things in the soil

3. Which of the following organisms are decomposers?
(1) fungi (3) protozoa
(2) algae (4) viruses

4. The role of the decomposer is to
(1) produce food during photosynthesis
(2) release oxygen to the environment
(3) return minerals in the remains of plants and animals to the soil
(4) change sunlight into chemical energy in food

5. Green plants make food. For this reason they are called
(1) consumers (3) producers
(2) decomposers (4) regulators

6–8. Base your answers to questions 6–8 on the diagram of the food web shown below.

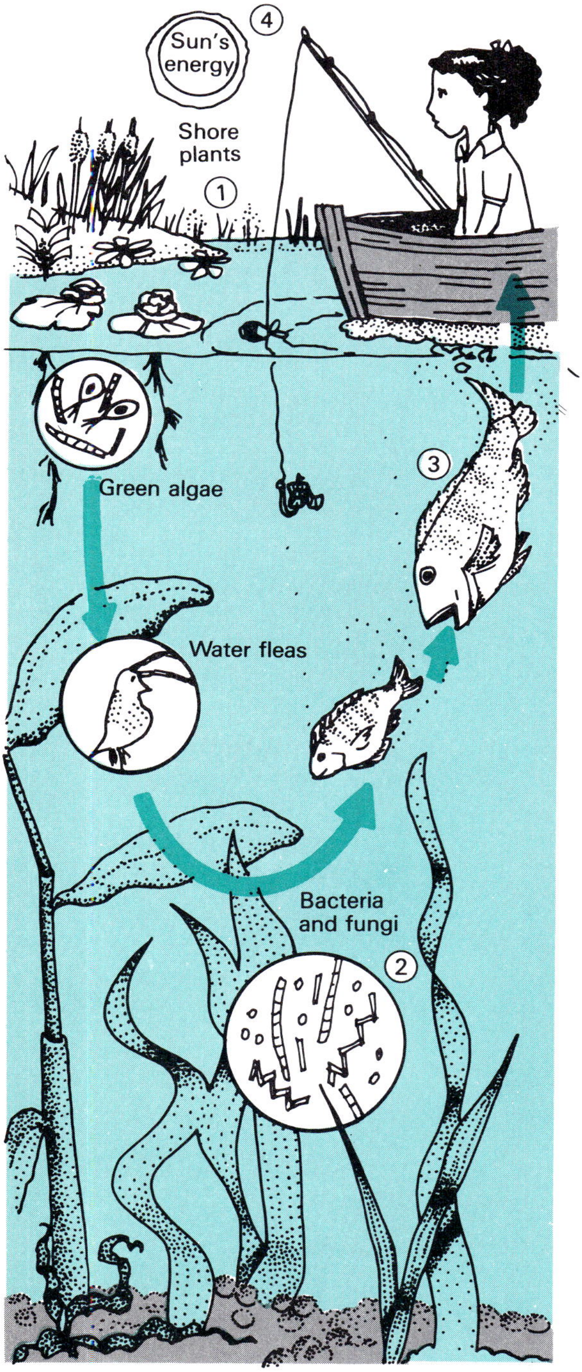

6. Which number on the diagram represents the consumer?

7. Which number on the diagram represents the decomposer?

8. Which one of the following represents a correct food chain?
   (1) green algae eaten by big fish eaten by girl
   (2) water flea eaten by small fish eaten by big fish
   (3) fungi eaten by big fish eaten by girl
   (4) water flea eaten by big fish eaten by girl

9–12. Base your answers to questions 9–12 on the diagram of the balanced aquarium containing water, soil, green plants, a snail, a goldfish, and a catfish.

9. Which represents a correct activity in the aquarium?
   (1) The fish breathes in carbon dioxide dissolved in water.
   (2) The fish eats the green plant.
   (3) The catfish eats the snail.
   (4) The snail uses the fish for its food.

10. Which organism is the producer in the aquarium?
(1) catfish
(2) snail
(3) gravel
(4) green plant

11. Which gas do the snail and fish release into the water?
(1) oxygen
(2) nitrogen
(3) carbon dioxide
(4) hydrogen

12. A gas released by the green plant is used by the snail for
(1) photosynthesis
(2) digestion
(3) excretion
(4) respiration

13. A student wants to prove that a plant needs minerals from the soil to grow. She places a plant in the sun as shown in the diagram below.

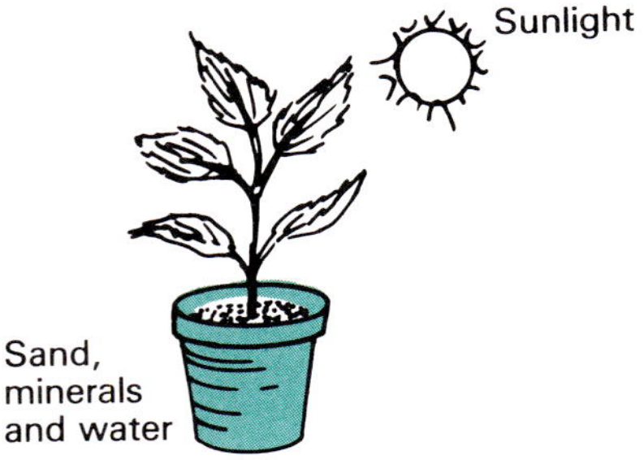

To check her idea, she also sets up a control. Which diagram below represents the control in her experiment?

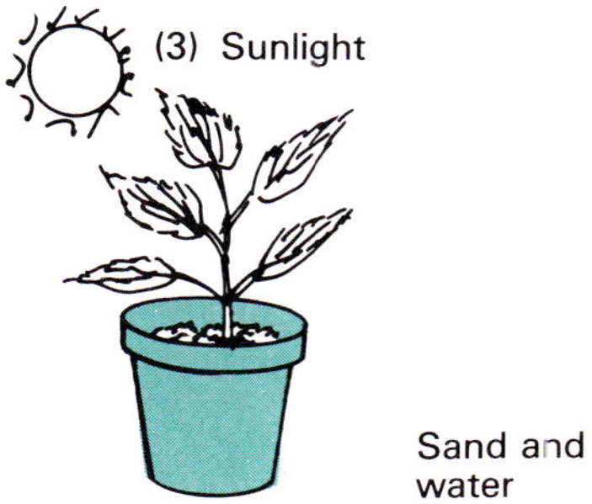

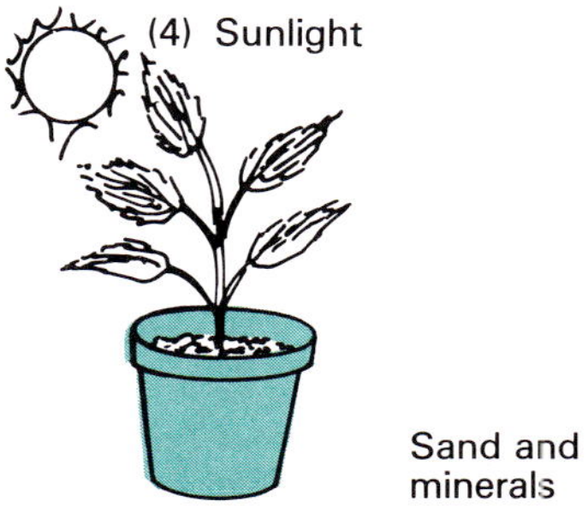

III. THE CHANGING ECOSYSTEM

1. Disturbing the Balance

(A20, A22)

Sometimes the balance present in an ecosystem is disturbed. The result may be changes in a community or the replacement of one community by another.

Some disturbances are due to natural causes. For example, a disease may destroy a population of wolves. With predator wolves absent, the population of moose may increase dramatically. Soon, however, the moose population grows too large for its food supply, causing a drop in the number of moose.

Some disturbances may be due to human causes. A forest fire or flood may temporarily destroy an entire ecosystem. Humans may excavate a pond, destroying the soil habitat of many animals and plants. During the process of **biological succession** new communities may be reestablished in these barren areas. For example, after a forest fire the soil is rich in organic matter. Weeds begin to grow in the rich soil. In later years taller weeds and low-growing shrubs appear. As time goes on, woody plants crowd out the soft-stemmed weeds. Finally tall trees replace the weeds and shrubs, completing the cycle of succession. A sequence of succession in a forest is shown in Figure 1–10.

If a pond is left alone, it too changes. Eventually the pond will fill in again, recreating a soil environment.

2. People Disturb the Natural Balance *(A23)*

When people change natural communities they often create disturbances that are undesirable or even harmful to their own welfare. For example, people may remove forests for lumber. The loss of forests eliminates the habitats of wildlife, resulting in a reduction in the numbers of species of living things. When forests are destroyed the bare soil that remains may be washed away, or *eroded*. This is just one example of how the activities of humans may disturb the natural balance in an ecosystem.

Figure 1–10. The order of succession in a forest. The first tree to appear is the cottonwood. It gives way to pine, which is then followed by oak. The final community is a mature forest of maple and beech trees.

Science Skill

EXPLAINING EXPERIMENTAL TECHNIQUE

A large field at the base of a mountain is periodically flooded when heavy rains in the mountains cause a nearby stream to overflow. Each time the flooding occurs, more soil washes away.

The owners of the land want to perform a test to see how different types of plants could help to reduce the soil erosion. They choose five areas of ground that are the same size, have the same kind of soil, and receive the same amount of sun. A different type of plant is planted in each area. Measurements of soil erosion are made after each time it rains in the mountains.

1. What is the manipulated variable in this experiment?
   (1) the type of soil
   (2) the types of plants
   (3) the size of the areas planted
   (4) the amount of soil erosion

2. What is the responding variable?
   (1) the type of soil
   (2) the types of plants
   (3) the size of the areas planted
   (4) the amount of soil erosion

3. What hypothesis is being tested?
   (1) Soil erosion is affected by the strength of the wind.
   (2) Flooded areas have greater soil erosion than nonflooded areas.
   (3) Plants can reduce the amount of soil erosion.
   (4) Some types of plants reduce soil erosion more than others.

4. Which of the following variables is *not* controlled in this study?
   (1) the amount of soil erosion
   (2) the amount of sun the area receives
   (3) the size of the planted areas
   (4) the type of soil in the areas

Earth's resources and its ability to recycle them is limited. Therefore, people must not exploit these resources. Otherwise we will be faced with serious shortages or even the elimination of natural resources.

Although soil, forests, and water are **renewable resources**, long periods of time are required to recycle them. Therefore they must be conserved.

Humans depend upon good soil. Soil provides the minerals from which green plants make their food. Damage to soil is often the result of human activity. People have depleted soil by overcropping, leaching, and mismanagement. One good example of mismanagement is the destruction of agricultural land and forests by land developers. Through techniques such as crop rotation, chemical fertilizers, contour plowing, and cover crops, damage to the soil may be reduced.

Humans need water for a great variety of activities. As the human population grows, the need for water steadily increases. Although water is constantly recycled, less than half of the water used by people is returned to the environment in usable condition. Therefore, people must conserve water. They must make better use of the available supply, prevent pollution, and capture a greater percentage of the runoff. Some methods of water conservation include reservoirs, reforestation (planting new trees to replace those cut down), watershed management, pollution control, and filtration processes.

Forests are of great value for wood products and lumber, soil and water conservation, wildlife habitat, and beauty and recreation. Human activities, such as starting forest fires and misusing and wasting trees, result in the loss of forest resources. Forests may also be destroyed due to the ravages of insects and diseases. Methods of forest conservation include fire protection and prevention, reforestation, insect and disease control, selective cutting, and the recycling of forest products.

3. Nonrenewable Mineral Resources *(A24)*

Minerals are **nonrenewable resources.** If we do not conserve them, they may eventually run out. People must use minerals wisely and develop new techniques for recycling them. For example, technology exists for recycling aluminum soda cans and glass bottles. Mineral resources will be preserved only if we make use of these and other technologies.

Sample Questions

1–4. Base your answers to questions 1–4 on the brief reading and the graph below, which shows changes in a population of deer in the Kaibab Plateau of Arizona from 1905 to 1940.

In order to protect the deer from their enemies the wolves, the United States government offered a cash reward for each wolf killed. The graph below shows how the population of deer changed.

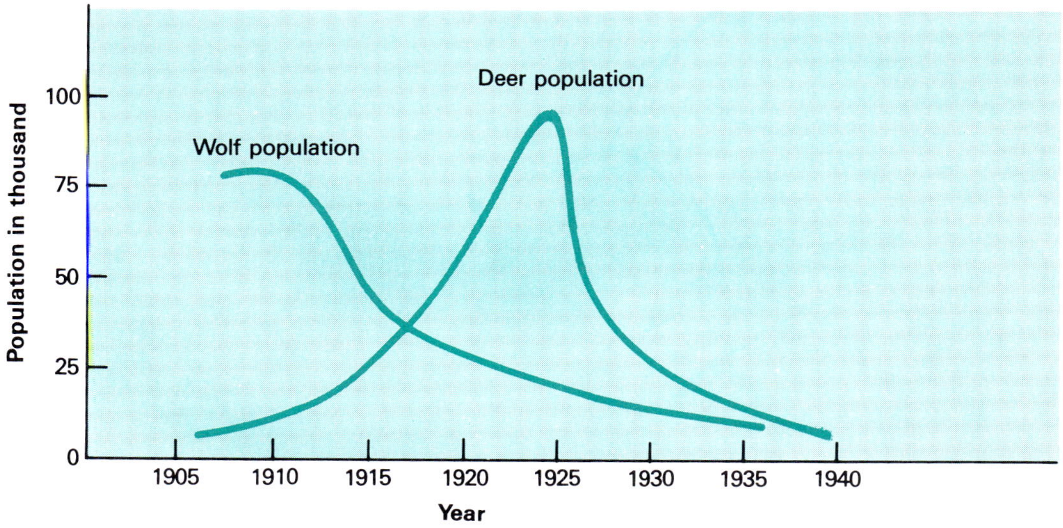

1. As the wolf population decreased, the deer population
   (1) increased
   (2) decreased
   (3) remained the same

2. From the data shown on the graph, which of the following relationships is correct?
   (1) The deer eat the wolves.
   (2) The wolves eat the deer.
   (3) The deer and wolves are eaten by a common enemy.
   (4) The deer and wolves have no natural enemies.

3. In the year 1925 there was a sudden and large drop in the population of deer due to
   (1) an increase in the population of wolves
   (2) a decrease in the population of wolves
   (3) a decrease in the amount of grass available for the deer to feed on
   (4) an increase in the amount of grass available for the deer to feed on

4. The graph illustrates which important ecological principal?
   (1) The balance present in this ecosystem was disturbed by people.
   (2) The balance present in this ecosystem was disturbed by natural causes.
   (3) Living and nonliving things are affected by each other.
   (4) The sun is needed by plants to make food.

5–6. Base your answers to questions 5 and 6 on the diagram above at the right and your knowledge of life science.

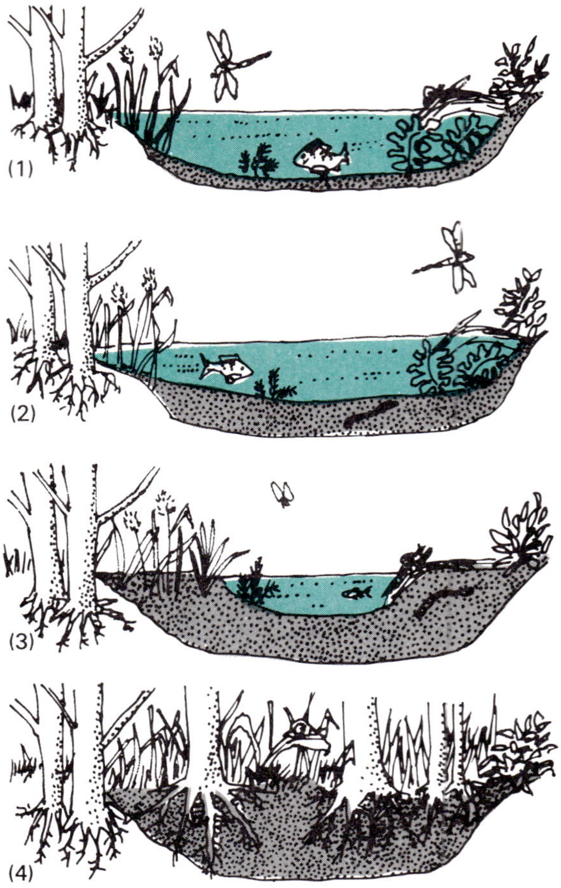

5. The diagram shows which important ecological principal?
   (1) One community can be replaced by a quite different community over time.
   (2) All living things come from other living things.
   (3) Soil, plants, and water are renewable resources.
   (4) Minerals are renewable resources.

6. Which natural process is most responsible for filling the pond with soil?
   (1) decomposition (3) evaporation
   (2) erosion (4) condensation

Issues in Science, Technology, and Society

Acid Rain

Sulfur dioxide and nitrogen oxide are pollutants released to the atmosphere from the burning of fossil fuels. These pollutants combine with moisture in the air to form acid rain. The acid rain destroys the natural balance in lakes and streams and kills many species of fish. Some lakes in the Adirondack Mountains have become ten times more acidic since 1940. Forests also are affected by acid rain. It causes a decline in the growth of trees and may cause some of them to die.

Acidic conditions affect not only lakes and forests but also the buildings and statues found in many cities. Limestone and marble, two commonly used building stones, are damaged by acid rain. Other materials, such as metals, ceramics, glass, paints, and leather, are also affected by acid rain.

In North America, the effects of acid rain have been most severe in the eastern United States and eastern Canada. Scientists think this is because these areas are downwind of the heavily industrial Ohio River valley. Studies have shown that ten midwestern and eastern states (Missouri, Illinois, Indiana, Tennessee, Kentucky, Michigan, Ohio, Pennsylvania, New York, and West Virginia) account for 53 percent of the sulfur dioxide emissions and 30 percent of the nitrogen oxide emissions in the United States. Recent studies done in the western states have shown that acid rain is becoming a serious problem there also.

In 1987 the federal government pledged 2.5 billion dollars for the development of technological devices to stop acid rain. The money will be used to develop and install new pollution control devices in power plants and factories in order to prevent sulfur dioxide and nitrogen oxide from entering the atmosphere.

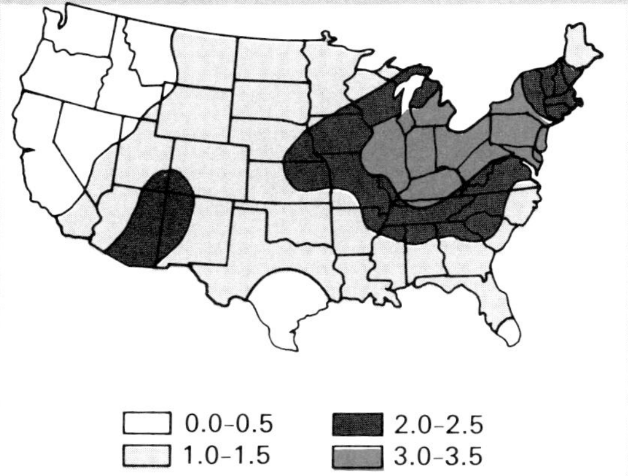

Acid rain concentration in the United States (in milligrams of acid per liter).

Do research to answer the following questions.

1. What effect does acid rain have on organisms?
2. Lakes in the Adirondack Mountains of New York State have been destroyed by acid rain. What effects does acid rain have on lakes? How does acid rain affect people?
3. Should society monitor the discovery and use of technological devices and processes that result in acid rain? Why or why not?

CHAPTER 2 Living Systems: Human Systems

I. ORGANIZATION OF THE HUMAN BODY

1. *Interdependence of Body Systems* *(B1, B2)*

The human body is complex. It is built of a variety of systems, each of which performs some functions necessary for life. For example, the digestive system prepares nutrients for use by the cells. The circulatory system delivers digested nutrients to all the cells. The nervous system provides a means for communication among the organs of the body. Although each body system performs its own functions, all the systems must work together to keep the human body alive.

2. *Structures of the Human Body* *(B3)*

A human being is a multicellular organism made of trillions of cells. **Cells** are the units of structure and function in the human body.

There are many different kinds of cells. Human body cells include skin cells, muscle cells, red blood cells, nerve cells, and many others. All cells are alike in some ways. For example, they have the same basic parts—nucleus, cell membrane, and cytoplasm (Figure 2–1).

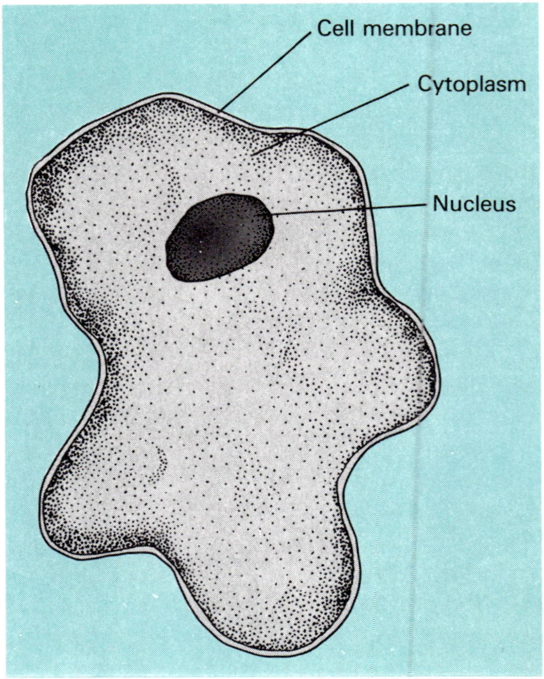

Figure 2–1. Parts of a cell.

There are also differences, however. Figure 2–2 shows the structure of some different kinds of human cells. Notice how they differ. These structural differences enable different kinds of cells to perform different functions. Table 1 lists some of the different kinds of human cells and their functions.

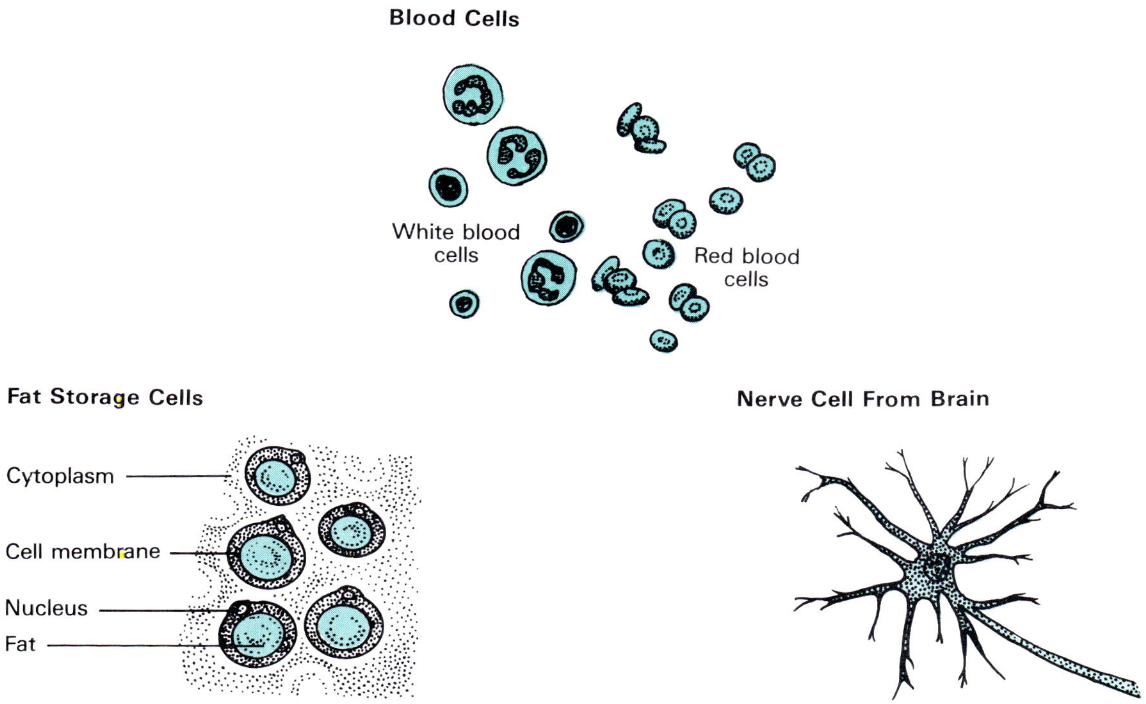

Figure 2–2. Some different human cells.

Table 1 Structure and Function of Some Human Cells

Cell Type	Function
Lining	Cover and protect body parts
Muscle	Expand and contract for movement
Blood	
red blood cells	Carry oxygen
white blood cells	Fight disease
Bone	Protect and support
Nerve	Carry messages from organ to organ
Fat	Store food

Cells in the human body are grouped together into tissues. A **tissue** is a group of similar cells working together to do the same job. The following is a list of some tissues and their functions:

Skin tissue — Covers and protects the body
Muscle tissue — Enables the body to move
Blood tissue — Carries materials throughout the body
Bone tissue — Supports the body and provides sites for the attachment of muscle

The human body contains a number of parts called organs. An **organ** is a group of tissues that work together to do a special job. For example, the kidney is an organ that cleans wastes from the blood. The heart pumps blood to all parts of the body.

Table 2 lists some human organs and their functions.

Table 2 Some Organs and Their Functions

Organ	Function
Heart	Pumps blood
Kidney	Cleans blood
Small intestine	Digests food
Ovary	Produces eggs
Lung	Exchanges gases
Skin	Cools the body
Eye	Receives light
Ear	Receives sound

Human organs are grouped together into **organ systems**, such as the digestive and circulatory systems. Organ systems perform specific functions. For example, the digestive system prepares nutrients for use by the body cells. The circulatory system distributes materials to all the cells. The human body is made of a number of organ systems, listed below. Each of these systems is discussed in this chapter.

Human Organ Systems

Skeletal system	Respiratory system
Muscular system	Nervous system
Digestive system	Endocrine system
Excretory system	Reproductive system
Circulatory system	

In summary, cells are organized into tissues, tissues into organs, and organs into systems. Organ systems build the human organism.

Sample Questions

1. In the human body, a group of similar cells functioning together to do one job is known as a(n)
(1) tissue (3) system
(2) organ (4) organism

2–4. For each phrase in questions 2 through 4, select the correct tissue type from the list below.

Tissue Types
skin
muscle
blood
bone

2. Enables the body to move

3. Transports material throughout the body

4. Supports the body and provides sites for the attachment of muscles

5. Which of the following lists parts of the human body in order from simple to complex?
(1) cell – organ – tissue – organ system
(2) cell – organ – organ system – tissue
(3) cell – tissue – organ – organ system
(4) organ system – organ – tissue – cell

6. Which cell is specialized for body movement?
(1) blood cell (3) skin cell
(2) muscle cell (4) fat cell

II. BONES AND MUSCLES

1. The Human Skeletal System *(B5)*

The human skeletal system is the internal framework or support system of the body. It works together with the muscular system to support and move the body. The skeletal system also protects the internal organs.

The skeletal system (Figure 2–3) consists of the skull, the spinal column, the breastbone and ribs, and the bones that form the limbs. It also includes soft tissue called cartilage.

The **skull** is a group of flat bones that surround and protect the brain. The **spinal column**, or backbone, runs up and down the middle of the back. It is made of many small bones called *vertebrae*. In the center of each vertebra is a hole through which the spinal cord runs (Figure 2–4). (The spinal cord is part of the nervous system, discussed on pages 35-36.)

The **breastbone** is located in the top part of the chest. Attached to the breastbone are pairs of curved bones, the **ribs**. The breastbone and ribs surround and protect the heart and lungs.

The **limbs** (arms and legs) are made of long bones, which work together with the muscles for movement.

Cartilage, a flexible tissue, is located in several places in the skeletal system. For example, disks of cartilage lie between each of the vertebrae. The cartilage disks cushion the vertebrae so that they do not rub against and damage each other. Cartilage is also found at the end of bones and in the nose and ears. In general, cartilage cushions the bones and provides flexibility.

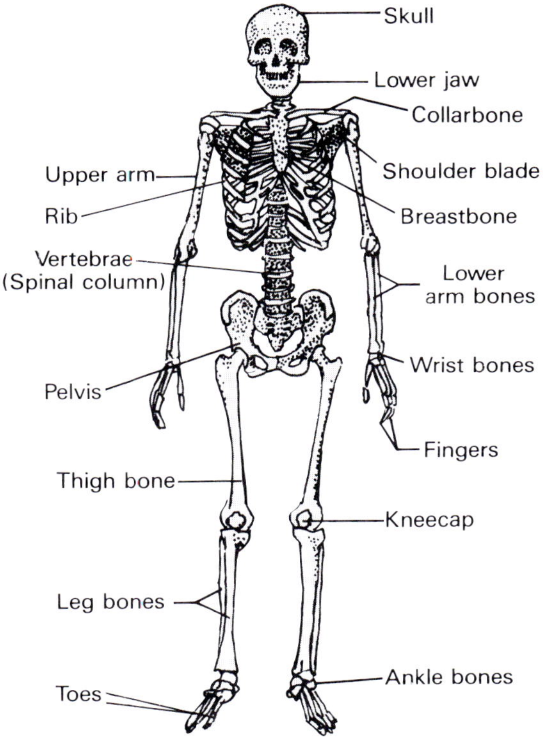

Figure 2–3. The skeletal system.

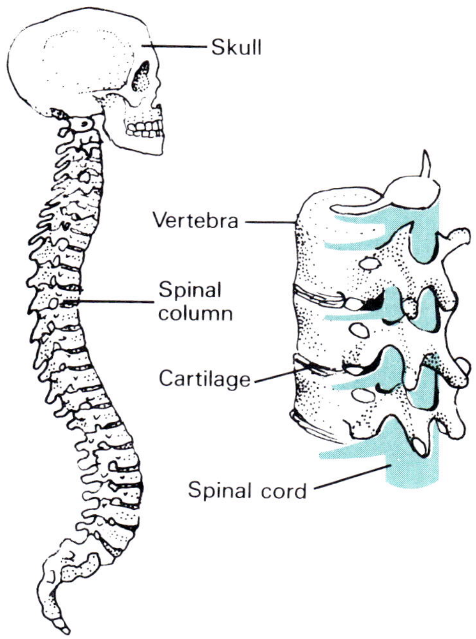

Figure 2–4. The spinal cord runs through the spinal column.

Joints are places in the skeleton where bones are connected to each other (Figure 2–5). Elbows, hips, and knees are examples of joints. Joints make the motions of the body possible.

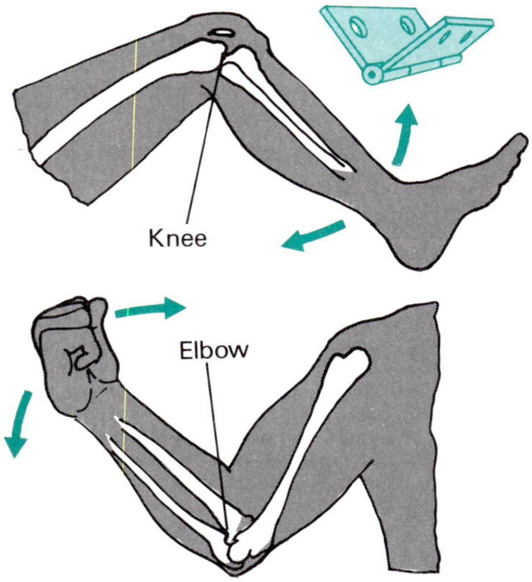

Figure 2–5. **The elbow and knee joints work like hinges.**

Figure 2–6. **Ligaments in the ankle.**

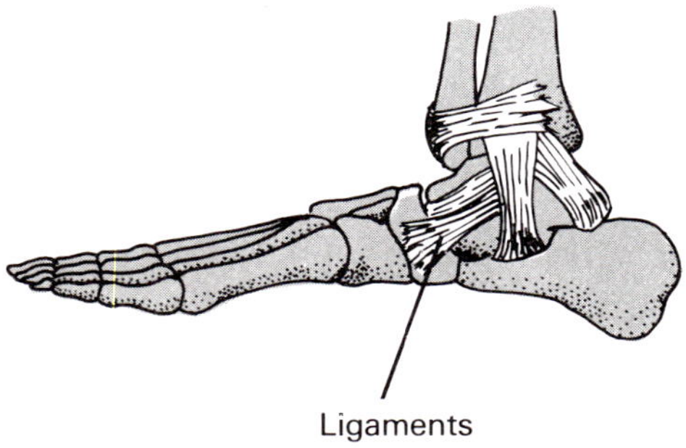

Bones are connected to bones at joints by a kind of connective tissue called **ligaments** (Figure 2–6). Ligaments stretch slightly as the bones move.

Bones provide surfaces for muscle attachment. Muscles are connected to bones by another kind of tissue called **tendons** (Figure 2–7). Tendons help the bones move when muscles expand or contract.

Figure 2–7. **Tendons attach muscles to bones.**

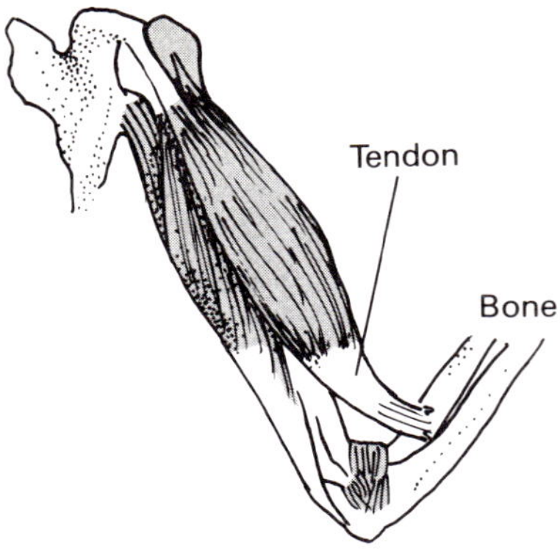

2. The Muscular System (B6)

The human muscular system is made of over 600 **muscles**. Muscles expand and contract to move the joints and some organs. The heart, diaphragm, arms, and legs are all are moved by muscles.

The muscular system is made of voluntary and involuntary muscles. **Voluntary muscles** are consciously controlled. For example, *skeletal muscles* are voluntary. These are long, slender muscles attached by tendons to bones in the limbs. When skeletal muscles contract, they pull on tendons. The tendons, in turn, pull on bones, causing movements at the joints.

Involuntary muscles cannot be consciously controlled. One kind of involuntary muscle is *smooth muscle*. Smooth muscle is found in the digestive, circulatory, and respiratory systems. Smooth muscles are generally short and slender, and are usually wrapped around or embedded in tissue where squeezing actions are required. Smooth muscle in the esophagus, for example, causes a squeezing action that pushes the food toward the stomach. *Cardiac muscle* is another kind of involuntary muscle. Cardiac muscle, which is found in the heart, is responsible for the heart's pumping action.

3. Bones and Muscles Work Together *(B4)*

The skeletal and muscular systems function together to move body parts and to control **locomotion**, the movement of the entire body. Figure 2–8 shows how bones, muscles, and tendons in the forearm and upper arm cause movements at the joints. When the *biceps* muscle contracts, it pulls on tendons. The tendons in turn pull in one direction on a bone, causing the arm to bend at the elbow joint. When the *triceps* muscle contracts, it pulls on other tendons. These tendons, in turn, pull the bone in the other direction, causing the arm to straighten. This action of a pair of muscles, the biceps and triceps, together with bones and the tendons, is just one example of how the skeletal and muscular systems work together to move parts of the body.

Figure 2–8. Bones and muscles work together.

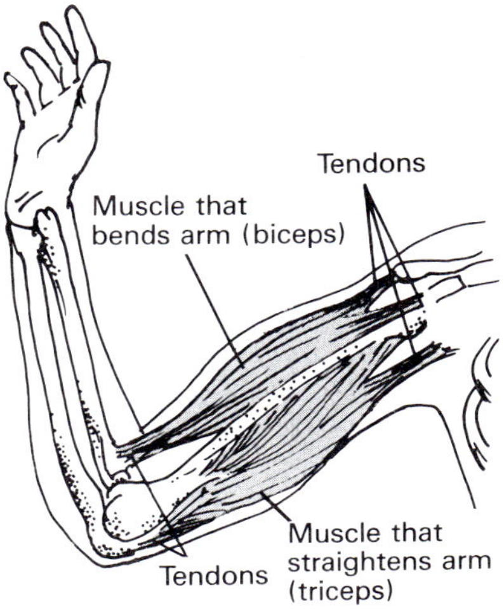

Sample Questions

1. The human skeletal and muscular systems work together to
(1) filter the blood of its wastes
(2) pump fluids through the heart
(3) move the parts of the body
(4) coordinate and control body activities

2. Which student activity is the result of the work of voluntary muscles?
(1) breathing in air
(2) digesting food
(3) walking to school
(4) transporting blood

3. During exercise, the human heart beats faster due to an increase in the activity of
(1) involuntary muscle
(2) voluntary muscle
(3) skeletal muscle
(4) stomach muscle

4–5. Base your answers to questions 4 and 5 on the diagram below, which represents the human arm.

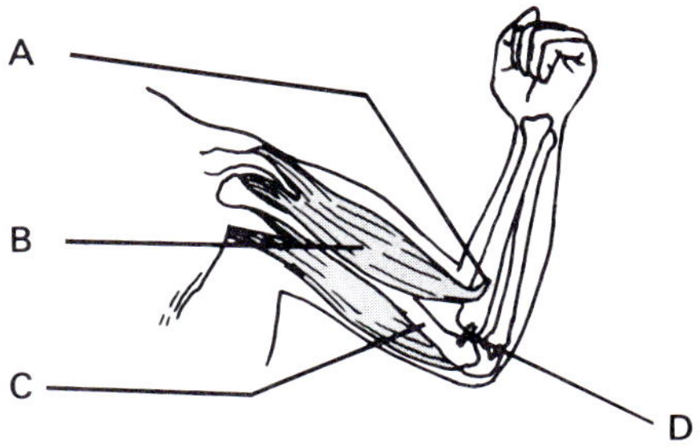

4. Which structure is a skeletal muscle?
(1) A (2) B (3) C (4) D

5. Which structure is a bone?
(1) A (2) B (3) C (4) D

6. Which part of the human body contains skeletal muscles?
(1) heart (3) lung
(2) small intestine (4) leg

7. The skeletal system is composed of all of the following parts except the
(1) skull (3) spinal column
(2) heart (4) ribs

III. DIGESTION AND EXCRETION

1. The Role of the Digestive System *(B10)*

The digestive system consists of a group of organs that work together to prepare foods to enter (be absorbed) into the circulatory system, where they are transported to all the cells. Food is digested both physically and chemically as it moves through the digestive system.

During **physical digestion**, food is broken into smaller pieces. The small pieces provide a greater surface area on which digestive juices work to chemically digest the food. During **chemical digestion**, the *nutrients* in foods are changed into a dissolved or *soluble* form that can be absorbed into the bloodstream. Table 3 lists some nutrients and the end products of their chemical digestion by various digestive juices.

Table 3 Examples of Chemical Digestion

Nutrient	Digestive Juice	Where Digestion Occurs	End Product
Starch	Saliva	Mouth	Maltose
Protein	Gastric and intestinal juices	Stomach and small intestine	Amino acids
Fat	Bile; intestinal juice	Small intestine	Fatty acids, glycerol

2. Parts of the Digestive System *(B11)*

The digestive system (Figure 2–9) consists of the mouth, esophagus, stomach, and the small and large intestines. In addition to these are the liver, gallbladder, and pancreas, also known as *accessory organs*.

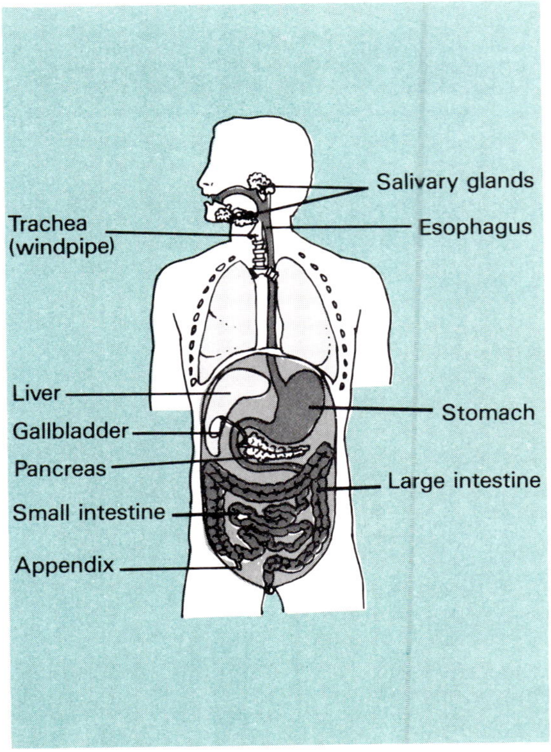

Figure 2–9. The digestive system.

Digestion begins in the **mouth**, where the teeth break the food into small pieces. Juices called *saliva*, carried in ducts from the *salivary glands* to the mouth, moisten the small pieces of food. Saliva contains chemicals called *enzymes*, which begin the chemical digestion of starch.

The act of swallowing moves the partially digested food from the mouth to the esophagus. The **esophagus** connects the mouth with the stomach. In the esophagus a series of wavelike contractions continues physical digestion and squeezes the food toward the stomach. Similar wavelike contractions in the stomach and small intestine move the food along there also.

In the **stomach** the wavelike contractions continue the physical digestion of food. At the same time, gastric juices secreted from the gastric glands in the stomach wall begin the chemical digestion of protein.

When the food leaves the stomach it enters the **small intestine**. Here both physical and chemical digestion continue. Chemical digestion is completed in the small intestine, helped by the action of

Science Skill

GRAPHING; INTERPRETING DATA

A scientist performed an experiment to show the length of time needed to digest protein. She placed 10 small pieces of hard-boiled egg white (a protein) in a test tube containing hydrochloric acid, water, and the enzyme pepsin. She then measured the rate at which the egg white was digested over a 24-hour period, and recorded the information in the data table below.

Data Table

Percent of Egg White Digested	Time (hours)
5%	2 hours
10%	4 hours
20%	8 hours
50%	12 hours
70%	16 hours
80%	20 hours
85%	24 hours

Use the directions below to graph the data on a grid. Then answer the questions that follow.

A. Draw and label the horizontal and vertical axes.
B. Mark an appropriate scale on each axis.
C. Plot the data.
D. Connect the points.

1. During which 4-hour period did the most digestion take place?
(1) 0–4 hours
(2) 4–8 hours
(3) 8–12 hours
(4) 20–24 hours

2. How much digestion occurred in 12 hours?
(1) 5% (2) 50% (3) 75% (4) 90%

3. The amount of digestion after 10 hours was probably about
(1) 10% (2) 12% (3) 35% (4) 80%

intestinal juices secreted by glands in the wall of the small intestine and by juices secreted by the liver and pancreas. These juices complete the chemical digestion of starch, protein, and fat. The end products of digestion (glucose, amino acids, fatty acids, and glycerol) are absorbed from the small intestine into the bloodstream for distribution to the body cells.

3. The Role of the Large Intestine *(B12)*

Some materials in food cannot be digested. These indigestible materials, along with some undigested materials, pass from the small intestine to the **large intestine**. Undigested and indigestible foods make up solid human wastes, or **feces**. Feces move through the large intestine and are eliminated from the body. As feces pass through the large intestine, water is reabsorbed from them into the bloodstream.

4. Structure and Function of the Excretory System

(B18, B19)

As a result of cellular activities, chemical wastes are produced. If these wastes were not removed, they would poison the cells. The removal of wastes from the cells into the blood and eventually from the body occurs during the the process of **excretion**.

The human excretory system consists of the skin, lungs, kidneys, and the liver. The **skin** (Figure 2–10) contains *sweat glands*, which excrete wastes such as water, salts, and nitrogenous substances. These wastes are absorbed from the capillaries to the sweat glands and then pass through ducts in the skin. The wastes exit through tiny openings at the surface of the skin called *pores*. The mixture of wastes and

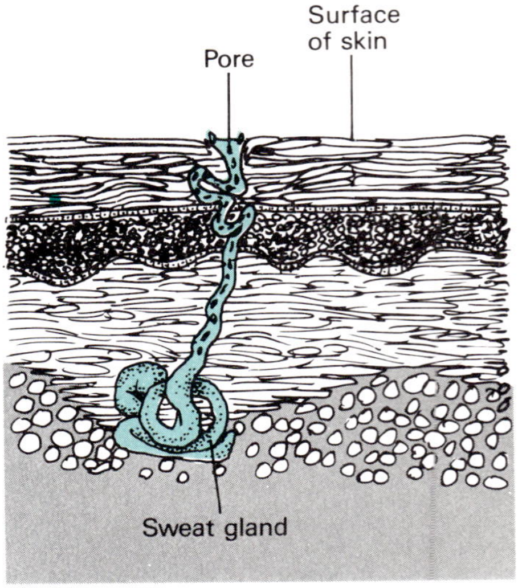

Figure 2–10. Cross-section of skin.

Figure 2–11. The urinary system.

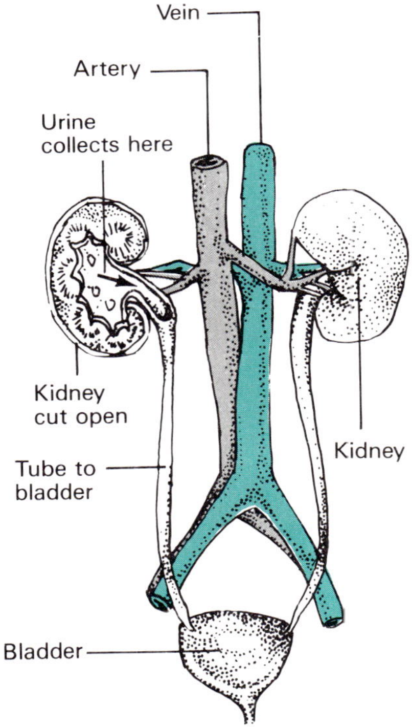

water leaving the skin is called *perspiration*, or sweat. In addition to serving as a vehicle for the elimination of wastes, the work of the sweat glands lowers the body temperature. The evaporation of water from the pores cools the body.

Excretion occurs in the lungs. The large number of air sacs in the lungs provide an enormous surface area from which wastes (mostly carbon dioxide) are exhaled to the external environment.

The **kidneys,** shown in Figure 2–11, are a pair of bean-shaped organs located in the back of the stomach on either side of the spine. Water, urea, minerals, and other wastes are filtered from the blood as it flows through the kidneys. In this process, the kidneys help control the water and mineral balance in the blood. Tubes leading from the kidneys carry the filtered wastes, called *urine*, to the *bladder*. Urine is held in the bladder until it is passed out of the body.

The **liver** destroys red blood cells. The products resulting from the breakdown of red blood cells are absorbed into the bloodstream and carried to the kidneys, where they are eliminated. The liver also makes urea from nitrogenous wastes. The urea is absorbed into the bloodstream and carried to the kidneys.

Sample Questions

1. The main activity of the human digestive system is to
(1) make minerals
(2) add vitamins to food
(3) break down food
(4) excrete water

2. After food is digested most of it is
(1) eliminated by the body
(2) stored in the small intestine
(3) changed into waste products
(4) absorbed into the circulatory system

3. Which activity does *not* take place in the human digestive system?
(1) Food is broken down physically and chemically.
(2) Digested food is absorbed into the circulatory system.
(3) Undigested and indigestible materials form feces.
(4) Food combines with oxygen to release energy.

4. Substances in food that humans cannot digest are called
(1) fat
(2) protein
(3) indigestible material
(4) excretory wastes

5. Which two organs belong to the human excretory system?
(1) heart and lungs
(2) skin and kidneys
(3) ribs and muscles
(4) skin and esophagus

6. One function of the skin is to
(1) secrete hormones
(2) exchange gases
(3) release wastes
(4) digest food

7–9. Base your answers to questions 7–9 on the diagram of the human digestive system shown below.

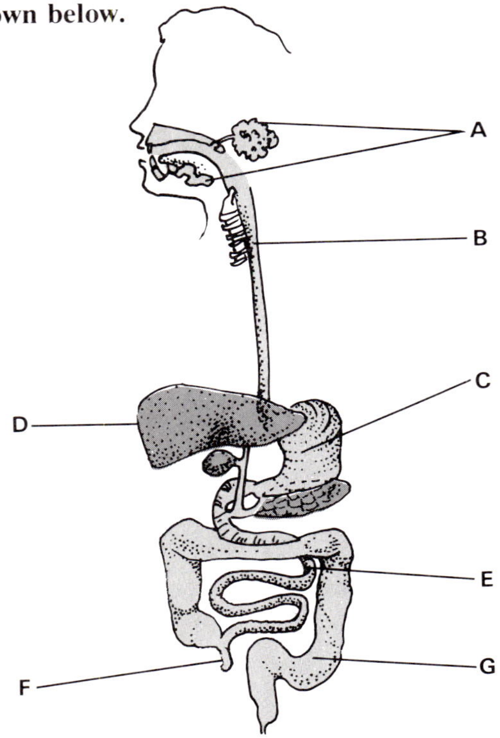

7. Which structure is an accessory organ?

8. In which structure does the chemical digestion of protein begin?

9. Which structure is the esophagus?

10. Which organ is *not* a part of the human digestive system?
    (1) stomach
    (2) liver
    (3) kidney
    (4) esophagus

11. The human excretory system
    (1) releases energy from digested foods
    (2) removes wastes from the blood
    (3) transports digested food to the cells
    (4) controls and coordinates the body

12. The major role of the kidneys is to
    (1) protect and support the reproductive organs
    (2) control the water and mineral balance of the body
    (3) produce enzymes and hormones
    (4) produce solid wastes

IV. CIRCULATION AND RESPIRATION

1. Structure and Function of the Circulatory System

(B13, B14)

The circulatory system consists of the blood, the heart, arteries, veins, capillaries, lymph, and lymph vessels. Locate some of these parts in Figure 2–12.

Blood is a liquid tissue composed of different types of cells, including red and white blood cells and platelets (Figure 2–13). Blood transports digested food, water, and oxygen to the cells of the body. It transports carbon dioxide and other wastes from the cells.

The **heart**, which is made of muscle tissue, pumps blood to all parts of the body. The heart has a right and left side, each made of an upper and lower chamber (Figure 2–14). Blood travels from the body through **veins** to the right side of the heart, where it is pumped to the lungs. In the lungs, the blood becomes oxygen-rich.

From the lungs the blood travels to the left side of the heart, where it is pumped through arteries to the organs of the body. **Arteries** have thick muscular walls, which can expand to accommodate large amounts of blood coming from the heart.

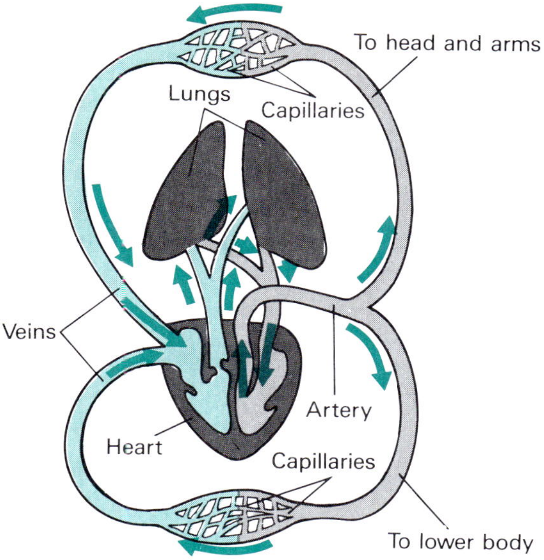

Figure 2–12. The circulatory system.

Arteries branch into tiny blood vessels called **capillaries**. Capillaries, which surround the body tissues, permit the exchange of materials between the blood and the body cells.

Digested food, water, and oxygen leave the blood at the capillaries and enter the body cells, while carbon dioxide and other wastes leave the cells and enter the blood (Figure 2–15). Blood flows from the capillaries to veins, which carry blood back to the heart.

In the veins the pressure of the blood flow to the heart is very low. *Valves* in the veins (Figure 2–16) prevent the blood from flowing backward and enable the blood to continue its path toward the heart.

Lymph vessels, like capillaries, are tiny vessels. Lymph vessels surround all the body tissues. They collect extra fluid, called **lymph**, which bathes the body cells. Lymph is carried by the lymph vessels back to the circulatory system, where it empties into the blood (Figure 2–17).

Type of Blood Cell	Function
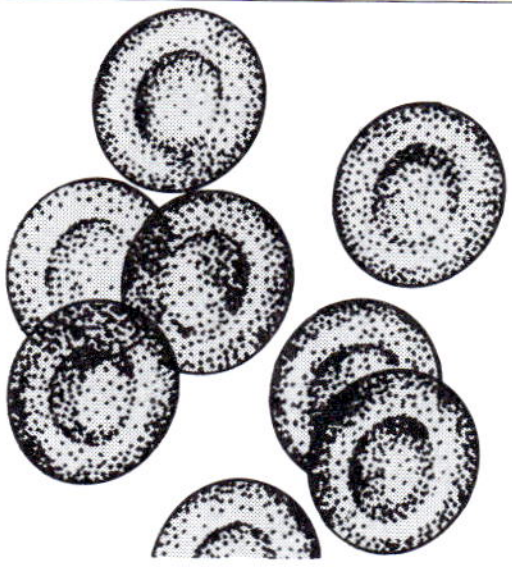 Red Blood Cells	Transport oxygen to the cells
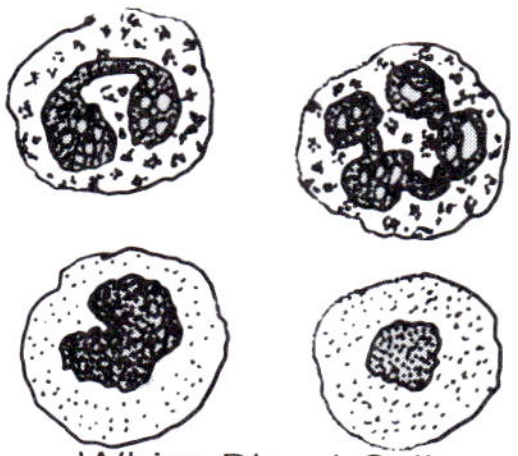 White Blood Cells	Fight diseases
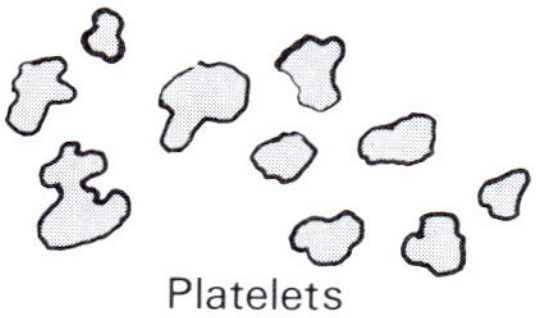 Platelets	Assist in blood clotting

Figure 2–13. Types of blood cells and their functions.

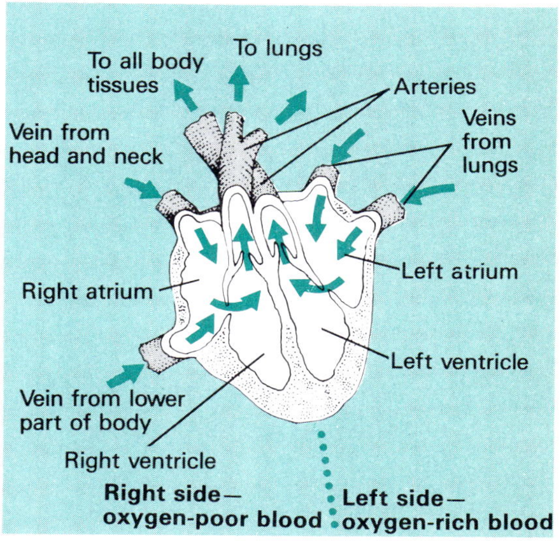

Figure 2–14. Chambers of the heart.

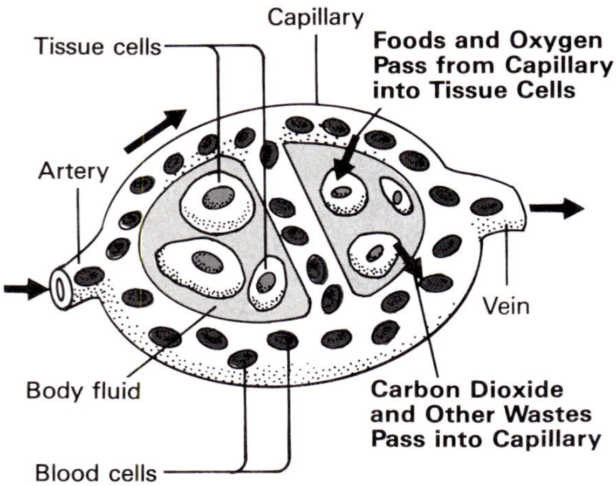

Figure 2–15. Exchange of materials between capillaries and cells.

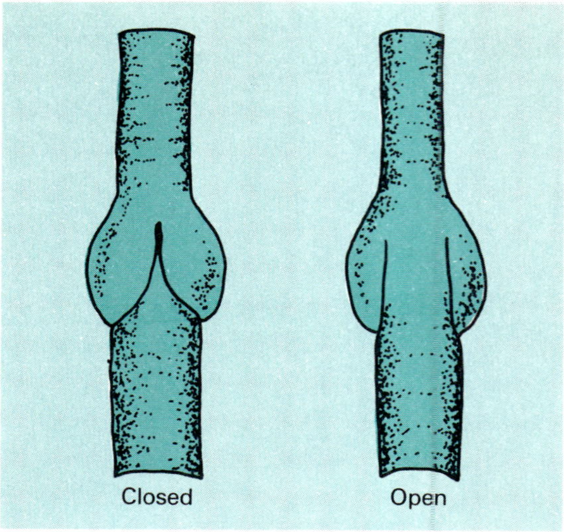

Figure 2–16. A valve in a vein.

Figure 2–17. The lymph circulation. The lymph nodes purify lymph and produce some types of blood cells.

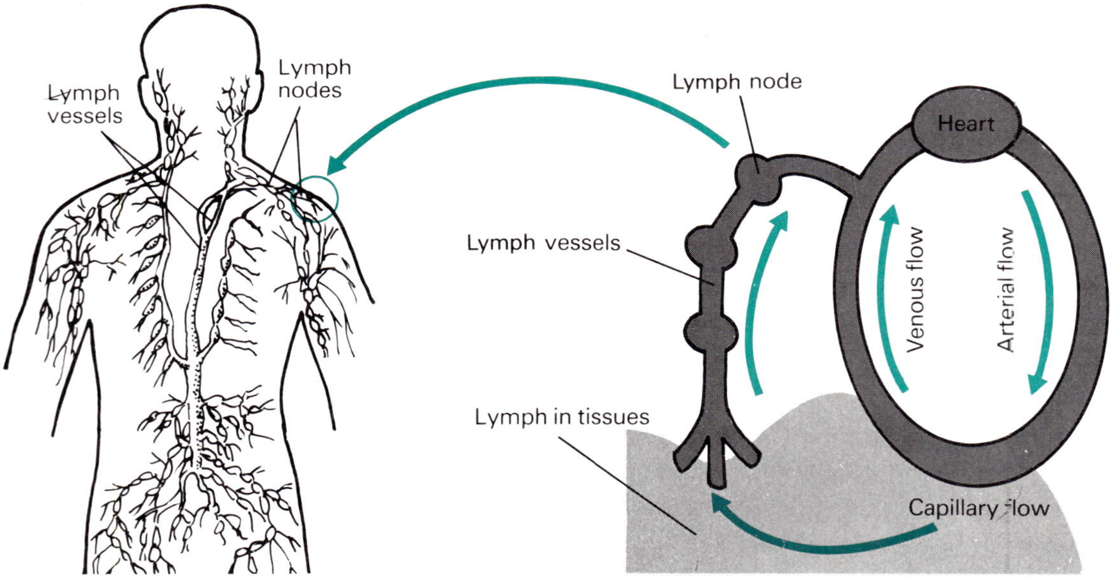

2. Structure and Function of the Respiratory System

(B16, B17)

The process of taking in (inhaling) oxygen and releasing (exhaling) carbon dioxide is known as **respiration**. This process is the job of the *respiratory system*.

As shown in Figure 2–18, the respiratory system consists of the mouth, nose, trachea, bronchi, and lungs. Oxygen-rich air is inhaled through the mouth and through two openings in the nose called *nostrils*. The nostrils carry the air into the *nasal passages*. *Mucous membranes* lining these passages moisten and warm the air and also trap dust and bacteria. Tiny hairs called *cilia* move mucus that contains dust and bacteria toward the nostrils, where it is expelled.

From the nasal passages air enters the **trachea**, or windpipe. The trachea is supported by rings of *cartilage*. The trachea divides further into two large branches called **bronchi**, which carry oxygen-rich air to the lungs.

The **lungs** are two spongy organs made of millions of tiny *air sacs* (Figure 2–19). Each air sac is surrounded by a network of capillaries. Oxygen passes through the walls of the air sacs and moves into the capillaries, where it is dissolved in the blood. At the same time, carbon dioxide moves from the capillaries into the air sacs. When you exhale, the carbon dioxide is breathed out into the air.

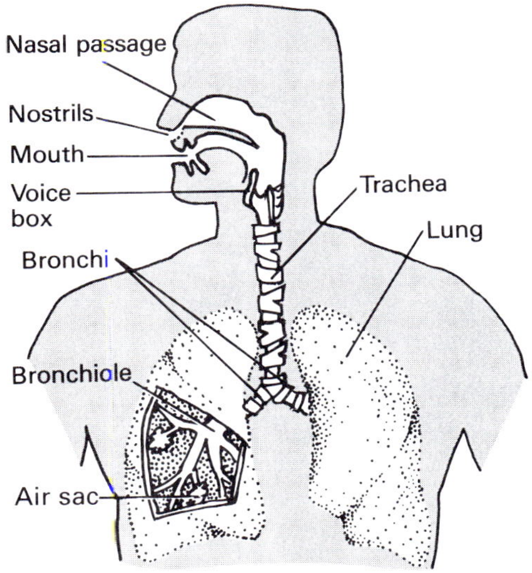

Figure 2–18. The respiratory system.

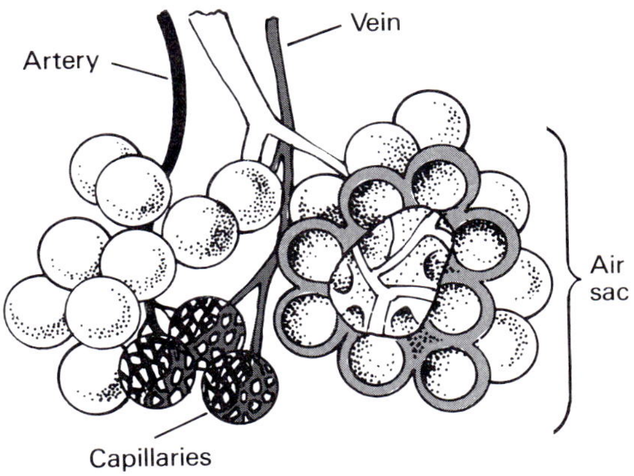

Figure 2–19. Oxygen and carbon dioxide are exchanged in the air sacs.

Respiration can be divided into three stages: breathing, transport of respiratory gases, and cellular respiration. During breathing, air rich in oxygen is inhaled and air rich in carbon dioxide is exhaled. At the air sacs in the lungs the respiratory gases are exchanged with the bloodstream. In the bloodstream oxygen is transported from the air sacs to the body cells, while carbon dioxide is transported from the body cells to the lungs. After oxygen is absorbed from the blood into the body cells, it is used for cellular respiration.

3. Cellular Respiration *(B15)*

Cellular respiration takes place in all the cells of the body. During cellular respiration usable energy is released from glucose, a form of sugar carried in the blood. To release energy, glucose combines with oxygen. Carbon dioxide and water are formed as waste products.

The following chemical reaction occurs during cellular respiration:

Glucose + Oxygen →
Carbon dioxide + Water + Usable energy

Sample Questions

1. Which is a function of the human circulatory system?
   (1) transports carbon dioxide and other wastes from the cells
   (2) releases energy from digested food
   (3) coordinates and controls body activities
   (4) controls the locomotion of the body

2. Materials move into and out of the blood through special blood vessels called
   (1) hearts (3) veins
   (2) arteries (4) capillaries

3–4. Base your answers to questions 3 and 4 on the diagram of the circulatory system shown below.

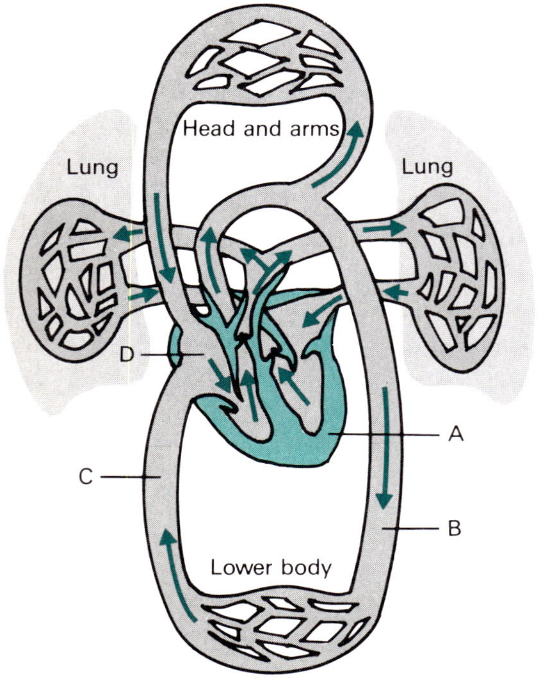

3. Which vessel receives oxygen-poor blood from the organs of the body?

4. Which vessel carries oxygen-rich blood to the organs of the body?

5. The major parts of the circulatory system are the
   (1) veins, arteries, heart
   (2) skin, lungs, kidneys
   (3) nose, bronchi, lungs
   (4) trachea, bronchi, lungs

6. A jogger's pulse rate at rest was 60 beats per second. After running in a 100-yard dash his pulse rate was 120 beats per second. From the data presented above one can conclude that pulse rate
   (1) always doubles while exercising
   (2) increases while exercising
   (3) decreases while exercising
   (4) is unaffected by exercising

7. Which cellular activity releases energy from digested food?
   (1) circulation
   (2) regulation
   (3) cellular respiration
   (4) cellular excretion

8. The life function that supplies the body with necessary oxygen is
   (1) secretion (3) absorption
   (2) excretion (4) respiration

9. Which gas is found in greater amounts in inhaled air than in exhaled air?
   (1) carbon dioxide
   (2) oxygen
   (3) nitrogen
   (4) hydrogen

10–11. Base your answers to questions 10 and 11 on the diagram of the human respiratory system shown below.

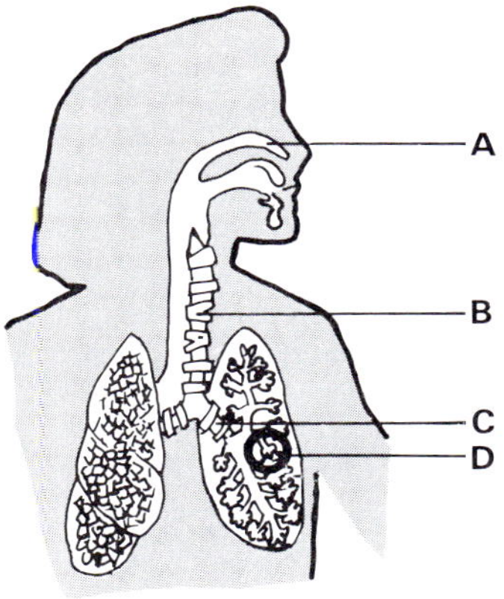

10. Which structure is the site for the exchange of respiratory gases?
(1) A (3) C
(2) B (4) D

11. Which part is the trachea?
(1) A (3) C
(2) B (4) D

12. Two major organs of the respiratory system are
(1) brain and nerves
(2) nerves and muscles
(3) arteries and veins
(4) trachea and lungs

V. COORDINATION, CONTROL, AND REPRODUCTION

1. *The Control Systems* *(B7)*

The human body continuously receives information, or *stimuli*, from the environment. Humans detect, process, and then respond to stimuli (react) by using their nervous system and their endocrine system. The nervous and endocrine systems help to coordinate and control body activities.

Here is an example of how the nervous system controls body activities. If you see danger, you use your legs to move away. The danger seen by your eyes is communicated to the legs through the nervous system. Chemicals produced by special glands called *endocrine glands* control human body activities too. For example, *adrenaline*, a special chemical produced by an endocrine gland called the adrenal gland, prepares the body to move away from danger by increasing heartbeat and blood flow and by increasing the amount of blood sugar.

2. *The Parts of the Nervous System* *(B8)*

The nervous system, shown in Figure 2–20, consists of the brain, spinal cord, nerves, and sense organs. The cells that make up the nervous system are nerve cells called **neurons**.

The parts of the nervous system work together to enable humans to detect, process, and then respond to stimuli. The **sense organs**—the eyes, ears, nose, taste buds, and receptors in the skin—are adapted to receive stimuli. Eyes, for example are adapted for perceiving light, ears for perceiving sound, and the nose for perceiving odors.

When a sense organ receives a stimulus, *sensory nerves* carry the stimulus as *impulses* (messages) to the brain and spinal cord. From the brain and spinal cord, *motor neurons* carry the impulses to muscles and glands for an appropriate response.

Figure 2–20. (A) The nervous system. (B) A neuron, or nerve cell.

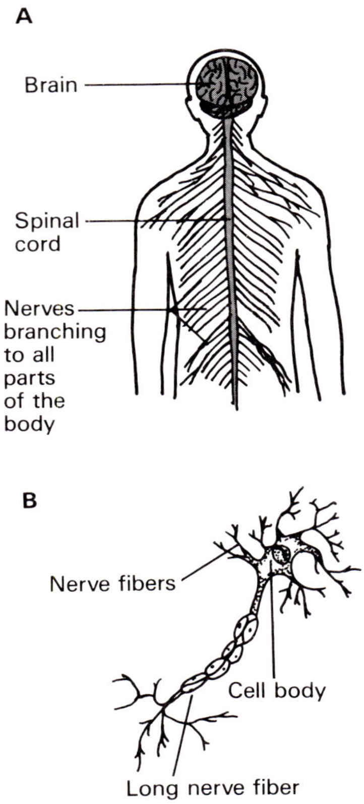

Figure 2–21. The path of a reflex.

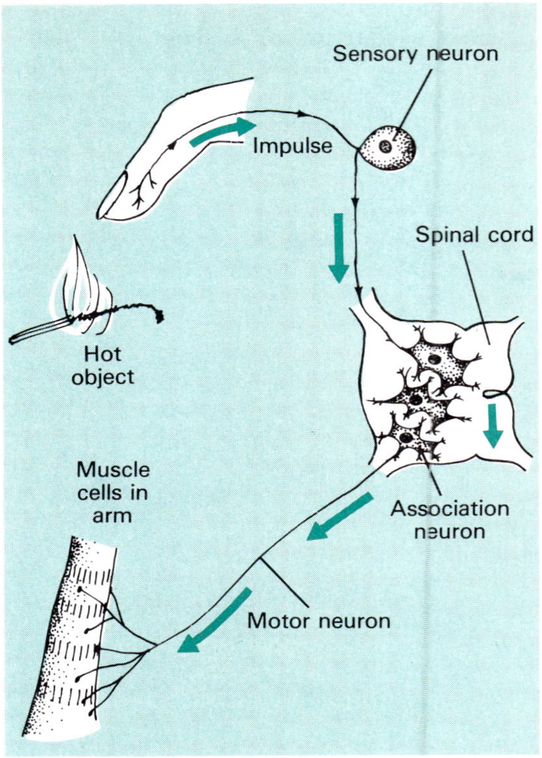

Humans are born with the ability to respond automatically to some stimuli. These automatic, inborn responses are called **reflexes**. Figure 2–21 traces the path of one such reflex.

Together the **brain** and **spinal cord** make up the *central nervous system*. Impulses are interpreted in the central nervous system and are then directed through nerves to other parts of the body for an appropriate response.

3. The Endocrine System *(B9)*

Along with the nervous system, the endocrine system coordinates and controls the activities of the body.

The endocrine system consists of a group of glands called *endocrine glands*. Endocrine glands secrete special chemicals, called **hormones**, which are released directly into the bloodstream. The hormones are transported through the blood to target organs where they produce their effects. Figure 2–22 gives the names and locations of some endocrine glands.

Figure 2–22. The endocrine system.

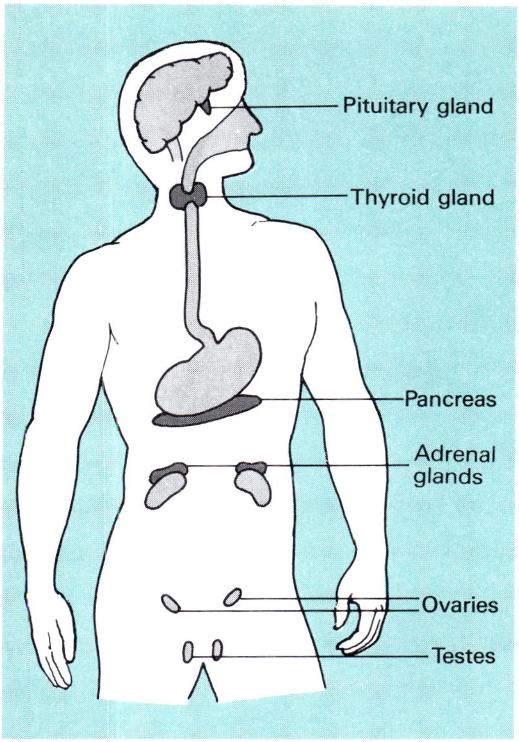

The pancreas is an endocrine gland that secretes the hormone *insulin*. Insulin travels through the blood to the liver. With the help of insulin, the liver absorbs and stores sugar from the blood. Ovaries are a pair of endocrine glands found in the human female. They secrete female sex hormones, which control the development of reproductive organs. Hormones produced by the thyroid and pituitary glands regulate growth and development and help control metabolism.

4. The Reproductive System *(B21)*

The male and female reproductive systems are needed to produce offspring. The

Figure 2–23. The female reproductive system.

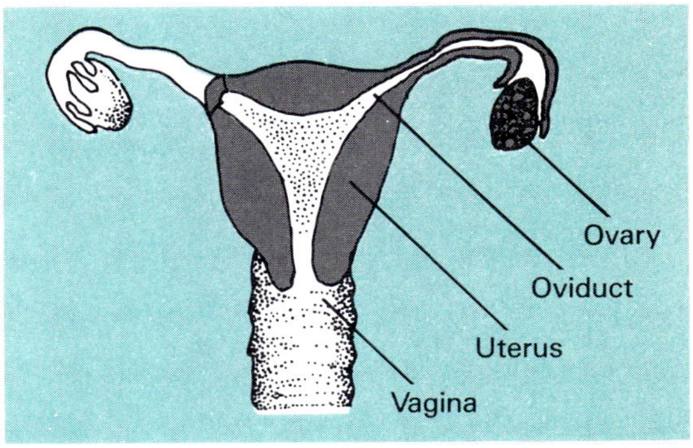

male reproductive system produces male reproductive cells, called sperms. The female reproductive system produces female reproductive cells, called eggs.

5. The Female Reproductive System *(B22)*

The female reproductive system, shown in Figure 2–23, consists of the ovaries, oviducts, uterus, vagina, and mammary glands.

The **ovaries** are located in the lower part of the abdomen. Approximately once a month, one of the ovaries releases an egg cell. The eggs are carried through tubes called **oviducts** to a muscular organ called the **uterus**.

While it is in the oviduct, an egg may participate in a process called *fertilization*. During fertilization an egg cell joins with a sperm cell. If fertilization occurs, a new cell called a *zygote* forms. The zygote is the beginning of a new offspring. As soon as the zygote forms it begins to develop. The developing zygote travels through the oviduct to the uterus, where it implants itself and continues to develop for nine months (see

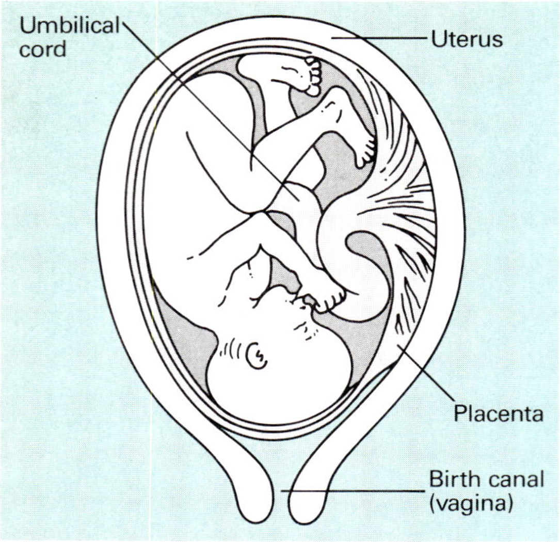

Figure 2–24. The developing offspring is protected and nourished within the uterus.

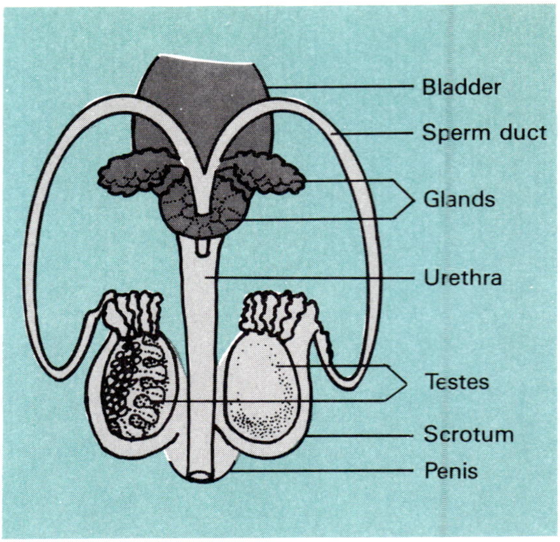

Figure 2–25. The male reproductive system.

Figure 2–24). After nine months, at birth, the offspring passes through the **vagina**, or birth canal.

After the offspring is born it may feed on milk from the **mammary glands**, or breasts.

6. The Male Reproductive System (B23)

The male reproductive system, shown in Figure 2–25, consists of the testes, the sperm ducts, and the penis. The **testes**, which produce sperm cells, are located in a pouch of skin called the *scrotum sac*. Sperm cells pass from the testes into the **sperm ducts**, which carry them back into the body. Glands located near the sperm ducts secrete a fluid which mixes with the sperm to form *semen*. From the sperm ducts, semen is carried to a tube in the **penis**. The penis places semen into the vagina of the female.

Sample Questions

1. The major parts of the nervous system are
(1) bones and muscles
(2) veins and arteries
(3) kidneys and sweat glands
(4) brain and spinal cord

2. The endocrine system consists of glands that
(1) eliminate wastes
(2) secrete hormones
(3) exchange gases
(4) digest food

3–4. Base your answers to questions 3 and 4 on the diagram of the cell shown below.

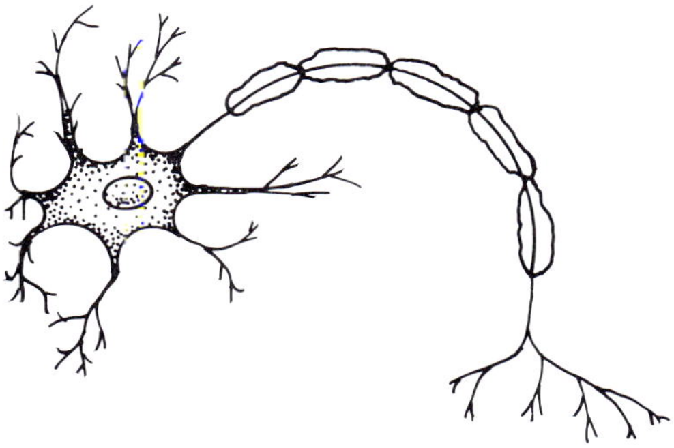

3. This cell is the building block of the
   (1) digestive system
   (2) circulatory system
   (3) excretory system
   (4) nervous system

4. This cell helps to
   (1) coordinate and control body activities
   (2) secrete hormones
   (3) release waste products
   (4) support the organs of the body

5. Simple reflexes, such as pulling your hand away from a hot stove, are most closely associated with the
   (1) nervous system
   (2) excretory system
   (3) digestive system
   (4) respiratory system

6–9. For each phrase in questions 6–9, select the correct reproductive structure from the list below.

Reproductive Structures
   (1) ovary
   (2) testes
   (3) vagina
   (4) mammary glands
   (5) uterus

6. The organ that produces egg cells

7. The birth canal

8. The organ where the human embryo develops

9. The structure that produces milk

10–12. Base your answers to questions 10 through 12 on the diagram of the reproductive system of a female shown below.

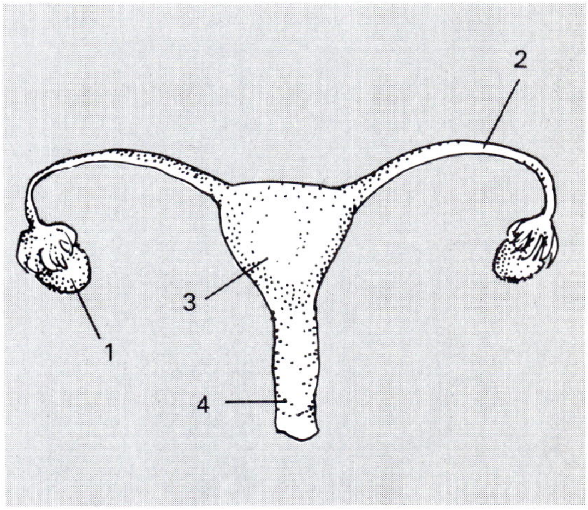

10. Within which structure does the human embryo develop?

11. In which structure is the zygote usually formed?

12. Where is the egg produced?

13. Egg is to sperm as ovary is to
   (1) oviduct
   (2) sperm duct
   (3) testis
   (4) penis

Issues in Science, Technology, and Society

Reducing Pollution

In recent years, people have become more aware of the problem of environmental pollution. The air is polluted by automobile exhausts and wastes from factory chimneys. Rivers are polluted with sewage and with wastes dumped from factories located along their banks. Some of these wastes pollute a large area when they are carried into lakes, ponds, and oceans.

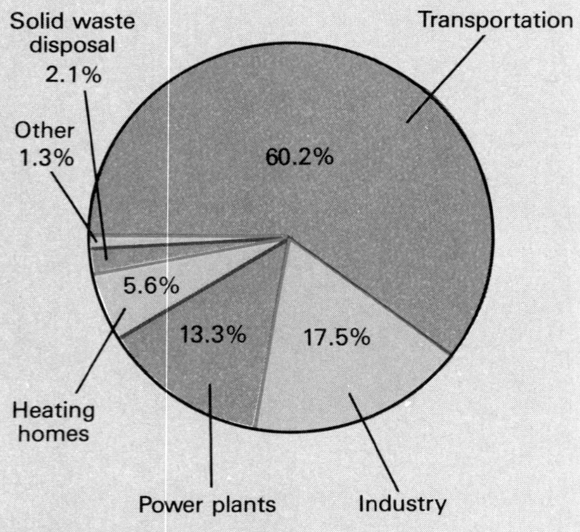

Sources of air pollution.

Solving the pollution problem is a major challenge faced by society today. A number of technological devices have been developed.

Emission Control Devices All new automobiles sold in the United States must be equipped with an emission control device. This device cleans the automobile exhaust before it passes into the air.

Trash Compactors In some cities, burning trash is prohibited in order to reduce the amount of smoke and soot entering the air. Trash compactors crush trash into small packages that can easily be carried away to landfill sites.

Sewage Treatment Plants To prevent sewage from polluting the land and water, it is passed through sewage treatment plants. Here the sewage is chemically treated to eliminate disease-causing bacteria and other harmful wastes. After being treated in the plant, the sewage can safely be emptied into waterways.

Although these devices have helped reduce pollution, technology alone cannot solve the pollution problem. Society must make a commitment to keep a constant watch on the cleanliness of the environment. People must take whatever steps are necessary to make certain that the environment is safe for all living things.

1. How can factories in one part of the country cause pollution in another part of the country?
2. What acts of "progress" can you name that have since been associated with polluting the environment?
3. Who should be responsible for maintaining the quality of the environment: individuals, industry, local government, or national agencies? Why?

CHAPTER 3 Living Systems: Microorganisms

I. CELLS

1. The Cell and Its Parts (C1, C2)

Every living organism is made of **cells.** Cells carry on the basic life activities of the organism.

Most cells are too small to be seen with the unaided eye. To see these cells, biologists use an instrument called a **microscope.** Biology students use a *compound microscope*, shown in Figure 3–1, to see cells. A compound microscope contains two lens systems. Some compound microscopes can magnify cells up to 4000 times.

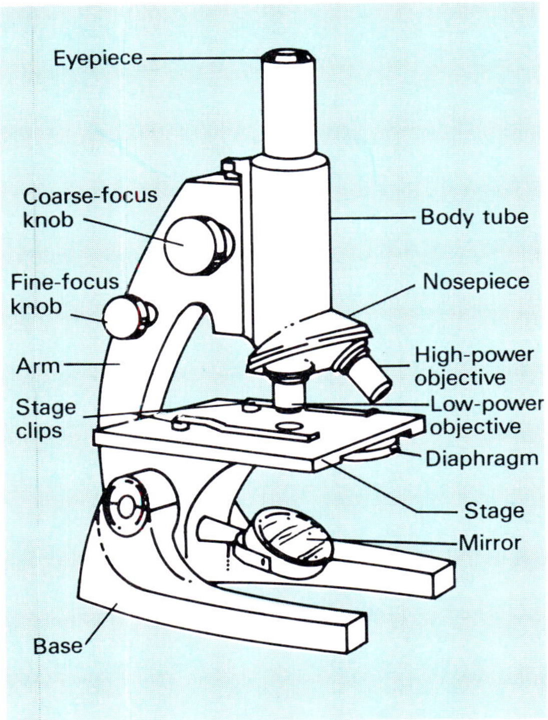

Figure 3–1. Compound microscope.

Figure 3–2 shows the parts of the cell that can be seen with a compound microscope. The following parts of the cell can be seen: the cell membrane, the cytoplasm, and the nucleus. The *cell membrane* encloses the cytoplasm and regulates the passage of materials into and out of the cell. The *cytoplasm*, a jellylike material, contains

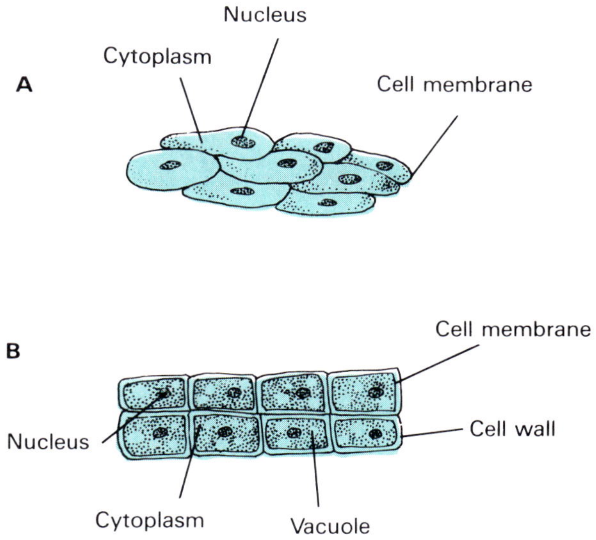

Figure 3–2. How cells look viewed under a compound microscope. (A) Human cheek cells; (B) onion skin cells.

the nucleus and the other parts of the cell. The *nucleus* contains the genetic material of the cell.

To see cells in greater detail, biologists use a very powerful microscope, the *electron microscope*. The electron microscope can magnify cells as much as 400,000 times. It has enabled biologists to identify many more parts of the cell. Table 1 lists some of these structures and their functions.

Table 1 Structures of a Cell

Structure	Function
Cell membrane	Surrounds cell; regulates passage of materials into and out of the cell
Cytoplasm	Jellylike substance that contains the parts of the cell
Nucleus	Houses the genetic material (chromosomes and genes)
Mitochondria	Powerhouse of the cell; releases useful energy
Ribosomes	Manufacture proteins
Endoplasmic reticulum	Tubelike membranes on which chemical reactions take place
Golgi bodies	Manufacture, store, and secrete carbohydrates and proteins

Plant cells and animal cells differ in some ways. A plant cell, shown in Figure 3–3, has a *cell wall*. The cell wall is made of a tough material called cellulose, which stiffens the cell wall and makes it hard. The cell wall protects and helps to support the plant. Plant cells also have *chloroplasts*. Chloroplasts contain a green pigment, chlorophyll, which is important in the process of photosynthesis.

Animal cells have neither cell walls nor chloroplasts. However, every animal cell has a pair of *centrioles*. Centrioles play an important role in cell division. Plant cells have no centrioles. Figure 3–4 shows an animal cell.

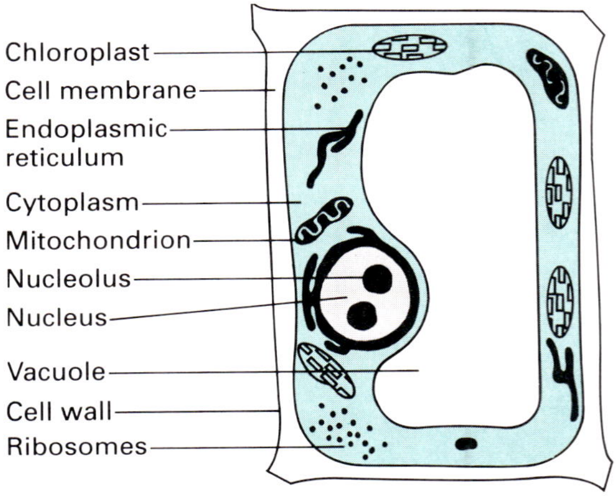

Figure 3–3. A plant cell.

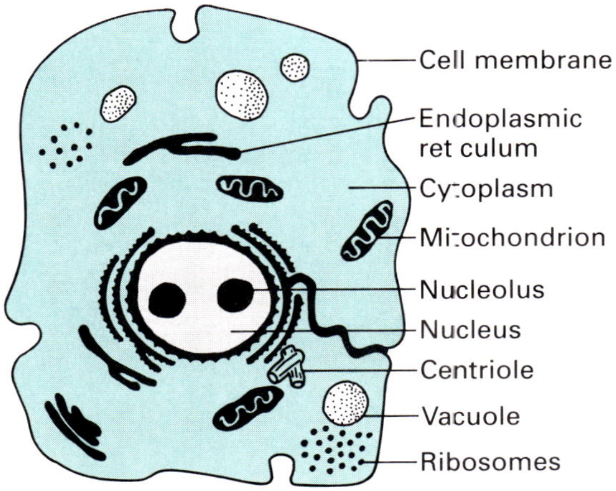

Figure 3–4. An animal cell.

The various parts of plant and animal cells perform activities necessary for the survival of the organism. For example, cell respiration, an energy-releasing process, takes place in the *mitochondria* of plant and animal cells. Proteins are manufactured in the *ribosomes*. In plant cells, photosynthesis occurs in the chloroplasts.

2. Cell Division *(C3)*

Cells grow to a particular size and then they divide, or reproduce. To put it another way, new cells come from preexisting cells.

All life continues through cell division. For life to continue, some instructions must be passed down from generation to generation. These instructions are carried in the nucleus of the cell. The cell's nucleus contains genetic material called *chromosomes* and *genes*. Chromosomes and genes are the cell's blueprints. They provide the instructions for building the offspring. Genes and chromosomes are passed on to the offspring during cell division (reproduction).

Some organisms reproduce asexually. In **asexual reproduction**, one or more of the cells of one parent develops into an offspring. Some types of asexual reproduction are shown in Figure 1–5 on page 7. The offspring is created by a type of cell division called *mitosis*. In **sexual reproduction**, an offspring is produced by the union of two reproductive cells called **gametes** (sperm and egg). Sperm and egg cells are created during a type of cell division called *meiosis*.

Mitosis **Mitosis** is a kind of cell division that results in the reproduction of new cells. The following events take place during mitosis:

1. The nuclear material (chromosomes) double, forming two sets. Each daughter cell receives one set of chromosomes (Figure 3–5).

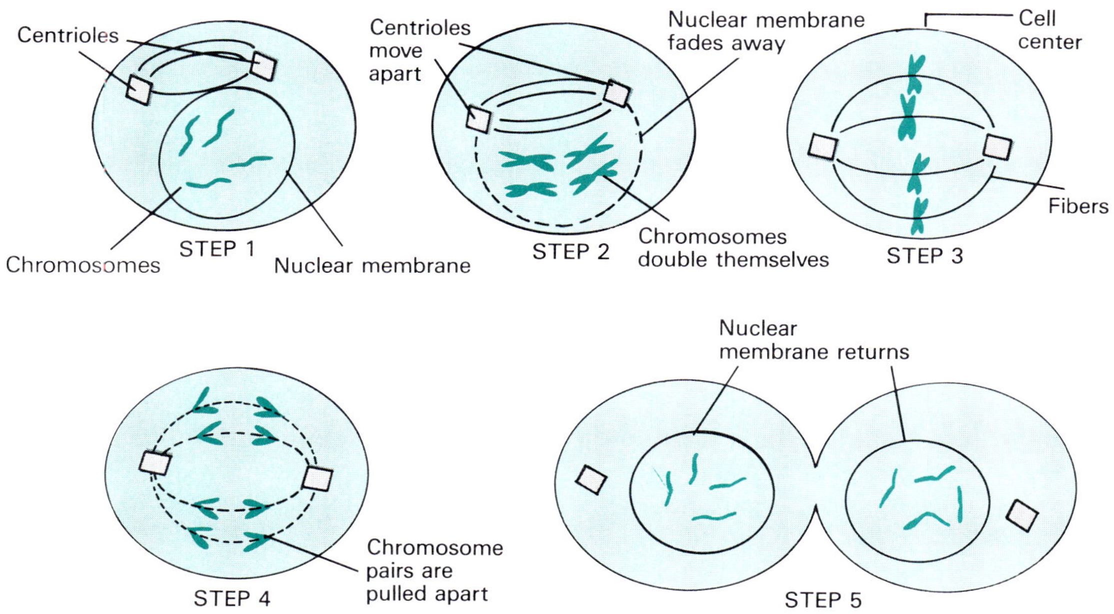

Figure 3–5. The steps of mitosis.

2. The cytoplasm divides to form two daughter cells (offspring).

Each particular kind of plant or animal cell has its own definite number of chromosomes. All the body cells of a particular organism have this same chromosome number. For example, each body cell of a human contains 46 chromosomes (23 pairs). Each body cell of a fruitfly contains 8 chromosomes, or 4 pairs (Figure 3–6). Because mitosis doubles the chromosomes and then distributes a set to each daughter cell, this ensures that the number of chromosomes in all cells of a particular organism remains constant.

Mitosis is important for the continuation of life. In unicellular organisms, such as the ameba and the paramecium, mitosis results in the reproduction of new individuals. The result of mitosis for unicellular organisms is the production of two offspring, each with the same number and kinds of chromosomes, making the offspring and parent identical. To put it another way, asexual reproduction usually produces offspring with no genetic variations.

In addition to its role in the reproduction of unicellular organisms, mitosis in multicellular organisms is linked to development, growth, and repair. For example, a human begins life as a single cell, called a **zygote**. The zygote undergoes repeated mitotic divisions to become an organism of many identical cells. The cells that arise as a result of mitosis grow, specialize, and form the various organs of the human. As in humans, mitosis in all organisms provides new cells, tissues, and organs.

Meiosis In sexual reproduction two gametes, a sperm and egg, unite during fertilization to form a zygote. Sperms and eggs form in the testes and ovaries during a kind of cell division called **meiosis**. During meiosis the number of chromosomes in some cells in the testes or ovaries is reduced in half to form sperm and egg cells (Figure 3–7).

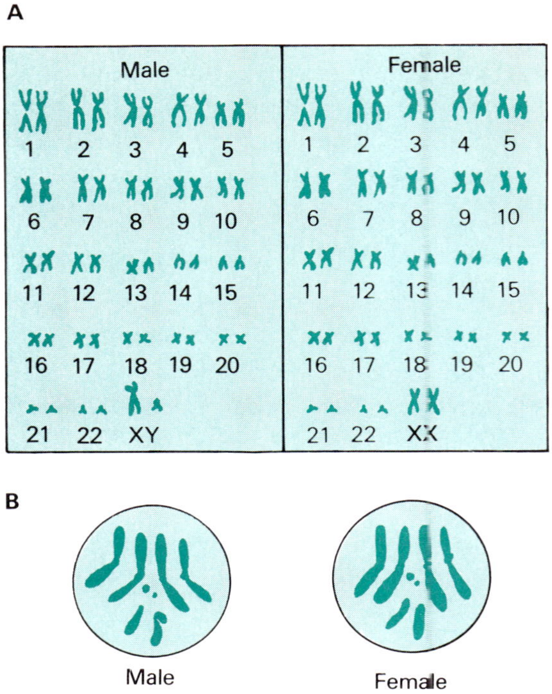

Figure 3–6. (A) The 23 pairs of human chromosomes; (B) the 4 pairs of fruitfly chromosomes.

Notice in the figure that the chromosomes line up in pairs and separate from each other. As a result of meiosis, each sperm or egg cell has only half as many chromosomes as do cells in the other parts of the body (only one of each chromosome pair). During fertilization a sperm and egg cell, each with half the chromosome number of the species, fuse. This fusing causes the correct number of chromosomes for that species to appear in the zygote.

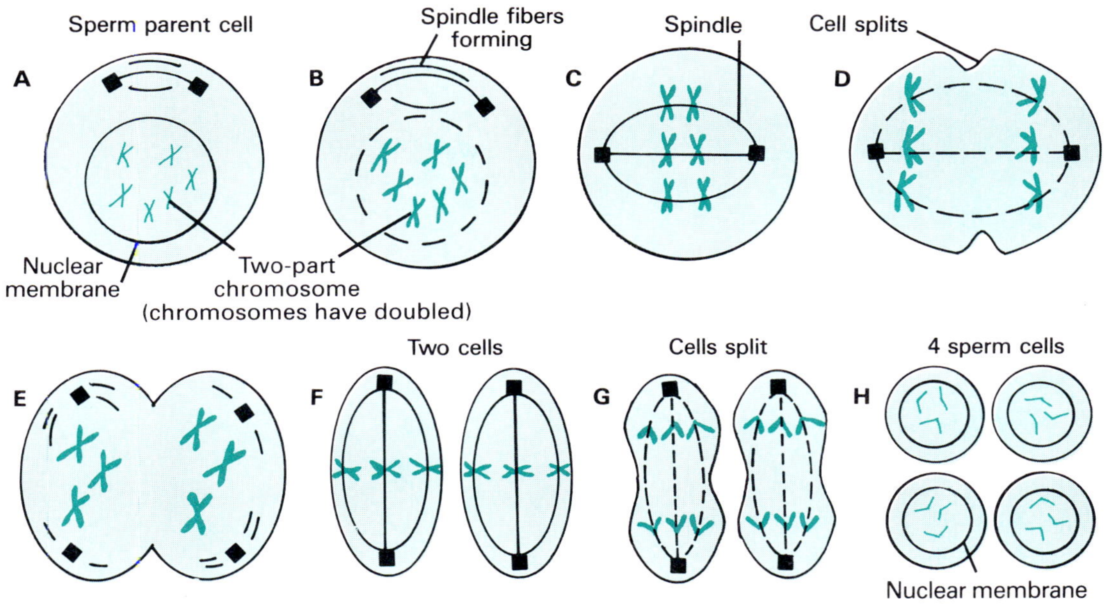

Figure 3–7. During meiosis one cell divides twice, producing four cells. This illustration shows a sperm parent cell dividing into four sperm cells. A–E illustrate the first cell division. F–H illustrate the second cell division, sometimes called reduction division.

In humans, for example, the zygote contains 46 chromosomes. The sperm cell brings 23 chromosomes (paternal chromosomes) from the father to the zygote. The egg cell carries 23 chromosomes (maternal chromosomes) from the mother to the zygote. Half the chromosomes come to the offspring from the mother, half from the father (Figure 3–8).

In brief, meiosis is a kind of cell division that reduces to half the chromosome number in sperm and egg cells. At fertilization, the sperm and egg join together, restoring the chromosome number characteristic of the species.

3. Sexual Reproduction Creates Variations *(C4)*

In asexually reproducing organisms, as a result of mitosis, offspring look identical

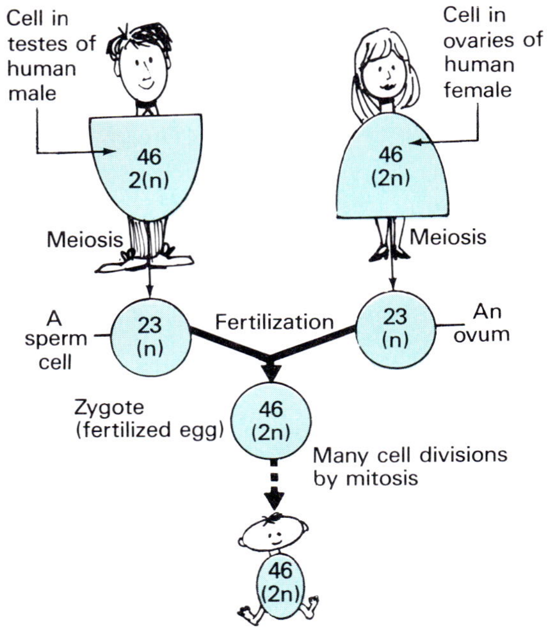

Figure 3–8. In humans, 23 chromosomes come from the father and 23 chromosomes come from the mother.

to the parent. In sexually reproducing organisms this is not so. Organisms arising from sexual reproduction resemble their parents in some ways but differ in other ways. To understand this variation in offspring it is necessary to look once again at what takes place during meiosis. Figure 3–9 shows the many different possible combinations of chromosomes that can appear in the gametes. The figure shows a zygote produced by the union of a sperm and egg cell. (The chromosomes from the father are shown in blue; the chromosomes from the mother are shown in white.)

After undergoing repeated mitotic divisions, the zygote becomes a multicellular organism, each cell bearing four pairs of chromosomes characteristic of this species. When this multicellular organism produces gametes through the process of meiosis, each gamete will receive either the maternal or paternal chromosome of each pair.

The figure shows the many possible combinations of chromosomes in the gametes. Since any one of these gametes may participate in the fertilization process, individuals in the next generation will exhibit genetic variations. For this reason, children born of the same parents are often quite different from each other.

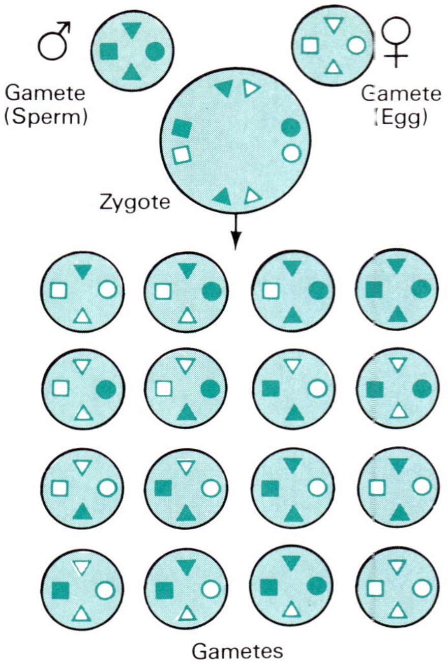

Figure 3–9. Many different combinations of chromosomes can appear in the gametes.

Sample Questions

1. Which of the following statements about cells is *not* true?
   (1) Cells make up a living thing.
   (2) Cells carry on the basic life functions of living things.
   (3) Cells contain structures that carry on life functions.
   (4) Most cells cannot reproduce.

2–5. Base your answers to questions 2–5 on the diagrams at the right, which illustrate two cells observed under a compound microscope.

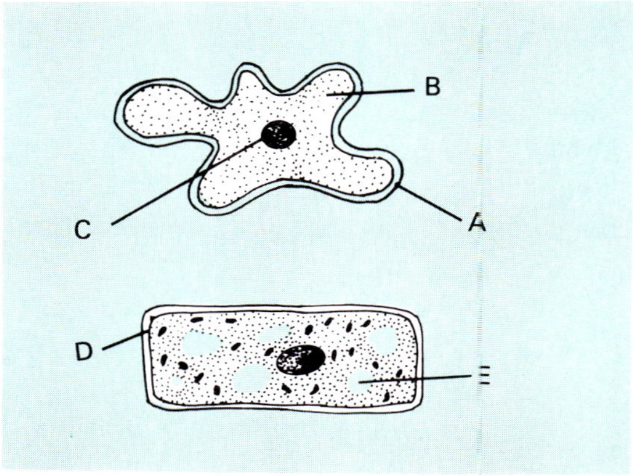

2. Which cell structure contains genetic material?

3. Which cell structure produces food?

4. Which cell structure controls the passage of material into and out of the cell?

5. Which cell structures are not found in animal cells?

6. A few bacteria are placed in a sugar solution. After several hours, thousands of bacteria are present. Which life activity is responsible for this event?
(1) digestion (3) reproduction
(2) circulation (4) respiration

7–9. Base your answers to questions 7–9 on the growth curve showing the rate of division of a bacteria culture.

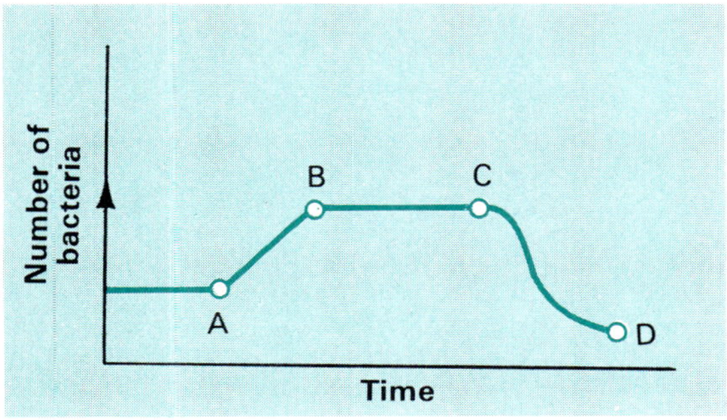

7. During which growth period was the growth rate of the bacteria the fastest?
(1) A through B
(2) B through C
(3) C through D

8. Between which two time periods did the bacteria start to decline in number?
(1) A to B
(2) B to C
(3) C to D

9. What condition was probably *least* responsible for the decline in the number of bacteria between time periods C and D?
(1) The bacteria used up the nutrients in the environment.
(2) Waste products poisoned the environment.
(3) The bacteria only survive for a few hours in the environment in the laboratory.

10. The process of mitosis results in
(1) two cells with identical nuclei
(2) four cells with identical nuclei
(3) four sperm cells
(4) one egg cell

11–13. Base your answers to questions 11–13 on the diagram of the human reproductive cycle shown below.

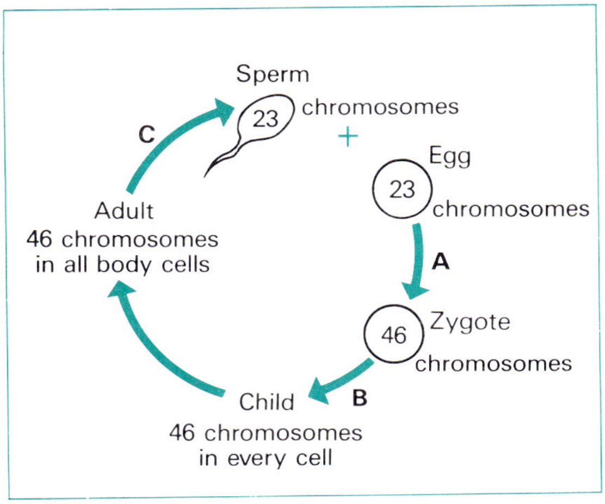

11. The process of mitosis is shown by letter
(1) A (2) B (3) C

12. The process of fertilization is shown by letter
(1) A (2) B (3) C

13. The process of meiosis is shown by letter
(1) A (2) B (3) C

14. A child has the same number of chromosomes as each parent because of the processes of fertilization and
(1) circulation
(2) respiration
(3) growth
(4) meiosis

15. If a lobster loses a claw, it is capable of growing a new one. Which life process is responsible for this event?
(1) meiosis
(2) fertilization
(3) mitosis
(4) sexual reproduction

16. Children born of the same parents are usually very different from each other. This difference is caused mainly by the process of
(1) mitosis
(2) meiosis
(3) asexual reproduction
(4) cytoplasmic division

II. MICROORGANISMS – HELPFUL AND HARMFUL

1. *Kinds of Microorganisms*

A **microorganism** is an organism that is too small to be seen with the unaided eye. Therefore biologists must use a microscope to observe them.

The greatest number and variety of all living things fall into the microorganism category. Bacteria, protozoa, viruses, and some fungi are microorganisms.

Protozoa are unicellular (single-celled) plants and animals. Each protozoan contains its own nucleus with genetic material bound by a nuclear membrane. Examples include the paramecium and the ameba (Figure 3–10).

Bacteria are tiny one-celled organisms. Each contains a cell wall and some genetic material not bound by a nuclear membrane. There are three basic cell shapes among the bacteria: rod-shaped, round, and spiral-shaped (Figure 3–11).

Fungi are sometimes called nongreen plants. Fungus cells have a cell wall, but lack food-making structures (chloroplasts).

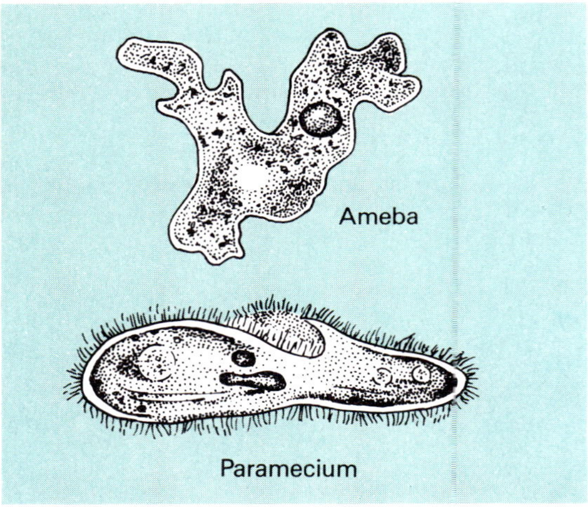

Figure 3–10. Ameba and paramecium.

Figure 3–11. Three shapes of bacteria: coccus (round), bacillus (rod-shaped), and spirillum (spiral-shaped).

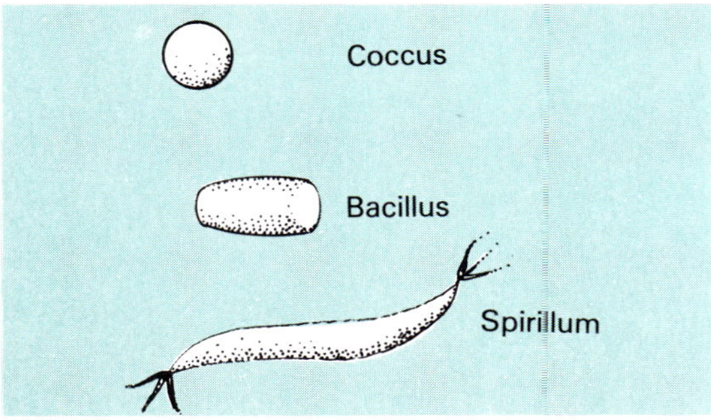

Therefore, fungi must obtain food from other living things. Figure 3–12 shows some types of fungi.

Viruses are the smallest known microorganisms. Viruses are not made of cells. Each virus contains an inner core of genetic material and an outer coat of protein (Figure 3–13).

Figure 3–12. Four types of fungus.

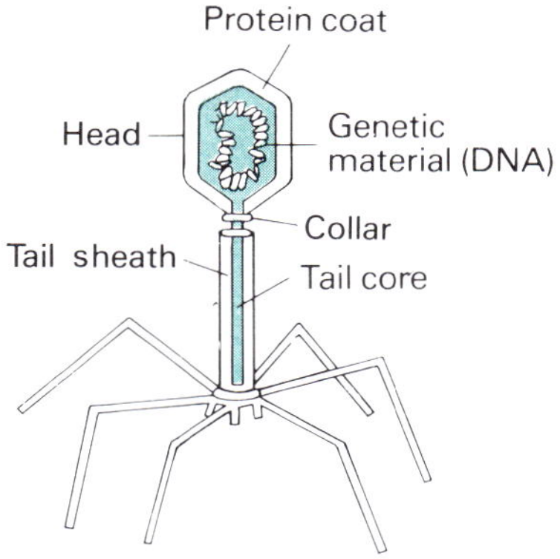

Figure 3–13. Structure of a virus.

2. Many Microorganisms Are Beneficial *(C7)*

Many microorganisms are beneficial to other organisms. Some are even essential. For example, microorganisms in the soil, called bacteria of decay, decompose (break down) the bodies of dead organisms and the wastes of living organisms. The decomposed materials may serve as foods or fertilizer for other living things. Many foods, such as bread, cheeses, and wines, obtain their tastes from cultures of microorganisms. Yeast, a kind of fungus, is used to ferment sugars to produce wines and beers. Molds (another kind of fungus) are used to produce blue cheese. Many foods, including sauerkraut, yogurt, buttermilk, cottage cheese, and butter, are prepared with the assistance of bacteria. Bacteria in the human digestive system assist in the digestion of food.

3. Microorganisms: The Cause of Infectious Diseases *(C5)*

Some microorganisms are harmful to other organisms. These harmful microorganisms, including some bacteria, viruses, fungi, and protozoa, are called **pathogens**.

Pathogens cause infectious diseases that can spread from one individual to another in different ways:

By air—Microorganisms can be spread through the air as a result of a cough or sneeze.

By water—Microorganisms are found in drinking water. Often they enter the water along with human wastes.

By contact—Microorganisms may pass from person to person on contact by touching, kissing, or by sexual contact.

When harmful microorganisms enter an organism they multiply in it, causing disease. Table 2 lists some common infectious diseases caused by microorganisms.

Table 2 Infectious Diseases Caused by Microorganisms

Diseases	Microorganism
Cold, polio, measles hepatitis, warts, mononucleosis, flu, smallpox, mumps, cold sores, herpes, AIDS	Virus
Athlete's foot, ringworm	Fungus
Tuberculosis, pneumonia, diphtheria	Bacteria
Sleeping sickness, malaria, black fever, diarrhea, bleeding gums	Protozoan

4. Controlling Undesirable Microorganisms *(C8)*

It is important to control the spread of harmful microorganisms (pathogens) so that food, water, and air do not become contaminated with them and cause an increase in infection in human populations.

To prevent infection, contamination, and spoilage, microorganisms are controlled by removing or killing them or by slowing their growth. To do this the following techniques are used:

Sterilization—A process in which all the microorganisms in an area are completely destroyed. Sterilization involves the use of chemicals or intense heat. Doctors sterilize medical instruments after using them to destroy all microorganisms on them.

Disinfection—A process used to destroy most harmful microorganisms (some of the more resistant bacteria may not be destroyed). Disinfection may or may not result in sterilization. To disinfect an area, chemicals called germicides are used. Examples of germicides include bactericidals and fungicidals. Boiling water or flowing steam may also be used to disinfect.

Pasteurization—A process in which substances such as milk and fruit juices are heated in order to kill harmful microorganisms.

Canning—A process used to preserve foods. First the food is sealed in airtight cans. Then the cans are heated to a high temperature to sterilize the foods.

Refrigeration—A method of preserving foods. The cool temperature inside a refrigerator (about 4°C) slows the growth of microorganisms in food but does not destroy them. As a result, foods last longer; that is, they will not spoil as quickly when placed in the refrigerator.

Freezing—Another method of preserving foods. Freezing does not destroy microorganisms in foods, but does slow their growth. Foods last longer when in the freezer instead of the refrigerator. However, not all foods freeze well.

Scientists are continually working on new methods to prevent the spread of mi-

Science Skill

EXPLAINING EXPERIMENTAL TECHNIQUE

A solution of an unknown chemical was spilled into a petri dish containing disease-causing bacteria. The dish was placed in a dark closet for three days. At the end of the three days, all the bacteria in the dish were dead.

1. Which of the following conclusions can be drawn from this observation?
   (1) Darkness killed the bacteria.
   (2) The unknown chemical killed the bacteria.
   (3) The bacteria died of old age.
   (4) More research must be done to determine the cause of death of the bacteria.

2. To make a fair judgment regarding the cause of death of the disease-causing bacteria, it is necessary to
   (1) heat the petri dish to see if a high temperature kills the bacteria
   (2) cool the petri dish to see if a low temperature kills the bacteria
   (3) place a second petri dish with the same disease-causing bacteria but without the unknown chemical in the closet for three days
   (4) place a second petri dish with the same disease-causing bacteria and with the unknown chemical in the closet for a week

3. In 1929 Dr. Alexander Fleming discovered a mold called penicillin. Research the experiment he did that led to the discovery of penicillin and its effects. Why is this discovery of pencillin considered a great breakthrough in medicine?

croorganisms in the air, in water, and in food. As human populations grow and as urban areas become more crowded, it is important to slow the growth of disease-producing microorganisms.

5. Noninfectious Disease *(C6)*

Infectious diseases are caused by microorganisms passed on from one person to another. Some human diseases, however, are not passed from one person to another. These noninfectious diseases, such as cancer, heart disease, diabetes, and allergies, are becoming more prevalent in the United States today.

Cancers are a group of noninfectious diseases caused by uncontrolled growth of cells. The causes of some cancers are unknown. Scientists think that viruses may cause some cancers. Other cancers may be caused by industrial chemicals in the environment. Scientists are working hard to find the many causes of cancer.

Diabetes is another noninfectious disease. Its major symptom is abnormal amounts of sugar in the blood. A malfunctioning endocrine gland is its cause.

Deficiency diseases are a group of noninfectious diseases caused by deficiencies in the diet. Vitamin deficiency diseases, such as beriberi and scurvy, are caused by lack of vitamins. Goiter, a mineral deficiency disease, occurs when the body receives no iodine. The lack of iron in the diet may cause anemia, a condition in which the blood cannot carry enough oxygen.

An **allergy** is an abnormal sensitivity to certain substances in the environment. Examples of these substances include pollen, dust, and certain foods. Allergic people may sneeze, cough, and develop skin problems when exposed to these substances.

Science Skill

INTERPRETING DATA

The graph at the right shows the incidence of three diseases between the years 1940 and 1970. Study the graph and then answer the questions below.

1. The greatest number of cases of bacterial pneumonia occurred in
   (1) 1940
   (2) 1950
   (3) 1960
   (4) 1970
2. The best possible explanation for the decrease in the number of cases of bacterial pneumonia from 1940 to 1970 is that
   (1) more people were immune to this disease in 1970
   (2) scientists have developed drugs to prevent and treat bacterial infections such as pneumonia
   (3) doctors did not report all cases
   (4) more people died from the disease

Incidence of Three Diseases From 1940 to 1970

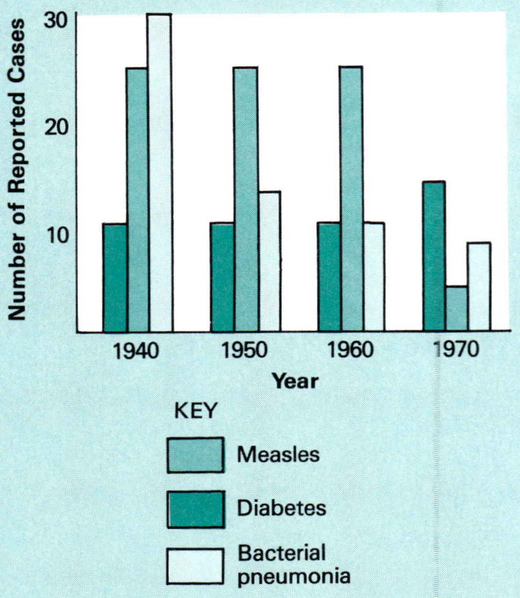

Sample Questions

1. Which one of the following diseases is caused by pathogens?
(1) diabetes
(2) high blood pressure
(3) heart disease
(4) chicken pox

2. Infectious diseases are caused by which of the following?
(1) microorganisms
(2) vitamin deficiencies
(3) lack of sleep
(4) lack of exercise

3–5. Base your answers to questions 3–5 on the graph below, which provides information concerning the spread of AIDS in New York City. AIDS is an infectious disease caused by a virus. AIDS may be spread from one individual to another by sexual contact.

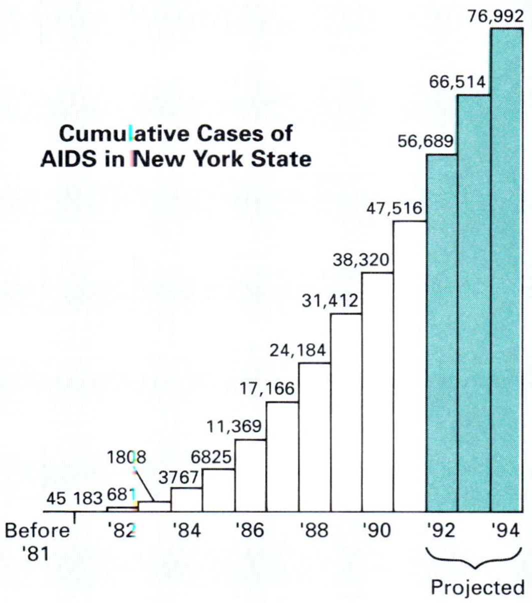

3. As of the end of 1990, how many cases of AIDS have been reported in New York State?
(1) 1808 (3) 38,320
(2) 17,166 (4) 47,516

4. What information concerning AIDS is correct?
(1) The number of cases of AIDS is increasing at a rapid rate.
(2) Since 1979 there have been fewer cases of AIDS reported each year.
(3) The number of AIDS cases doubles each year.
(4) More cases of AIDS were reported in 1990 than in any other year.

5. Which information cannot be determined from the graph?
(1) the cumulative cases of AIDS in 1989
(2) the cumulative cases of AIDS from 1981–1990
(3) the projected cumulative cases of AIDS through 1994
(4) the number of reported cases of AIDS in 1980

6. Which statement concerning pathogenic bacteria is true?
(1) They cannot spread from one individual to another.
(2) They may spread through the air as a result of a cough or sneeze.
(3) They die as soon as they enter the human body.
(4) They are the causes of allergies and heart disease.

7. Microorganisms are harmful to humans in which one of the following ways?
(1) Microorganisms decompose dead organisms.
(2) Cultures of microorganisms are used to make wines and beers.
(3) Microorganisms in the human digestive system assist in the digestion of food.
(4) Some microorganisms are the causes of infectious diseases.

8. The best method for preventing the spread of the common cold in school would be
(1) vaccinating all children
(2) keeping pupils with colds at home
(3) making all pupils take aspirin
(4) injecting students with hormones

9–10. Base your answers to questions 9 and 10 on the diagram below, which appears on the side of a milk container.

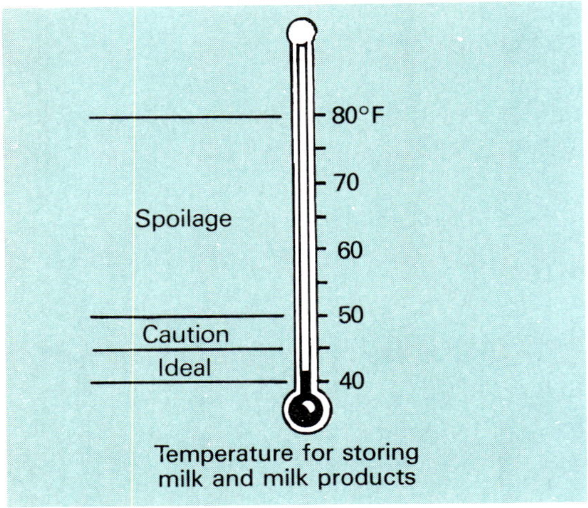

9. For storing milk, what would be a good temperature inside a refrigerator?
(1) 1–8°F (3) 35°F
(2) 30°F (4) 45°F

10. What general statement about milk products could be made based on the diagram?
(1) Milk products kept at high temperatures will not keep as long.
(2) Milk products can be stored only at temperatures above 0°F.
(3) Do not drink milk at 6°F.
(4) The length of time that milk products keep is not related to temperature.

11. Which two noninfectious diseases have become the major causes of death in the United States today?
(1) polio and mumps
(2) diabetes and allergies
(3) heart disease and cancer
(4) pneumonia and tuberculosis

12. Asbestos particles in the environment have been shown to cause some cancers in the human respiratory system. This is one example of how some diseases are caused by
(1) allergies to foreign substances
(2) microorganisms in the environment
(3) particles and chemicals introduced into the environment
(4) deficiences in the human diet

13. A scientist discovered a mold that is capable of slowing the growth of certain disease-causing bacteria. The mold may be used to
(1) grow more disease-causing bacteria
(2) fight the disease
(3) eliminate the disease-causing bacteria
(4) produce wine and cheese

14–16. For each statement in questions 14–16, select the term from the list below that is most closely associated with that statement.

A. Pasteurization C. Disinfection
B. Sterilization D. Freezing

14. Milk and milk products are heated to kill most pathogenic organisms.

15. A doctor's instruments are heated to a very high temperature to destroy all organisms on them.

16. Germicides are used to destroy all pathogenic organisms.

Tools that Improve and Extend Human Lives

Electron Microscope The electron microscope can magnify cells as much as 400,000 times. With it biologists are able to view the tiniest parts of the cell.

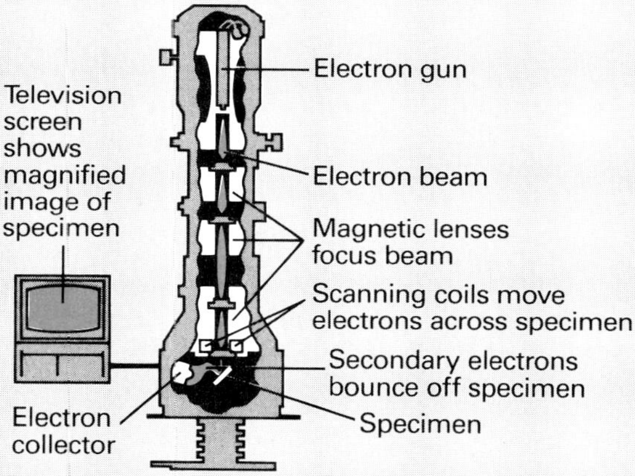

This electron microscope can magnify very tiny objects.

The use of the electron microscope has increased our knowledge of infectious diseases. Biologists can now see and identify many disease-causing bacteria and viruses. Once these pathogens are identified, scientists can try to develop vaccines to control them. As a result of vaccinations, some diseases, such as smallpox, have been wiped out worldwide.

Observations of cancer cells made with the electron microscope may help identify how they differ from normal cells. Using the electron microscope, scientists can compare the cycle of growth and division of cancer cells and normal cells. As scientists continue to study cells and learn about their structures and functions, they may eventually find cures for the many types of cancer.

Microsurgery Today biologists can perform surgery on some cells. Devices called microdissection instruments have enabled biologists to perform cell surgery under the microscope. With microdissection instruments, biologists can remove the nucleus from a cell and transplant it into another cell.

In one experiment, a biologist surgically removed a nucleus from the intestinal cell of a frog and transplanted it into an unfertilized frog egg whose own nucleus had been destroyed. The second frog grew up to be identical to the first frog. This process, called **cloning**, results in the production of offspring genetically identical to the parent whose nucleus was used.

Producing "Better" Organisms Researchers have successfully removed genetic material from one organism and injected it into the fertilized eggs of another organism. They hope that this technique will produce "better" organisms. For example, agricultural researchers hope to produce cows that give more milk and chickens that lay more eggs. In fact, researchers foresee the day when genes can be mixed to produce entirely new kinds of plants and animals.

1. How has the invention of the electron microscope helped in the battle against infectious and noninfectious diseases?
2. Although biologists have successfully cloned frogs and some plants, they have not yet cloned human beings. Eventually they may be able to do so. Should society permit biologists to clone human beings? Why or why not?
3. Should society permit researchers to use genetic techniques to produce "better" humans? Why or why not?

CHAPTER 4 The Earth's Changing Surface

I. THE EARTH'S SURFACE

1. Surface Features Undergo Change *(D1)*

Earth's surface features are continually undergoing change. Two sets of opposite forces shape and change the surface. One set of forces wears away Earth's surface. Another set of forces builds up Earth's surface.

2. Rock Fragments and Bedrock *(D2)*

Most of Earth's solid outer crust is covered by loose soil and rock fragments. Beneath this loose material lies unbroken solid rock called **bedrock**. Bedrock that is exposed at the surface is called an *outcrop* (Figure 4–1). Outcrops can often be seen in mountains, cliffs, and roadcuts.

Soil and rock fragments are formed by the breakdown of bedrock. **Soil** is a combination of finely broken up bedrock and organic matter (the remains of dead organisms and the wastes of living organisms). Plants grow in soil. Rock fragments are pieces of bedrock ranging in size from great boulders to tiny grains.

3. Minerals *(D3)*

Rocks are made of substances called minerals. A **mineral** is a solid inorganic substance with definite physical and chemical properties. A few minerals, such as sulfur, copper, silver, and gold, occur as elements. The great majority of minerals, however, are compounds of two or more elements. Over two thousand minerals are known, but only a few (about ten) make up most of Earth's crust. For example, the two most abundant minerals, feldspar and quartz, make up more than half of Earth's crust. Some common minerals are listed below.

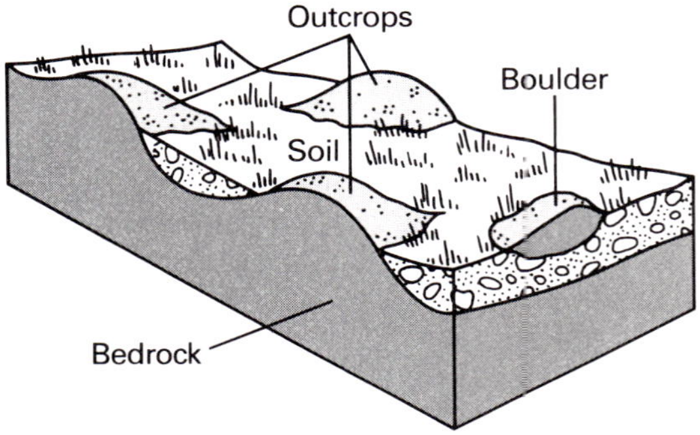

Figure 4–1. An outcrop is bedrock that is exposed at the surface.

Common Minerals

Feldspar	Diamond
Quartz	Mica
Sulfur	Pyrite
Malachite	Galena
Cinnabar	Hornblende
Asbestos	Calcite

Each kind of mineral has its own unique color, shape, and chemical composition. Most minerals have a definite geometric or crystalline shape. A crystal has a definite shape because of the way its ions are packed together in repeating patterns. Some mineral crystals are large enough to be seen in rocks with the unaided eye. Some are so tiny that a microscope must be used to see them.

4. *Identifying Minerals* *(D3)*

Minerals are identified by some of their physical and chemical properties.

Physical Properties A number of physical properties are useful in identifying minerals. These properties include hardness, cleavage, fracture, streak, luster, color, crystal form, and density.

Hardness is the ability of a mineral to resist scratching. Table 1 shows the scale used by scientists to measure mineral hardness. The higher the number, the harder the mineral. An important rule to remember when determining hardness is that a mineral can be scratched by a harder one.

Table 1 Scale of Hardness for Minerals

Hardness	Mineral
1	Talc
2	Gypsum
3	Calcite
4	Fluorite
5	Apatite
6	Feldspar
7	Quartz
8	Topaz
9	Corundum
10	Diamond

For example, quartz can scratch all minerals with a lower number on the hardness scale, including feldspar, apatite, fluorite, calcite, gypsum, and talc.

Some minerals break in definite directions along smooth surfaces or faces. These minerals possess **cleavage**. Mica, for example, cleaves into thin sheets. Halite breaks in three directions. Minerals may have two, three, four, or even six different directions of cleavage (Figure 4–2).

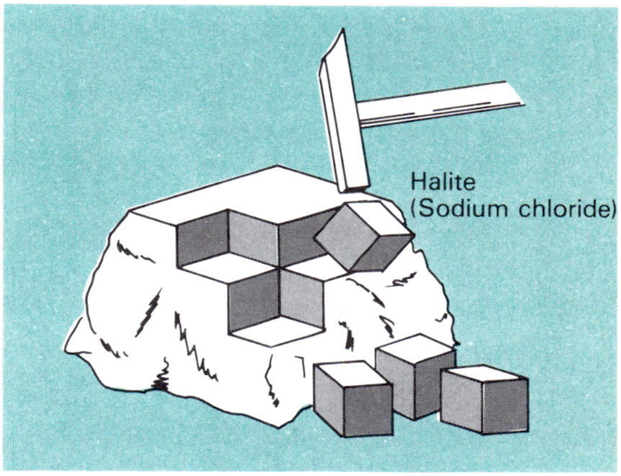

Figure 4–2. When a piece of halite is broken, it breaks into roughly cubic pieces because it has three directions of cleavage.

Some minerals do not have cleavage. Instead of breaking in definite directions along smooth surfaces these minerals may **fracture**, or break, leaving splintered or jagged surfaces.

The **streak** of a mineral is the color of its powder. A mineral can be powdered by rubbing it on an unglazed porcelain plate known as a streak plate (Figure 4–3).

The way a mineral reflects light is known as its **luster**. The luster of a mineral may make it look like a metal or a nonmetal, depending upon how its surface reflects light.

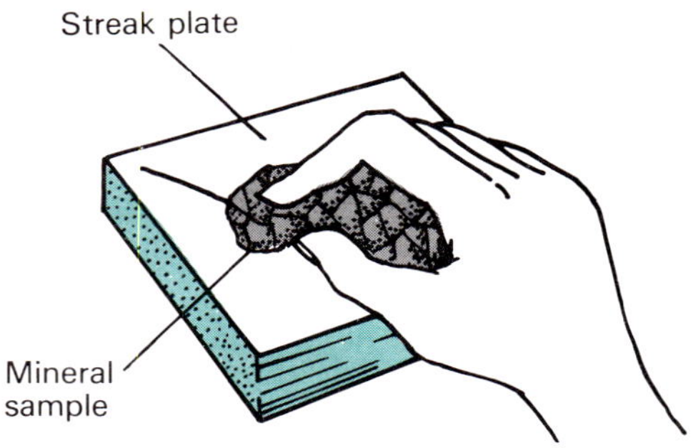

Figure 4–3. Streak test.

The **color** of a mineral is obvious. However, different samples of a mineral may be different colors. Color, therefore, is not as reliable for identifying a mineral as streak.

Most minerals have a definite geometric or crystalline shape. **Crystal form** is determined by the internal arrangement of the atoms making up the mineral.

Density is the ratio of the mass of a substance to its volume. For example, a mineral with a mass of 2 grams that occupies 4 cubic centimeters has a density of 0.5 g/cm^3. A mineral with a mass of 2 grams that occupies 2 cubic centimeters has a density of 1 g/cm^3. To put it another way, density compares how heavy something is to the space it occupies. Table 2 lists some minerals and their densities.

To determine the density of a mineral it is necessary to do the following. First, use a balance to determine the mass of the sample. Then calculate the volume of the sample by placing it in a graduated cylinder partially filled with water. The difference between the readings before and after the sample is added is the volume. To determine the density of the mineral use the formula

$$\text{Density} = \frac{\text{Mass}}{\text{Volume}}.$$

Table 2 Densities of Some Different Minerals

Mineral	Density (g/cm^3)
Quartz	2.5
Calcite	2.7
Talc	2.8
Topaz	3.5
Pyrite	5.0
Magnetite	5.2
Galena	7.6
Cinnabar	8.1
Gold	19.3

Chemical Properties Some minerals can be identified by their chemical properties. One commonly performed chemical test is called the **acid test**.

Calcite, the main mineral in marble, can be identified by the acid test. Calcite is calcium carbonate ($CaCO_3$). If a few drops of hydrochloric acid (HCl) are placed on a piece of calcite, bubbles of carbon dioxide are released. In general, any mineral containing carbonates reacts similarly when an acid is added to it.

5. Rocks *(D4)*

Earth's crust is made of rocks. **Rocks** are naturally occurring substances made of one or more minerals. There are three different classes of rocks—igneous, sedimentary, and metamorphic. Each forms in its own special way.

Igneous rocks Beneath Earth's crust lies hot liquid (molten) rock called **magma**. When magma cools and hardens, above or below Earth's surface, it forms **igneous rock**.

Science Skill

PERFORMING CALCULATIONS

The illustration below shows the water level in a graduated cylinder before and after a rock sample was placed into it. The rock has a mass of 50 grams.

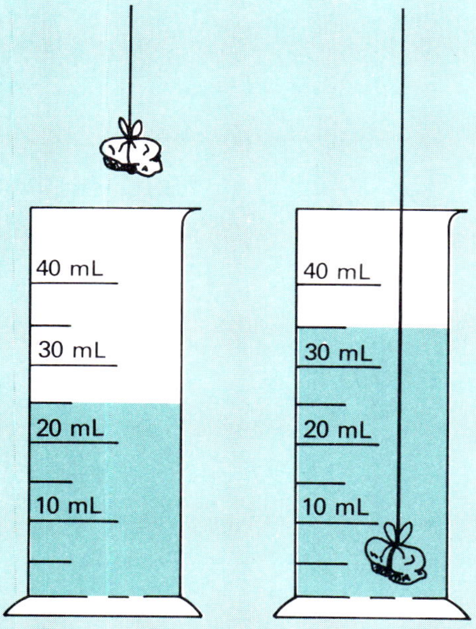

1. What is the volume of the rock?
2. How did you compute the volume?
3. Calulate the density of the rock using the formula Density = $\frac{\text{Mass}}{\text{Volume}}$.

There are two types of igneous rocks, shown in Figure 4–4. *Extrusive* igneous rock forms when hot liquid magma cools at Earth's surface. This occurs when a volcano erupts and hot magma pours out of it. *Intrusive* igneous rock forms when hot liquid magma cools and hardens beneath Earth's surface. This occurs when magma finds its way into cracks between layers of rock. Intrusive igneous rock may later be exposed if the rock that covers it is removed.

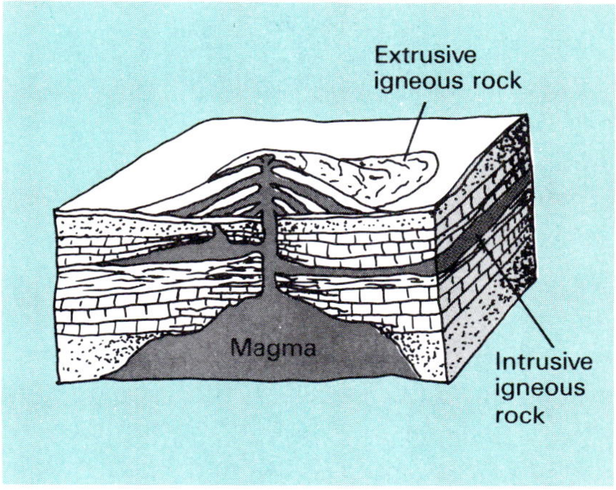

Figure 4–4. Intrusive igneous rock forms when magma squeezes between rock layers and cools below the surface. Extrusive igneous rock forms when magma cools at the surface.

The properties of igneous rocks can be used to identify them. One property is the size of the mineral crystals in the rock. The slower an igneous rock cools, the larger the mineral crystals. Another property is the color of its minerals. Some common igneous rocks are listed below.

Some Common Igneous Rocks

Granite	Gabbro
Obsidian	Basalt
Pumice	Diabase

Sedimentary Rocks A second kind of rock is called **sedimentary rock.** Sedimentary rocks form when layer upon layer of rock fragments build up. The fragments are called *sediments*. Under extreme pressure, the rock layers are cemented together, forming sedimentary rock (see Figure 4–5).

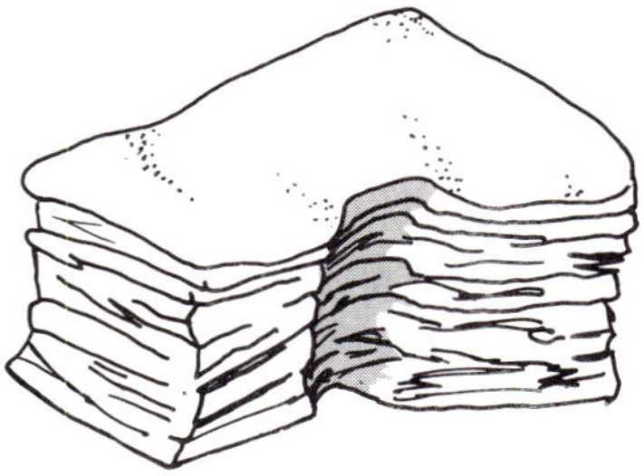

Figure 4–5. Sedimentary rocks form in layers.

Most sedimentary rock is formed on the ocean floor. Today sedimentary rocks are found under the oceans where they were formed. They are also found in many places on land, including the tops of high mountains, as a result of movements of Earth's crust. Some common sedimentary rocks are listed above at the right.

Some Common Sedimentary Rocks

Sandstone	Gypsum
Shale	Bituminous coal
Limestone	

Metamorphic Rocks **Metamorphic rock** forms from igneous or sedimentary rock that has been subjected to intense heat, pressure, chemical action, or any combination of these three. Metamorphic rock usually forms deep beneath Earth's surface where very high temperatures and pressures exist. Some common metamorphic rocks are listed below.

Some Common Metamorphic Rocks

Slate	Marble
Schist	Anthracite coal
Gneiss	

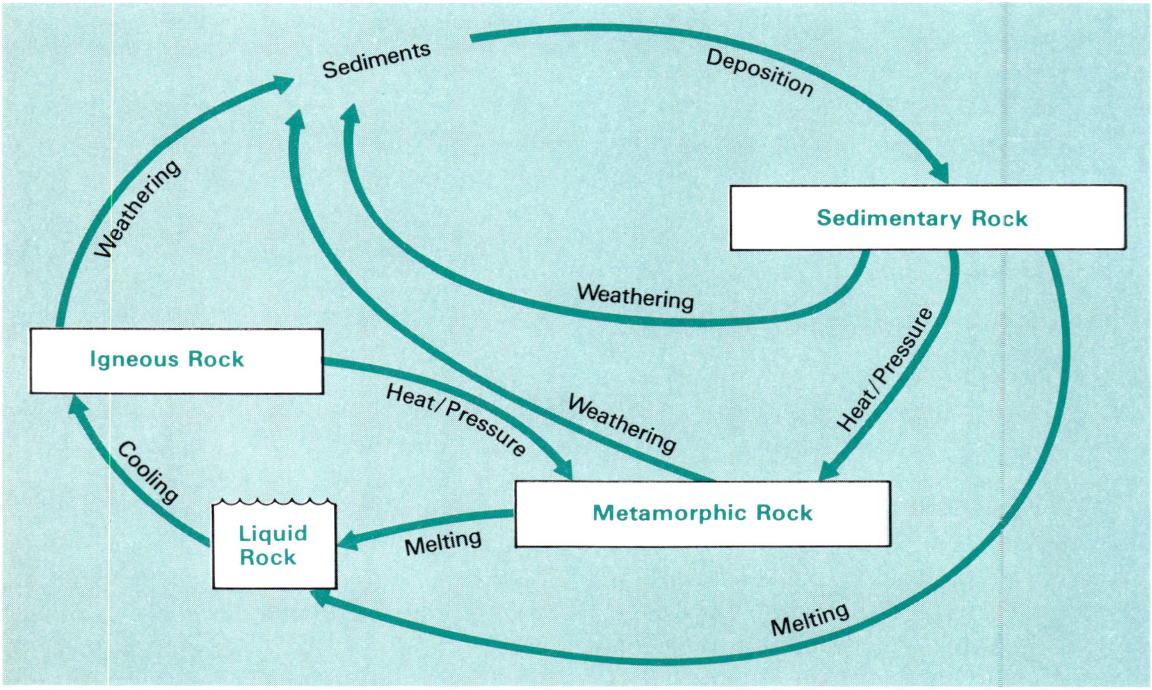

Figure 4–6. The rock cycle. Any type of rock can change to any other type.

The Rock Cycle Scientists think that all rock originated as igneous rock. With time, some igneous rocks broke down, forming sedimentary rock. Others were subjected to heat and pressure, forming metamorphic rock. Today rocks are continually changing from one type to another. This interrelationship among rock types is known as the **rock cycle** (Figure 4–6).

6. The Ocean Floor (D5)

The ocean covers nearly three fourths of Earth's surface. Most of the world ocean lies in the Southern Hemisphere. The average depth of the ocean is about 4 kilometers, although in places it reaches a depth of about 11 kilometers.

Sea water contains about 96.5% water and 3.5% salts. About 25% of the salt is common salt, or sodium chloride. The oceans are getting saltier because streams continue to bring more salt from the land while evaporation removes fresh water.

Shape of the Ocean Floor There are three sections of the ocean floor (Figure 4–7). The first section is the **continental shelf**. The continental shelf slopes away gently from the beach or shore. For every kilometer from the shore the level of the water drops only 2–3 meters. In some areas the continental shelf is several hundred kilometers wide. In these areas the depth of the continental shelf can be over 150 meters at its edge. Continental shelves are formed by material carried from the land by running water and deposited offshore.

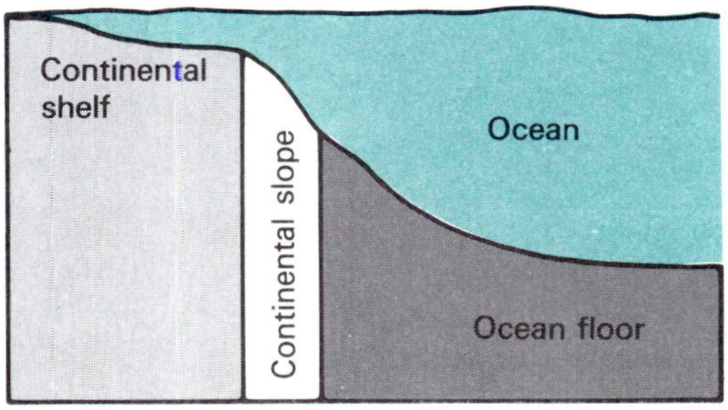

Figure 4–7. This cross section shows the continental shelf, continental slope, and ocean floor.

Where the continental shelf ends the **continental slope** begins. The continental slope is steeper than the continental shelf.

Eventually the continental slope levels off at the **ocean floor**. The ocean floor stretches from continent to continent. The Atlantic Ocean floor, for example, reaches from the edge of the North and South American continental slopes all the way to the European and African continental slopes.

Although the ocean floor begins where the continental slope ends, the floor is not smooth and level. The ocean floor is covered with *mountains*, *valleys*, *ridges*, and *deeps*. Even though many of these mountains are several kilometers high, they are totally underwater. Some of the taller mountains, however, poke through the ocean's surface to form chains of islands. These tall mountains are much higher than the tallest mountains on land.

Valleys are found all over the ocean floor. The deepest valleys are called **trenches**.

Economic Importance of the Oceans The oceans are economically important in several ways.

1. They are a source of food. Fish, shellfish, and sea plants provide food for humans.

2. They modify the climate. Ocean currents tend to move warm water from the tropics to the polar regions. Cold water moves from the polar regions to the tropics. Coastal areas tend to be

warmer in winter and cooler in summer than inland areas of the same latitude. This occurs because water heats up and cools off more slowly than land. Human populations are high in coastal areas, where climate is comfortable.

3. They are a source of minerals. Many important minerals are found in great abundance in the oceans. Magnesium and bromine are obtained commercially from salts found in sea water. Other minerals, including diamond, gold, tin, iron, copper, phosphate, and manganese, are found in sea water. However these minerals are very difficult to mine. Scientists have not yet developed all the technology required to extract dissolved minerals or to reach mineral deposits deep on the sea floor. Until scientists discover a way to obtain these minerals, people will be unable to make use of these valuable mineral resources.

Sample Questions

1. Rocks are made of inorganic substances called
(1) water (3) minerals
(2) alcohol (4) humus

2–5. For each definition in questions 2–5, choose the correct mineral property from the list below.

Mineral Properties
(1) hardness
(2) cleavage
(3) density
(4) streak

2. Breakage in definite directions

3. Color obtained by finely powdering a mineral

4. Ability to resist scratching

5. Ratio of the mass of a substance to its volume

6. Liquid rock found beneath Earth's surface is called
(1) lava (3) sandstone
(2) quartz (4) magma

7. A chemical test that is sometimes used to identify a mineral is the
(1) acid test (3) hardness test
(2) streak test (4) luster test

8. When magma cools, which type of rock forms?
(1) sedimentary (3) metamorphic
(2) igneous (4) mudstone

9. When igneous rock is subjected to intense heat and pressure it may become
(1) sedimentary rock
(2) limestone
(3) metamorphic rock
(4) sandstone

10. Three fourths of Earth's surface is covered by
(1) deserts (3) lakes
(2) forests (4) oceans

11. The oceans are a rich source of all of the following *except*
(1) mineral deposits
(2) food
(3) salt
(4) clay

12–13. Base your answers to questions 12–13 on the diagram of the rock cycle below.

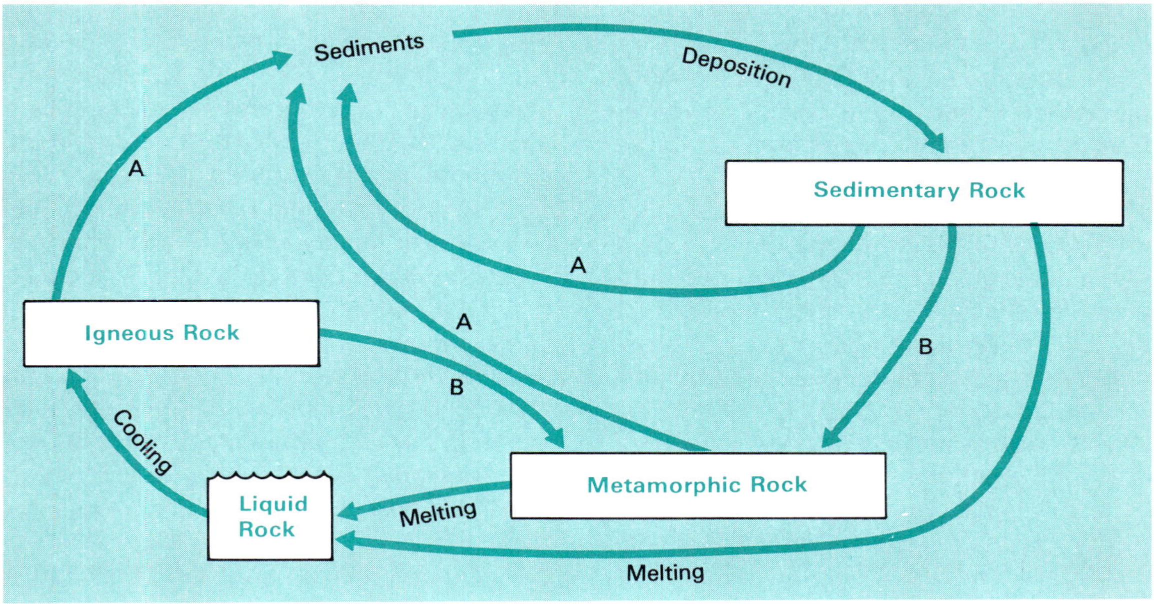

12. The process shown by letter *A* is called
(1) weathering (3) mining
(2) petrification (4) solidification

13. Sedimentary and igneous rock may become metamorphic rock, as shown by the arrows labeled *B*. One condition necessary for this to occur is
(1) low temperature
(2) little pressure
(3) intense heat
(4) high humidity

14. Some minerals break in definite directions along smooth surfaces. This property is known as
(1) streak (3) luster
(2) color (4) cleavage

15. An example of an igneous rock is
(1) limestone (3) shale
(2) sandstone (4) granite

16. The major portion of Earth's crust is made of
(1) rock (3) water
(2) air (4) organic matter

17. Scientists have not yet developed the technology required to
(1) capture food from the sea
(2) extract gold dissolved in sea water
(3) remove salt from sea water
(4) use the oceans for navigation

18. Which is *not* found on the ocean floor?
(1) mountains (3) ridges
(2) valleys (4) ice caps

19. The hardness of a mineral can be determined by
(1) doing a scratch test
(2) dissolving it in water
(3) breaking it
(4) determining its density

II. CHANGES IN EARTH'S SURFACE

1. Forces That Wear Away Earth's Surface *(D6)*

Forces are at work constantly to move exposed rocks into the oceans. The movement results from the processes of weathering and erosion.

Weathering Rocks at or near Earth's surface crumble and decay when exposed to the atmosphere. This process of crumbling and decaying is called **weathering**. There are three types of weathering – physical, chemical, and biological. All three produce rock fragments.

Physical weathering is the breaking of rock into smaller pieces without changing its chemical makeup. For example, physical weathering occurs when water freezes in the cracks of rocks. The freezing water expands and breaks the rocks (see Figure 4–8). Freezing (frost action) accounts for considerable weathering in New York State. This may be seen happening at road cuts marked "Fallen Rock Zones." Here in winter rocks break and fall due to repeated freezing and thawing of water in cracks.

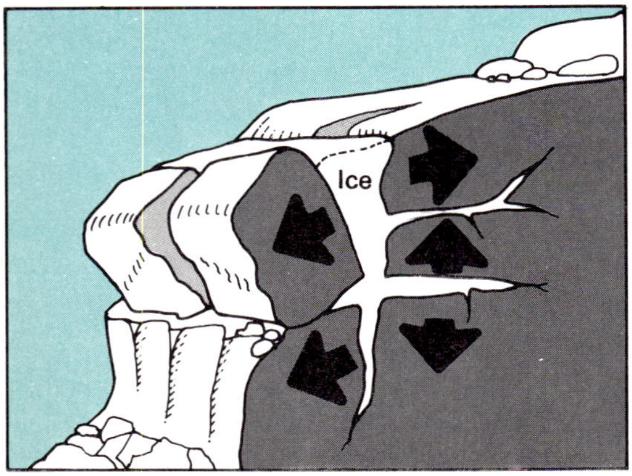

Figure 4–8. Freezing water can break rocks apart.

Chemical weathering is the breaking down of rock due to changes in its chemical composition. Chemical changes can occur when substances in the atmosphere combine with materials in rocks. These chemical combinations may result in chemical weathering. A rusting nail is an example of chemical weathering. Rusting results when oxygen in the atmosphere combines with iron. Likewise, oxygen in the air may combine with other minerals in rocks, causing them to change chemically and then break down. In another kind of chemical weathering, water and carbon dioxide may combine to form a weak acid called carbonic acid. Carbonic acid can dissolve some of the minerals in rocks.

Biological weathering occurs when rocks are broken down by plants and animals. For example, plant roots growing between the cracks in rocks create pressure that can cause further cracking and weathering (see Figure 4–9).

The rate of weathering depends upon the physical and chemical properties of the rocks, the climate in which weathering occurs, and the amount of rock surface exposed to the atmosphere. Weathering is greatest in regions that have a moist climate with hot summers and cold winters.

Erosion The process of breaking up and carrying away rock material is known as **erosion**. Erosion is carried out by such moving forces as running water, ground water, wind, and glaciers. These forces move rock material from the land into the ocean basins. Most erosion is driven by the water cycle and the force of gravity.

Running water causes most of the erosion on Earth's surface. The running water in streams moves by gravity from higher elevations to lower elevations, carrying rock materials with it. Streams empty into lakes

Figure 4–9. The roots of plants can cause biological weathering.

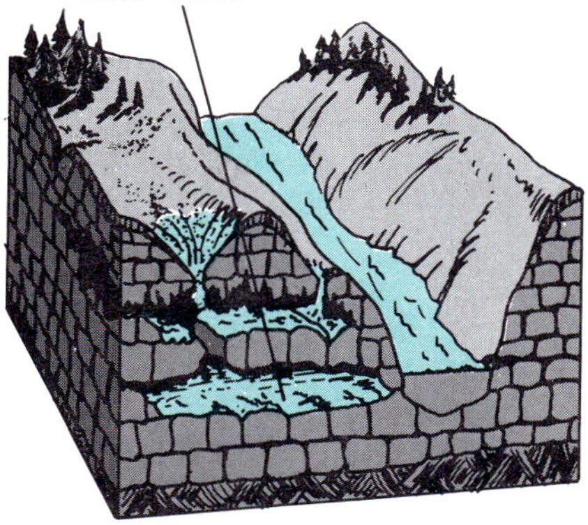

Figure 4–10. Ground water that is slightly acid can cause underground caves to form.

or oceans, where they deposit the rock materials they carry.

Ground water forms when rainfall sinks into the ground. Ground water moves slowly, often dissolving and carrying away rock materials in its path. For example, if ground water is slightly acid it can dissolve limestone, sometimes leaving underground caves (Figure 4–10). The dissolved limestone may later come out of solution and form iciclelike deposits in the ceilings and floors of the caves. Like the running water in streams, ground water moves by gravity through rocks to the lowest levels of the land.

The **water table** is the level below which rock or rock fragments are saturated with ground water. The ground water below the water table is a source of water for drinking.

The **wind** changes the surface of the land, especially in dry (arid) places like the desert. As the wind moves across Earth's surface it carries with it small pieces of rock material, including sand, silt, and clay. In dry areas in the midwest, strong winds often produce dust storms. During dust storms small pieces of rock material are picked up and carried over large distances. The wind-blown material grinds and scours surfaces it hits, smoothing rock surfaces and forming unusual landscape features. When the winds die down, the soil materials stop moving and are deposited. The best known wind deposits are *sand dunes*. Sand dunes are found in deserts and beaches.

A **glacier** is a large mass of ice found all year round at high altitudes, such as in a mountain valley, or at high latitudes, such as the polar regions. Glaciers form from snow that builds up above the snow line in areas where winter snowfalls exceed summer melting. Freezing and thawing and increasing pressure change the accumulated snow to ice.

In mountain regions a glacier may move downhill in response to gravity. A moving glacier may break fragments of bedrock loose. These rock fragments become part of the glacier and move along with it. The rock fragments act as cutting tools and erode the surfaces over which they pass. The larger rock fragments may produce big grooves and scratches on the surfaces over which they move. The smaller rock fragments may act like sandpaper, polishing the surfaces over which they move.

As glaciers move, they carve Earth's surface and create some interesting landforms. Table 3 lists some kinds of landforms carved by glaciers and locations in New York State where these landforms are found.

Table 3 Glacial Landforms in New York State

Feature	Location
Terminal moraine	Long Island
Outwash plain	Hempstead
Eskers	Saranac
Drumlins	Palmyra
Finger lakes	Geneva

Due to gravity, rock fragments accumulate at the lower end of a glacier in a *terminal moraine* (Figure 4–11). When the ice melts, rock piles are released. Long Island in New York State is a terminal moraine built from rock piles deposited by melting ice. Much of the topography of New York State is the direct result of the work of glaciers.

2. Evidence of Crustal Movement *(D7)*

Scientists think that Earth's crust has risen and the seas have deepened many times through the ages. They think that these changes take place due to forces that operate at the surface and beneath Earth's crust. Their ideas are based upon observations of present changes that provide clues to what may have happened in the past.

For example, mountains are strongly folded and contain broken rock. Strong forces had to act in order to fold these mountains. Most sedimentary rocks are formed under the ocean in horizontal layers. Today, in many places on Earth, sedimentary rock layers are no longer horizontal. They

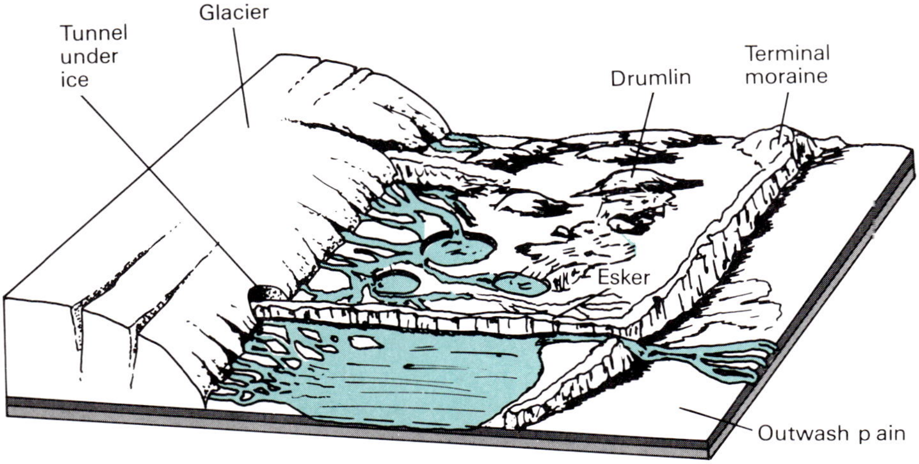

Figure 4–11. Glacial landforms.

Science Skill

DESIGNING A CONTROLLED EXPERIMENT

A student wants to test how different types of grasses affect soil erosion. He constructs ten trays of the same size and fills them with the same kind of soil. Then the student plants a different kind of grass in each tray and places all the trays in an area where they will receive the same amount of sunlight. After the grass has grown, the student places each tray at an angle and pours water down into it. This process is repeated once each week for two months. The student measures and records the amount of soil eroded from each tray each week.

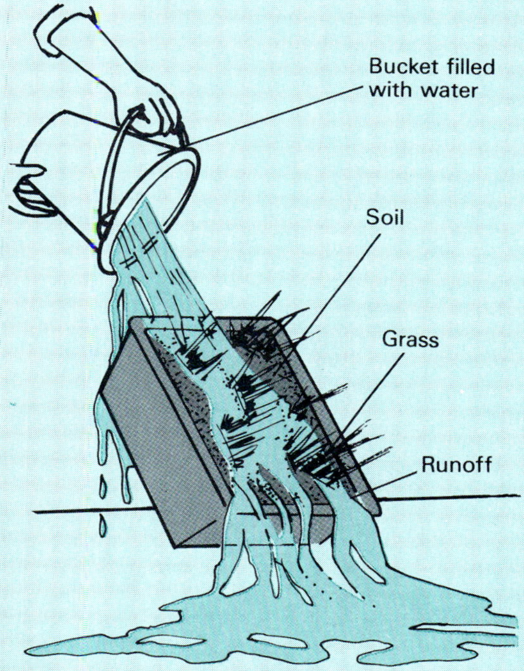

1. What is the variable in the student's experiment?
   (1) type of soil
   (2) light
   (3) water
   (4) type of grass
2. What hypothesis is the student testing?
   (1) The amount of erosion depends upon the type of grass growing in an area.
   (2) The amount of erosion depends upon the slant of the land.
   (3) The amount of sunlight an area receives determines the rate of erosion.
   (4) The amount of erosion increases as the amount of grass decreases.

may be folded, tilted, or fractured (Figure 4–12). Sedimentary rock is found at the tops of high mountains, far away from the ocean floor where it formed. These changes in structure and location of sedimentary rock must have been caused by strong forces beneath Earth's crust.

Fossils are the remains or imprints of ancient animals or plants trapped in layers of sedimentary rock. Fossils of marine

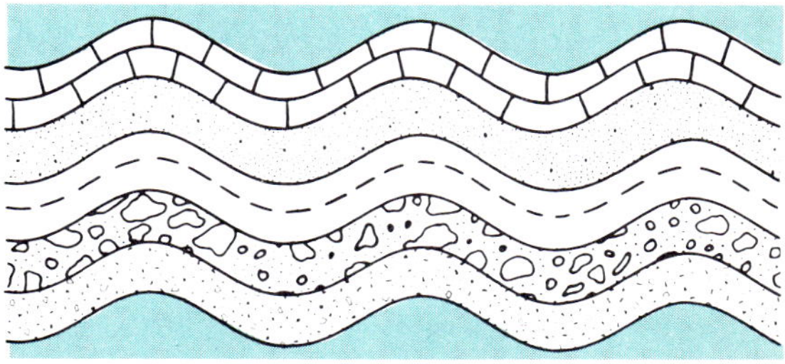

Figure 4–12. Rock layers can be squeezed into folds.

animals are often found in rocks high above sea level. Forces beneath the crust have moved these rocks and the fossils they contained up from the ocean floor where they formed to their current positions in the mountains.

3. Forces that Build Up Earth's Surface *(D7)*

The evidences listed above show that forces beneath Earth's crust and at its surface cause movements that build up the surface. But what causes Earth to move? What forces create these movements?

Continental Drift and Plate Tectonics Figure 4–13 shows the continents. As you can see, the east coast of South America matches the west coast of Africa. Although of a somewhat less perfect fit, the east coast of North America matches the west coast of North Africa and Europe. The matching shapes of the continents suggest that all the present continents came from one large landmass. Scientists call this large landmass *Pangaea*.

Forces within Earth's mantle provided the energy to break Pangaea into large pieces and then move them apart. The moving apart of these pieces is called *continental drift*. At the present time, the continents continue to drift apart very slowly.

How and why does Earth's crust move? According to the theory of **plate tectonics**, Earth's crust is not an unbroken shell of rock. Instead, its surface is split into a number of blocks or *plates*. The plates have different sizes and shapes. Six major plates cover most of Earth's surface and form the continents (Figure 4–14). They include the American, African, Eurasian, Indian, Pacific, and Antarctic plates. Smaller *subplates* fill the spaces between the major plates. Both the major plates and the subplates move.

Here are some examples of the movements of the major plates. The American and Eurasian plates are moving away from each other at the mid-Atlantic Ridge. The Eurasian and Indian Plates are moving toward each other. The Pacific and American plates slide alongside each other. As the plates move, the continents move along with them. *Convection currents* caused by heat in Earth's mantle provide the energy for plate movement.

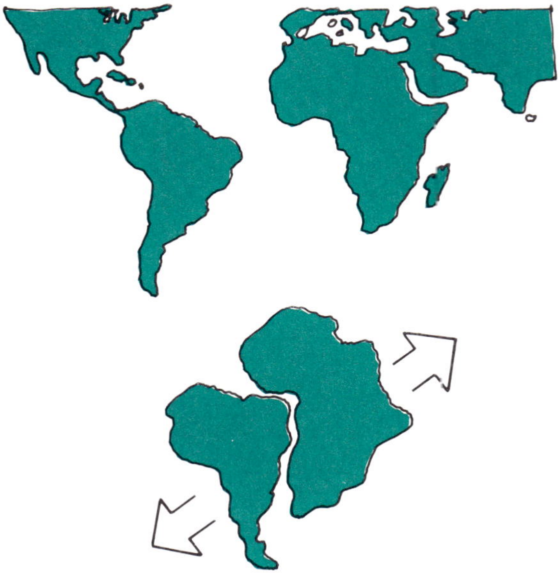

Figure 4–13. The matching coastlines of South America and Africa suggest that these continents were once joined.

4. Features that Result From Plate Movements *(D7)*

The movements and interactions of these plates over millions of years helps to explain the present locations of the continents. The movement of the plates also helps to explain many landscapes.

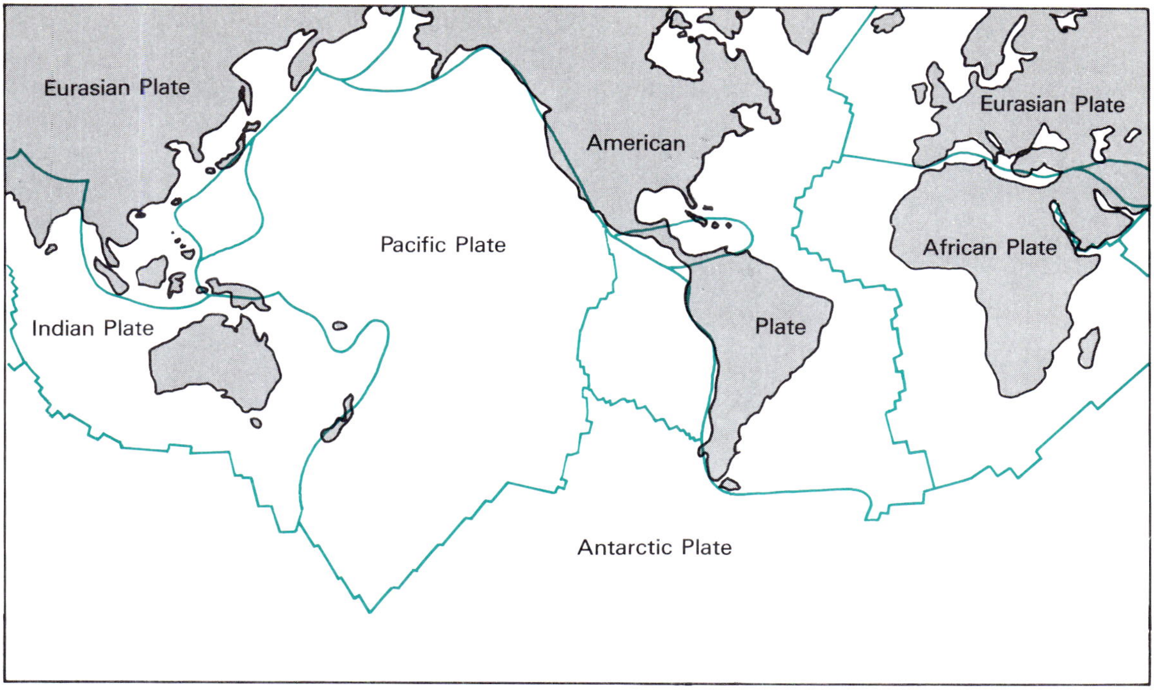

Figure 4–14. The major crustal plates.

Mountain Building The fact that sedimentary rocks that originally formed below sea level are found in many mountains provides evidence that mountains were raised from lower levels to their present heights. Pressure from crustal movements causes mountain building.

Sideways pressure from crustal plate movements squeezes rocks into folds (Figure 4–15). The process of squeezing rocks into folds is called **folding**. Most of Earth's greatest mountain ranges (Himalayas, Alps, Rockies) are made of folded sedimentary rocks.

When plates collide, sedimentary rocks are folded or squeezed together, shortening and raising them. The rocks are folded into upfolds, or *anticlines*, and downfolds, or *synclines* (Figure 4–16).

Faulting Rocks may contain cracks (fractures) called faults. A **fault** is a crack

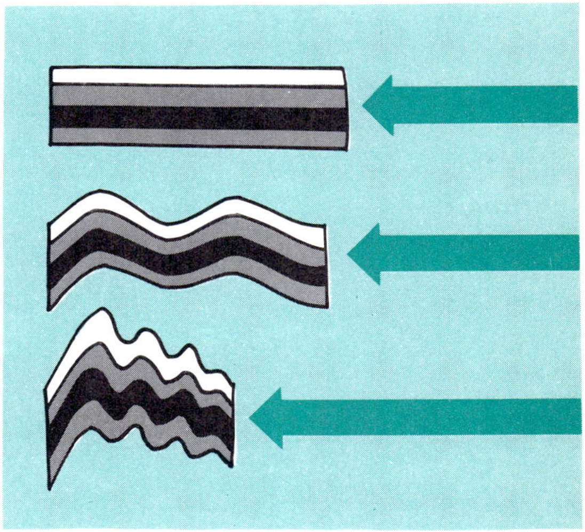

Figure 4–15. Sideways pressure causes rocks to fold.

in Earth's crust along which movement has occurred (Figure 4–17). The city of San Francisco lies over a fault called the San Andreas fault.

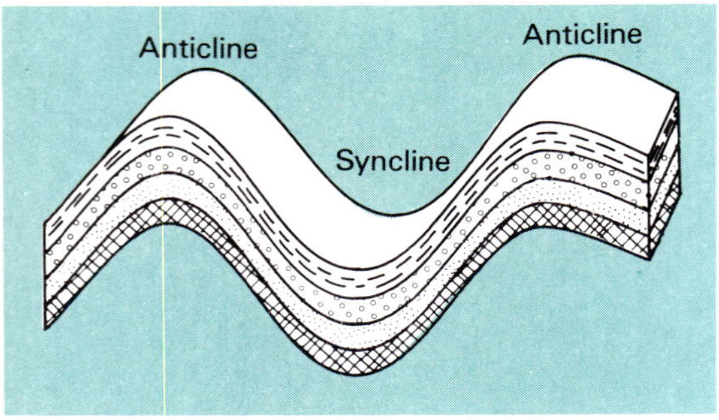

Figure 4–16. An anticline is an upfold. A syncline is a downfold.

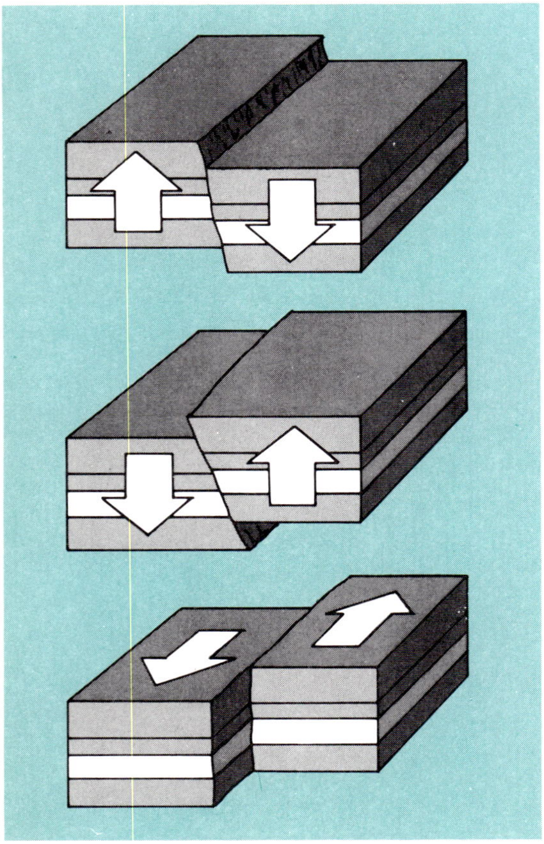

Figure 4–17. Three types of faults.

When faulting takes place, new landforms may result. Large pieces of Earth's crust may be raised by faulting to form mountains. The Sierra Nevadas in California were formed in this way. Faulting may also result in the formation of cliffs and plateaus. Faulting often takes place along boundaries between crustal plates. Movements of these plates at their boundaries leads to faulting.

Earthquakes Earthquakes occur along faults at boundaries between crustal plates. Here adjacent crustal plates move against each other, creating a force. This force causes faulting and earthquakes.

The major earthquake areas of the United States are along the coasts of California and southern Alaska. Both of these areas are near the boundary between the North American and Pacific plates. In these areas earthquakes have resulted in sudden large uplifts of rocks. These uplifts have helped form the cliffs along the coastline of California and Alaska. The occurrence of an earthquake is detected with an instrument called a *seismograph*. A siesmograph records earthquake waves.

Volcanoes A **volcano** is an opening in the crust through which liquid (molten) rock called *magma* may erupt. Magma comes from inside Earth. When magma erupts from a volcano and cools it is called *lava*. The movement of magma at or near Earth's surface is called *volcanism*.

What makes magma rise and erupt from a volcano? Volcanoes are located along the boundaries of adjacent crustal plates. When the plates move away from each other, cracks are created through which magma may rise. As the plates spread apart, the magma pours out.

Sometimes magma may pour out when adjacent plates move toward each other.

This pushing together creates a pressure that causes an eruption to occur.

As lava flows from a volcano, it may form a mountain (Figure 4–18). Mount Rainier in the United States is one example of a mountain that formed from volcanic eruptions.

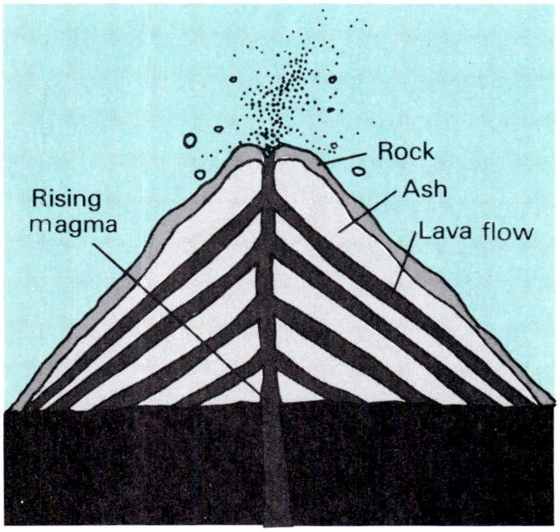

Figure 4–18. Lava flowing from a volcano may form a mountain.

5. Major Landforms *(D7)*

The processes just described, including folding, faulting, earthquakes, and volcanism, result in a number of landforms.

Plains **Plains** are broad, flat regions of undisturbed sedimentary rocks with little variation in elevation. Plains originate from uplifted continental shelves, river deposits, glacial deposits, lake floors, or lava flows. They are found at low altitudes.

Plateaus **Plateaus** are areas of undisturbed horizontal sedimentary rocks that sit at high altitudes (greater than 1000 meters). Some plateaus have been raised above sea level by faulting. The Colorado Plateau in the southwestern United States was raised in this way. Other plateaus have formed from the slow uplift of land without faulting. Some plateaus have formed from lava flows.

Mountains Mountains contain disturbed nonhorizontal sedimentary rock. They may form as a result of folding, faulting, or volcanism.

Sample Questions

1. A rock may fall apart due to repeated freezing and thawing of water found in its cracks during the winter. This is an example of a process called
(1) cracking (3) folding
(2) faulting (4) weathering

2. Iron rusts when it combines with oxygen. This is an example of
(1) chemical weathering
(2) physical weathering
(3) biological weathering
(4) mineral weathering

3. What is mainly responsible for the movement of sediment toward the ocean in the diagram below?

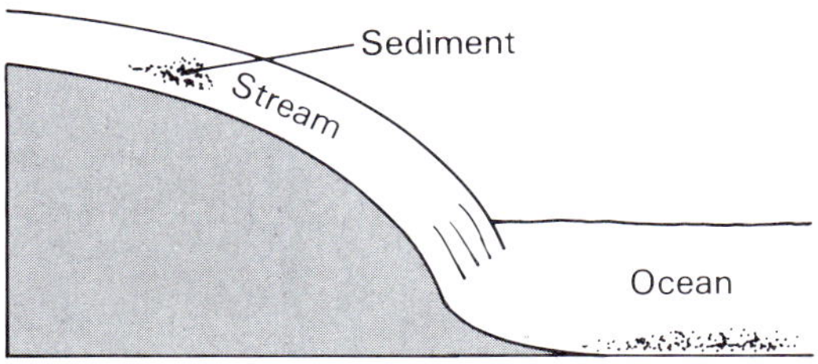

(1) animals (3) gravity
(2) wind (4) humans

4. A heavy rainstorm removed a large amount of soil from the side of a mountain. This is the result of a process called
(1) precipitation (3) evaporation
(2) erosion (4) elimination

5. A large mass of ice found at high altitutes all year round is a
(1) dune (3) plate
(2) glacier (4) plain

6. An example of a process that builds up Earth's surface is
(1) weathering (3) volcanism
(2) erosion (4) evaporation

7. A pothole in the pavement of a highway occurs due to
(1) evaporation (3) faulting
(2) weathering (4) condensation

8. An example of a landscape feature that forms due to the action of winds is a(n)
(1) terminal moraine
(2) pothole
(3) sand dune
(4) hill

9–11. Questions 9–11 are based on the diagram below, which shows a cross section of rocks.

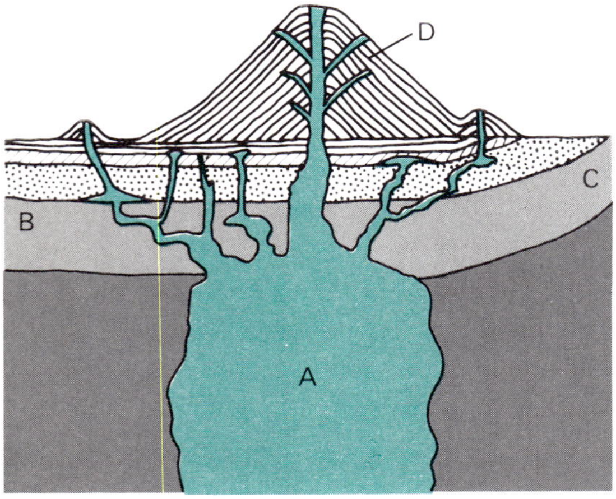

9. Magma is represented by the letter
(1) A (2) B (3) C (4) D

10. A mountain that formed as a result of volcanism is represented by letter
(1) A (2) B (3) C (4) D

11. The sedimentary rock shown by letter C has bent upward due to a process called
(1) faulting (3) volcanism
(2) cracking (4) folding

12. Rocks that form from the cementing of settled pieces of other rocks are called
(1) igneous rocks
(2) sedimentary rocks
(3) metamorphic rocks
(4) sand rocks

13. A theory that explains how continents move is the theory of
(1) evolution (3) plate tectonics
(2) relativity (4) gravity

14. The moving of the continents is called
(1) faulting and folding
(2) volcanism
(3) continental drift
(4) rock formation

15. Which is *not* a result of plate tectonics?
(1) erosion of soil
(2) earthquakes
(3) eruption of a volcano
(4) folding of a mountain

16. All the following processes help build mountains *except*
(1) folding (3) volcanism
(2) faulting (4) precipitation

17. A large crack or fracture in bedrock is called a(n)
(1) fault (3) anticline
(2) fold (4) plateau

18. Sudden vibrations in Earth's crust result from

(1) erosion
(2) weathering
(3) earthquakes
(4) dunes

19. The occurrence of frequent earthquakes along the coastline of California is due to its location along a(n)
(1) ocean
(2) plateau
(3) fault
(4) fold

20. Plains and plateaus differ in which of the following ways?
(1) Plains sit at low elevations while plateaus sit at high elevations.
(2) Plateaus sit at low elevations while plains sit at high elevations.
(3) Plains are formed by erosion while plateaus are formed by volcanism.

III. AGE OF THE EARTH

What were conditions like on Earth during the different geologic eras? What events took place throughout Earth's geologic past? Scientists learn about Earth's history by studying rocks. They study what rocks are made of, how they formed, where they are located, and what kinds of fossils are embedded in them. A study of the *rock record* provides clues about what may have happened in the past.

Earth's features as they are at present and the events that change and shape them today also provide clues about what may have happened in the past. Scientists think that the events that shape Earth today have always taken place. The water cycle and the rock cycle worked the same millions of years ago as they do today. Rocks have weathered and eroded in the same fashion throughout geologic time. By studying the present, scientists can infer what has happened in the past.

1. Studying Sedimentary Rock *(D8)*

Sedimentary rock is formed when sediments are cemented together. Scientists learn about Earth's history by studying sedimentary rocks.

Figure 4–19 shows some sedimentary rock layers. Notice how the rock layers are arranged in horizontal fashion. The oldest layer is on the bottom. The youngest layer is on top. The relative age of a sedimentary rock layer is usually indicated by its position in the rock layers.

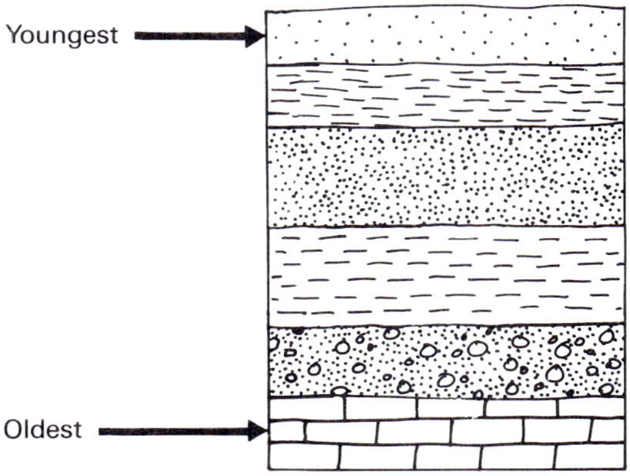

Figure 4–19. The oldest sedimentary rock layers are on the bottom.

However, the story is not quite that simple. The events that operated in the past sometimes changed the position of the horizontal layers in sedimentary rock. Erosion may have occurred, taking away a part of a layer or parts of several layers of rock (Figure 4–20). Folding or faulting may have taken place, changing the angle or tilt of some of the layers. Magma may have filled the spaces between the rock layers and caused them to separate. Crustal uplifts may have occurred, breaking away large sections of rock. Breaks in the rock layers due to the processes described above provide clues about Earth's geologic past.

Scientists use **radioactive dating** to find out the actual age of most rocks. Most rocks contain radioactive elements such as *uranium*. The atoms in these radioactive elements break down to form simpler atoms. The time in which the breakdown occurs varies from one radioactive element to the next. Scientists base their measurements of age of a rock on the amount of time it takes for half the atoms in a sample to change to simpler atoms. For example, it takes 4.5 billion years for half of the uranium atoms in a rock sample to change to lead. By comparing the amount of lead to uranium in a rock sample, scientists can determine the absolute age of a rock.

Assume that a rock had a certain amount of radioactive uranium when it first formed and now has equal amounts of uranium and lead. Scientists conclude that the rock is 4.5 billion years old. If the rock now has 3/4 uranium and only 1/4 lead, the rock is about 2.25 billion years old. The regular rate of decay of radioactive elements in a rock sample is used by scientists as a measure for dating rocks.

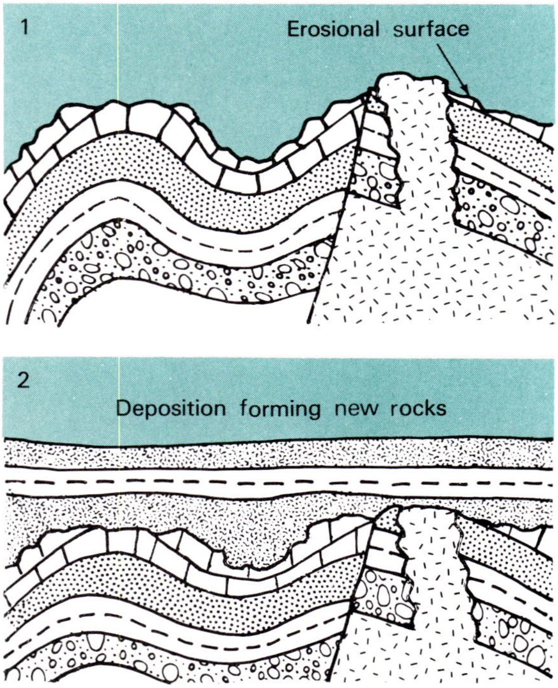

Figure 4–20. Erosion, folding, faulting, and igneous intrusions are some of the processes that can complicate the rock record.

2. Fossils in Sedimentary Rock *(D8)*

What was life like on Earth in the distant past? Scientists find out by studying fossils. **Fossils** are the remains or evidences of animal and plants that lived in the geologic past (Figure 4–21).

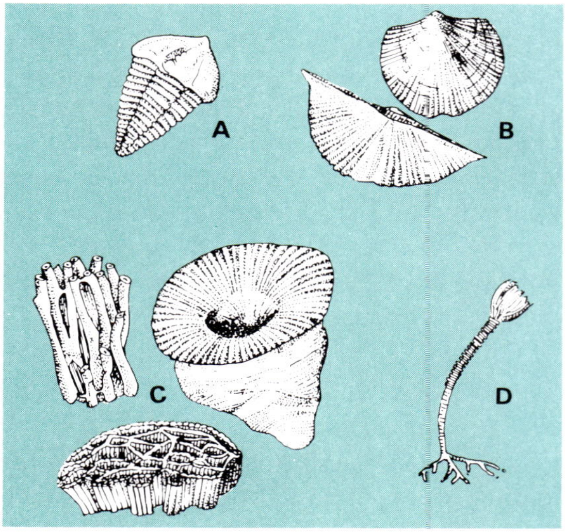

Figure 4–21. Some common fossils: (A) trilobite, (B) brachiopods, (C) corals, (D) crinoid.

When an organism dies, its soft parts decay. Its hard parts (shells, bones, and teeth) may become trapped in the sand or mud at the bottom of an ocean or a lake. With time, layers of sand or mud (sediment) cover the remains. The layers of sediment eventually harden and become layers of sedimentary rock. The remains are trapped as fossils in this rock.

By studying fossils, scientists learn a great deal about Earth's geologic history. They can determine the conditions in which the sedimentary rock formed. For example, the presence of the shells of marine organisms is evidence that the rock was formed in the ocean. The presence of imprints of large fern leaves is evidence that the rock containing these imprints was probably formed during an era when the climate was tropical.

Scientists can determine the relative age of the sedimentary rock by studying the fossils they contain. Rock layers containing similar fossils are probably the same age. Scientists look for index fossils in sedimentary rock. **Index fossils** are fossils of organisms that existed for only a short period of time and were relatively abundant. Index fossils are markers to scientists. Their presence in widely separated rock layers tells scientists that these rock layers are about the same age.

From the fossil record, scientists learn a great deal about life on Earth: where and when it originated, why new species formed, why some organisms became extinct and others survived. In brief, scientists learn from their study of fossils how life evolved.

3. Geologic History (D8)

Scientists have learned enough about Earth's history to divide geologic time into long periods called *eras*. Each era is separated from the next one by changes in the fossil record and by intervals of mountain building.

Life forms in each era differ because of major climate changes. Many species could not survive these climate changes and died out. New species that were more adapted survived and continued to evolve.

Table 4 lists the geologic eras and describes the important events and the kinds of life that existed during each era.

Table 4 Geologic Eras

Millions of Years Ago	Era	Major Events in North America	Life
70	Cenozoic	North America reaches its current shape; ice ages	Development of mammals
225	Mesozoic	Continents moving apart; Rockies form at end of era	Reptiles dominant; flowering plants develop at end of era
600	Paleozoic	Continents split apart; Appalachians form at end of era	Marine animals at beginning, then amphibians and reptiles; seed plants and tree ferns develop
4500	Precambrian	Volcanic activity, glaciation	Algae, fungi, bacteria, then worms and mollusks

Sample Questions

1. To learn about the geologic past, scientists look at
   (1) weather data
   (2) rock records
   (3) cloud formations
   (4) climate zones

2–5. Base your answers to questions 2–5 on the diagram of rock layers shown below.

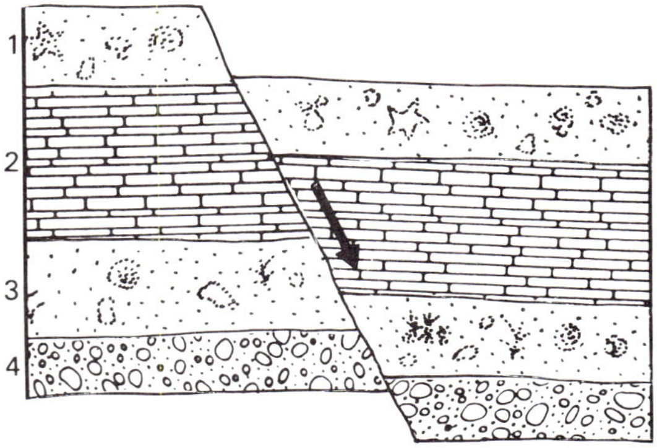

2. The oldest rock layer is represented by number
   (1) 2 (3) 4
   (2) 3 (4) 5

3. Which pair of rock layers is probably the same age?
   (1) 1 and 2
   (2) 2 and 3
   (3) 2 and 7
   (4) 3 and 7

4. The youngest rock layer is represented by number
   (1) 1 (3) 3
   (2) 2 (4) 4

5. The arrow in the diagram points to the direction in which the rock shifted along a
   (1) fold
   (2) fault
   (3) sediment
   (4) syncline

6. The remains or imprint in sedimentary rock of life of long ago is called a(n)
   (1) element
   (2) artifact
   (3) fossil
   (4) trace

7. To determine the absolute age of a rock, scientists use
   (1) position in the rock layers
   (2) radioactive dating
   (3) mineral analysis
   (4) streak tests

8. Fossils that are relatively abundant and have existed for short periods of time are called
   (1) index fossils
   (2) fern fossils
   (3) marine fossils
   (4) bones and teeth

9. Scientists have divided geologic time into long periods called
   (1) centuries
   (2) years
   (3) eons
   (4) eras

Issues in Science, Technology, and Society

Radon—A Toxic Waste From Rocks

Radon is a radioactive gas that occurs in nature. You cannot see it, smell it, or taste it. Radon is produced in soil or rocks through the normal decay of uranium and radium. Most of the radon in the Middle Atlantic States has been found in a granite bedrock formation that begins at Reading, Pennsylvania, and stretches through northwestern New Jersey into southern New York and western Connecticut.

Radon may also be found in soils contaminated with certain types of industrial wastes from uranium or phosphate mining.

Since it is a gas, radon can move into air spaces in our homes, such as basements and crawl spaces. It can also dissolve in well water and be released into the air from running tap water. Once inside our homes, radon can accumulate. Well-insulated houses, which have little air exchange, generally have higher indoor radon levels than draftier houses.

When radon undergoes radioactive breakdown, it decays into other radioactive elements called *radon daughters*. Radon daughters are solids, not gases. They stick to surfaces such as dust particles in the air. If contaminated dust is inhaled, these particles can stick to the airways of the lungs. Here they release small bursts of energy that can damage lung tissue and increase the risk of lung cancer. The risk increases as the levels of radon and the length of exposure increase.

What can be done to reduce exposure to indoor radon? From the standpoint of radiation exposure, "energy conservation" could be a dangerous trade-off.

If you want to find out the level of radon in your home, you might consider having your home tested. If you have further questions about radon, contact your local Department of Health.

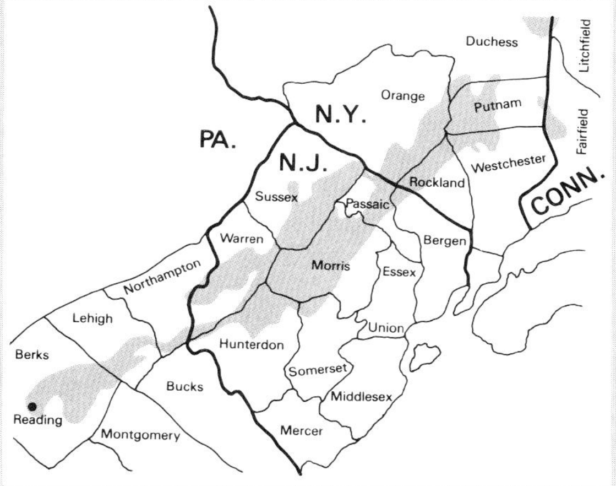

The Reading Prong is a granite bedrock formation containing radon. It stretches through a number of counties in Pennsylvania, New Jersey, New York, and Connecticut.

1. If society follows government recommendations to insulate homes and if as a result there is an increase in cases of lung cancer, is the government responsible?

2. Should society prohibit the mining of uranium and phosphate in populated areas, thereby reducing radon levels in these areas? This would cause uranium to be in shorter supply.

3. Should money be spent researching and developing the technology required to eliminate radon from our homes? Or should we depend on increased ventilation in our homes to remedy the problem?

CHAPTER 5 Weather and Climate

I. BROAD-SCALE WEATHER SYSTEMS

The following is a local weather report for a city in New York State:

Today will be partly cloudy. The temperature will be in the low 70s (around 22°C). The winds will be moderate, from the southwest. There will be a slight chance of rain late this afternoon

The weather service releases weather reports like this one each day. **Weather** is the condition of the atmosphere (air) in a certain place at a certain time. One of the conditions of the atmosphere is its temperature. Another is the amount of moisture. A third is the wind direction and speed. Weather does not remain constant. It changes gradually, due to the movement of air masses.

1. Air Masses *(E1, E2, E3)*

Sometimes the weather turns sharply cooler. Weather forecasters would say that a very cold air mass moving across the region caused this change in weather. An **air mass** is a large body of air that has the same conditions throughout. An air mass forms when air stays over a large portion of Earth's surface, its *source region.*

Since conditions throughout an air mass are uniform, it has uniform temperature and humidity. An air mass is named for these two characteristics (temperature and humidity). An air mass may be either cold or warm, dry or moist. The characteristics of an air mass depend on where it forms. For example, if an air mass forms over an ocean it will probably be very moist, because water from the ocean evaporates into it. Table 1 names and describes the four principal air masses affecting the United States and identifies their source regions. These source regions are also shown in Figure 5–1.

Table 1 Air Masses

Air Mass	Source Region	Characteristics
Continental polar (cP)	Central and northern Canada	Cold and dry
Maritime polar (mP)	Northern Atlantic and Pacific oceans	Cold and humid
Continental tropical (cT)	Desert region of southwestern United States	Hot and dry
Maritime tropical (mT)	Tropical seas	Warm and humid

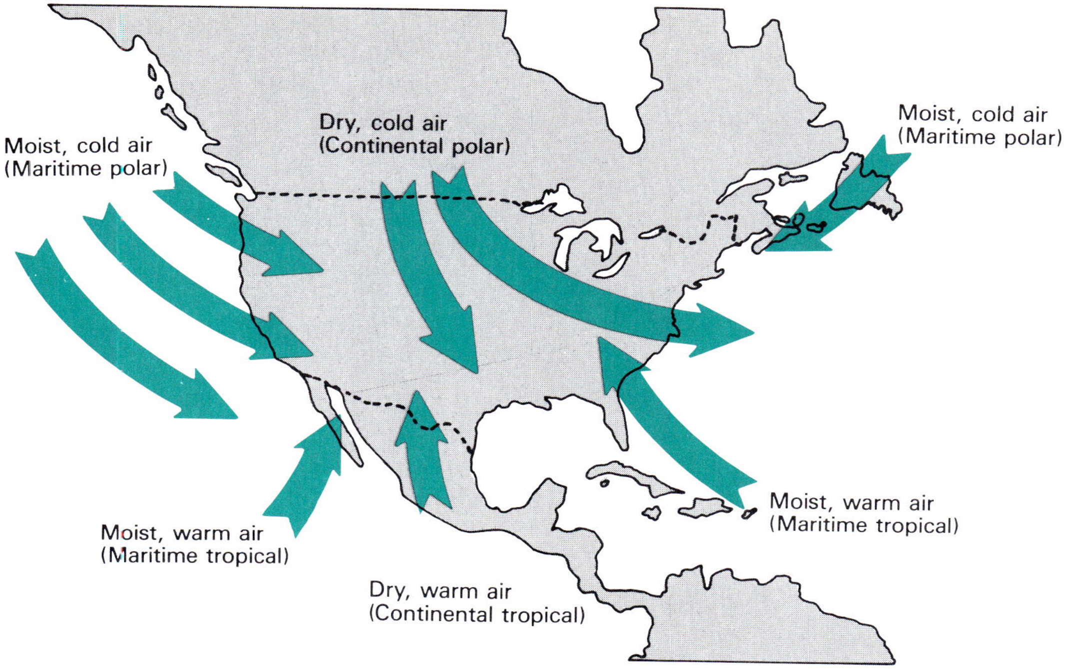

Figure 5–1. Source regions of air masses that affect the continental United States.

An air mass usually remains over its source region for some time. Then it begins to move, carrying with it the temperature and moisture characteristics of the source region over which it formed.

As an air mass moves from its source region across the United States, it causes the weather to change. For example, if an air mass from a cold source region moves over another area, the weather in that area becomes colder. If an air mass from a warm source region moves over an area, then the weather in that area becomes warmer. In the same way, air masses from humid or dry source regions cause weather to be wet or dry. In the winter months in the United States, polar air masses bring very cold weather.

2. Weather Fronts *(E5)*

It would be simple for **meteorologists**, or weather scientists, to predict the weather if only one air mass affected an area at one time. However, it is not that simple. Air masses are always forming and changing. They move around and meet other air masses. The areas where air masses meet one another are called weather **fronts**. Abrupt changes in weather often occur across a front and sometimes make predicting weather very difficult.

Weather fronts form because different air masses have different densities. To understand this, think about what happens when water and cooking oil are poured into a jar (Figure 5–2). The oil and water do not mix—they separate. The oil floats on top of

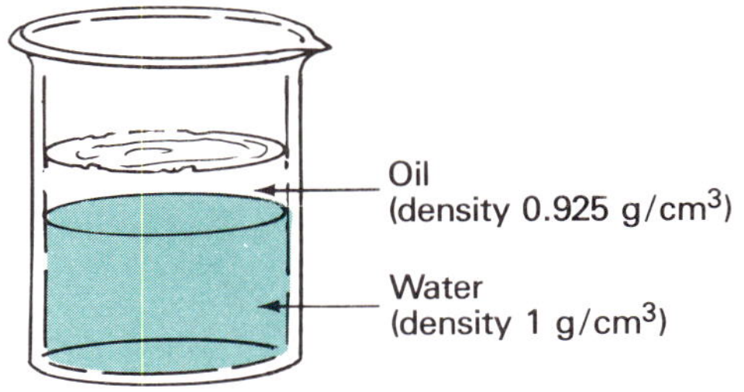

Figure 5–2. Oil and water don't mix because they have different densities.

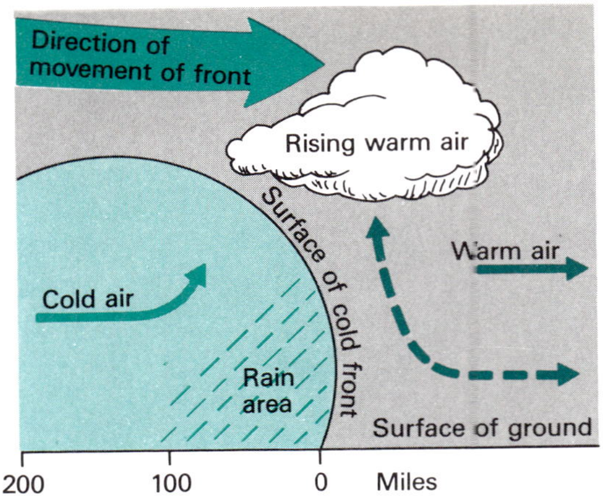

Figure 5–3. Cross section of an advancing cold front.

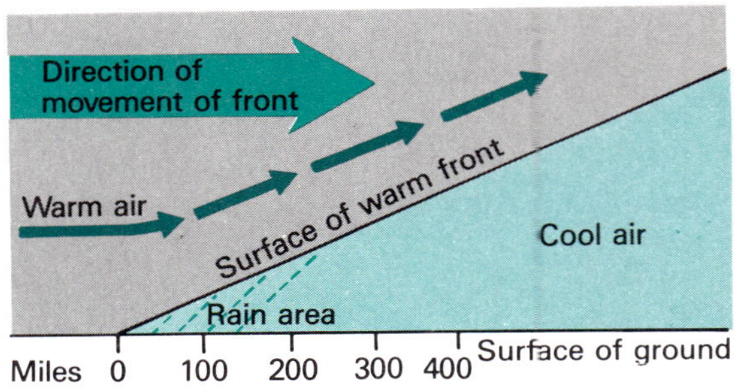

Figure 5–4. Cross section of an advancing warm front.

the water, because oil is less dense than water.

Air masses act somewhat like oil and water. Air masses have different temperatures. Cold air is heavier (more dense) than warm air. When two different air masses come together their different densities keep them from mixing, and a weather front forms. The kind of front that forms depends on how the air masses meet.

Figure 5–3 shows a cold air mass moving into a warm air mass. The weather front that forms is called a **cold front**. Whenever a colder air mass pushes against a warm air mass a cold front forms.

Usually a cold front moves quickly. The cold, dense air pushes into the lighter, warmer air like a wedge and forces the warm air to rise. As the warm air is pushed higher and higher, it becomes cooler. Since the cooler air cannot hold as much moisture, the water vapor in it condenses to form clouds. It begins to rain. Because a cold front moves quickly, the rain stops very soon and the sky clears. However, the cold air of the air mass remains in the area for a while, until it is forced away by another air mass.

Figure 5–4 shows what happens at a **warm front** when a fast-moving mass of warm air meets a slower-moving cold air mass. Describe what happens to the warmer air. What weather changes take place? Why? Locate the warm front in the illustration.

3. Air Pressure *(E4, E6, E7, E10)*

Air is a form of matter. Like all matter, air has certain characteristics. One of these characteristics is weight. Weight is the effect of gravity on a certain mass. As Earth's gravity pulls on air, the air presses down on Earth. The force with which air presses down on Earth is called **air pressure**.

Air pressure is not the same everywhere. For example, it is affected by height.

Air pressure at the top of a high mountain is less than air pressure at sea level. Similarly, temperature plays a role in changing air pressure. Cold air, for example, is heavier (more dense) than warm air. Therefore, cold air exerts more pressure than warm air.

It is easy to prove that cold air is heavier than warm air. Figure 5–5 shows the weight of two balloons of equal volume, one filled with cold air and the other with warm air. The one with the cold air weighs more.

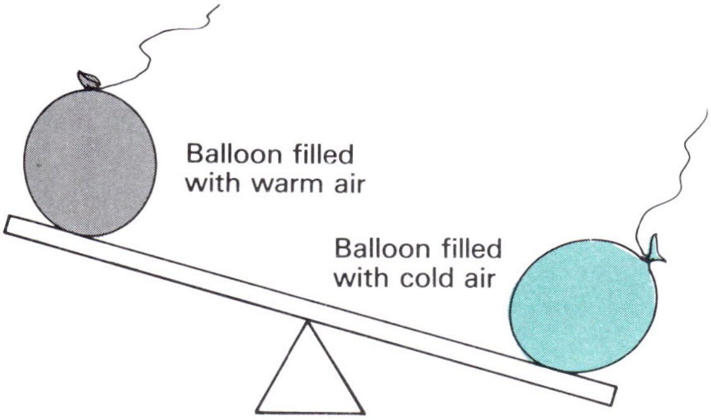

Figure 5–5. Cold air is heavier than warm air.

The cold air is heavier (more dense) than the warm air—more of it is packed into the same amount of space. Since there is more air in the same space, cold air must be heavier than the same amount of warm air. And, because it is heavier, cold air exerts more pressure on the ground.

Highs and Lows Air masses can be either cold (polar air masses) or warm (tropical air masses). Because cold air is heavy, cold air masses exert much pressure on Earth. Cold air masses therefore are usually called high-pressure areas, or simply **highs**. Highs tend to be fair-weather systems. Warm air masses, on the other hand, are made of lighter air, so they exert less

Science Skill

INTERPRETING DIAGRAMS

The diagram at the right shows a cold front as it approaches Town *A*. Study the diagram and then answer the questions that follow.

1. What happens to the warm air over Town *A* as the cold front wedges into the air?
2. What effect will the approaching cold front have on the weather conditions in Town *A*?
3. Explain why it will probably rain as the cold front passes over Town *A*.

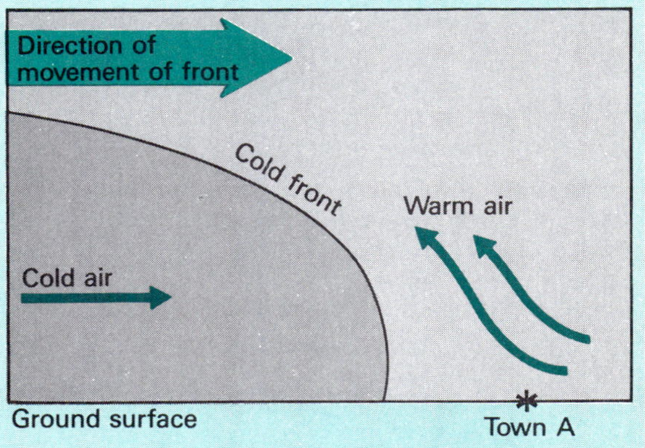

pressure on Earth. They are called low-pressure areas or **lows**. Low-pressure areas often form along fronts. Lows are the major storm systems in the United States. The movement of air in high- and low-pressure areas causes different weather.

The air pressure in a low is not the same throughout the air mass. It is lowest in the center (Figure 5–6). The higher-pressure air around the outside of the low blows inward, toward the center of the low.

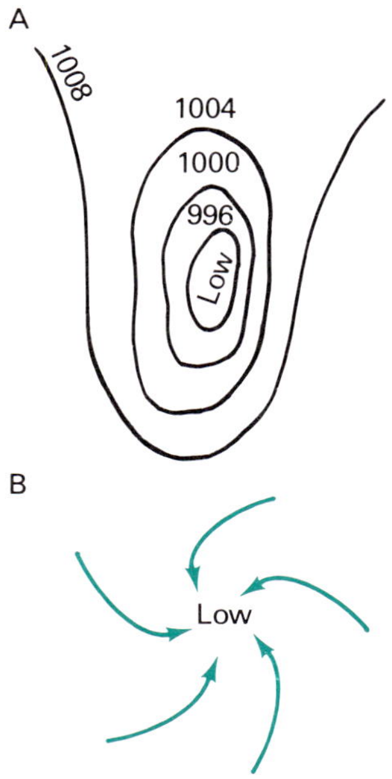

Figure 5–6. (A) Pressure is lowest in the center of a low. (B) Winds blow inward toward the center of a low.

As the heavier, higher-pressure air moves in, it forces the lighter, lower pressure air to rise. As this air moves upward, its temperature drops. Water vapor in the rising air condenses, forming clouds. This is followed by some form of precipitation. Lows usually bring rain and stormy weather.

Highs are just the opposite of lows. The air pressure in a high is highest in the center. The higher-pressure air blows outward from the center of the high. As the heavier, higher-pressure air moves out it falls toward Earth (Figure 5–7). As the air falls, it gets warmer. Since warm air can hold more water vapor than cooler air, the water vapor doesn't condense as in a low.

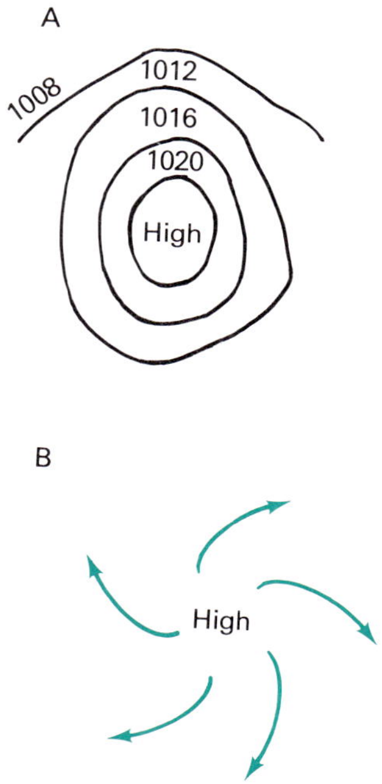

Figure 5–7. (A) Pressure is highest in the center of a high. (B) Winds blow outward from the center of a high.

There are few clouds and very little precipitation in a high. Highs usually bring clear, pleasant weather. Because highs are large, they tend to move slowly and cause gradual changes in the weather.

Sample Questions

1. An air mass that forms over the ocean is a(n)
   (1) maritime air mass
   (2) continental air mass
   (3) tropical air mass
   (4) polar air mass

2. When one air mass meets another air mass, a boundary forms. This boundary is called a
   (1) high (3) front
   (2) low (4) current

3. Cold air masses are usually associated with what kind of pressure?
   (1) low pressure (3) medium pressure
   (2) high pressure

4. The map shows the source areas for different air masses. Which air mass brings very cold, dry weather to New York State during the winter?

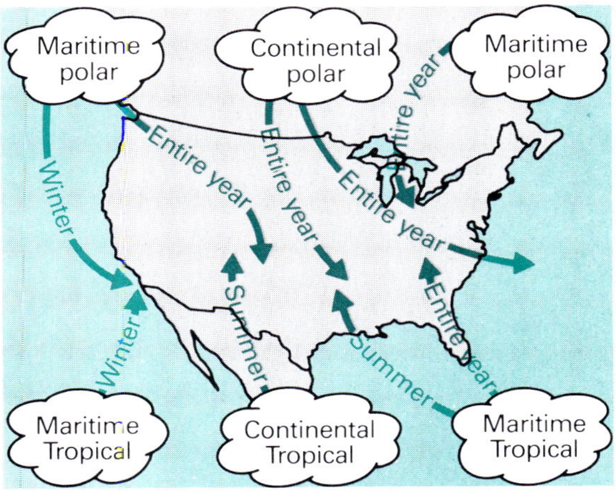

   (1) maritime tropical
   (2) continental tropical
   (3) continental polar
   (4) maritime polar

5. An air mass that forms at the North Pole most likely will be
   (1) cold and moist
   (2) cold and dry
   (3) warm and moist
   (4) warm and dry

6. A low-pressure area usually results in what kind of weather?
   (1) stormy (2) clear (3) dry

7. The diagram below shows a fast-moving mass of warm air meeting a slower-moving cold air mass.

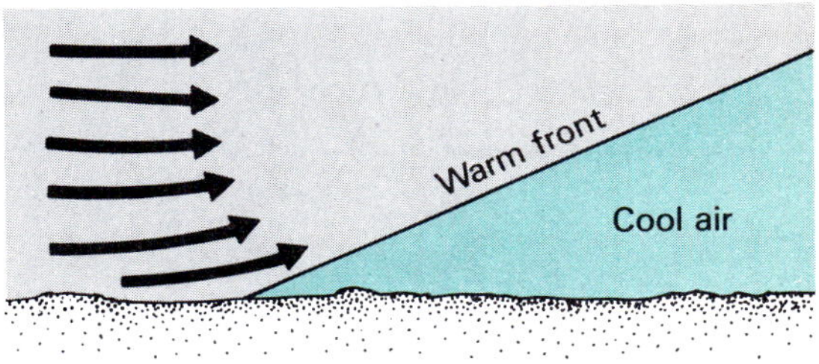

   As the warm front passes over this area, the weather most likely will become
   (1) warm and rainy
   (2) cool and dry
   (3) warm and dry
   (4) cool and rainy

8. As a cold front approaches an area, air pressure usually
   (1) increases
   (2) decreases
   (3) remains the same

9. The following weather changes were reported in a certain area: *The temperature dropped 15°C in the last 12 hours. The winds shifted from southeast to northwest*. The sudden change in the

weather was probably due to an approaching
(1) warm front
(2) cold front
(3) maritime tropical air mass
(4) continental tropical air mass

10. Which statement is true for a low-pressure area?
(1) It is usually associated with fair weather.
(2) It is usually associated with a storm system.
(3) It is associated with a cold air mass.
(4) It is associated with a cold front.

11. The passing of highs and lows is usually associated with
(1) changes in air pressure
(2) no changes in air pressure
(3) no changes in weather
(4) increases in solar radiation

12. Air pressure is usually highest when the air is
(1) cold and dry
(2) cold and moist
(3) warm and dry
(4) warm and moist

13. A source of maritime polar air is
(1) northern Canada
(2) the Gulf of Mexico
(3) the north Pacific Ocean
(4) southern Canada

14. In the polar regions, the atmosphere is cold and the air pressure is
(1) high
(2) low
(3) medium
(4) zero

II. LOCAL WEATHER

1. Weather Elements *(E8)*

The study of weather requires a collection of data for a number of weather elements. Weather elements include temperature, humidity, wind direction and speed, air pressure, solar radiation, cloudiness, and precipitation. The weather forecaster uses this data to describe current weather and to make an accurate prediction of future weather. Let's look at the weather elements—what they are and how they are measured.

Air Temperature Meteorologists measure the air temperature to find out about the weather. They want to find out how hot or cold it is. The air temperature often provides a clue about where the air has come from.

The instrument used to measure air temperature is the *thermometer*. Most thermometers are made of a hollow glass tube filled with a liquid. The liquids most often used in thermometers are mercury and alcohol. When the air around the thermometer becomes warmer it heats the liquid in the tube. The liquid expands. The only place for the expanding liquid to go is up the tube. When the air around the thermometer cools, the liquid contracts and goes back down the tube.

Lines drawn on the tube help in reading the temperature. These lines stand for **degrees**. There are different scales for measuring temperature, but the one used by meteorologists is called the *Celsius scale*. The temperature of freezing water is 0°C. Water boils at 100°C. Human body temperature is about 37°C. The temperature on a pleasant spring day is about 23°C (Figure 5–8).

Humidity The amount of water vapor in the air is called **humidity**. The humidity of the air is affected by the temperature. The

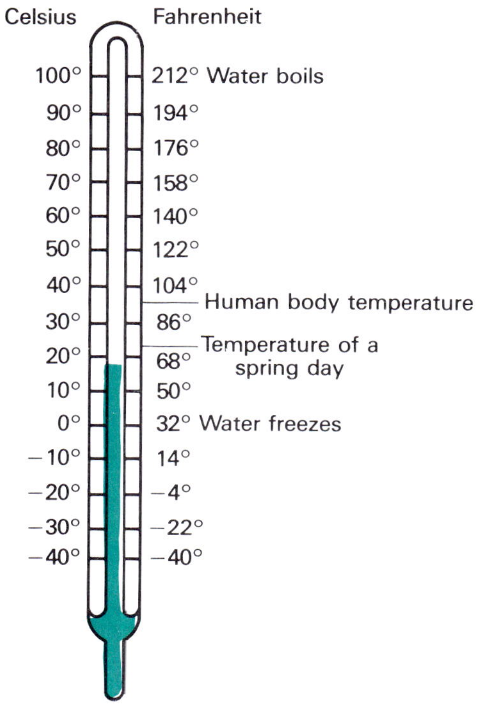

Figure 5–8. Temperature scales.

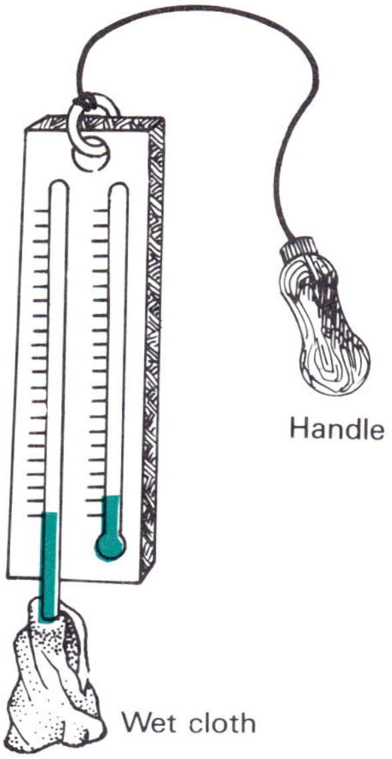

Figure 5–9. Wet-and-dry-bulb thermometer.

higher the temperature, the more water vapor the air can hold. The lower the temperature, the less water vapor the air can hold. As the air temperature changes so can the humidity.

Air does not always hold as much water vapor as it can. In fact, most of the time the air has less water vapor than it could hold. The amount of water vapor in the air is a measure of *relative humidity*. Relative humidity is usually given as a percentage. If the air is holding all the water it can hold, the relative humidity is 100%. If the air is holding only half of the water vapor that it can absorb, the relative humidity is 50%.

By knowing the relative humidity and temperature of the air, meteorologists can make some predictions. They can tell if clouds are going to condense in the sky. They can tell if it is going to rain or snow. They can tell how comfortable the weather will be during the day.

Measuring relative humidity is done with a tool called a *wet-and-dry-bulb thermometer* (Figure 5–9). Sometimes this tool is called a *psychrometer* or *hygrometer*. The wet-and-dry-bulb thermometer is made of two thermometers held together on a base. Over the bulb of one of the thermometers is a wet cloth or sponge. The bulb of the other thermometer is left uncovered and dry.

When the two thermometers are whirled around, they act differently. The temperature reading on the dry-bulb thermometer (the one without the wet cloth) usually doesn't change at all. Because of the water evaporating from the wet cloth, though, the wet-bulb thermometer's temperature drops. If the air around the thermometers has a low relative humidity, then a lot of water will evaporate from the cloth and the temperature will drop more.

By taking the readings from both the wet-bulb and the dry-bulb thermometers we can figure out the relative humidity of the air. All that is needed to do this is a chart that gives the percent of relative humidity when both temperatures are known.

Wind Direction and Speed The branches of trees sway back and forth. A kite soars high in the sky. A flag waves in the air. These motions are caused by moving air. Any kind of moving air, whether it is a breeze or an air current, is called **wind**.

Winds affect weather. Some winds are cool, others are warm. One of the conditions that makes up the weather is the temperature of the air. Warm and cool winds, then, cause the weather to change because they change the air's temperature. As winds move air from place to place they also move the water vapor that is in the air, and as a result cause weather to change.

Winds are measured in two ways. The first measurement, called *wind speed*, describes how fast the winds are blowing. Wind speed is measured in kilometers per hour. Wind speed tells the meteorologist just how fast air masses and weather fronts are moving. This information helps in predicting changes in the weather.

Wind speed is measured with an *anemometer* (Figure 5–10). This instrument is somewhat like a pinwheel. It spins around as the wind blows against it. By counting how many times the anemometer rotates, the speed of the wind can be determined.

The second wind measurement is *wind direction*. Wind directions are named according to where the winds are coming from, not where they are blowing to. For example, a wind blowing from the Pacific Ocean toward the Atlantic Ocean is called a west wind or a westerly. It is blowing from west to east. Usually wind direction is given by using a combination of the four directions: north, east, south, or west. The wind direction can be any one of these four; a combination of two of the directions, such as northwest; or a combination of three of the directions, such as east southeast.

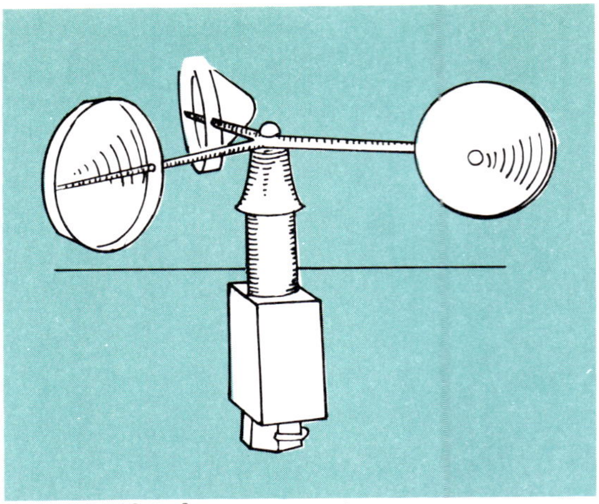

Figure 5–10. An anemometer measures wind speed.

Wind direction is measured with a *wind vane*. Most wind vanes look like arrows. The wind vane's tail is always bigger and heavier than its head (Figure 5–11). A

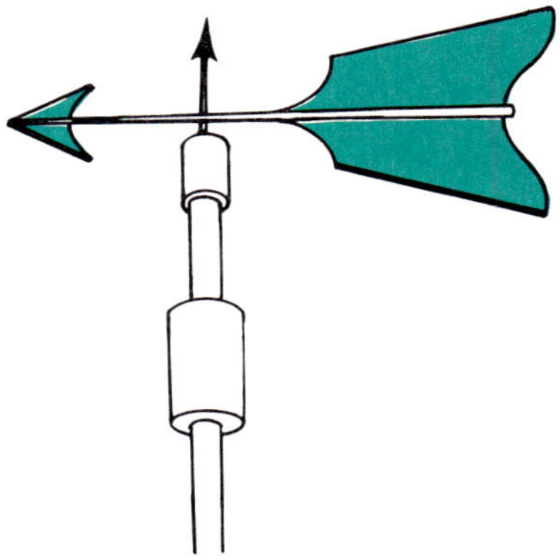

Figure 5–11. A wind vane indicates wind direction.

blowing wind exerts more force against the bigger tail, swinging the arrow to point in the direction from which the wind blows. For example, if the arrow points to the south, the wind is blowing from the south.

Wind direction tells where the air masses have been. It tells if the air mass is polar or tropical, maritime or continental. Wind direction often tells what kind of air will come to a region.

Air Pressure Air pressure, the force with which air pushes down on the earth, is measured with an instrument called a *barometer*. The first barometers were made using a long tube filled with mercury. The tube was turned upside down in a dish. The force of the air pressing down on the mercury in the dish kept the rest of the mercury in the tube. As the air pressure changed, so did the height of the mercury in the tube. Mercury barometers very much like the first one are still used today (Figure 5–12).

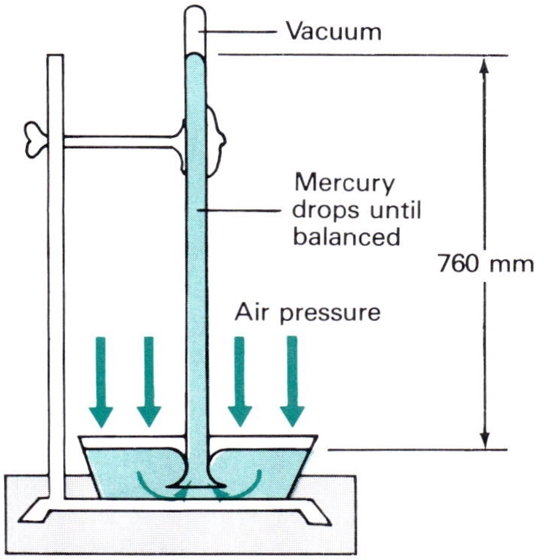

Figure 5–12. Mercury barometer.

The *aneroid barometer* is also used by weather forecasters. The aneroid barometer is made of a sealed box or a can. Some of the air is removed from the can before it is sealed, however. This makes it very sensitive to air pressure outside the can. As the outside air pressure rises, the top of the can falls in slightly. As the outside air pressure drops, the top of the can springs back. A needle attached to the can's top points to a scale that indicates the air pressure.

Originally, air pressure was measured by how tall the column of mercury was in the tube. For example, at sea level on an average day normal air pressure might be 760 millimeters of mercury. If a high-pressure air mass moves into the area, the air

Science Skill

GRAPHING DATA

The data table below shows the average temperature in five cities in New York State during the month of April.

Data Table

City	Average Temperature (°F)
Buffalo	44
Rochester	45
Riverhead	48
New York City	50
Lake Placid	38

On a piece of graph paper, plot the points for the average temperature for each city given in the data table. Draw a line through the points.

presses down harder on the mercury in the dish and it rises higher in the tube. If a low-pressure air mass moves over the area, the air presses down with less force on the mercury and it falls lower in the tube. The barometer then indicates an air pressure below the normal 760 millimeters of mercury.

Most modern barometers don't have tubes of mercury—they are aneroid barometers. Scientists have developed a new unit to measure air pressure. This unit is the *millibar*. Normal air pressure, 760 millimeters of mercury, is equal to 1013.25 millibars.

To the meteorologist, it is as important to know if the air pressure is changing as it is to know exactly what the measurement is. For example, if the air pressure is steady there will probably be no change in the weather. If the air pressure is increasing there will probably be an improvement in the weather. (Remember, high-pressure air masses usually bring clear weather). However, if the air pressure is dropping there is probably bad weather ahead. (Remember, low-pressure air masses usually bring stormy weather).

Solar Radiation Sunlight heats Earth. Earth, in turn, gives off some of its heat to the air.

Because Earth is round, light from the sun (solar radiation) strikes Earth at different angles in different places. For example, sunlight strikes Earth at the equator directly for most of the year. The farther away from the equator, however, the more slanted the rays that strike Earth.

Earth is heated most at the equator, where the sun's rays are direct. The direct rays cover only a small area (Figure 5–13). All of the sun's energy heats that small area. Slanted rays, on the other hand, cover a larger area. Therefore, away from the equator, the sun's energy is spread over a larger area. These areas are heated less than the areas at the equator. This explains in part why the temperature at the equator is higher than at latitudes north or south of the equator.

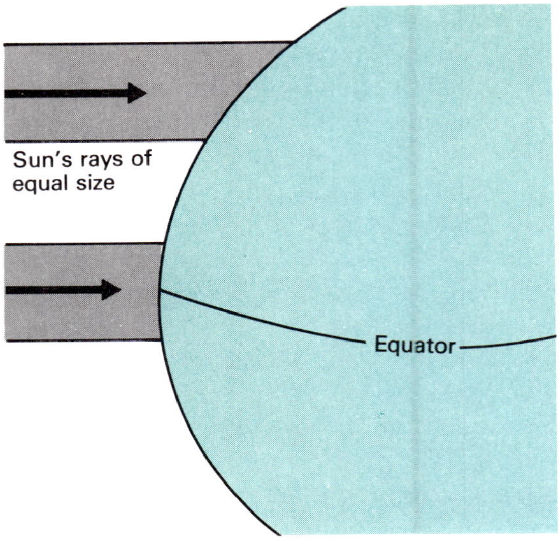

Figure 5–13. Away from the equator, the sun's energy is spread over a larger area.

Clouds A **cloud** is a large mass of tiny, condensed water drops. Clouds form as warm, moist air rises. As warm, moist air moves higher and higher, it becomes cooler. The temperature keeps falling as the warm air continues to rise. Since cool air cannot hold as much water vapor as warm air, the water vapor condenses to form clouds. There are many different types of clouds. Table 2 lists and describes the three main types of clouds.

Precipitation **Precipitation** is the name given to any kind of condensed water that falls from the sky. Rain, snow, sleet, and hail are the four kinds of precipitation. They all condense from water vapor in the air and fall from clouds. They are all forms of water.

Table 2 Main Types of Clouds

Cloud Type	Appearance	Characteristics
Cirrus	Look like curls of smoke	Occur at high altitudes; made of ice crystals; usually indicate rain or snow in a few days
Cumulus	Look like puffs of cotton	Flat on the bottom with puffs above; accompany fair weather; dark grey cumulus are thunderstorms
Stratus	Layers that cover the sky	Occur at low altitudes; associated with stormy weather

2. Predicting the Weather *(E9)*

Meteorologists use the data they collect to predict what kind of weather might be expected in a region in a few hours, a few days, or even a longer period of time.

An important part of predicting the weather is writing down all of the measurements that have been taken. Weather forecasters use a **weather map** to record all of the information they gather at hundreds of local weather stations. Special symbols or codes are used to show air pressure, weather fronts, wind speed and direction, and so on. In fact, there are symbols on a weather map for every kind of information that is used to predict the weather.

A sample weather map is shown in Figure 5–14. Around it are the keys. These keys show all the symbols used in the map.

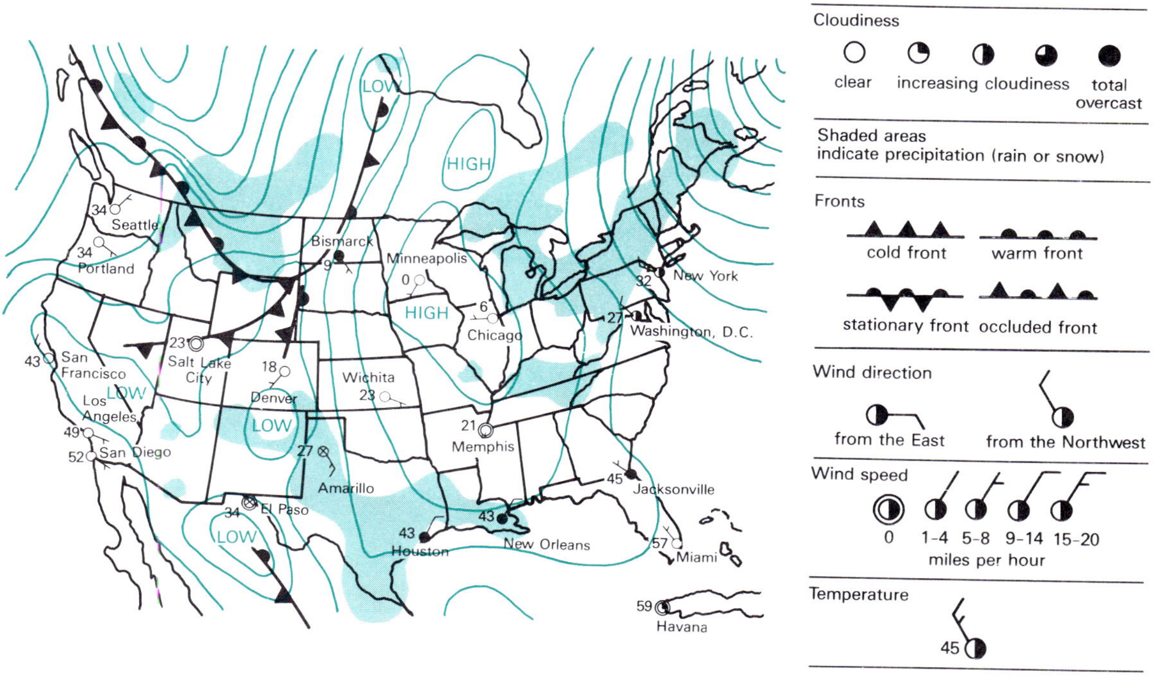

Figure 5–14. Weather map.

The keys also explain what the symbols mean and how they are used.

From the data collected and recorded on the map, forecasters can determine the locations of high- and low-pressure systems and cold and warm fronts. The speed and direction of movement of pressure systems and fronts can be determined too. These kinds of information are used by forecasters to predict changes in the weather.

Predicting the weather is a very difficult job. Sometimes the predictions made by the weather forecaster are accurate. Sometimes the forecasters seem to make big mistakes. There are many factors (e.g., temperature, wind humidity, pressure, etc.) that can affect the weather. Every one of these factors must be considered when making a prediction of the next day's weather.

Science Skill

PREDICTING

Study the weather map. Then answer the questions that follow.

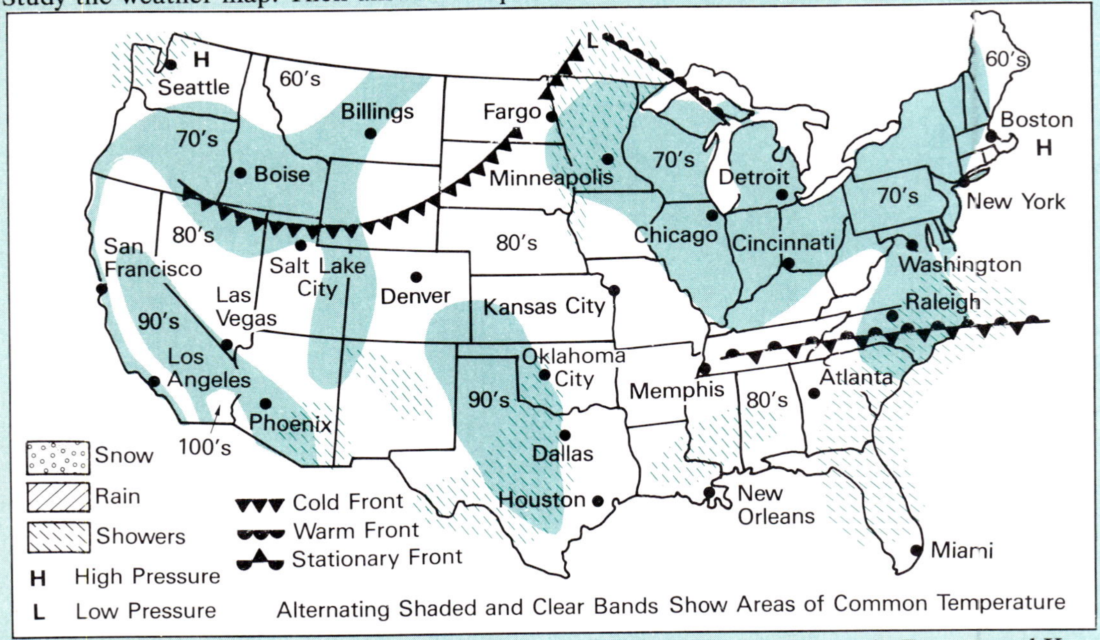

1. Where is there a cold front on the map?
2. Examine the temperature reported at stations on both sides of the cold front. Why is it warmer in Denver than in Seattle?
3. What are some possible causes of the rain in Fargo and Minneapolis?
4. Will the temperature in Denver and Kansas City increase or decrease in a day or two? Explain your answer.
5. What is represented by the shading on this map?

Sample Questions

1–3. Base your answers to questions 1–3 on the table below, which shows temperature readings at different times on three days.

Day	6 A.M	9 A.M.	12 noon	3 P.M.	6 P.M.
Monday	15°C	17°C	20°C	21°C	19°C
Tuesday	15°C	15°C	15°C	10°C	9°C
Wednesday	8°C	10°C	14°C	14°C	13°C

1. When was the highest temperature recorded?
(1) noon on Monday
(2) 3 P.M. on Monday
(3) noon on Tuesday
(4) noon on Wednesday
(5) 6 P.M. on Wednesday

2. Which thermometer below shows the temperature at 6 A.M. on Wednesday?

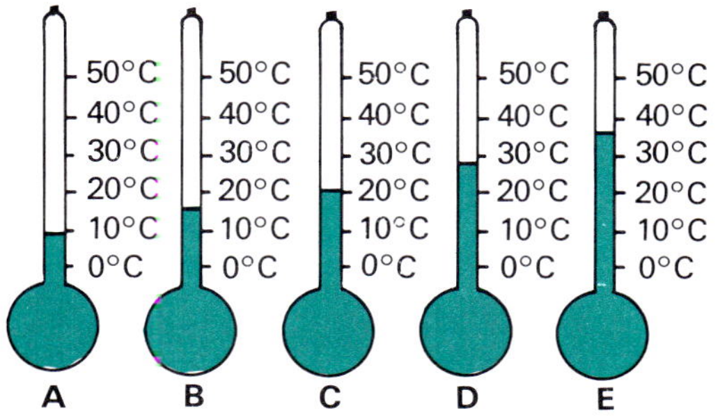

(1) A (2) B (3) C (4) D (5) E

3. On one day a cool wind began to blow. When did this most likely occur?
(1) Monday morning
(2) Monday afternoon
(3) Tuesday morning
(4) Tuesday afternoon
(5) Wednesday afternoon

4. The graph below shows the total amount of precipitation for five cities in New York State in April.

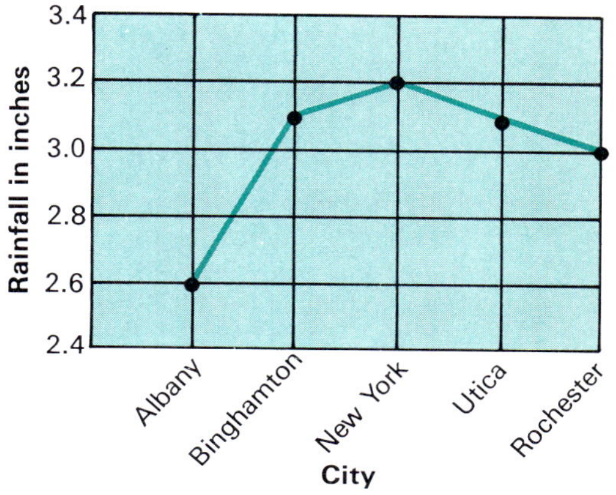

Which is the total amount of precipitation in Binghamton for the month of April?
(1) 2.6 inches
(2) 2.6 centimeters
(3) 3.1 inches
(4) 3.2 centimeters

5. On a certain day the air over New York City held only one fourth of the water vapor it could absorb. The relative humidity of this air was
(1) 25% (2) 50% (3) 75% (4) 100%

6. The sun's rays hit Earth most directly at the
(1) North Pole (3) equator
(2) South Pole

7. Wind direction is described by
(1) where the winds are coming from
(2) where the winds are blowing to
(3) the speed at which winds move
(4) the amount of water vapor carried by the wind

8. The relative humidity readings in a certain region at 1 P.M. on three consecutive days were as follows: Day 1 – 87%; Day 2 – 50%; Day 3 – 25%. Based on the data, it can be concluded that
(1) warm, moist air moved into the region
(2) cool, dry air moved into the region
(3) there was no change in the air over this region for three days
(4) a low-pressure system covered the region for three days

9. The force with which air pushes down on Earth is called
(1) relative humidity
(2) temperature
(3) air pressure
(4) gravity

10. Air pressure is measured with an instrument called a(n)
(1) thermometer (3) barometer
(2) psychrometer (4) anemometer

11. The weather forecast indicates that there is an 80% chance of rain. This means that the chances of rain occurring are
(1) 0 out of 10 (3) 8 out of 10
(2) 2 out of 10 (4) 10 out of 10

12. The weather service reports that the humidity is rising and the air pressure is falling. It is likely that
(1) the weather will be fair
(2) the weather will be rainy
(3) cool, dry air will arrive
(4) warm, dry air will arrive

13. Air pressure is a measure of the
(1) amount of rainfall
(2) force of air
(3) relative humidity
(4) air temperature

14. Humidity is measured with an instrument called a(n)
(1) psychrometer (3) weather vane
(2) barometer (4) thermometer

15. The graph below shows temperature readings taken on July 5.

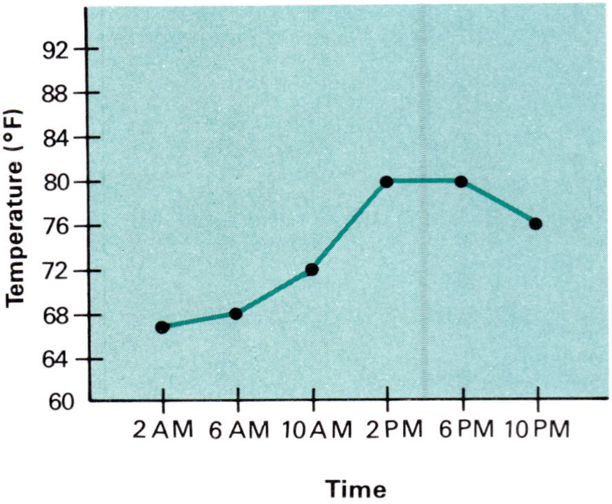

What is the temperature reading at 6 A.M.?
(1) 67° (2) 68° (3) 72° (4) 80°

16. Thin, feathery ice-crystal clouds are called
(1) cirrus (3) cumulus
(2) nimbostratus (4) nimbus

17. The passing of a high or low is associated with a change in
(1) climate (3) air pressure
(2) latitude (4) state

III. ENERGY AND MOTION IN THE ATMOSPHERE

1. The Sun—Primary Source of Energy *(E12, E13, E14)*

The sun is the primary source of energy for Earth. The sun warms the land, the water and the atmosphere. Its energy causes water to evaporate into the atmosphere. The sun's energy also causes the winds. Light from the sun is absorbed and used by green plants during photosynthesis to produce food.

Energy from the sun reaches Earth in the form of **radiation**. Hardly any sunlight is absorbed by the atmosphere. Most of the sunlight reaches Earth's surface. Then it is absorbed by the land and water and becomes heat (Figure 5–15). In this way Earth's surface becomes warmer than the air above it.

Only the lower layer of air touches the surface of the land and water. Some of the heat from the land and water flows into the lower layer of air, warming it. As the land and water warm the air, the warmed air becomes lighter. The cooler air above it falls and pushes the lighter air up. Thus differences in the air temperatures cause air movements known as *currents*.

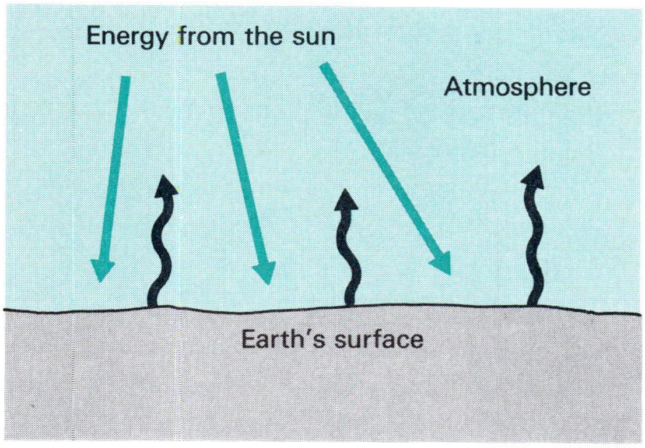

Figure 5–15. Energy from the sun is absorbed by Earth's surface. Reradiated energy from the surface is absorbed by the atmosphere.

Air currents can also move across Earth's surface, causing the **winds**. Winds result from the unequal heating of Earth's surface.

2. Uneven Distribution of Energy in the Atmosphere *(E13)*

On a hot summer day the sand on the beach feels very hot. The water feels much cooler. The land absorbs more heat from the sun's rays than the water does. Because the land absorbs more heat, the air over the land becomes warmer than the air over the water. This unevenness in heating causes air currents to form.

First, the warm air over the land rises. Then cool air over the water rushes in to take the place of the rising warm air. This current causes a cool breeze to blow in from the water toward the land. The cool breeze is called a *sea breeze*.

At night, just the opposite occurs. The land loses its heat faster than the water. The warmer air over the water rises. Cool air from over the land rushes toward the water, forming a *land breeze*.

3. Prevailing Winds and Wind Belts *(E15)*

Earth is heated most at the equator, where the sun's rays are direct. As the heated air over the equator rises, cooler air rushes in to take its place. The cooler air comes from areas near the poles. A huge convection current is set in motion. Hot air rises from the equator and flows north and south toward the poles. Cool air sinks at the poles and flows toward the equator.

Prevailing Winds The pattern of the currents of air on Earth should look like Figure 5–16. However, it doesn't. Besides the sun's energy and Earth's shape, another factor – Earth's rotation – affects air currents.

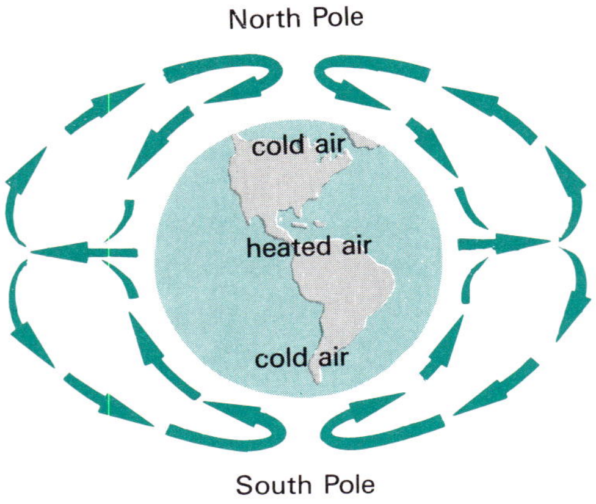

Figure 5–16. Winds on a nonrotating Earth.

Earth rotates on its axis. It spins around like a top. Rotation causes night and day. Rotation causes the sun to seem to move across the sky. Also, rotation causes the pattern of the air currents (winds) around the world.

Earth spins from west to east. The air around Earth spins in the same direction but not as fast. The spinning makes the air currents bend. Figure 5–17 shows the patterns of Earth's winds. Compare this with the way the winds would blow if Earth did not rotate. In reality, the winds do not flow straight north and south. North of the equator the path of the winds bends to the right. South of the equator the path of the winds bends to the left. These winds that always blow in the same patterns are called **prevailing winds.**

If Earth did not rotate, the winds would be simple currents moving between the equator and the poles. However, Earth does rotate, and the rotation changes the direction of the winds.

Wind Belts The patterns made by the prevailing winds are called the **wind belts**. The wind belts circle the globe parallel to the equator. Each belt has its own characteristics. These characteristics are caused by very complicated changes that take place as the air currents cool off and warm up. Figure 5–17 shows the wind belts and how the winds blow in each one.

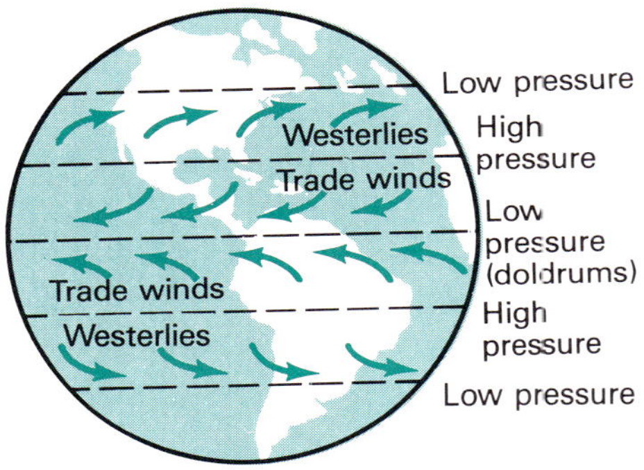

Figure 5–17. Earth's major winds and pressure zones.

Surrounding the equator is a belt with almost no winds. The heated air rises almost straight up. There is very little air moving in any other direction. This calm area is called the **doldrums**.

Heated air at the equator rises. As the air rises, it cools and moves north and south toward the poles. Some of this cooled air sinks back to Earth's surface about one fourth of the way to the poles in both the Northern and Southern hemispheres. The rest of the air continues north and south toward the poles. The air that sinks back to Earth divides north and south, forming some wind belts. The winds moving south form the **trade winds**. The winds moving north form the **prevailing westerlies**. The prevailing westerlies usually blow in the same direction all the time, from the southwest to the northeast. These winds play an important part in determining the weather for the United States. Due to the prevailing westerlies the highs and lows that dominate the weather in the United States move from west to east.

The air that continues to the poles becomes colder and heavier. At the poles this air sinks, moving back toward the equator to form the **polar easterlies**.

Sample Questions

1. The primary source of energy for Earth is
(1) the sun (3) clouds
(2) the water (4) gases

2–4. Base your answers to questions 2–4 on the diagram below, which shows the movement of air in a convection box.

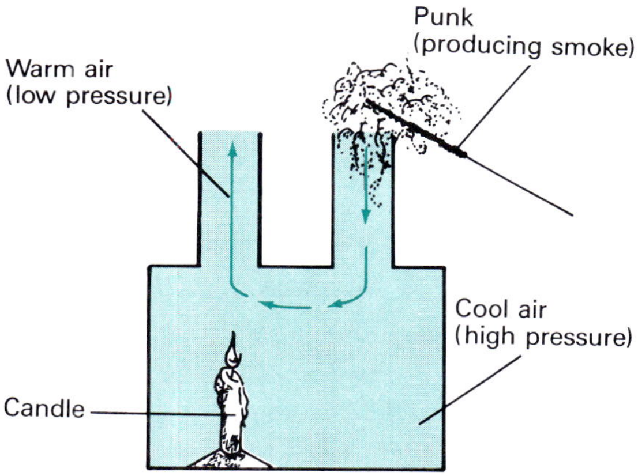

2. The arrows indicate that
(1) warm air rises and cool air sinks
(2) cool air rises and warm air sinks
(3) both cool and warm air rise
(4) both cool and warm air sink

3. The demonstration proves that
(1) warm air is heavier than cool air
(2) cool air is heavier than warm air
(3) warm air pushes cooler air and makes it rise
(4) warm air exerts higher pressure than cool air

4. This demonstration can be used to explain the formation of
(1) air currents (3) cold fronts
(2) water vapor (4) warm fronts

5. The diagram below shows the direction of prevailing winds on Earth. Which statement best explains the direction of the prevailing winds?

(1) Wind direction is affected by Earth's rotation.
(2) Wind direction is affected by mountains and valleys.
(3) Wind direction is affected by water.
(4) Wind direction is affected by the sun's movements.

6. In the United States, the highs and lows that dominate the weather move from west to east due to the
   (1) trade winds
   (2) prevailing westerlies
   (3) prevailing easterlies
   (4) polar easterlies

7. During the day, cool air blows in toward the beach from the water. This cool air is a result of a(n)
   (1) land breeze
   (2) sea breeze
   (3) drop in temperature
   (4) drop in humidity

8. Warm air rises because it is
   (1) heavier than cool air
   (2) lighter than cool air
   (3) denser than cool air

9. Wind direction is determined by an instrument called a(n)
   (1) anemometer
   (2) sling psychrometer
   (3) barometer
   (4) wind vane

10. A balloon was attached to the narrow neck of a flask. Then the flask was heated over a Bunsen burner.

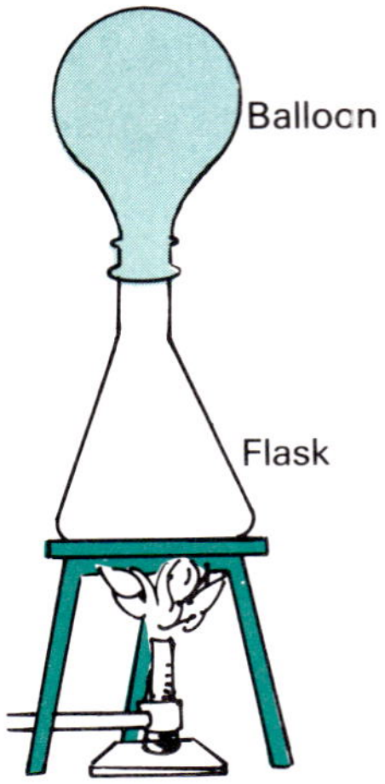

The balloon becomes inflated because
   (1) molecules in the air move farther apart when heated
   (2) molecules in the air move closer together when heated
   (3) warm air takes up less space than cool air
   (4) warm air takes up as much space as cool air

IV. THE WATER CYCLE

1. Evaporation (E16)

After a rainstorm, the sidewalks may be covered with puddles of water. Soon the puddles are gone. The water **evaporates** – it enters the atmosphere. Water evaporates from oceans, river, bays, and lakes just as it does from a puddle.

Water is made of tiny particles called *molecules*. These molecules are always moving. They move back and forth and up and down, and bounce into each other. Sometimes molecules near the surface of the water move in just the right direction and escape into the air. These molecules are no longer part of the body of water. They have become part of the air. They have *evaporated*. The water has changed from a liquid state to a gaseous state. Water in the gaseous state is called **water vapor**.

The amount of water vapor in the air is called *humidity*. The higher the temperature, the more water vapor the air can hold. Also, the lower the temperature the less water vapor the air can hold. Cool air cannot hold as much water vapor as warm air.

2. Condensation (E17)

When the temperature drops, water vapor may start **condensing** into *water droplets*. The temperature at which the water vapor starts condensing into water drops is called the **dew point**. Here is an example. Suppose the temperature of the air is 15°C and the relative humidity is 90%. The temperature begins to fall. As it does, the air can hold less and less water, so the relative humidity goes up. Soon, the temperature has dropped low enough that the relative humidity becomes 100 percent (even though the total amount of water vapor in the air has not changed) . If the temperature drops any more, water will start to condense out of the air. The temperature at which water vapor begins to condense into water droplets is the dew point.

Warm air is lighter than cool air. Warm air can hold more water vapor than cool air. Warm, moist air rises. As it moves higher and higher, the air becomes cooler. The temperature keeps falling as the warm air continues to rise. Eventually the temperature falls to the dew point. Water vapor condenses into water droplets. Large masses of water droplets form clouds.

Clouds are not the only form of condensation. *Fog*, *dew*, and *frost* are other forms of condensation. Unlike clouds, however, each of these forms near the surface of Earth.

Fog is a cloud that forms right next to the ground. It forms when a large mass of low air cools to its dew point. Drops of water condense. The water droplets are so small and light that the slightest breeze keeps them floating in the air. A fog can also form when air is blown across a cooler surface. This kind of fog often occurs near the shore. As warm air passes over cooler land, the water condenses to form a fog.

Dew forms when warm air comes in contact with a cool surface. The air that touches these cool objects becomes cooler too. When the air temperature drops below the dew point, the water vapor condenses into dewdrops. Dew usually forms on grass, windowpanes, and car tops.

Frost is similar to dew. Frost forms when the dew point is below 0° Celsius, the freezing point of water. When frost forms, the water vapor condenses right into frozen ice crystals. Sometimes on evenings in spring or fall the ground temperature falls below freezing, causing frost to form.

Fog, dew, and frost condense near or on the ground. Clouds, on the other hand, condense high in the sky. Clouds are made of water drops. Under certain circumstances, the drops may fall to the ground as rain or snow.

Precipitation is the name given to any kind of condensed water that falls from the sky. Rain, snow, sleet, and hail are the four kinds of precipitation. They all fall from clouds. They are all forms of water.

In summary, water enters the atmosphere by evaporation. The water vapor condenses into water droplets and falls to the surface as precipitation. This continuous movement of water between Earth's surface and the atmosphere is known as the **water cycle** (Figure 5–18).

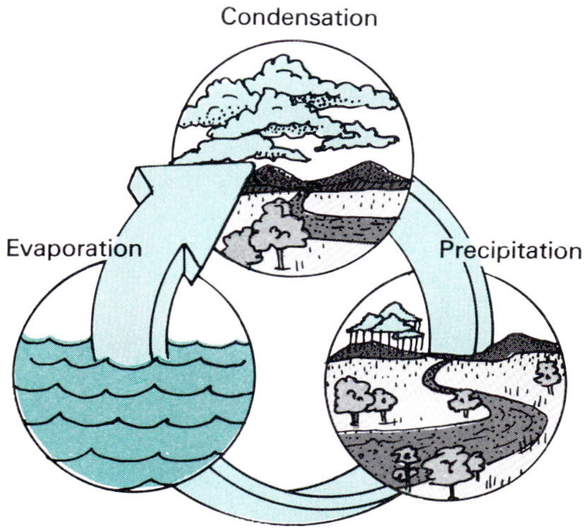

Figure 5–18. The water cycle.

Sample Questions

1. The amount of water vapor in the air is called
(1) air pressure
(2) air temperature
(3) humidity
(4) radiation

2. When moisture condenses on cool objects, such as grass and windowpanes, it is known as
(1) hail (3) fog
(2) snow (4) dew

3. A kind of cloud that forms next to the ground is called a
(1) cirrus cloud (3) fog
(2) cumulus cloud (4) dew

4–6. Base your answers to questions 4–6 on the diagram of the water cycle shown below.

4. The process of evaporation is shown by the arrow labeled
(1) A (2) B (3) C

5. The process of precipitation is shown by the arrow labeled
(1) A (2) B (3) C

6. Which process is most closely associated with the formation of clouds?
(1) evaporation
(2) precipitation
(3) condensation
(4) erosion

7. Rain is to snow as dew is to
(1) fog (3) frost
(2) cloud (4) vapor

8. A flask containing some ice-cold water was set at an angle over a drinking glass filled with boiling water as shown below.

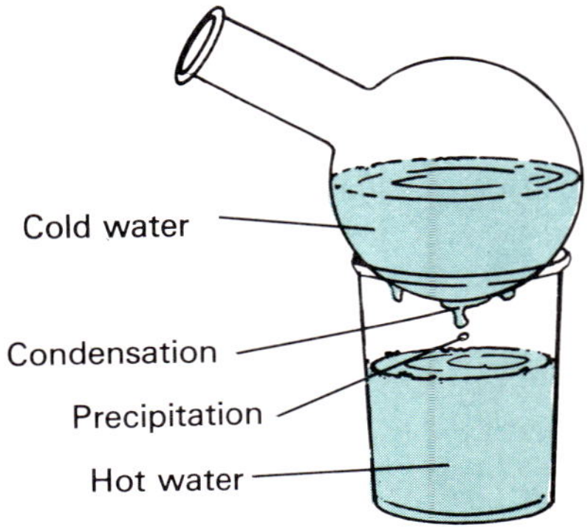

Water droplets formed on the outside of the flask. Which statement *best* explains why this happened?
(1) Some water leaked through the crack in the flask.
(2) Water from the glass evaporated.
(3) Water vapor from the glass condensed on the flask.
(4) Some water from the glass splashed on the flask.

9. The process by which water vapor changes to a liquid is called
(1) evaporation
(2) condensation
(3) regulation
(4) erosion

10. The processes of evaporation, condensation, and precipitation are part of the
(1) oxygen cycle
(2) carbon cycle
(3) nitrogen cycle
(4) water cycle

V. HAZARDOUS WEATHER

Hazardous weather conditions can threaten life and property. When people are aware of the dangers of hazardous weather, they can prepare for and do what is needed to save life and property. Hazardous weather conditions include severe thunderstorms, tornadoes, hurricanes, and winter storms.

1. Thunderstorms *(E18)*

A **thunderstorm** is a local storm. It is called a local storm because it occurs in one small area. A thunderstorm may occur along a front. It may occur within an air mass when warm humid air is forced upward. In any case, it comes to a local area quickly. The most reliable sign of a thunderstorm's arrival is the presence of large thunderhead, or *cumulonimbus*, clouds.

The day may be clear and hot. But a thunderstorm is in the making as heat from the ground causes the moist air over it to rise. As this air rises, the water vapor in it condenses into clouds. Thunderhead clouds begin to form. As the clouds build, raindrops begin to fall and the storm begins.

Lightning always accompanies thunderstorms. Lightning is a huge electrical discharge. As lightning cuts through the air the heat from it causes the sudden expansion of the air. The sudden expansion results in a loud noise called *thunder*.

Thunderstorms are dangerous. Lightning is a major killer. Heavy thunderstorms can bring sudden flooding and strong, damaging winds. You should always remain indoors when a thunderstorm is in your area.

2. Tornadoes *(E18)*

Tornadoes are violent circular winds associated with severe thunderstorms. They may strike suddenly, do not last long, and cause great destruction and death.

A tornado with wind speeds of more than 300 miles per hour may travel across Earth's surface for as long as 25 km, destroying everything in its path. A funnel-shaped cloud may be the first sign of an oncoming tornado.

3. Hurricanes *(E18)*

Hurricanes are gigantic whirling storms with high winds, torrential rains, and storm surges capable of causing widespread flooding and destruction.

Hurricanes tend to form over ocean surfaces during the warmest part of the year. August through October is when Atlantic hurricanes are most likely to form.

As hurricanes approach and cross shorelines they bring wind-blown waves and torrential downpours. Most hurricane-related deaths are due to high winds, flooding, and heavy rainfall.

Sample Questions

1–4. From the list below, choose the correct name for each weather condition described in questions 1–4.

A. Thunderstorm
B. Tornado
C. Hurricane
D. Lightning

1. Dangerous storm that forms over ocean surfaces in summer

2. Huge discharge of electricity

3. Violently rotating local wind storm with wind speeds of over 300 miles per hour

4. Local storm with lightning, strong winds, and heavy rain

VI. CLIMATE AND POLLUTION

1. Climate *(E19)*

At the beginning of this chapter *weather* was defined as the condition of the atmosphere at a particular place and time. It includes conditions that may change from hour to hour and day to day. **Climate**, on the other hand, describes the changes of air conditions at a particular place over a *long* period of time. Climate is the average or general weather at a particular place from season to season and from year to year. In particular, climate includes the average amount of rain (and snow), average temperature, and the amount of sun at a location from season to season, year to year.

For example, in the northeastern part of the United States the winters are cold and snowy and the summers are warm and moist. In the southwest the climate is hot and dry much of the year.

Scientists learn about the climate of an area by collecting weather information over a number of years. Every day they note the temperatures and amounts of precipitation – rain, snow, sleet, and hail. They note the winds that pass over the area during the year. They note the fronts that pass through and the changes that come with them. Every day of the year this information is recorded on weather maps, charts, and graphs.

2. Factors that Affect Climate

Several factors affect the amount of rainfall and the temperature – and therefore, the climate – in an area. These factors include latitude, altitude, and closeness to large bodies of water.

Latitude The **latitude** of a place is a measure of how far to the north or south of the equator the place is (Figure 5–19). Lines of latitude are drawn around a globe as circles parallel to the equator. Above the equator, the lines show north latitude. Below the equator, the lines show south latitude. Areas near the equator, both north and south, have low latitudes. The farther away from the equator, the higher the latitude.

Near the equator, the sun's rays reach Earth at nearly right angles. At higher latitudes (above and below the equator), the sun's rays reach Earth at more and more of a slant. The angle of the sun's rays can affect the temperatures of an area.

Direct rays (rays reaching Earth at right angles) can result in high average temperatures. The more slanted the rays are, the lower the average temperatures are. All year long the sun's rays are most direct at areas near the equator. These areas have high temperatures all year.

The higher the latitude, the more slanted the sun's rays are. So the higher the latitude, the lower the average temperature of an area. This explains why the average temperature in New York State is lower than the average temperature in Panama.

Altitude Kansas City, Missouri, and Denver, Colorado, are at the same latitude north of the equator. The two cities are near each other, so near that they can both be covered by the same air mass at the same time. However, the average yearly temperatures of the two cities are different. Denver is about 10° cooler than Kansas City.

Denver is at much higher altitude than Kansas City. **Altitude** is the height of a place above sea level. At any given latitude, a place with a high altitude has a lower average temperature than a place with a low altitude. In fact, for every 300-meter increase in altitude, the average temperature decreases about 2°C.

Closeness to Bodies of Water Large masses of air move across Earth's surface. Air masses that move from the ocean to land often bring moisture with them. As a moist air mass moves over the land, moisture "falls out" of the air mass in the form of rain or snow. The closer a land area is to an ocean or some other large body of water, the more rain or snow the area will have each year.

Suppose an air mass from an ocean travels across a large continent. Rain falls from the air mass as it travels. The farther inland the air mass travels, the less moisture the air mass has left. Areas far inland get less and less rain from the air mass. In general, the farther away an area is from a large body of water, the less rainfall the area gets each year. Areas far inland tend to have dry climates.

Temperatures tend to change more quickly far inland than near the coast. Land heats up more quickly than water during the day. As a result, the temperature of air above land is usually higher than the temperature of air above water. During the summer, inland areas reach high temperatures. Since water stays cooler throughout the summer, air masses from the ocean can have a cooling effect on areas along the coast. That is why summer temperatures are lower near a large body of water than they are farther inland.

During the night, land cools off more quickly than water. Water stays warmer longer. The temperature of the surface of an ocean or other large body of water can remain high well into the winter. During

Figure 5–19. **The meaning of latitude. Parallels of latitude are circles parallel to the equator.**

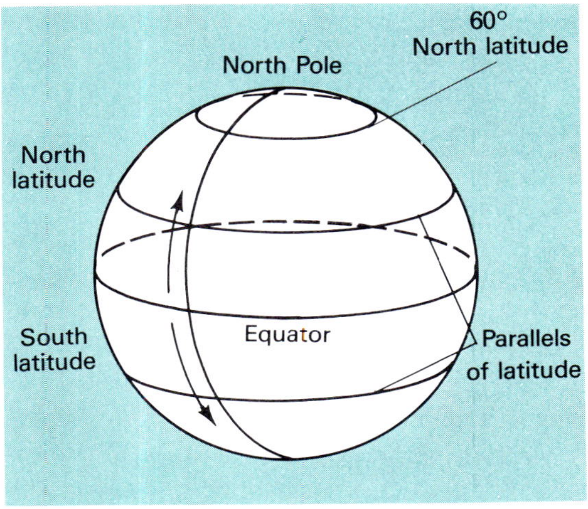

the winter, air masses from the ocean can warm the land near the coast. Farther inland, however, winter temperatures are usually lower than along the coast.

So large bodies of water can affect the climate of areas along the coast in two ways. Areas along the coast have more rain and snow per year than inland areas. In general, temperatures along the coast do not get as high in summer or as low in winter as temperatures farther inland.

3. Climate of New York State

New York State lies in the middle latitude zone and therefore has a temperate climate. **Temperate** climates have warm summers and cold winters. Precipitation occurs throughout the year. Figure 5–20 shows Earth's major climate zones.

4. People Affect the Air *(E11)*

Air is a mixture of a number of gases. Air consists of 78% nitrogen, about 21% oxygen, a very small amount of carbon dioxide (.03%), less than 1% argon, and traces of a few other gases. Air also contains varying amounts of water vapor.

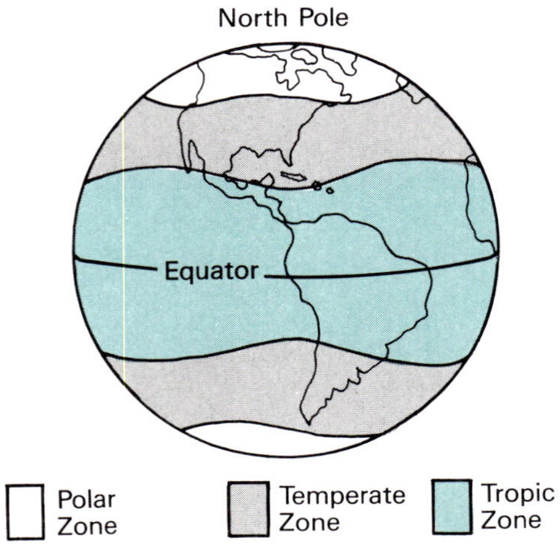

Figure 5–20. Earth's major climate zones.

Air is held to Earth by gravity. Air is densest at sea level and becomes less dense at increasing altitudes. At increasing altitudes the temperature of the air drops.

Natural Contaminants and Air Pollutants **Natural contaminants** are substances added to the air by such natural happenings as volcanic eruptions, forest fires, and decaying vegetation. Some natural contaminants include pollen, dust, volcanic ash, and smoke from forest fires.

Air pollutants are the products of human activity. They are released from factories, mines, or other industrial settings. Air pollutants include undesirable gases, liquids, and solid particles. Examples include the gases carbon monoxide and sulfur dioxide, incompletely burned rubbish, smog, radioactive materials, and human wastes. Air pollutants have harmful effects on humans and other animals and plants.

Air Pollutants and the Weather The conditions of the air (weather elements) play a major role in spreading air pollutants. When air currents and winds are strong, air pollutants may be carried long distances. A fast-moving front may carry air pollutants with it. On the other hand, when the air is calm (when there is little wind) air pollutants may accumulate in one place.

During an **inversion**—which occurs when the surface air is cooler than the layer above it—the air cannot rise and pollutants may accumulate.

In cities during the summer months, tall buildings may block the movement of heated air. Pollutants may accumulate in this stagnant air.

Air pollutants are dangerous. They may result in human illness, even death. Government agencies, industries, and individuals must work together to monitor and prevent the contamination of the air.

Sample Questions

1. A description of air conditions at a particular place over a long period of time is called
(1) weather (3) radiation
(2) climate (4) condensation

2. The sun's rays strike Earth at nearly right angles at
(1) the poles (3) 30°S
(2) 30°N (4) the equator

3. Natural contaminants include all of the following *except*
(1) pollen (3) volcanic ash
(2) dust (4) sulfur dioxide

4. Air pollutants increase in an area when
(1) air currents and winds are strong
(2) a fast-moving cold front passes through
(3) the air is calm
(4) the humidity is low

5–7. Questions 5–7 are based on the graph below, which is a record of the monthly average precipitation for an area in New York State.

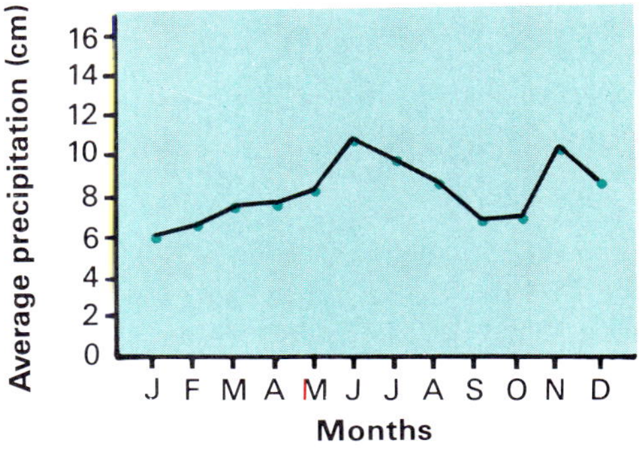

5. During which months does the *least total* amount of precipitation occur in this area?
(1) January, February, March
(2) April, May, June
(3) July, August, September
(4) October, November, December

6. Which of the graphs below best represents the relationship between the average precipitation and the time of year for this location?

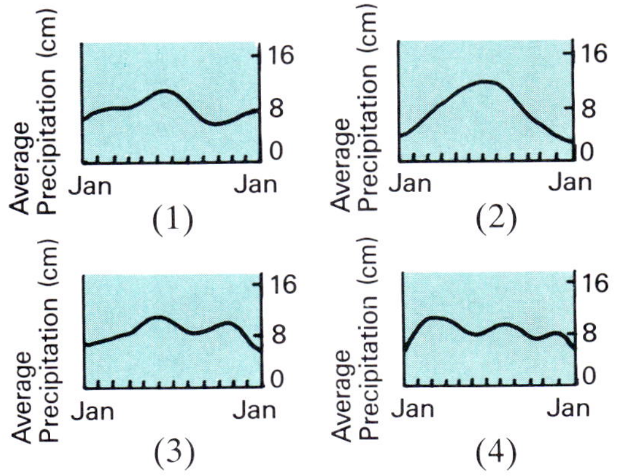

7. During which month does the *greatest* amount of precipitation occur?
(1) January (3) June
(2) February (4) November

8. It is cooler at the shore than inland during the summer because
(1) land heats up more quickly than water
(2) water heats up more quickly than land
(3) land and water heat up at the same rate
(4) water and air mix at the beach

9. New York State lies in which climate zone?
(1) tropical (3) polar
(2) temperate (4) sun belt

10. One major cause of air pollution is
(1) photosynthesis (3) climate
(2) weather (4) industry

How Accurate Is Weather Forecasting?

On November 21, 1980, the National Weather Service forecast was for fair weather. Hearing this report, a fisherman left Hyannis, Massachusetts, for an offshore fishing ground. The next day an unpredicted dangerous storm with 100-mph winds destroyed the boat and drowned the fisherman.

The fisherman's family sued the federal government. They claimed that he would have stayed home if the weather forecast had been correct.

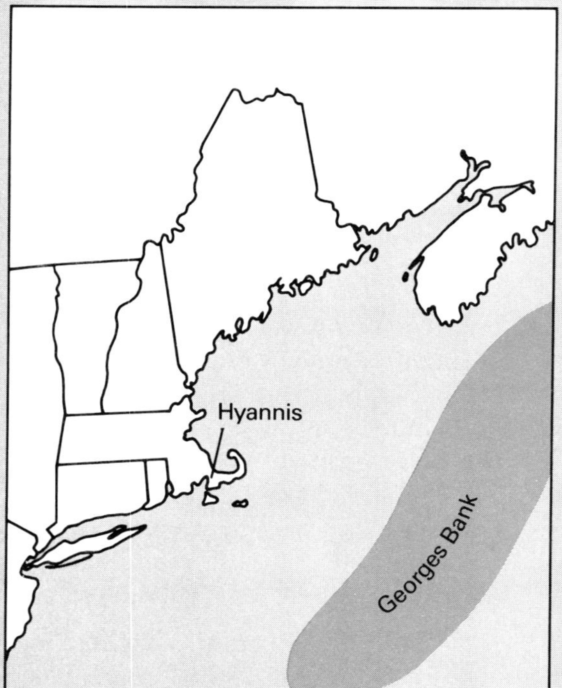

The locations involved in the lawsuit. Georges Bank is the offshore fishing area.

An investigation showed that for two and a half months before the disaster the National Weather Service had failed to repair a weather buoy in this area. Data provided by the weather buoy might have helped predict the storm. In court, a private meteorologist convinced the judge that readings from the buoy would have enabled the National Weather Service to more accurately track the storm and predict the weather. The judge ruled that the government had neglected its duty to make certain that forecasts be as accurate as possible. The judge also ruled that the government had neglected its duty to warn the fisherman that its forecast was based on incomplete data.

Many meteorologists were upset with this decision. They claimed that the science of weather forecasting has many unanswered questions. They felt that a great deal needs to be learned before weather can be predicted with accuracy. They felt that even if the buoy had been operating, its information would not have been sufficient to predict the course of the storm and save the fisherman's life. A court of appeals later reversed the judge's decision and denied the family any damages.

1. Do you think that forecasters should be responsible for predicting the weather? Should they be held responsible for the fisherman's death?
2. How much should people depend on weather forecasts?
3. Should more government money be spent on research in meteorology? Why or why not?

CHAPTER 6 Astronomy and Aerospace Science

I. EARTH IN SPACE

1. The Movements of Objects in the Sky *(F1)*

Ancient people watched the sky very carefully. They noted objects, motions, and changes in the sky that can still be observed today. The most obvious motion is that the sun rises in the east, travels across the sky, and sets in the west every day. Many people do not realize that this same motion occurs at night also. The moon, the stars, and any planets that are visible move across the sky, hour by hour, every night.

Careful observations and photographs reveal that these night objects move in circular paths that have one center point in the sky (Figure 6–1). The night sky turns like a record on a turntable. The star Polaris is near that center of turning, so Polaris does not change its place during the night as the other stars do. Polaris is also called the North Star or the Pole Star.

Ancient people thought the sun, moon, and stars were gods or special lights that raced around Earth, moving through the sky and then returning underground. Today we know that these objects in the sky are not moving, but that Earth is spinning. The objects in the sky *seem* to move because we are on a rotating planet. This effect is known as **apparent motion**, because the motions *appear* to be true.

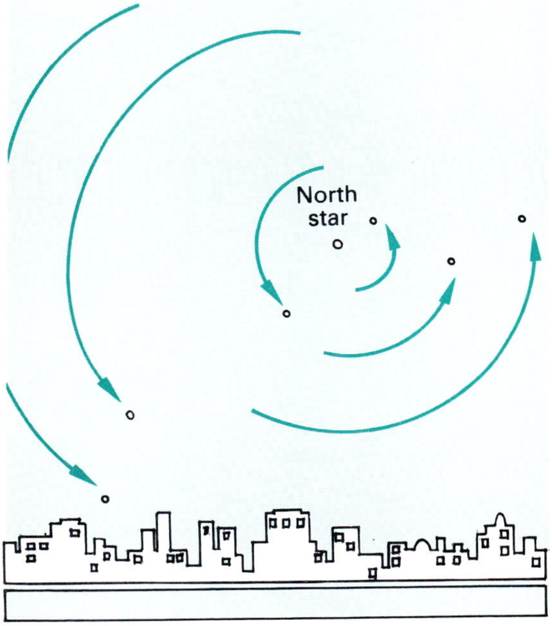

Figure 6–1. Movements of objects in the sky during the night.

2. Day and Night

As Earth rotates, half of it faces the sun. The people on that side of Earth have daylight. Later, however, those people will turn with Earth and will be facing away from the sun toward the blackness of space. This is nighttime. Because the sun's brightness is not lighting up the sky, the stars, moon, and planets can be seen. At any time, half of the world is in daylight, facing the sun, and half is in nighttime, facing away from the sun.

This change occurs everywhere on Earth except near the poles. At certain times of the year, people within the northern Arctic Circle and the southern Antarctic Circle have several weeks of continuous daylight or nighttime. This occurs because Earth's axis of rotation is slightly tipped (Figure 6–2). During summer in these places, the sun moves in a circle (because Earth is rotating) but never drops below the horizon for several weeks. The result is continuous sunshine.

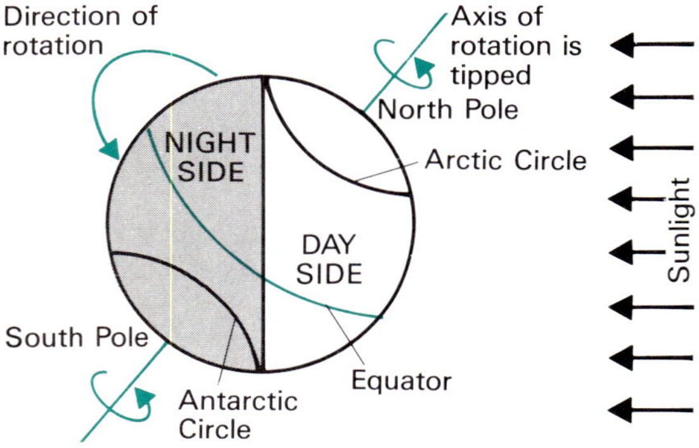

Figure 6–2. Earth's spinning causes night and day.

3. Earth Rotates in 24 Hours

(F3)

It takes 24 hours for Earth to **rotate**, or spin, once. This is why one full day, daylight and nighttime, takes 24 hours and why all clocks are based upon 24 hours. When a spot on Earth is facing directly toward the sun it is 12:00 noon at that spot. The sun is at its highest point at that moment. Twelve hours later that same spot will be facing away from the sun, making the time 12:00 midnight. All other times and time zones are based on these facts (see Figure 6–3).

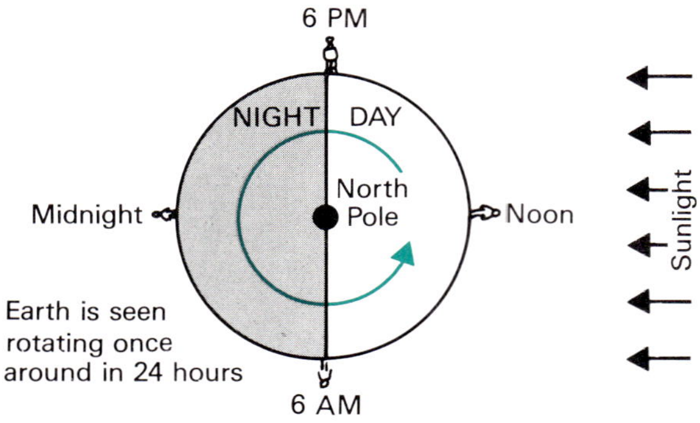

Figure 6–3. Rotation and time. This is a view of Earth looking down on the North Pole.

4. Earth Revolves Around the Sun *(F4)*

Besides rotating, Earth is also moving around the sun. The shape of Earth's path around the sun is an ellipse. An **ellipse** is an oval shape, somewhat like an egg or a football (Figure 6–4). Earth's path is close to being circular, but is still an ellipse.

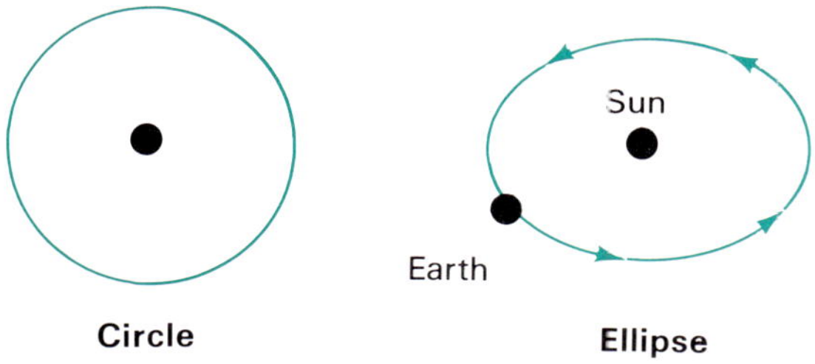

Figure 6–4. An ellipse is a flattened circle, or oval.

Earth's motion around the sun is called **revolution** and the path is called the **orbit**. It takes 365¼ days for Earth to go once around in orbit; therefore, 365¼ days is called one year. One year is the time needed for Earth to revolve once around the sun.

As Earth revolves around the sun our view out to space changes (Figure 6–5). As a result, month after month different stars and star groups (constellations) can be seen at night. However, after a year the cycle of changes begins again. This is very much like taking a walk around the block. During one revolution we see the entire surrounding neighborhood and return back to the starting point.

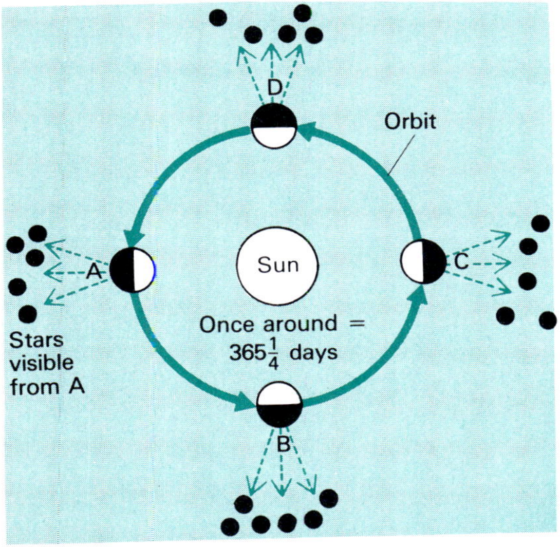

Figure 6–5. Earth revolving around the sun. At each position in Earth's orbit around the sun, different stars are visible from Earth.

5. *The Cause of the Seasons*

(F5)

Earth's revolution around the sun also triggers the seasons: summer, fall, winter, and spring. The real cause of the seasons is that Earth's axis of rotation is tilted. Instead of being vertical to the orbit Earth takes around the sun, the axis is tilted 23 degrees.

The axis of rotation is like the axle of a car. A tire turns around the axle; Earth turns around its axis. Earth's axis is an imaginary line that runs from the North Pole, through Earth's center, down to the South Pole.

The axis always points in the same direction in space as Earth moves around the sun (Figure 6–6). Therefore, during some months the Northern Hemisphere is tilted toward the sun while the Southern Hemisphere is tilted away from the sun. This causes the heating effect of the sun to be very different in each hemisphere.

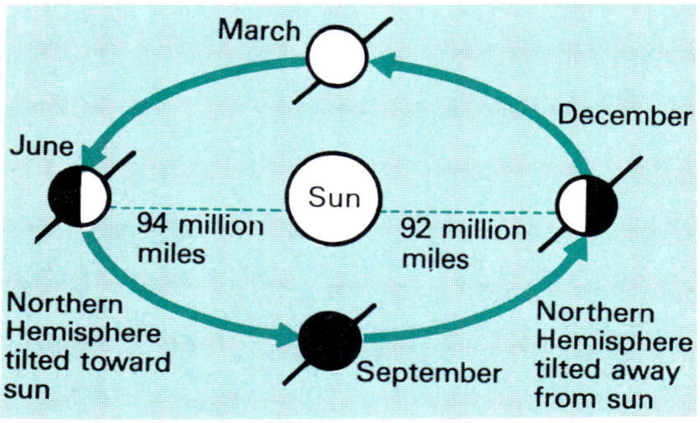

Figure 6–6. Earth revolving around the sun. Notice that Earth's axis of rotation is always tilted in the same direction.

Many people incorrectly think that the seasons are caused by changes in the distance between Earth and the sun. This is wrong. In fact, during June, Earth is *farther* from the sun than during December. If distance controlled the seasons, New York State and all other areas in the Northern Hemisphere would be colder in June than in December. But it is Earth's tilt toward the sun, not its distance from the sun, that causes the seasons. During June the Northern Hemisphere is tipped toward the sun and so June is hot, not cold.

6. *The Four Seasons* ***(F6, F7, F8)***

During the summer months the Northern Hemisphere is tilted toward the sun. The sun's rays shine more directly on Earth, creating a greater heating effect. Also the tilt makes the daylight last longer, so the heating effect lasts longer too. From the point of view of people, the summer sun appears to move in a high and long path through the sky and therefore it gives great warmth (see Figure 6–7).

During winter months the Northern Hemishphere is tilted away from the sun. This makes the sun's rays shine less directly on Earth, creating a reduced heating effect. Also the tilt now makes the daylight shorter, so there is less time for heating during the day but more time for cooling at

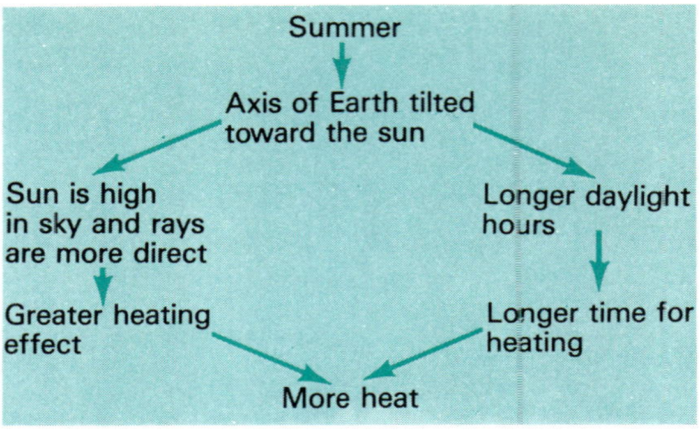

Figure 6–7. The equation of summer.

Science Skill

CALCULATING

Finding Circumference Suppose you want to find the distance around the equator. Start by picturing Earth as a circle or globe. The distance around the equator is the circumference.

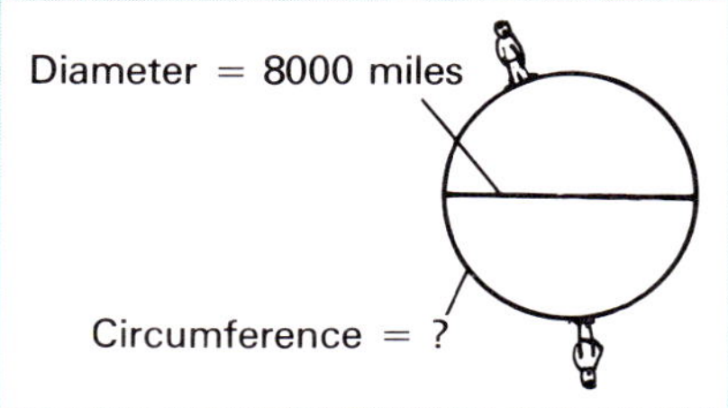

The equation used to calculate circumference is

$$\text{Circumference} = \text{Diameter} \times \pi,$$

where the symbol π is the number *pi* and is equal to about 3.14.

1. If Earth's diameter is 8000 miles, what is the circumference?

Finding Speed of Rotation Suppose you live at the equator and want to know how fast you and everything else at the equator are rotating. In 24 hours you turn once around Earth's circumference, which you calculated above.

The equation used to calculate speed is

$$\text{Speed} = \frac{\text{Distance (circumference)}}{\text{Time}}.$$

2. Find the speed of rotation at the equator, in miles per hour.

3. New York City is not on the equator. In 24 hours New York City turns in a circle that is smaller than the equator, about 18,000 miles around. How fast is New York City spinning, in miles per hour?

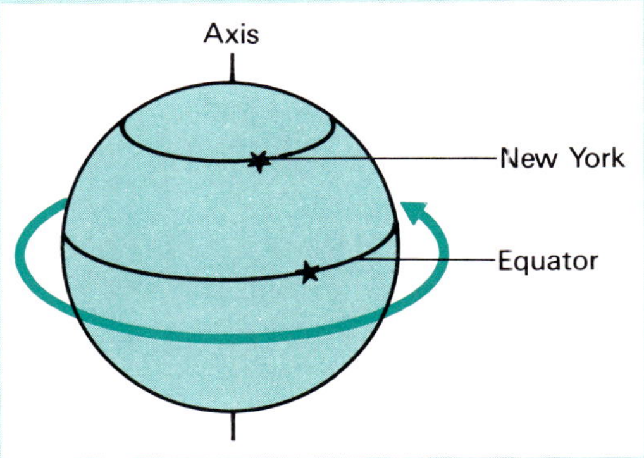

night. From the point of view of people, the winter sun appears to move in a low and short path through the sky and therefore it gives little warmth (see Figure 6–8).

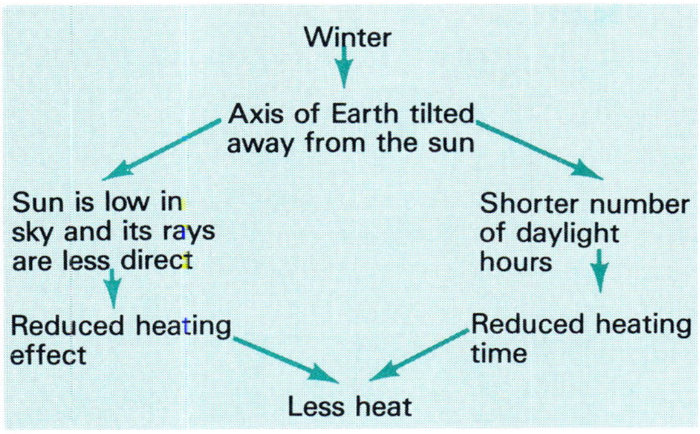

Figure 6–8. The equation of winter.

During spring and fall Earth is not strongly tilted toward or away from the sun. The heating effect in both hemispheres is about equal and daylight and nighttime hours are about equal, resulting in moderate temperatures. See Table 1 and Figure 6–9.

The seasons in the two hemispheres are reversed. When the Northern Hemisphere has winter, the Southern Hemisphere has summer.

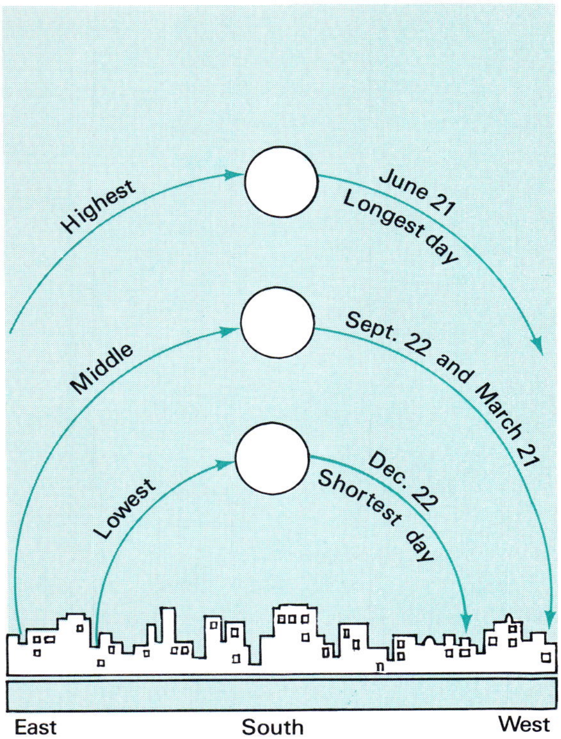

Figure 6–9. Path of the sun through the sky at different seasons.

7. Lessons from Shadows (F9)

We can learn a lot from shadows. For example, as the sun moves through the sky the *direction* of shadows changes. This changing direction is how a sundial works to tell the time. The shadow on the sundial acts like the hand on a clock: it points to the time. Shadows can also tell the seasons. During the summer shadows are *shorter*

Table 1 Important Seasonal Dates in the Northern Hemisphere

Season	Starts On	Angle of Sun in Sky	Day and Night Hours
Winter	Dec. 22	Lowest	Shortest day, longest night
Spring	March 21	Mid-angle (directly overhead at the equator)	Day and night each 12 hours
Summer	June 21	Highest	Longest day, shortest night
Fall	Sept. 22	Mid-angle (directly overhead at the equator)	Day and night each 12 hours

than they are during the winter. The shadows are shorter because in summer the sun is high in the sky and so forms short shadows. In winter the sun is low in the sky and so forms long shadows.

Shadows can also show *compass direction*. In the United States the sun never travels through the exact center of the sky, even when it reaches its highest angle on June 21. It is always south of the center line of the sky. Therefore at noon on any day the shadows of all objects point north.

Sample Questions

1. Which statement correctly describes the movement of the sun and stars each day and night?
(1) The sun moves hour by hour, but the stars do not.
(2) The sun and stars move in straight paths from east to west.
(3) The sun and stars move in circular paths from east to west.
(4) The sun moves east to west, and the stars move west to east nightly.

2. What is the most direct result of Earth's rotation?
(1) the changing shape of the moon.
(2) the seasons
(3) the length of one full year
(4) day and night

3. What length of time is determined by Earth's rotation?
(1) one day of 24 hours
(2) one week
(3) one month
(4) one year

4. Shadows move continuously. However, at noon in the United States all shadows point in one direction. What is that direction?
(1) north (3) south
(2) east (4) west

5. How did ancient people explain the movements of the sun and stars each day?
(1) The sun and stars travel around Earth, which is fixed in place.
(2) Earth is spinning.
(3) The motion is an illusion caused by air movements.
(4) Earth is traveling around the sun.

6. In northern parts of Canada, Alaska, and Russia the people have continuous daylight for about three weeks each year. These places are located
(1) on the equator
(2) above the Arctic circle
(3) below the Antarctic circle
(4) within an extended eclipse of the sun

7. When in the future will you be able to see the same star patterns that are visible tonight?
(1) never again
(2) in 6 months
(3) in 1 year
(4) only after several thousand years

8. Where might a person go to enjoy warm, summer weather during December?
(1) New York (3) Rio de Janeiro
(2) Paris (4) Tokyo

9. Why don't the stars appear during the day?
   (1) There aren't any stars in the daytime direction of space.
   (2) Stars reflect sunshine, so they must be opposite the sun to be seen.
   (3) Stars turn on, like light bulbs, only during nighttime.
   (4) The sun's brightness obscures them.

10. Which factor is the major cause of Earth's seasons?
   (1) rotation
   (2) revolution
   (3) tilt of axis
   (4) distance to the sun

11. During which season is the sun's apparent size largest in the Northern Hemisphere? (This must occur when the sun is closest in distance.)
   (1) winter (3) summer
   (2) spring (4) fall

12. Which fact about Earth is the basis for defining one year?
   (1) Earth rotates on its axis.
   (2) Earth revolves around the sun.
   (3) Earth's axis is tilted.
   (4) The moon revolves around Earth.

13. Which is *not* true about summer in the Northern Hemisphere?
   (1) The Northern Hemisphere is tilted toward the sun.
   (2) The sun is seen at a high angle in the sky.
   (3) The heating effect of the sun is stronger.
   (4) The daylight is shorter than the nighttime.

14. Shadows grow longer as the sun moves to a lower angle in the sky. On what date are shadows in the Northern Hemisphere longest?
   (1) December 22 (3) June 21
   (2) March 21 (4) September 22

II. THE MOON AND EARTH

1. The Moon *(F10)*

The moon is our neighbor. It is the closest object in space to Earth, about 240,000 miles away. The moon circles around Earth just as Earth circles around the sun. This revolution, which takes about 28 days, is the basis for defining a month.

The moon is a solid ball about 2000 miles in diameter; Earth is 8000 miles in diameter. The moon has mountains, valleys, craters, and dark plains that can be seen clearly from Earth. Although it is made of rocks similar to Earth rocks, the moon has no air or water. The gravity on the moon is ⅙ that of Earth, so a 120-lb person would weigh 20 lb on the moon. That's why the astronauts could hop around on the moon, even wearing heavy suits and backpacks.

Only one side of the moon can be seen from Earth. The moon is said to keep "one face" toward Earth. The reason for this is an unusual fact: the moon itself rotates in exactly the same time that it revolves around Earth. This results in one side of the moon always facing Earth. Nevertheless, the unseen back side of the moon has been photographed and mapped by rockets and satellites sent there.

2. Moonlight Is Sunlight *(F11)*

The moon does not produce its own light. It reflects light from the sun. When a person looks at the moon, even in the middle of the night, that person is seeing sunshine, *reflected* sunshine.

Since Earth and the moon are both spheres in space, the sun always lights one half of each (Figure 6–10). The other half is dark. Both Earth and the moon always have one half of their surfaces lighted by the sun.

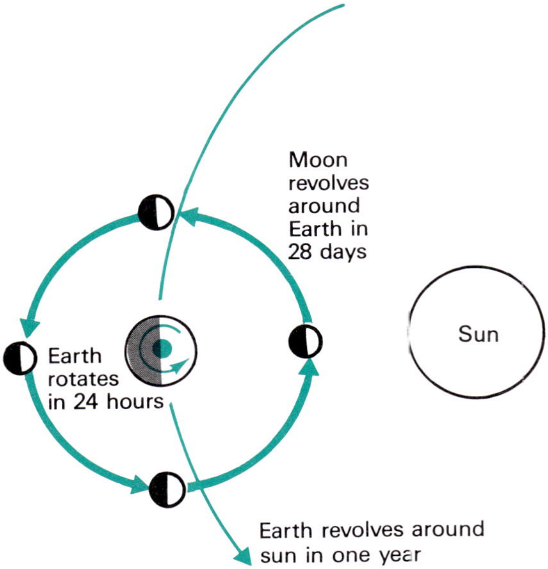

Figure 6–10. The relationship among the sun, moon, and Earth.

3. The Moon Appears to Change Shape Each Night *(F12)*

As the moon revolves around Earth every 28 days, its position keeps changing. Different amounts of its lighted surface can be seen from Earth. This explains why the moon seems to change shape. The changing shapes are called the **phases** of the moon (Figure 6–11).

For example, when the moon is located between Earth and the sun its dark side faces Earth, so the moon cannot be seen. This phase is called *new moon*. About 14 days later the moon is located on the opposite side of Earth from the sun. Now the entire lighted side of the moon faces Earth, so the moon is seen as a full circle. This phase is called *full moon*. The various phases of the moon are referred to as *apparent changes*, because the moon *appears* to change shape. In fact, the moon's shape is always the same (Figure 6–12).

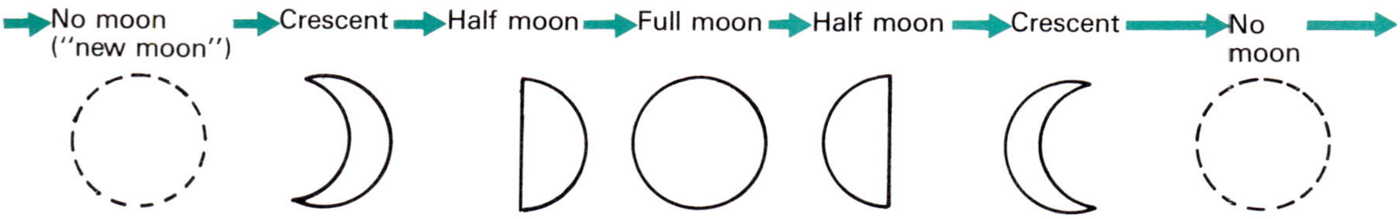

Figure 6–11. The phases of the moon over one month.

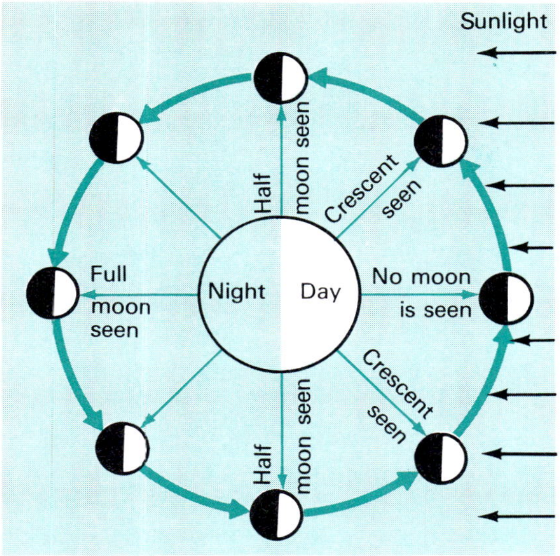

Figure 6–12. A top view of the moon and Earth, showing the moon's phases. Different amounts of the lighted side of the moon are seen as it revolves around Earth.

During the new moon phase, occasionally the moon's shadow may sweep across Earth, resulting in an eclipse of the sun. An eclipse of the sun lasts for only a few minutes. When the moon is in the full moon phase, occasionally it passes through Earth's own shadow. This results in an eclipse of the moon, which lasts for several hours.

4. The Origin of Ocean Tides

(F13)

The level of the ocean water at beaches and at docks continuously changes from high to low and then high again. It takes about six hours for each change, from high to low or from low to high, to occur. This changing water level is called the **tides**. Tides occur because the sun and moon pull upon Earth and its waters with a force called *gravitational attraction*. When the sun and moon are in a line with Earth, their pulls act together to create very high and very low tides. When the moon, sun, and Earth are not in a line the tides are not as high or low (See Figure 6–13).

Because the moon is so much closer to Earth than the sun is, the moon's gravitational attraction is stronger than the sun's gravitational attraction. Therefore, high tides occur at places on the Earth's surface that face directly toward the moon or directly away from the moon on the opposite side of the world.

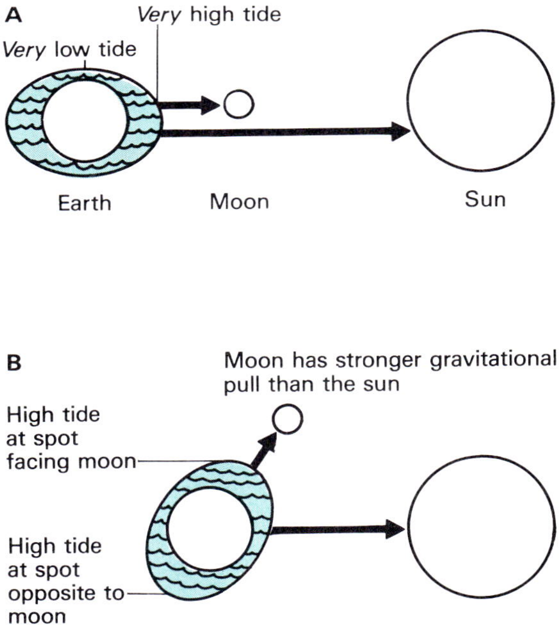

Figure 6–13. (A) High tides are highest when Earth, moon, and sun are in a straight line. (B) High tides are not as high when Earth, moon, and sun are not in a straight line.

Sample Questions

1. Which diagram shows the proper size comparison between the moon and Earth?

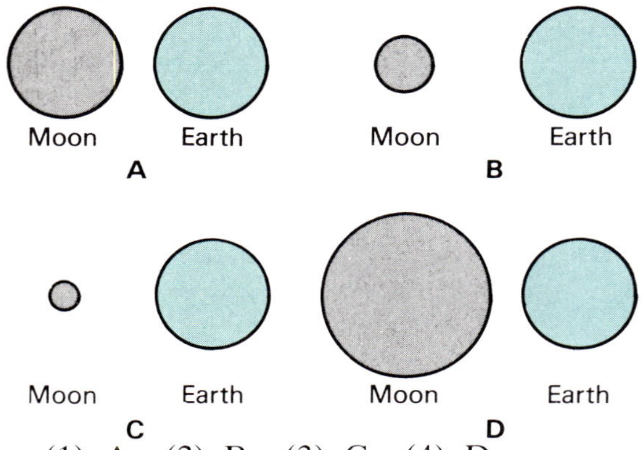

(1) A (2) B (3) C (4) D

2. The moon revolves around Earth in about
(1) one hour (3) 28 days
(2) one day (4) 365 days

3. How much would a 60-lb child weigh on the moon?
(1) 0 (3) 60 lb
(2) 10 lb (4) 360 lb

4. What features on the moon create the illusion of a face?
(1) dry land and oceans
(2) mountains and flat plains
(3) black dirt and white sand
(4) clouds

5. The moon revolves and rotates in a special way such that
(1) we only see one side of the moon
(2) we see all areas of the moon over 1 year
(3) we see all areas of the moon during 1 month
(4) we see all areas of the moon during 1 night

6. If the sun flashed on and off, then what would be true about the moon we see?
(1) It would stay constantly bright.
(2) It would stay constantly dark.
(3) It would flash on and off also.
(4) It would be visible during the day at all times.

7. The shape of the moon changes because
(1) the amount of its surface lighted by the sun changes
(2) it moves, so we see it from a different angle
(3) it changes its physical shape
(4) Earth's shadow hits the moon differently each night

8. What percentage of the moon is always lighted by sunlight?
(1) varies from 0 to 100%
(2) varies from 0 to 50%
(3) 50%
(4) 100%

9. The moon is "new" (not seen) on May 1. When will it be seen as a full moon?
(1) May 8 (3) May 22
(2) May 15 (4) May 29

10. At what spot on Earth in this diagram are the tides highest?

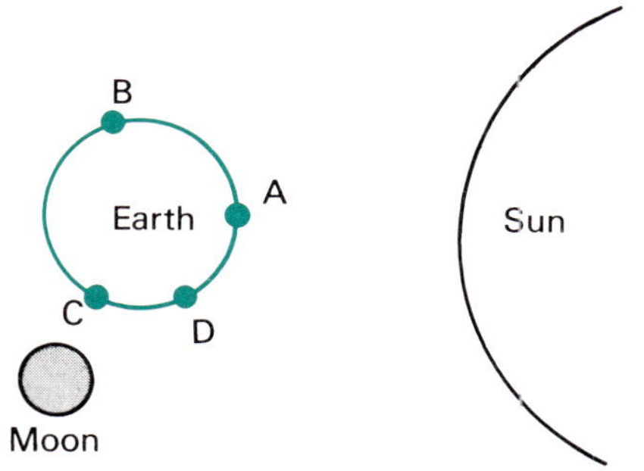

(1) A (2) B (3) C (4) D

III. THE SUN AND STARS

1. The Sun: Our Private Star (F14)

The sun is a star similar to the other millions of stars seen at night. The sun is an average star: average in age, average in size, average in temperature. However, for Earth the sun is a very special star. It is the star to which planet Earth is "attached." It provides the needed light, warmth, and energy to permit life to exist on Earth. Without the sun, life would not be possible.

The sun is many times larger than Earth. It has a diameter of 864,000 miles, more than 100 times the diameter of Earth. It weighs 300,000 times what Earth weighs. The temperature in the middle of the sun is about 15 million degrees Celsius and at its surface is about 6000 degrees Celsius. Like all stars, the sun is made mostly of hydrogen gas. This hydrogen gas is being converted into helium gas and other elements. During such conversions, enormous amounts of energy are released. So hydrogen is the fuel of the sun and all stars, producing energy, heat, and light.

2. The Stars Are Very Far Away (F15)

The universe is full of stars. Some are much bigger than the sun. But all stars are at such vast distances that we see them only as points of light in the sky. The closest star to Earth, after the sun, is 26,000,000,000,000 miles away. Other stars are ten, one hundred, even one million times farther than that. Because of such vast distances, space travel between stars seems only possible in stories and movies, not in reality. Distances between stars are so great that astronomers do not use miles to measure the distances. They use a unit called the **light-year**. One light-year is the distance light can travel in one year. Using this measurement, the closest star is 4½ light-years away.

Stars occur in groups called **galaxies**. *All* the stars we see at night, and the sun, are part of our galaxy, the Milky Way Galaxy. Far beyond our galaxy are millions of other galaxies, each containing billions of stars.

3. The Solar System (F16)

Closer to home than the stars is the sun and its family, the **solar system** (*solar* means "sun"). The major members of the solar system are the sun itself and the nine planets that orbit the sun. Each planet has its own special characteristics, described in Table 2 on page 116. Travel to the other planets is a strong possibility. Humans have already landed probes on Venus and Mars and have sent rockets to photograph almost all the other planets, with excellent results.

4. Hello! Is Anyone Else Out There? (F17)

Earth seems to be the only planet that supports life. Most other planets would be hostile to life because they are too hot, too cold, without water, or have a poisonous atmosphere. The United States landed a spacecraft on Mars that made chemical tests of the soil. It found no evidence of life, even microscopic life.

Many people believe there must be life elsewhere in the universe, however. Since every star is a sun, they may have planets. Perhaps life, even intelligent life, may exist on those faraway planets of faraway stars. Astronomers have been listening for radio signals that might indicate life out in space. So far, they haven't picked up any signals. We have no evidence of life beyond Earth . . . yet.

Table 2 Facts About the Planets

Name	Distance from Sun as Compared to Earth's Distance from Sun	Time Required to Revolve Once Around the Sun	Special Features
Mercury	0.4	88 days	Smallest planet; no moon; no atmosphere
Venus	0.7	225 days	Thick, deadly atmosphere; hottest planet because atmosphere traps heat; brightest planet; no moon
Earth	1	365¼ days (1 year)	Life; nitrogen-oxygen atmosphere; surface 75% water; one moon
Mars	1.5	2 years	Red, due to iron compounds in soil; small atmosphere; carbon dioxide (dry ice) covers poles; evidence of previous water erosion (no water now); two moons
Jupiter	5	12 years	Largest planet; mostly cold hydrogen gas; violent winds, including giant storm seen as a moving red spot; fourteen moons, each very unusual
Saturn	9.5	30 years	Second largest planet; mostly gas; rings made of ice, rocks, and dust surround the planet; ten moons
Uranus	19	84 years	Gaseous; its axis of rotation is tilted so much that the planet "rolls" in its orbit; five moons
Neptune	30	165 years	Frozen solid; two moons
Pluto	39	367 years	Frozen solid; little known; may be an escaped moon of Neptune; one moon

5. *"Falling Stars"* *(F18)*

On a clear night it is possible to see flashes of light streaking across the sky for a second or two. Best viewings require patience, locations away from lights, and moonless nights. Ancient people thought these flashes were stars that fell out of their places, so they called them shooting stars or falling stars. Today we call them **meteors**. Meteors are not stars at all. They are large rocks that come flying in from space at very great speeds. As they enter the atmosphere they heat up because of friction and start to burn. The burning causes the flash. Sometimes the meteor is so large that it doesn't completely burn up, and part of it hits the ground. The part that lands on the ground is called a **meteorite**. Many meteorites have been found. Some of them resemble igneous rocks. Others are made mostly of the metals iron and nickel.

Science Skill

GRAPHING

The table at the right contains information about some of the planets. Make a graph of the information. A sample graph has been provided for your use. Notice that the two axes of the graph have been numbered and labeled, and that the graph has been given a title.

Planet	Distance from Sun as Compared to Earth's Distance from Sun	Time Required to Revolve Once Around the Sun
Earth	1	1 year
Mars	1.5	2 years
Jupiter	5	12 years
Saturn	9.5	30 years

PLANET DISTANCES AND REVOLUTION TIMES

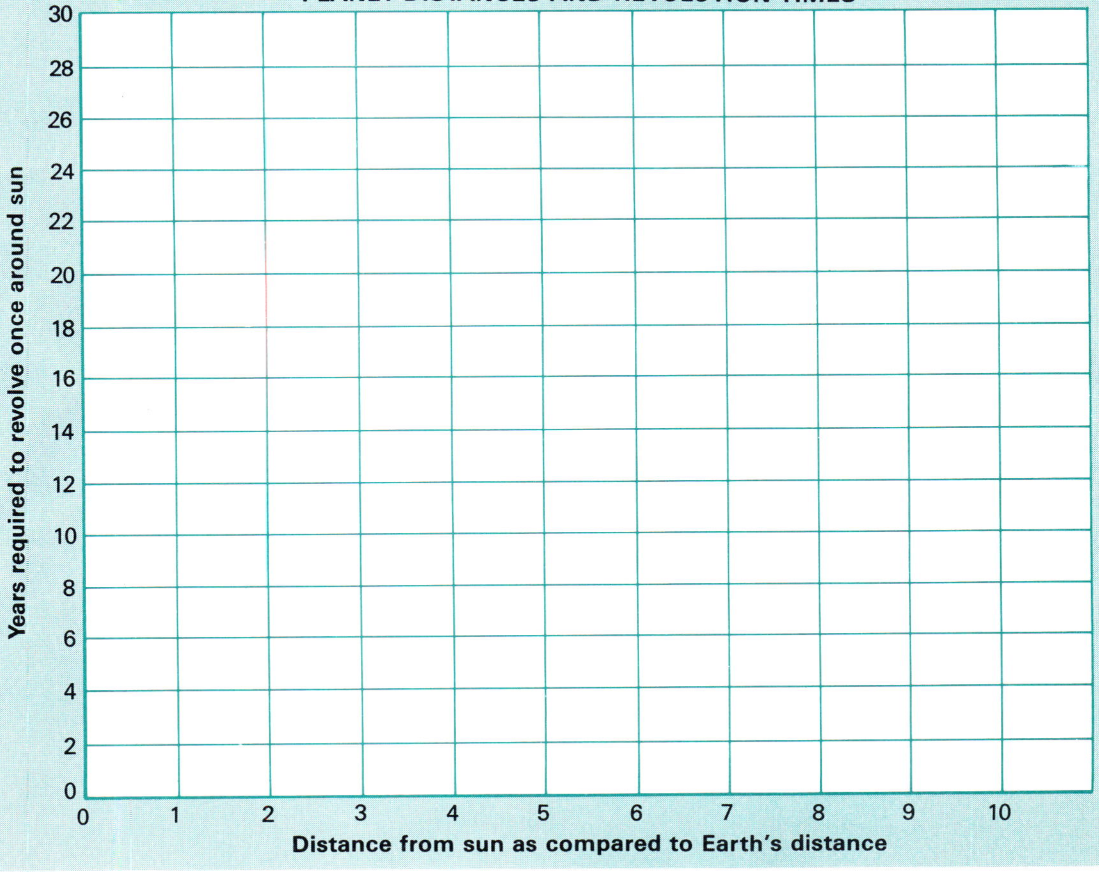

Sample Questions

1. Which statement about the sun is true?
(1) It is the only sun in the entire universe.
(2) It is a very hot planet.
(3) It receives its light by reflection from the stars.
(4) It is a star.

2. What is the chief fuel of all stars?
(1) uranium
(2) hydrogen
(3) organic compounds, such as gasoline and wood
(4) unknown at this time

3. Why is travel between stars most likely impossible?
(1) Space is a vacuum, so travel is hindered.
(2) We don't know how to design the right type of spaceship.
(3) Distances are too vast.
(4) Gravitational attractions and repulsions of stars would make such travel impossible.

4. Most of the universe is
(1) planets
(2) stars
(3) galaxies
(4) empty space

5. A star is 10 light-years away. This means that
(1) it moves around Earth in 10 years
(2) it is 10 years away by rocket
(3) Earth could approach it within 10 years
(4) light from the star takes 10 years to reach Earth

6. Which one of the following lists the objects in correct order of size from smallest to largest?
(1) moon, Earth, sun, big star, galaxy
(2) big star, moon, Earth, sun, galaxy
(3) moon, Earth, big star, sun, galaxy
(4) moon, Earth, galaxy, sun, big star

7. Which one is *not* within the solar system?
(1) planets
(2) moons
(3) the sun
(4) the Milky Way

8. If intelligent life exists somewhere else in the universe, where might it be found?
(1) on the inner planets of Mercury, Venus, and Mars
(2) on the large outer planets Jupiter, Saturn, and Neptune
(3) on moons of Jupiter
(4) on planets of other stars

9. Which is *not* true about the planet Mercury?
(1) It revolves fastest of all the planets.
(2) It is the hottest planet.
(3) It is the smallest planet.
(4) It has violent wind in its atmosphere.

10. A meteor is a(n)
(1) electric spark in the atmosphere
(2) burning rock from space
(3) small, fast travelling moon
(4) star dropping from its fixed position

Issues in Science, Technology, and Society

Trade-Offs Among Cost, Risk, and Benefits

The exploration of space shows us an important point about *all* science research: compromises may be necessary. These compromises are called **trade-offs**.

Many benefits come from space research. For example, it keeps our technology very modern and sophisticated. It also creates many "spin-off" products for people to use, such as home computers or improved insulating materials. Space satellites are used to study our Earth's resources and weather in order to improve our living here. Finally, people want to know about the universe. Space travel, space telescopes, and visits to other planets will tell us much about who we are and what's going on out there in the universe.

However, space research costs a lot of money and prevents scientists from working on more practical problems. Society, through its government, must constantly decide how much money can be given to space exploration, since funds are always needed for many other activities. Some projects, such as a proposal to send a rocket to investigate Halley's comet in 1986, are not approved. The benefits of many projects cannot balance out their burdens, their costs to society.

Trade-offs must also consider dangers and risks. The safety of astronauts is extremely important. However, all space flight involves risks and dangers. To remove these risks and dangers may be too costly and cause too many delays.

When making decisions about science research these three factors—benefits, costs, risks—must always be considered and trade-offs made.

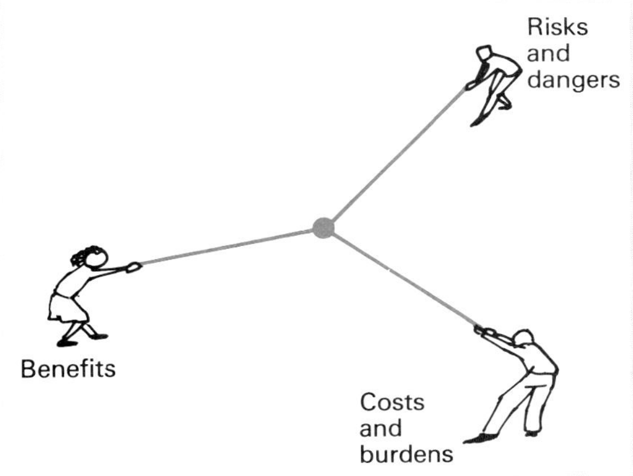

Trade-offs in making decisions—a three-way tug-of-war.

1. Why can't science study everything that might benefit people?

2. Suppose you are asked to help your family make a big decision about a new car, or moving, or making repairs at home. Make a chart that lists the benefits, the costs, and the risks to consider.

3. Suppose you're an assistant to a United States senator. Make a list of trade-offs the senator should consider about space research and space exploration before he or she votes on the requests. What personal opinion would you give as well?

CHAPTER 7 Energy and Motion

I. ENERGY AND WORK

1. What Are Work and Energy? (G1)

In science the word "work" has a special definition. **Work** is done if a force pushes or pulls over a distance.

Work = Force × Distance Acted

Pushing hard against a wall results in no work because there is no movement, no distance moved. However, dragging a box takes work, since the force of pulling acts over the distance pulled. See Figure 7–1.

In order to do work, energy is needed. **Energy** is the ability to perform work. For example, food contains energy. After the food is eaten this energy enables people to lift, pull, and push objects for a distance. In other words, the energy enables them to do work.

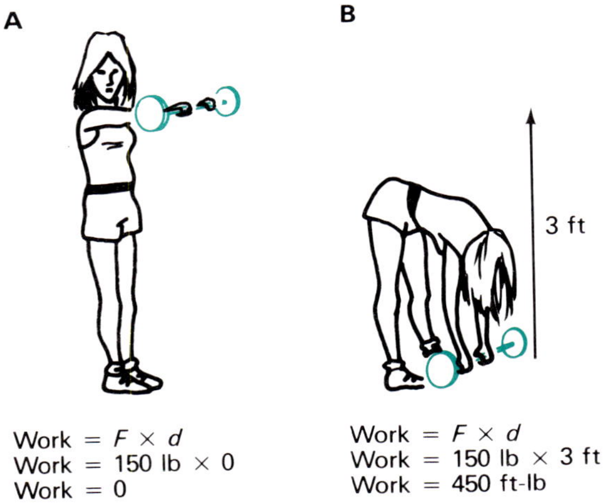

Figure 7–1. (A) Holding 150 lb in place requires no work. (B) Lifting 150 lb upward 3 ft requires work.

2. Potential Energy (G2)

Some objects contain energy because of their position. This energy of position is called **potential energy** or stored energy. For example, every object located above the ground has potential energy. When the object falls and hits the ground it can do work. A spring is another example of potential energy. When a spring is stretched or squeezed it has energy due to the position of its coils. This stored energy is released and does work when the spring pulls or pushes something. A magnet is another example of potential energy because it can pull on a piece of nearby iron. See Figure 7–2.

3. Kinetic Energy (G3)

Some objects contain energy because they are moving. This energy of motion is called **kinetic energy**. For example, the wind has kinetic energy, which can be used to push a boat or a windmill. A moving hammer has kinetic energy that pushes a nail into a piece of wood. The nail moves forward into the wood with a large force, which means work is required (Force × Distance). The kinetic energy of the moving hammer performs this work at each hit.

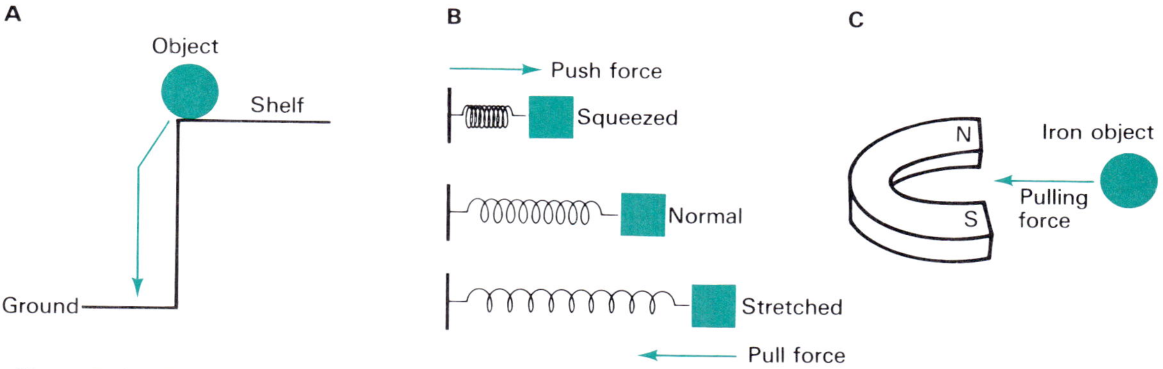

Figure 7–2. **Examples of potential energy. (A) The object has potential energy due to its position above the ground. (B) The box has potential energy due to the position of the spring coils. (C) The iron object has potential energy due to its position relative to the magnet.**

The amount of kinetic energy in a moving object depends on its mass and speed (Figure 7–3). If a fat person and a thin person run at the same speed, the fat person has more kinetic energy because of greater mass. If two identical balls are pitched at different speeds, the fastball has more kinetic energy than the slowball.

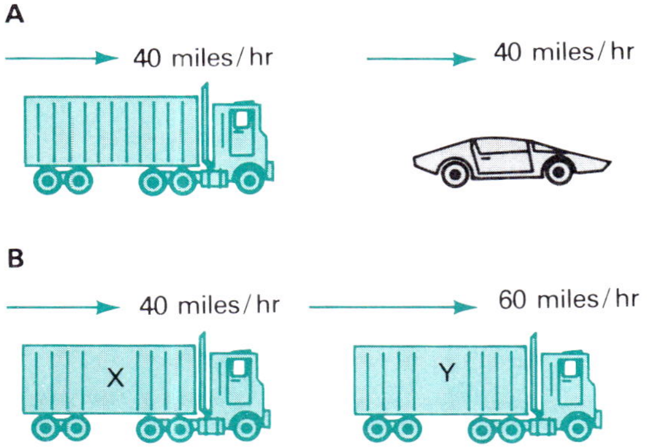

Figure 7–3. **Kinetic energy is due to mass and speed. (A) The truck has more kinetic energy than the car going the same speed, since the truck has more mass. (B) Truck Y has more kinetic energy than truck X, since truck Y has greater speed.**

4. *Energy May Be Transformed* *(G4, G5)*

Within the two main types of energy—potential and kinetic—energy occurs in many forms. Some of these forms are listed below, along with an example of each.

Forms of Potential Energy

Gravitational energy—in objects above the ground

Electrical energy—in an electric socket or battery

Chemical energy—in food or fuels

Magnetic energy—in ordinary magnets or electromagnets

Nuclear energy—in uranium atoms

Forms of Kinetic Energy

Mechanical energy—in any moving object

Light energy—in the vibrations of light and radio waves

Sound energy—in the vibrations of air molecules that create sound

Heat energy – in the vibrations of molecules that create an object's temperature

Energy can be transformed (changed) from one of these forms into another form, as shown in Figure 7–4. The *total amount* of energy always remains the same, even though it changes into various forms. Energy can be changed in form, but it can never be lost.

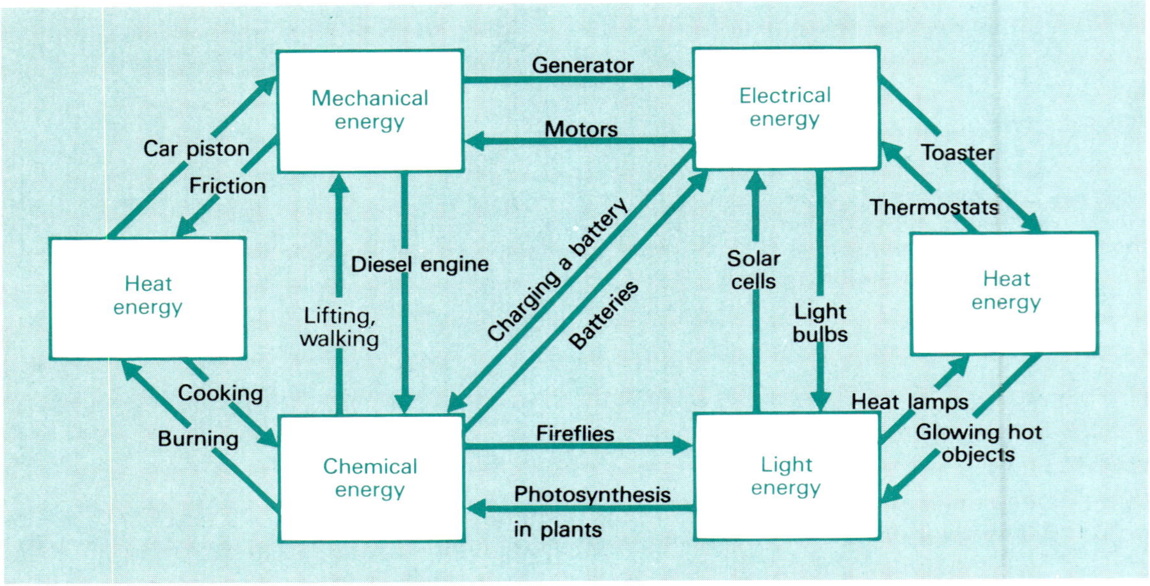

Figure 7–4. Examples of energy transformations.

Sample Questions

1. As defined in science, which person probably does the most work?
(1) a carpenter (3) a judge
(2) a typist (4) a writer

2. Which of the following events requires the most work?
(1) A heavy box rests on a high shelf.
(2) A heavy box is held steadily in someone's arms.
(3) A book is lifted from the floor to its shelf.
(4) A ball is rolled with no force for a distance of many yards.

3. Which one of the following is *not* necessary in order for work to be done?
(1) a force
(2) a distance moved
(3) energy made available
(4) use of a machine

4. During which one of the following processes does light energy change into chemical energy?
(1) photosynthesis
(2) burning
(3) running
(4) solar heating

5. Look at the illustration below, which shows a person diving into a pool.

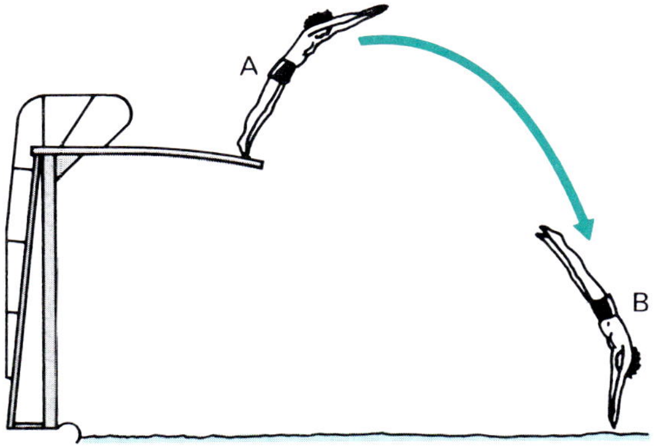

What is true about the diver at point *A* and point *B*?
(1) He has more energy at *A* than at *B*.
(2) He has more energy at *B* than at *A*.
(3) He has potential energy at *A* and kinetic energy at *B*.
(4) He has kinetic energy at *A* and potential energy at *B*.

6. The illustration shows a battery that is operating a small lamp, a small fan, and a toaster.

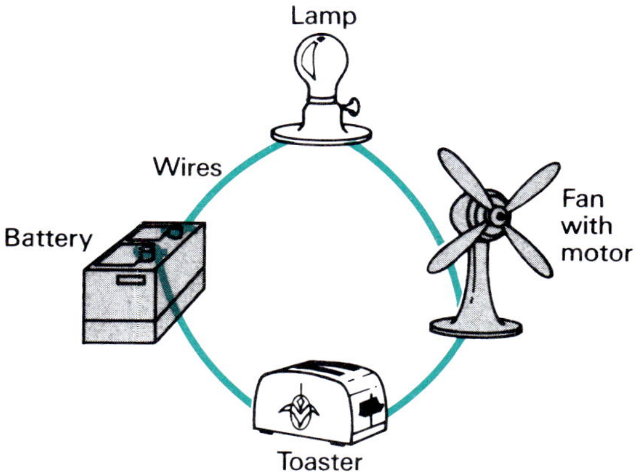

In which device shown is electrical energy being transformed into mechanical energy?
(1) battery
(2) lamp
(3) fan
(4) toaster

7. Which one of the following objects has kinetic energy?
(1) a powerful magnet
(2) a flying insect
(3) a tightly squeezed spring
(4) a hanging weight

8. What energy transformation occurs when you rub your hands together quickly?
(1) Electrical energy changes to chemical energy.
(2) Mechanical energy changes to heat energy.
(3) Chemical energy changes to nuclear energy.
(4) Magnetic energy changes to light energy.

9. In which device does sound energy change to electrical energy?
(1) motor (3) car horn
(2) electromagnet (4) microphone

10. The illustration shows four airplanes along with their weights and flying speeds.

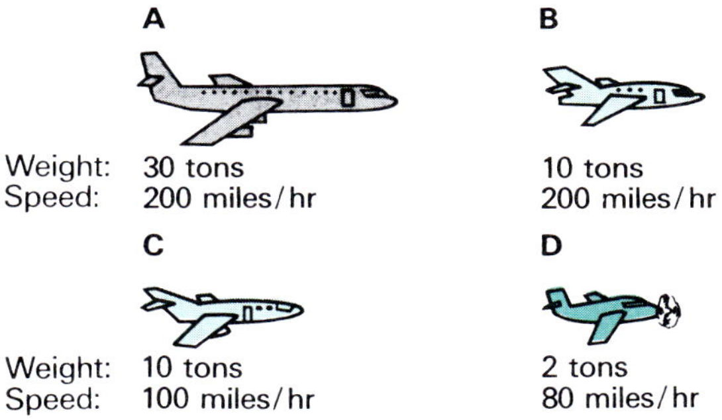

Which one of the airplanes has the greatest amount of kinetic energy?
(1) A (2) B (3) C (4) D

II. MACHINES

1. Machines Transfer Mechanical Energy (G6, G7)

Car engines, sewing machines, water pumps, elevators, and shop tools are complicated **machines**. Each contains many parts. However, the purpose of any machine is simply stated: *Machines transfer mechanical energy from one object to another object*. For example, a bicycle is a machine. It uses chains, gears, axles, and wheels to transfer mechanical energy from the rider's moving legs to the moving bike. In a water pump the mechanical energy of the spinning shaft is transferred by gears, blades, and pistons into the mechanical energy of the water it pushes. Machines do not create work or create energy. They merely transfer work and energy from one object to another object.

The amount of work *done by* a machine is always less than the amount of work *put into* the machine. This is true because some of the energy put in changes into heat energy and escapes. Less mechanical energy comes from a machine than goes into it, because of friction and rubbing inside the machine. This concept is illustrated in Figure 7–5.

In Figure 7–5 there are two losses of mechanical energy. (1) Loss in the motor: The motor takes in 1000 units of energy but gives out only 900 units of energy to the shaft. The missing 100 units of energy are changed into heat energy by friction and electrical heating inside the motor. (2) Loss in the elevator machinery: The spinning shaft puts 900 units of mechanical energy into the machinery. However, at the other end the lifting of the elevator only requires 700 units of energy. Once again,

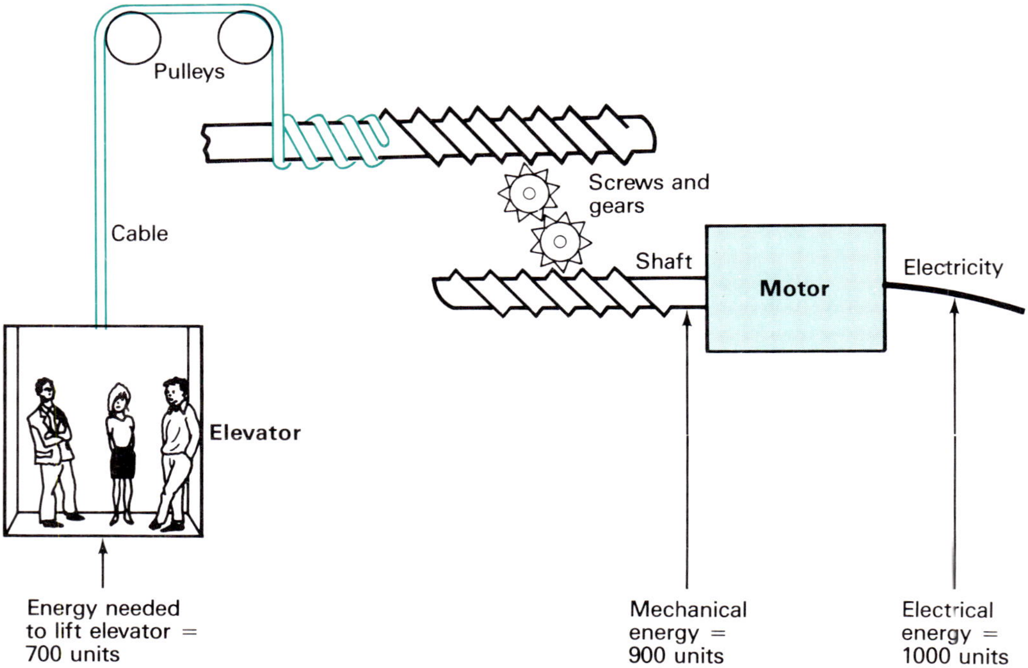

Figure 7–5. The energy given out is less than the energy put in.

the missing energy (200 units) is changed into heat by the friction between the screws, gears, cable, and pulleys.

This loss of mechanical energy occurs in all machines. Mechanical energy OUT is always less than mechanical energy IN, because some mechanical energy is always changed into heat by friction.

2. Making a Machine More Efficient *(G8)*

A machine is said to be very **efficient** if most of the energy put in also comes out, with very little "lost" as heat. A machine is *not* efficient if a large portion of the energy put in is changed into heat, with only a small portion actually left to do the machine's job. One way of making a machine more efficient is by reducing the amount of friction inside it. Ways of reducing friction include the following methods:

1. using oil or wax to make the gears turn more easily;
2. sanding and polishing machinery parts to make them smoother; and
3. using ball bearings in pulleys and axles to allow them to turn more easily.

3. Machines Make Work Easier *(G9)*

Look at Figure 7–6, which shows a garage mechanic lifting a heavy axle by means of many pulleys. Pulleys are machines.

The pulleys in the illustration make it easier for the mechanic to lift the 600-lb axle. She only needs to pull with 100 lb of force, and she can pull in a sideways-and-downward direction instead of upward. Machines can change the amount or the direction of a force. However, the *total amount* of work the mechanic must do is not reduced by using the machine. In

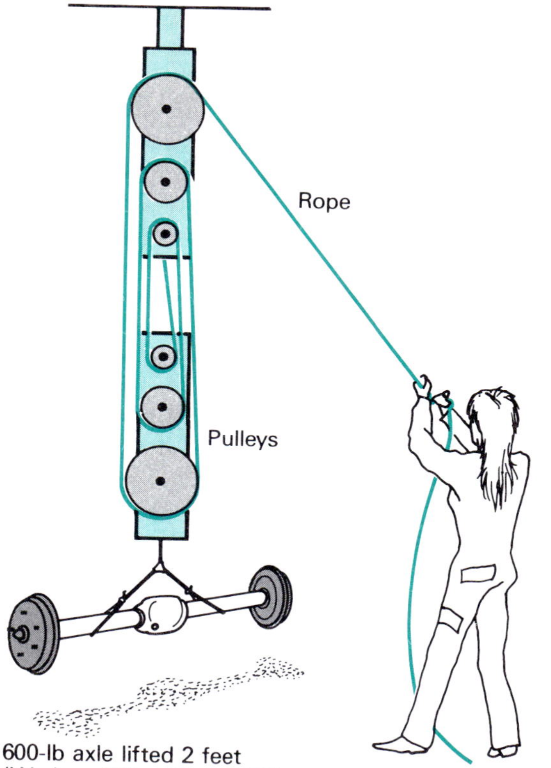

Figure 7–6. Machines do not make work any less.

order to lift the axle up 2 feet she will have to pull 12 feet of rope.

Work required to lift car axle:

Work (out) = 600 lb × 2 feet = 1200 ft-lb

Work done by mechanic using pulleys:

Work (in) = 100 lb × 12 feet = 1200 ft-lb

This machine, like all machines, has made the work easier to do but it has not reduced the amount of work required. In fact, it adds some extra work because of friction. Due to the loss of energy from friction, the mechanic has to pull the rope with *more* than 100 lb. She must put in more than 1200 ft-lb of work to get out 1200 ft-lb. Machines do not create work or energy. They transfer energy and change the *direction, amount,* and *distance* of a force.

4. *Simple Machines* *(G10)*

Complicated machines are made by combining simple parts, such as gears, inclined planes, pulleys, and levers. These parts are called **simple machines**. Figure 7–7 depicts various simple machines.

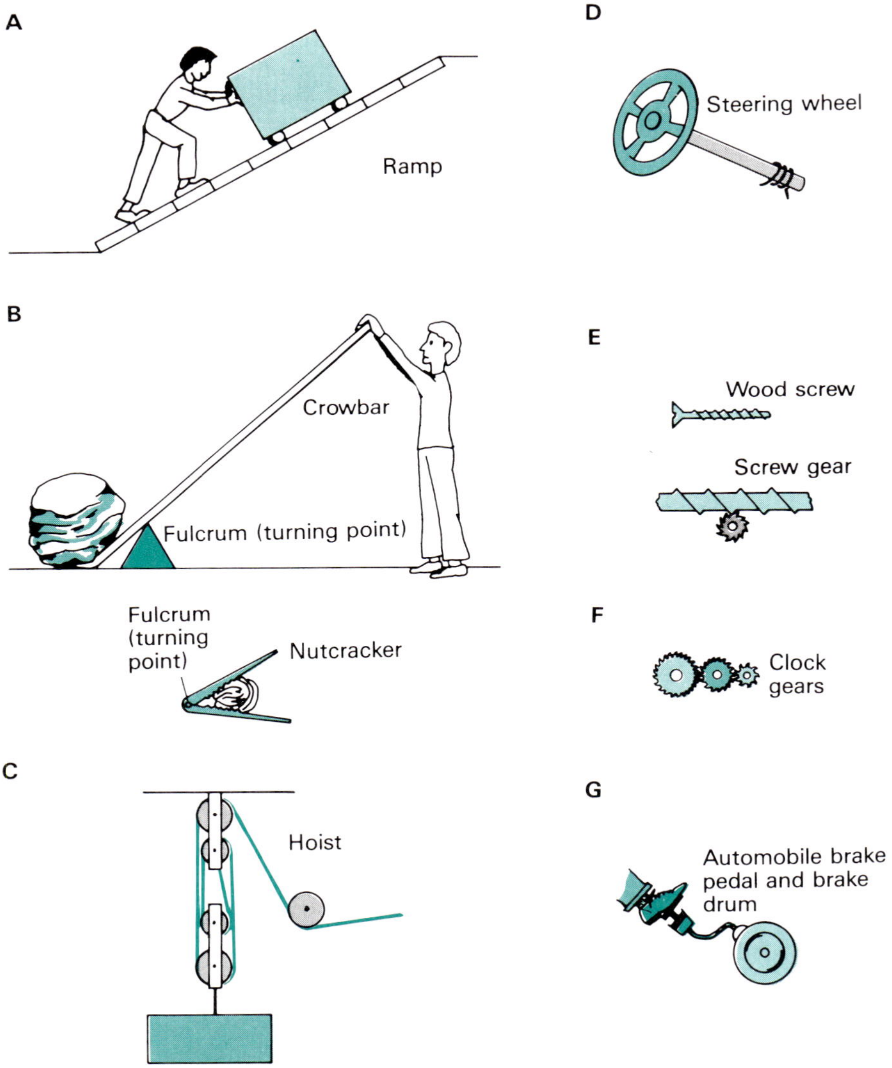

Figure 7–7. Simple machines. (A) The ramp is an *inclined plane*. (B) The crowbar and the nutcracker are *levers*. (C) The hoist is a system of *pulleys*. (D) The steering wheel is a *wheel-and-axle*. (E) The wood screw and screw gear are *screws*. (F) A clock uses *gears*. (G) The automobile pedal and brake drum are a *hydraulic press*.

Sample Questions

1. The diagram below shows a machine that uses wind to lift a weight.

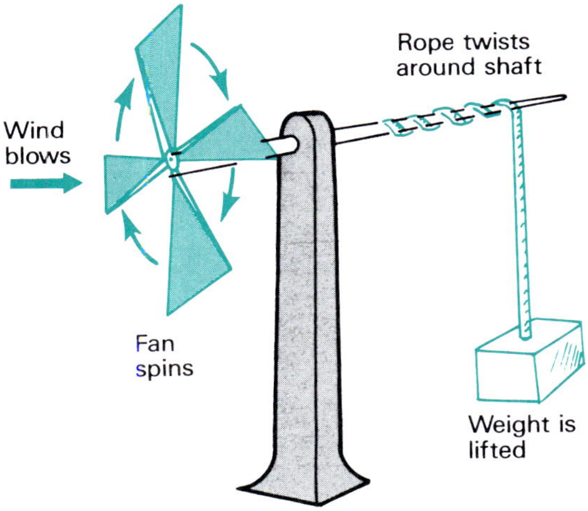

Why is this device called a machine?
(1) It creates energy.
(2) It creates work.
(3) It transfers mechanical energy.
(4) It has moving parts.

2. A hand drill is a machine that uses gears to change the turning of a handle into the turning of a drill.

If 600 units of energy are put into turning the handle, how many units of energy will be given to the drill?
(1) much more than 600
(2) a little more than 600
(3) exactly 600
(4) less than 600

3. Below are some suggestions that can make a bicycle easier to ride.

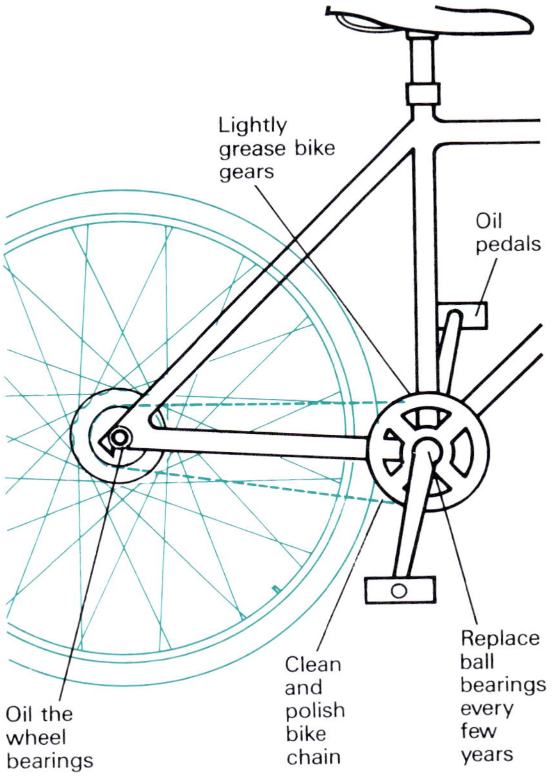

These suggestions work because they
(1) add energy
(2) reduce friction
(3) reduce efficiency
(4) transfer mechanical energy

4. Which one of the following statements about machines is *not* true?
   (1) Machines can change the amount of force transferred.
   (2) Machines can change the direction of the force that is applied.
   (3) Machines can change the distance over which a force acts.
   (4) Machines can decrease the work required to do a job.

5. Which one of the devices shown below is a simple machine?

A

Wind-up watch

B

Battery-operated watch

C

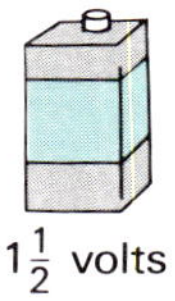

Battery

D

Can opener

(1) A (2) B (3) C (4) D

6. All machines give out less energy than they take in. Where does the missing energy go?
   (1) It is lost.
   (2) Unknown.
   (3) It changes to heat by rubbing of machine parts.
   (4) It changes to kinetic energy of motion.

7. As shown below, a lever can be used to lift a weight such as a heavy rock.

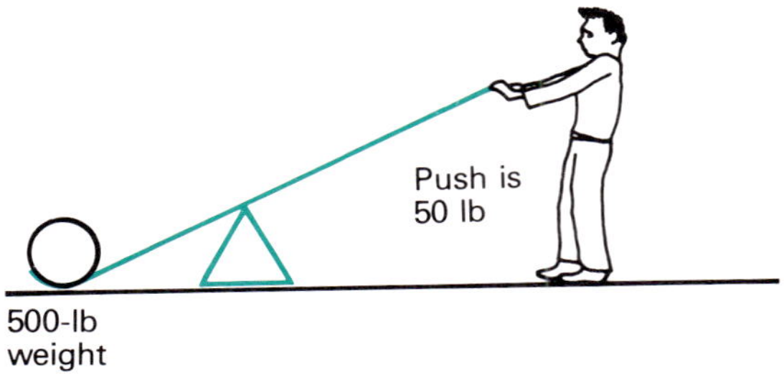

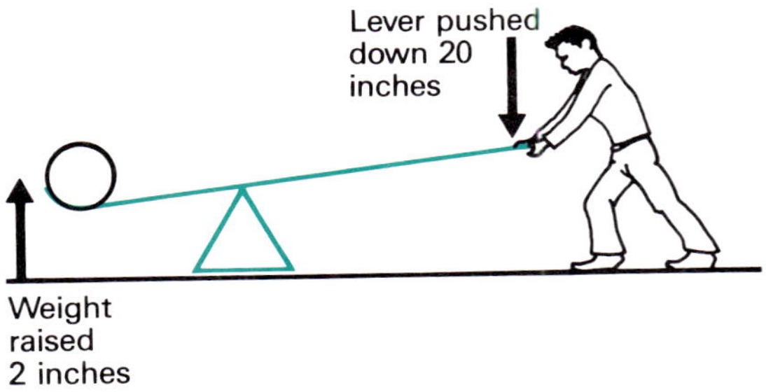

Measurements were taken when the lever was used to lift the rock. The results are shown in the table.

Action	Force	× Distance	= Work
Lifting the weight	500 lb	2 inches	1000 in-lb
Pushing down on the lever	50 lb	20 inches	1000 in-lb

The lever enabled the person to lift the heavy rock with
   (1) less force
   (2) less distance of action
   (3) less work
   (4) more work

8. The human arm, as shown at the right, is a simple machine. What type of machine is illustrated by the arm?
(1) a lever
(2) a pulley
(3) an inclined plane
(4) a hydraulic press

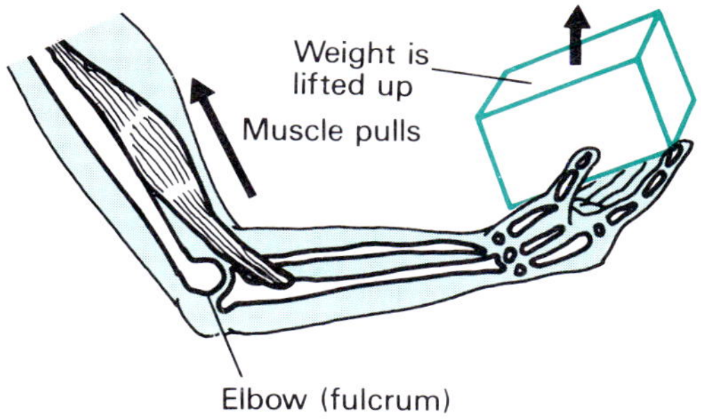

III. SOUND AND LIGHT

1. Sound Is Vibration *(G11, G12)*

Sound is a form of energy. It is produced when objects vibrate. Table 1 on page 130 lists some examples of vibrating objects that produce sound.

As objects vibrate, they push and pull gently and rapidly on the air. The air particles are rapidly squeezed back and forth. This motion produces air pressure waves that move through the air to a person's ear (Figure 7–8).

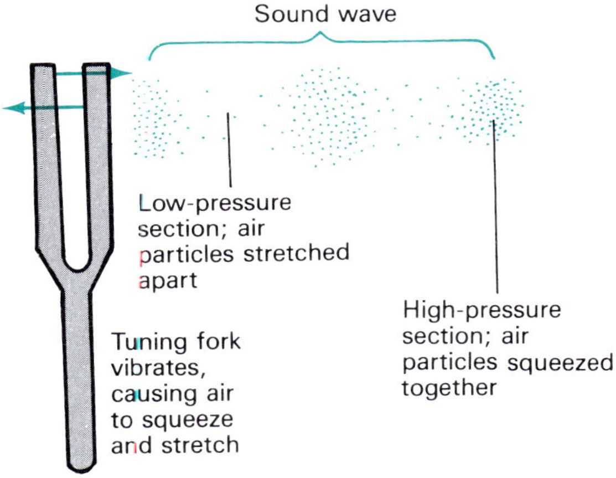

Figure 7–8. Sound waves are pressure vibrations moving in air.

2. Sound Cannot Travel Through a Vacuum *(G12)*

Sound can travel through air, water, glass, steel, and even rock. The substance through which sound waves travel is called the **medium**. The molecules of the medium bump against each other, causing the vibration to travel forward.

In a vacuum there are no molecules, no matter. Therefore, sound cannot exist in a vacuum. Once they hit a vacuum, sound waves stop. The bell jar experiment, shown in Figure 7–9, demonstrates this fact. When air is removed from the bell jar the sound of the ringing bell becomes softer and eventually disappears, even though the bell itself is still being hammered.

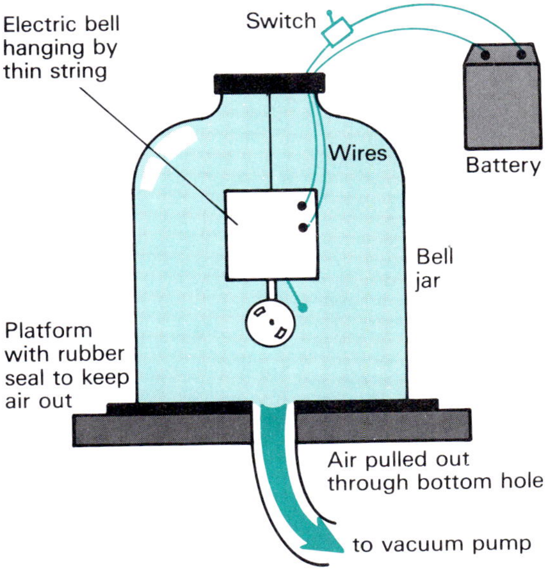

Figure 7–9. The bell jar sound demonstration.

Table 1 Vibrating Objects

Type of Object	Examples
Vibrating solid objects 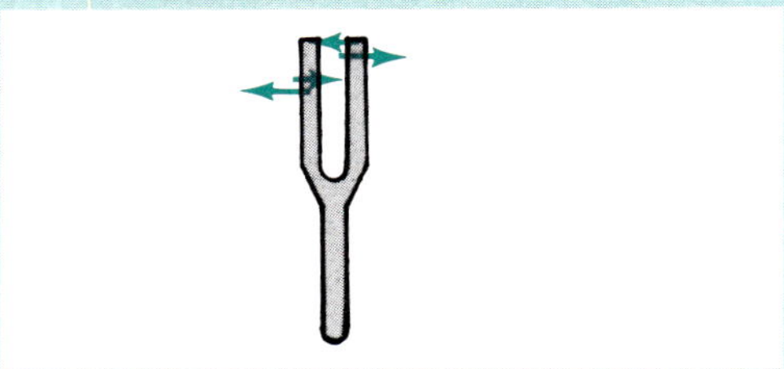	Tuning forks Harmonicas Reed instruments, such as clarinets Bells
Vibrating surfaces 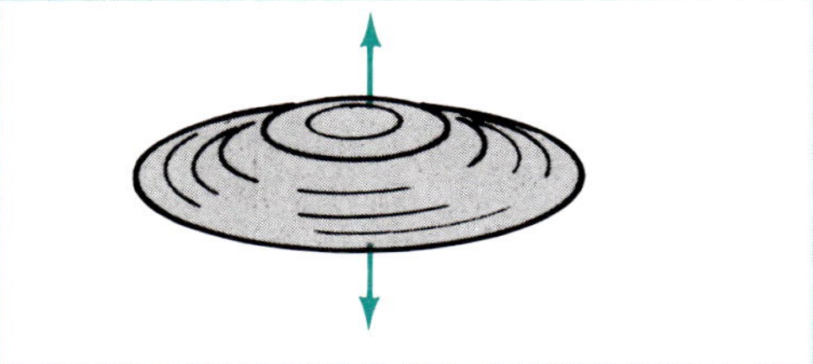	Drums Cymbals Human voice box (larynx) Audio speakers Earphones, telephone earpiece
Vibrating wires 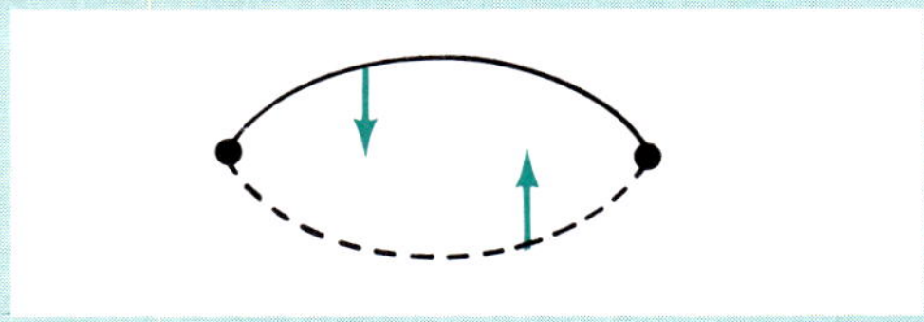	Guitars Violins Pianos Sitars
Vibrating air columns 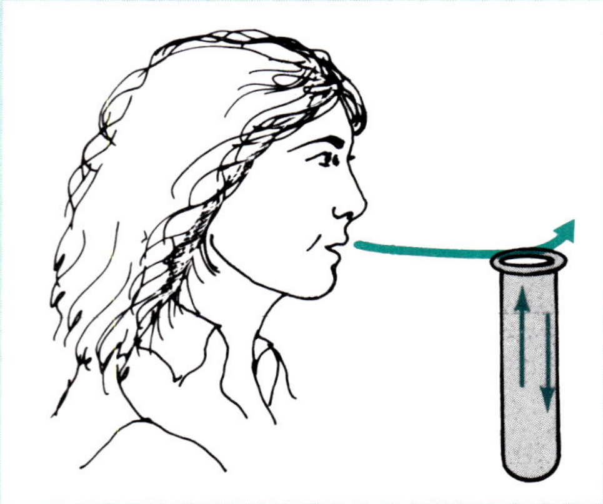	Organ pipes Wind instruments, such as trumpets Whistles

Table 2	Speeds of Sound and Light			
	Speed of Sound		Speed of Light	
Medium	meters/sec	miles/sec	meters/sec	miles/sec
Air	332	0.2	300,000,000	186,000
Water	1454	0.9	223,000,000	138,000
Stone	5971	3.6	___	___

3. *The Speed of Sound* *(G13)*

Sound travels at different speeds in different materials. Also, in any material the speed of sound is much slower than the speed of light. Table 2 gives some examples of how fast sound and light travel in different materials.

This tremendous difference in speeds of sound and light is made obvious during lightning. The flash of the lightning arrives almost instantly, but the sound caused by the lightning arrives after a brief delay (Figure 7–10).

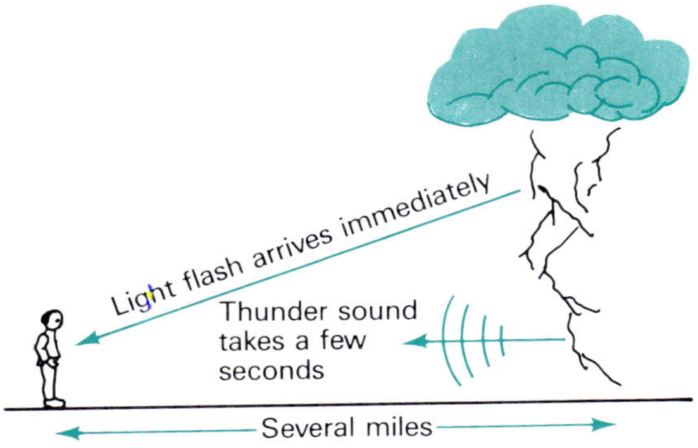

Figure 7–10. Lightning is seen before the thunder is heard.

4. *Pitch and Loudness* *(G14)*

The *number* of air vibrations that hit the ear each second determines the **pitch** (high note or low note) of the sound. For example, in music middle C is 256 vibrations per second, but high C (C′) is 512 vibrations per second. The human ear can hear from about 20 to 20,000 vibrations per second. Dogs can hear higher vibrations. Bats make and hear sounds with 80,000 vibrations per second.

The *strength* of the air vibrations that hit the ear determines the **loudness** (loud or soft) of the sound. A loud sound is made by strong pressure vibrations; a soft sound is made by weak pressure vibrations. A loud noise can damage ears temporarily or even permanently, especially if the loud noise is heard for a prolonged time. Evidence exists that loud music, even coming through small earphones, can damage hearing ability.

5. *Light* *(G15)*

Light waves travel in straight lines away from their source. Sound waves can bend and travel around corners; light waves cannot. For this reason, light waves are often drawn as straight rays coming from the light source (Figure 7–11).

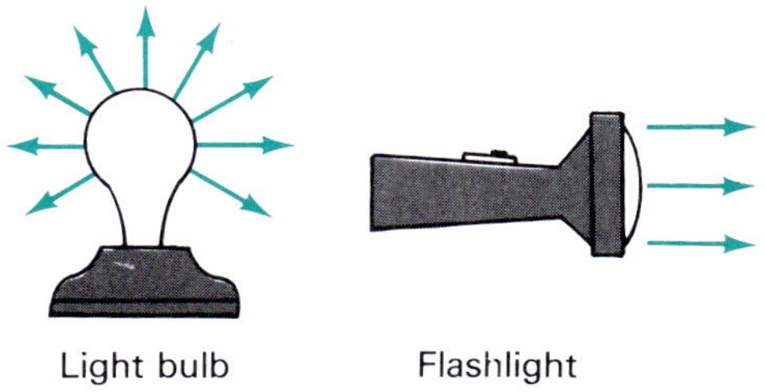

Figure 7–11. Light travels as straight rays.

One proof that light travels in straight lines comes from shadows made by a small (point) light source (see Figure 7–12).

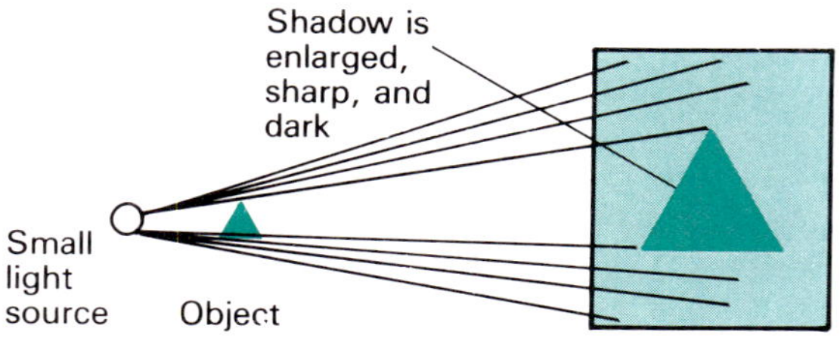

Figure 7–12. Only straight light waves can produce a large, sharp shadow.

These shadows are always larger than the object and are very sharp. If the light rays were able to bend, the shadows would neither be enlarged nor very sharp.

Another proof that light rays cannot bend is that a person can only see through a rubber hose if the hose is straight. Any bend or kink prevents the light from continuing (Figure 7–13).

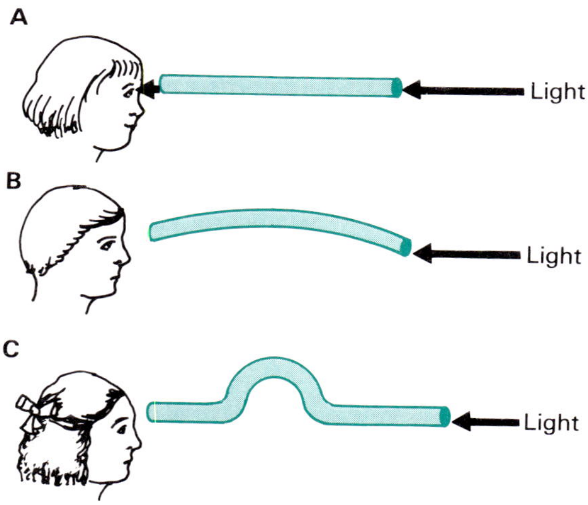

Figure 7–13. Light observed through a rubber hose. In (A), the light is visible. In (B) and (C), light does *not* continue through the hose and reach the eye.

6. Reflection, Absorption, and Transmission of Light *(G16)*

When light strikes a surface, three events occur.

1. Some of the light is **reflected** (bounced) off the surface.
2. Some of the light is **absorbed** (removed) by the material.
3. Some of the light is **transmitted** (passes through).

Figure 7–14 shows what happens when light strikes glass and when it strikes water.

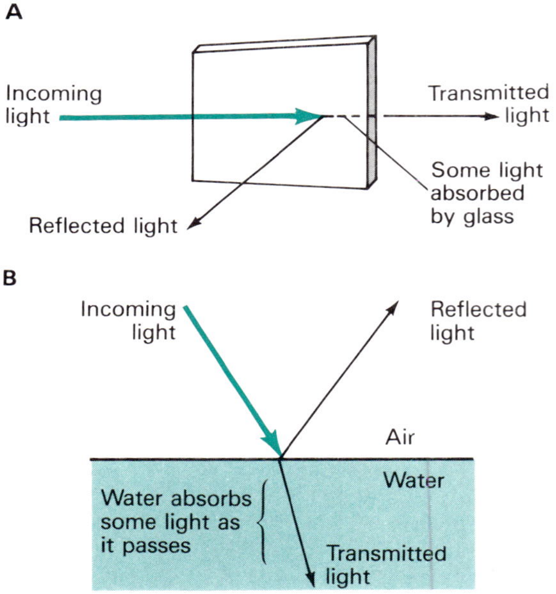

Figure 7–14. (A) Light striking a glass window; (B) light striking the surface of water.

For different purposes, the amounts of light needed to be reflected, absorbed, and transmitted vary. Table 3 shows characteristics of some objects that use light.

Table 3 Characteristics of Objects that Use Light

Use	Characteristics
In mirrors	% of light *reflected* must be very high
In sunglasses	% of light *absorbed* must be very high
In reading glasses	% of light *transmitted* must be very high

7. Lenses *(G17)*

Lenses are pieces of glass that have been ground to a special curved shape. This shape causes light passing through the lens to be bent in different directions, as shown in Figure 7–15.

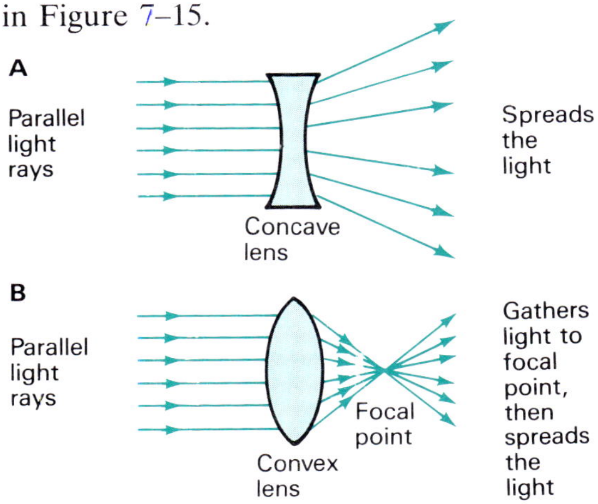

Figure 7–15. Lenses bend light rays in special ways. (A) Concave lens; (B) convex lens.

The ability of lenses to bend light rays is used in many devices to make images of objects. For example, a camera uses a lens to make a small image of an object on the film. A projector uses a lens to make a large image of the film on a screen. Images made by lenses may be smaller, larger, or equal in size to the object. Table 4 provides information about uses of lenses.

Table 4 Uses of Lenses

Use	Type of Lens	Size of Image
Peephole in door to see to outside hallway	Concave	Tiny compared to actual objects
Camera	Convex	Small compared to objects photographed
Photocopier	Convex	Same size as object being copied
Projector, telescope	Convex	Larger than object being viewed
Microscope, magnifying glass	Convex	Much larger than objects being viewed

8. Electromagnetic Waves *(G18, G19)*

Light waves are just one small portion of a much larger family of **electromagnetic waves.** Like sound waves, these electromagnetic waves vibrate at different rates. Unlike sound waves, however, they can travel through a vacuum. Table 5 on page 134 lists information about electromagnetic waves.

The table shows only a sample of the many helpful uses of electromagnetic waves. However, overexposure to electromagnetic waves may cause harmful effects as well. For example, too much sunlight allows too many ultraviolet waves to fall on human skin. This causes sunburning, and can lead to damaged skin and even skin cancer after many years of overexposure. Too many X-rays taken in dental or medical offices should be avoided for the same reasons. Researchers are still investigating possible harmful effects of the radio, TV, and microwaves that surround everyone today.

Table 5 Electromagnetic Waves

Type of Electromagnetic Wave	Approximate Vibrations per Second	Uses
Radio and TV waves	Millions	Broadcasting and other communications
Microwaves	Billions	Telephone communications and cooking food
Infrared waves	Trillions	Photography (in darkness); heating rays
Visible light	500 trillion	Sight
Ultraviolet waves	1000 trillion	Medical purposes (kills bacteria)
X-rays and gamma rays	Million trillion	X-ray photography, diagnosing diseases

Sample Questions

1. All sounds begin with objects that are
(1) hollow
(2) vibrating
(3) filled with excess energy
(4) filled with air

2. On the moon, astronauts talked to one another by radio phones even when they were next to each other. The reason they didn't talk directly without radios is that
(1) they wore thick helmets
(2) there is too much natural noise on the moon
(3) there is no gravity on the moon
(4) there is no air on the moon

3. Sound cannot travel in
(1) water
(2) dense rock
(3) steel
(4) a vacuum

4. In a concert the high sounds of the flutes are heard at the same time as the deep, low sounds of a tuba. What must be the same for all sound waves to account for this fact?
(1) their speed of travel
(2) their strength
(3) their vibration rate per second
(4) their pitch

5. Which statement about a fireworks display is true?
   (1) The flash and explosion are perceived together.
   (2) The flash is seen, then the explosion is heard.
   (3) The explosion is heard, then the flash is seen.
   (4) The flash is seen in all directions, but the explosion is heard only downwind.

6. Human hearing can be damaged by
   (1) high-pitched (high vibration) sounds
   (2) low-pitched (low vibration) sounds
   (3) loud noises
   (4) soft noises that last for some time

7. Light is different from sound in that
   (1) only light is a wave
   (2) light cannot travel through any liquids or solids
   (3) light cannot travel in a vacuum
   (4) only light travels in straight lines

8. Suppose you held a piece of paper behind a convex lens, like a screen. With slight adjustments you could see a small, upside-down picture of any houses, buildings, trees, and people nearby.

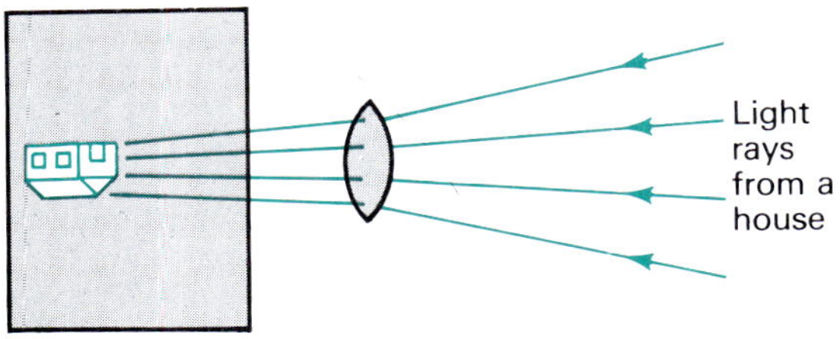

Which device uses a convex lens in this same way?
   (1) a camera
   (2) a magnifying glass
   (3) a slide projector
   (4) a microscope

9. Look at the diagram below, which shows a light ray passing through a glass prism.

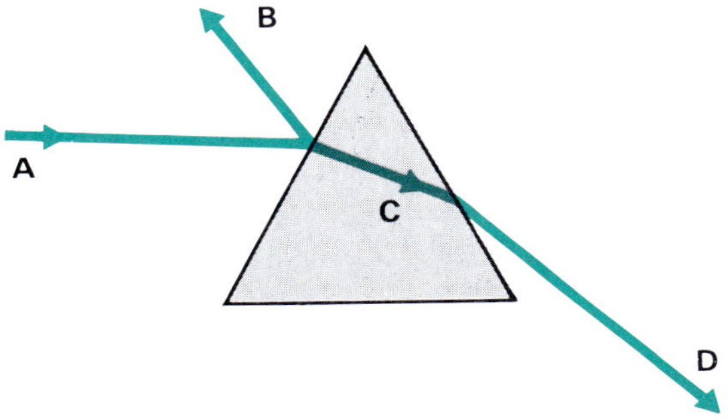

Which letter shows where absorption occurs?
   (1) A
   (2) B
   (3) C
   (4) D

10. The damage done to living cells by electromagnetic waves increases as the vibration rate increases. Which type of wave, therefore, is most dangerous to humans?
   (1) radio and TV
   (2) microwaves
   (3) visible light
   (4) X-rays

Science Skill

INTERPRETING TABLES

Visible light is only a tiny part of the whole electromagnetic family of waves. We can see only a certain spread of wave vibrations, from 460 trillion to 750 trillion vibrations each second.

460 trillion = 460,000,000,000,000

750 trillion = 750,000,000,000,000

Each color has its own number of vibrations and wavelength. Human eyes are very sensitive to certain colors and less sensitive to other colors. This information is summarized in the following table.

Color	Vibrations each second	Wavelength in millionths of a centimeter	Eye Sensitivity
RED	460 trillion	65	10%
ORANGE	500 trillion	60	60%
YELLOW	526 trillion	57	83%
GREEN	566 trillion	53	83%
BLUE	638 trillion	47	10%
VIOLET	750 trillion	40	1%

1. Which color has the greatest vibration rate?

2. Which color has the shortest wavelength?

3. Which statement is true about vibration amount and wavelength of light?
   (1) As vibrations increase, the wavelengths also increase.
   (2) As vibrations increase, the wavelengths decrease.
   (3) As vibrations increase, the wavelengths remain constant.
   (4) There is no relationship between vibrations and wavelength.

4. Which color of light is poorest for human vision?
   (1) red (3) blue
   (2) yellow (4) violet

5. Which color would probably have an eye sensitivity of 100%?
   (1) reddish-orange
   (2) yellowish-green
   (3) greenish-blue
   (4) bluish-violet

6. A certain light has 470,000,000,000,000 vibrations each second. As what color would we probably see this light?
   (1) red (3) yellow
   (2) orange (4) violet

7. Purple is between blue and violet. Which of the following could be a wavelength for purple?
   (1) 40 millionths of a centimeter
   (2) 43 millionths of a centimeter
   (3) 49 millionths of a centimeter
   (4) 53 millionths of a centimeter

8. Which vibration rate is not visible to humans?
   (1) 400 trillion per second
   (2) 500 trillion per second
   (3) 600 trillion per second
   (4) 700 trillion per second

IV. HEAT AND ELECTRICITY

1. Heat and Expansion *(G20)*

When materials are heated, they expand. Solid materials, such as steel and concrete, grow in length when they become hotter. This is why openings are left in bridges, in train tracks, and in sidewalks—to permit expansion without cracking or buckling. Liquids, such as water, alcohol, and mercury, also increase in volume when heated. Liquid expansion explains how thermometers show changes in temperature. Even gases expand when heated. Balloons and car tires swell up when they are made hotter.

Just as materials expand when they are heated, they contract when they are cooled. There is one unusual and important exception to this rule. As water is cooled, it shrinks in the normal way. However, as water begins to freeze and change into ice, it expands again. The expansion force created by water as it freezes is very large. It can cause cracks in streets (potholes), in rocks, and in metal pipes that carry water (Figure 7–16).

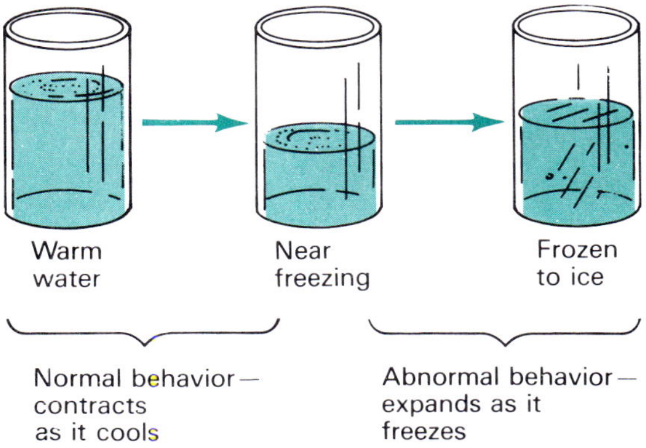

Figure 7–16. The unusual behavior of water when cooled.

2. The Flow of Heat Energy *(G21)*

Heat energy is actually the rapid movement and vibrations of the particles in any material. When a material is hot its particles move faster than when the material is cooler. For this reason, heat can only flow from warmer objects or parts to cooler objects or parts (Figure 7–17). Heat can never flow from colder to warmer parts.

Figure 7–17. The direction of heat flow—always from hot to cold.

Insulation may be used to reduce the amount of heat that flows from a warm area to a cold area. People wear coats to keep their body heat close to the body instead of allowing it to flow to the cool air. A coat is insulation. Fiberglass padding, double windows, air spaces, and curtains can all be used to insulate a home. They help keep the heat from flowing out to the cold outdoors.

3. Electricity *(G22, G23, G25, G27)*

Electricity is the flow of large numbers of tiny electrons. Electrons can move through solid metal wires as easily as water can move through a pipe. As the electrons move, they carry energy. We call this energy **electrical energy**. Some materials, such as metals, permit electricity to pass very well. These materials are called **conductors**. Some materials, such as rubber and glass, do not permit electricity to pass. These materials are called poor conductors *or* good **insulators**.

Electric wires are usually made of copper, silver, or aluminum, since these materials are good conductors. However, the wires are covered with plastic or rubber (insulators) so people are not hurt by the electricity. Electricians always protect themselves by wearing rubberized or fiberglass gloves and rubber shoes just in case they touch a "hot" wire (one that has powerful electricity in it). The electricity will not pass through these materials.

Electrical energy is dangerous. It can shock, injure, or kill living things, including humans. Electricity can cause muscles to tighten, the heart to stop, or seriously burn the skin depending on its strength and point of contact. Some electrical devices provide protection from accidents: they are **grounded**. Grounding involves attaching a wire to the outside of the machine (TV, refrigerator, or motor, for example) and then connecting that wire to pipes or other metal objects that are in contact with the ground. If electricity somehow manages to get to the outside of the machine, the electricity will immediately be drained to the ground instead of causing a shock to any person who touches the machine. Unfortunately, most small electrical devices, such as toasters, are not grounded. Objects that are grounded usually have a three-prong plug instead of a two-prong plug, as shown in Figure 7–18.

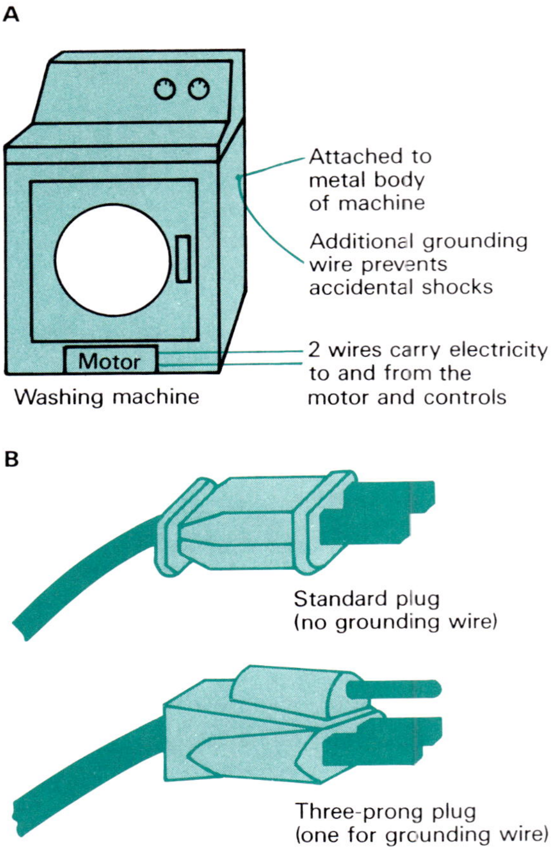

Figure 7–18. (A) Many electrical devices have a special wire for grounding. (B) A standard plug and a three-prong plug.

4. *Simple Circuits* *(G24, G26)*

A **circuit** is the path electricity takes as it flows. The simplest circuit consists of three items:

1. a source of electrical energy, such as a battery;
2. some device that uses the electrical energy; and
3. at least two connecting wires.

Figure 7–19 shows a simple circuit.

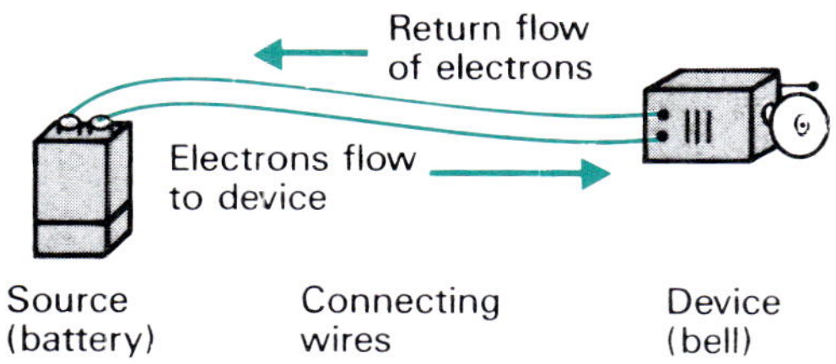

Figure 7–19. **A simple electric circuit.**

An expanded version of this simple plan is used in wiring a house. Electricity comes in from the main line and is distributed throughout the house. It is returned to the main line from all over the house by means of the second wire. The fuses and circuit breakers provide protection against fire. If too many electrical devices are turned on at the same time, an increased amount of electricity flows in the wires. This increase can cause the wires to heat up, possibly starting a fire. However, the fuse or circuit breakers will automatically stop the flow of electricity at a safe level. They will not permit electricity to overload in any one house line.

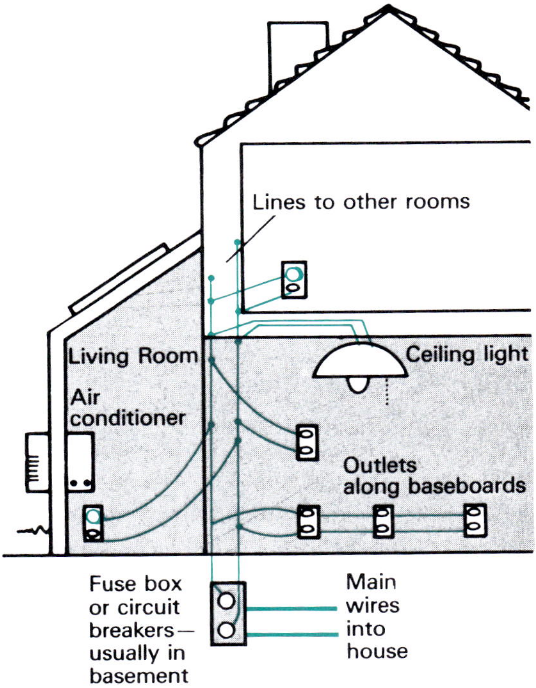

Figure 7–20. **The wiring of a house is an expanded version of a simple circuit.**

Sample Questions

1. A glass bottle is completely filled with cold water and then capped. It is placed into a freezer for several hours. What event will occur?
(1) The bottle will crack due to ice expansion.
(2) The ice made will be smaller in volume than the original water.
(3) The water will not freeze in a capped bottle.
(4) Ice will form and exactly fill the bottle.

2. People keep windows closed when using air conditioners during hot days. The best explanation for this is that closing windows
(1) prevents cold energy from leaving the room
(2) prevents heat energy from leaving the room
(3) prevents cold energy from entering the room
(4) prevents heat energy from entering the room

3. The illustration below shows telephone wires as seen on a cold winter day and a hot summer day.

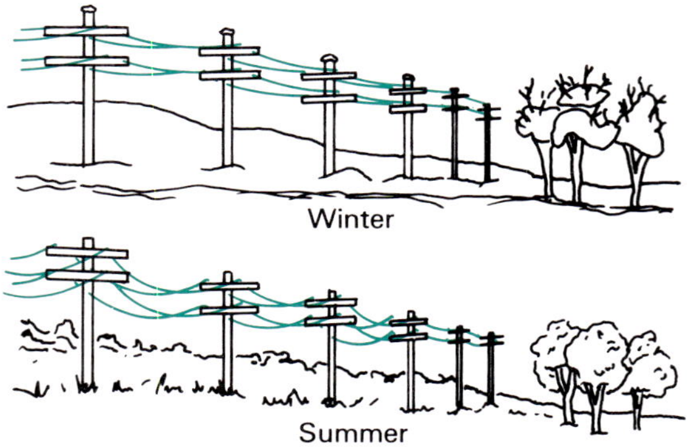

Why do the wires sag during the summer?
(1) They are longer because the weather is warmer.
(2) They support many birds.
(3) They partly melt and soften.
(4) They carry increased electricity and phone calls in summer.

4. Electric wires are covered by rubber because rubber is
(1) grounding
(2) durable
(3) a conductor
(4) an insulator

5. A Thermos bottle, shown below, can keep liquids hot for many hours because it uses several types of insulation.

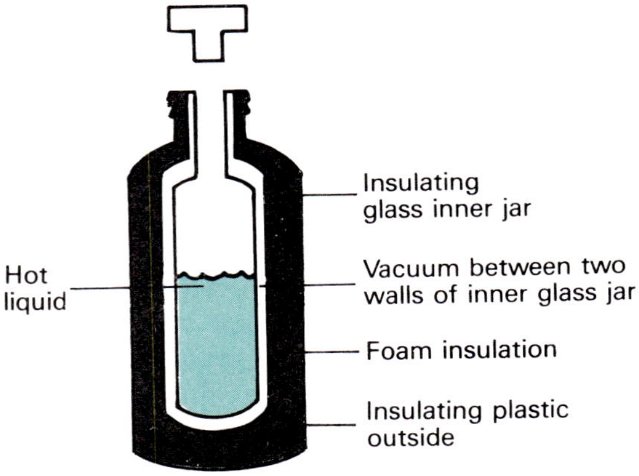

How does the insulation keep the liquid hot?
(1) It prevents heat from leaving the Thermos.
(2) It allows heat to leave the Thermos.
(3) It makes some heat energy.
(4) It uses up some heat energy.

6. Many electrical devices are grounded because grounding makes them
(1) safer
(2) cheaper to run
(3) more powerful
(4) more efficient

7. What does a fuse or circuit breaker do?
(1) It prevents too much electricity from flowing at one time.
(2) It increases the power of the electricity.
(3) It permits as much electricity to flow as is wanted.
(4) It prevents all heating in wires due to electricity.

8. The diagram below shows a common flashlight.

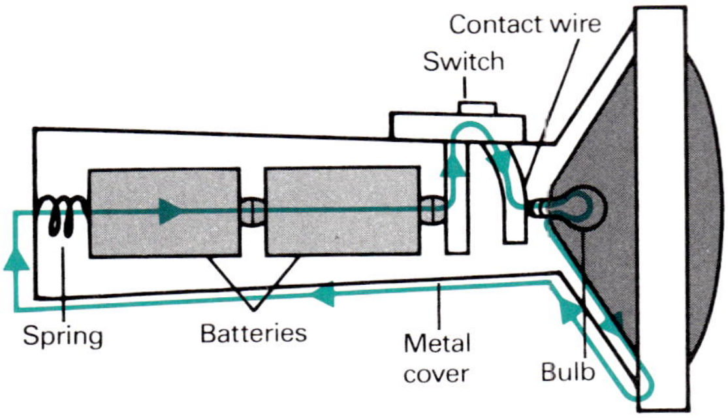

The blue line shows the movement of electrons when the switch touches the bulb. This flow of electrons is called the
(1) conduction channel
(2) electromotive force
(3) voltage
(4) circuit

Issues in Science, Technology, and Society

Business, Industry, and Employment

Science is the study of the facts of our natural world. Technology is the application of science understandings to practical uses. Technology tries to solve the problems of society and to meet society's needs using applied science knowledge. Together, science and technology have a great effect on business, industry, and employment opportunities.

For some time scientists have known that extremely cold temperatures increase the conductivity of metal. In other words, very cold temperatures (below −400°F or −250°C) permit electricity to flow with almost no resistance. Enormous amounts of electricity can be sent through ordinary wires. This increased flow is called **superconductivity**.

Superconductivity has many technology and business applications. For example, electricity is often sent over hundreds of miles. The resistance of the wires causes much electricity to be lost to heat during this transmission. If the wires could be kept extremely cold, then there would be no loss of electric power during long-distance transmission, resulting in a great saving for electric companies.

Superconductivity also has uses in creating powerful magnetism, since extra-large flows of electricity create extra-large magnets. The magnetism could be used to hold atomic and nuclear reactions using hydrogen fuel in one place. This may be a tremendous new source of energy for society some day.

The need to make wires extremely cold has led to an entirely new industry. Many people are now employed by companies that produce special pipes, liquids, and pumps in order to produce the cold temperatures needed.

Recently scientists discovered that certain ceramic materials (made from clay and sand) become superconductive at temperatures that are not as cold as the temperatures needed by metals. The electric industry is now employing thousands of scientists and engineers to learn how to produce, improve, and use these new materials. If materials are developed that are superconductive at ordinary room temperatures, billions of dollars will move into new industries. Society will benefit from new sources of energy, cheap transmission costs, new transportation methods, and improved medical techniques. The new industries will also create millions of dollars and thousands of jobs.

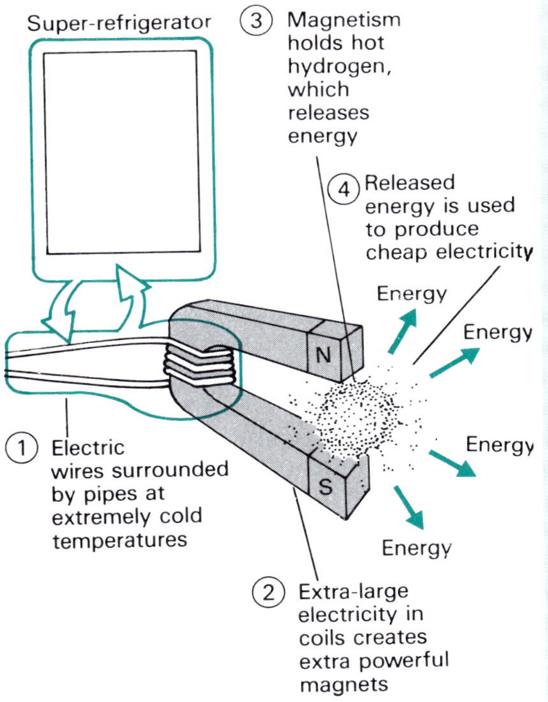

Superconductivity could be used to hold hydrogen fuel, providing a source of energy.

CHAPTER 8 The Chemistry of Matter

I. CHEMICAL SAFETY

1. *The World Is Made from Chemicals* *(H1)*

Chemistry is the study of what the world is made from. The name *chemistry* comes from the fact that *everything* is made from chemicals—people, stones, trees, food. There are billions of different materials in the world, but scientists have discovered that they are made from only a few chemicals. These chemicals are put together in different amounts, combinations, and patterns (Figure 8–1).

2. *Chemicals Can Be Dangerous* *(H2, H3, H4)*

Many chemicals used at home, in businesses, and in laboratories are dangerous. They must be handled carefully, using safe procedures. The laboratory equipment used to handle chemicals must also be used with safe procedures.

Some chemicals give off **vapors** (gas, fumes, odors). For example, ordinary ammonia water used for cleaning, vinegar, and bleach all give off vapors that are **toxic**, or harmful. This is especially true if no fresh-air ventilation is present when they are used. Gasoline, paint thinner, cleaning

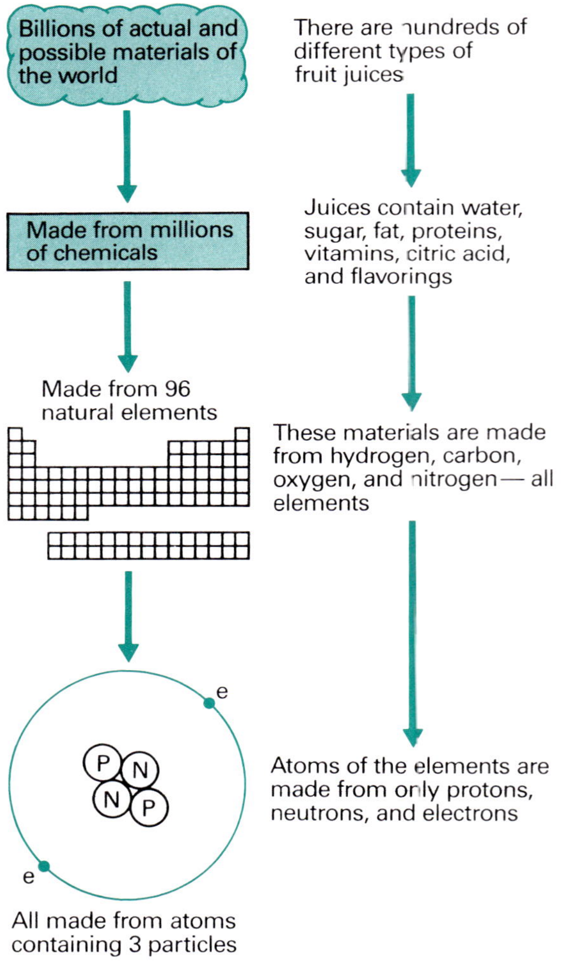

Figure 8–1. What is the world made of?

fluids, and heating oil are **flammable**. They can burn, and they give off vapors that can explode. Obviously, such chemicals should be used in well-ventilated places without flames or sparks.

Chemicals should not be mixed without specific instructions. Many chemicals can react and combine to create new materials that may be dangerous. For example, mixing ordinary ammonia water used for cleaning together with household bleach produces a poisonous gas.

Even mixing a substance with water can be unsafe at times. When very strong acid chemicals must be weakened (diluted) with water, the safe procedure requires that the acid be poured into the water. As Figure 8–2 shows, it is unsafe to pour the water into the acid. The heat produced on mixing can spatter the acid and water. Pouring acid into water is safe. The heavier acid sinks and mixes with the water. Heat is spread out.

Mixing can be dangerous. Therefore, always read instructions carefully when doing experiments and do not perform extra experiments without permission.

3. Pressurized Containers and Storage *(H5, H6)*

Some chemicals are kept in pressurized containers. For example, hair sprays, whipped cream, deodorants, and cleaning liquids are often in high-pressure cans. These cans can explode if they are punctured or heated. Handle them carefully and keep them away from sources of high heat.

Household chemicals should be stored in safe, closed places. They must be kept out of the reach of small children and pets. Cabinets with a childproof lock are advisable. Do not store chemicals on high shelves. Spills can occur easily when bottles are being taken down from high shelves.

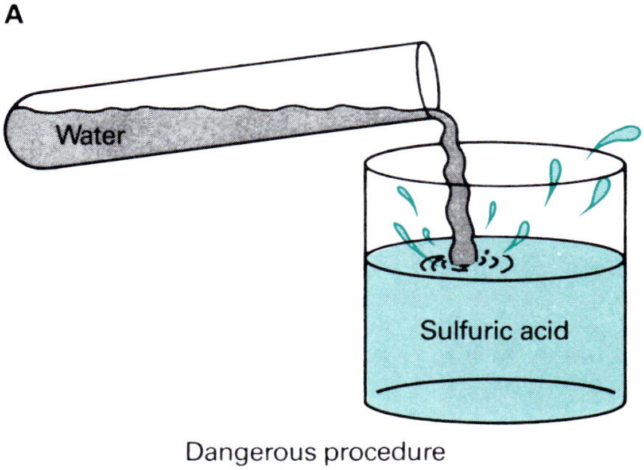

Figure 8–2. Diluting strong acid with water. (A) Pouring water into acid is dangerous. (B) Pouring acid into water is safe.

Science Skill

LAB SAFETY

Science textbooks, laboratory manuals, and laboratory equipment often contain international safety symbols. These symbols are used to call attention to situations that require extra caution.

Look at the safety symbols shown in the table below. Identify the hazard represented by each symbol. Then use the information in the table to answer questions 1–12 on the facing page.

A 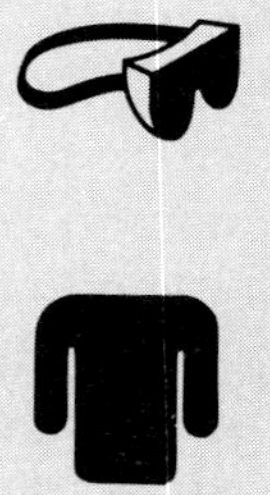	. . . indicate that safety goggles and a lab apron (or coat) are to be worn *at all times* when working in the lab.
B 	. . . indicates the presence of an open flame. Loose hair should be tied back or covered, and bulky or loose clothing should be secured.
C 	. . . indicates a caustic or corrosive substance—most frequently an acid. Avoid contact with skin, eyes, and clothing. Do not inhale vapors.
D 	. . . indicates an activity in which the likelihood of breakage is greater than usual, such as working with glass tubing, funnels, etc.
E 	. . . indicates the presence or production of poisonous or noxious vapors. Care should be taken not to inhale vapors directly. When testing an odor, use a wafting motion to direct the vapor toward your nose.
F 	. . . indicates that the potential for an explosive situation is present. When you see this symbol, read the instructions carefully and *follow them exactly*.
G 	. . . indicates the presence of a poisonous substance. Do not let such a substance come in contact with your skin and do not breathe its vapors.
H 	. . . indicates that the potential for an electrical shock exists. Follow all instructions carefully. Disconnect all apparatus when not in use.
I 	. . . indicates a radioactive substance. Follow instructions as to the proper handling of such substances.

1. Any material might give out dangerous vapors. Therefore, the best way to smell an unknown material is to
   (1) inhale the vapor directly under your nose
   (2) smell a cotton ball that has been dipped in the unknown material
   (3) put 2–3 drops of the substance on filter paper and smell the paper
   (4) use your hand to wave some of the odor toward your nose

2. The best protection for eyes when doing laboratory work is
   (1) a pair of safety glasses
   (2) a laboratory apron
   (3) being careful when heating, pouring, or mixing
   (4) holding chemicals and equipment a full arm's length away

3. What hazard is especially dangerous near loose hair and clothing, pressurized containers, and explosive vapors?
   (1) electricity
   (2) an open flame
   (3) radiation
   (4) caustic chemicals

4. A substance marked "poisonous" should only be
   (1) smelled (3) observed
   (2) tasted (4) touched

5. When they are not being used, electrical devices should be
   (1) turned off (3) covered
   (2) unplugged (4) removed

6–12. For each item in questions 6–12, choose the letter of the correct safety symbol or symbols. Some questions require more than one response.

6. All glassware, such as glass tubing
7. Strong acids
8. An AC/DC voltage source
9. Chemicals that contain lead, mercury, arsenic, or cyanide
10. Samples of radioactive iodine, uranium, and radium
11. A bottle of gasoline
12. Gas burners used to distill water

Sample Questions

1. Which one of the following has a toxic vapor?

(1)

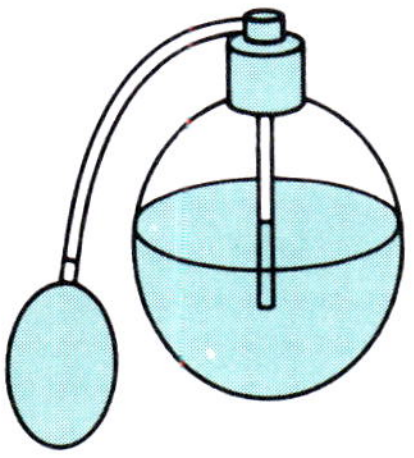

Perfume

(2)

Room freshener

(3)

Rubbing alcohol

(4)

Household ammonia water

2. The statement below is printed on a common household item.

> CAUTION: Do not set on stove or radiator or keep where temperature will exceed 120°F, as container may burst. Do not puncture or throw in fire. Keep out of reach of children.

The contents of this container are probably
(1) very caustic (harmful to skin and eyes)
(2) radioactive
(3) flammable
(4) pressurized

3. Which material has a flammable vapor?
(1) chlorine laundry bleach
(2) candle wax
(3) charcoal
(4) charcoal lighter fluid

4. Which of the statements below gives the best advice about mixing chemicals at home or in the laboratory?
(1) Never mix anything.
(2) Mix only as directed.
(3) Mix materials only if each material is safe to use alone.
(4) Experiment by mixing carefully.

5. When mixed, household ammonia water and laundry bleach produce
(1) a strong cleaning solution
(2) no additional products
(3) a solid soap
(4) a dangerous gas

6. The statement below is printed on a common household item.

> CAUTION: Do not use full strength. Mix with 2 parts water. Keep windows open for ventilation while drying.

The contents of this container probably
(1) are radioactive
(2) give off flammable vapors
(3) give off toxic vapors
(4) are highly pressurized

7. The statement below is printed on a common household item.

> DANGER: May cause burns to skin and eyes. Do not spray near eyes, nose, or skin. Do not take internally. FIRST AID: Eyes—Flush with water for 15 minutes. Skin—Wash thoroughly with soap and water. Internal—Do not induce vomiting; rinse mouth, drink large amounts of fluid. Call for medical attention immediately.

The contents of this container are probably
(1) very caustic
(2) radioactive
(3) flammable
(4) very poisonous

8. The statement below is printed on a common household item.

> CAUTION: Keep away from heat, sparks, and open flame.

The contents of this container are probably
(1) poisonous
(2) electrical
(3) flammable
(4) strongly acidic

II. ELEMENTS AND THEIR ATOMS

1. *What Is Matter?* *(H7, H11)*

Matter is anything that takes up space (volume) and has mass (weight). A piece of wood is matter, since it has both volume and weight. But light and electricity are not matter, since they have neither volume nor weight. Matter exists in three forms: solid, liquid, and gas. These forms are called **phases**.

Every chemical has its own characteristic physical properties. These properties help to identify it. Table 1 lists the physical properties of some chemicals.

The list below shows some of the standard physical properties that are used to describe chemicals.

Physical Properties Used to Describe Chemicals

1. Its usual phase – solid, liquid, or gas
2. Color
3. Odor
4. Taste
5. Density
6. Solubility in water
7. Melting temperature
8. Boiling temperature
9. Appearance (e.g., crystals, powder, softness)
10. Conduction of heat and electricity

2. *The Elements* *(H8, H9)*

All chemicals are made from one or more **elements**. There are 106 known elements, but less than half of them are commonly found on Earth. Table 2 shows some of the more common elements and their symbols.

Table 1 Physical Properties

Chemical	Physical Properties
Sugar	Solid, sweet, crystalline, white, dissolves well in water
Water	Liquid, colorless, freezes at 0°C, boils at 100°C, has a density of 1.000 grams per milliliter
Helium	Gas, colorless, less dense than air, not very soluble in water
Chlorine	Gas, light green, has very sharp odor, more dense than air, very soluble in water

Table 2 Common Elements and Their Symbols

Element	Symbol
Hydrogen	H
Helium	He
Carbon	C
Nitrogen	N
Oxygen	O
Fluorine	F
Sodium	Na
Magnesium	Mg
Aluminum	Al
Sulfur	S
Chlorine	Cl
Calcium	Ca
Iron	Fe
Copper	Cu
Silver	Ag
Gold	Au
Iodine	I
Lead	Pb
Uranium	U

3. Elements Can Combine *(H10)*

Some elements occur naturally in their pure form. Among these are gold, silver, sulfur, oxygen, and nitrogen. However, elements combine together to create millions of chemicals. These combinations of elements are called **compounds**. The word *compound* means "to join together." Most materials are made from elements that have joined together into compounds. Table 3 lists some common compounds and the elements from which they are made.

Table 3 Some Common Compounds and Their Elements

Compound	Symbols of Its Elements
Water	H, O
Salt	Na, Cl
Sugar	C, H, O
Gasoline	C, H
Soap	Na, C, H, O
Rust	Fe, O
Bleach	H, O, Cl
Ammonia water	N, H, O
Chalk	Ca, C, O
Battery acid	H, S, O
Stomach acid	H, Cl
Cavity-fighting ingredient in toothpaste	Na, F
Epsom salt	Mg, S, O

The smallest particle of any element is called an **atom**. Because atoms are extremely small, a sample of any pure element contains trillions of them. For example, an ordinary copper penny contains approximately 10,000,000,000,000,000,000,000 copper atoms. A helium balloon contains approximately 300,000,000,000,000,000,000,000 helium atoms.

Atoms join together in specific patterns (Figure 8–3). This is the reason why the elements can combine to make chemical compounds.

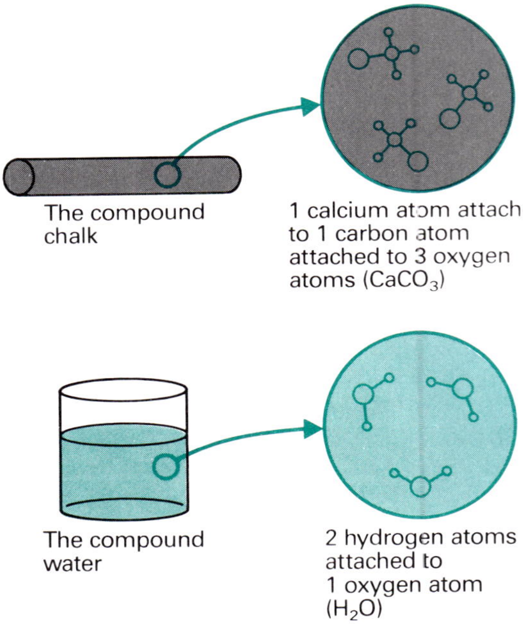

Figure 8–3. Atoms combine to form compounds.

4. Atoms Join by Chemical Bonds *(H10)*

The link that holds atoms together is called a **chemical bond** (see Figure 8–4). Such bonds contain chemical energy, and this energy can be released under certain conditions. When gasoline burns, food is digested, or gunpowder explodes, energy is being released from the bonds that hold their atoms together.

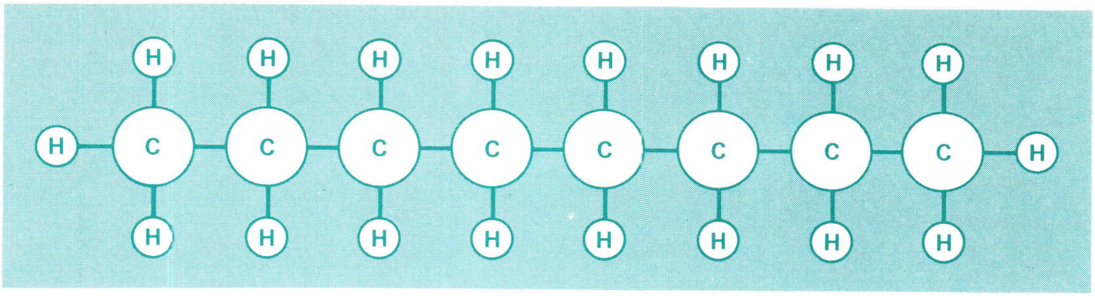

Figure 8–4. The chemical bonds in octane (gasoline). Octane, C_8H_{18}, is 18 hydrogen atoms linked to 8 carbon atoms. Each straight line represents a chemical bond.

5. *Phases and Particles* *(H12, H13, H14, H16)*

The arrangement of the atoms or particles in matter determines whether it is a solid, a liquid, or a gas. The important considerations are:

1. how close together the particles are,
2. how free they are to change position, and
3. how fast they move.

This is summarized in Table 4 and illustrated in Figure 8–5.

Table 4 Characteristics of the Three Phases

Phase	Description	Arrangement of Its Particles
Solid	Has a definite shape and a definite volume	Close together; resist changes in position; move relatively slowly
Liquid	Has no definite shape but does have definite volume	Farther apart; can change position more easily; move more quickly than solids
Gas	Has no definite shape and no definite volume	Much farther apart; can change position very easily; move relatively fast compared to solids and liquids

Figure 8–5. Arrangements of atoms in three phases of matter.

6. *Energy and Changes of Phase* *(H15, H17, H18)*

A change of phase occurs when matter changes from one phase into another. Table 5 lists the six kinds of phase changes.

Such phase changes can only take place if energy is given to or taken from matter. The energy allows the particles to have a new arrangement, thereby creating a new phase (see Figure 8–6). These phase changes can only happen at certain fixed temperatures for each type of material. Table 6 lists some examples of temperatures at which phase changes occur.

Notice that the melting point and the freezing point are usually the same. The boiling point and the condensation point are also usually the same.

Figure 8–6. Energy and phase changes.

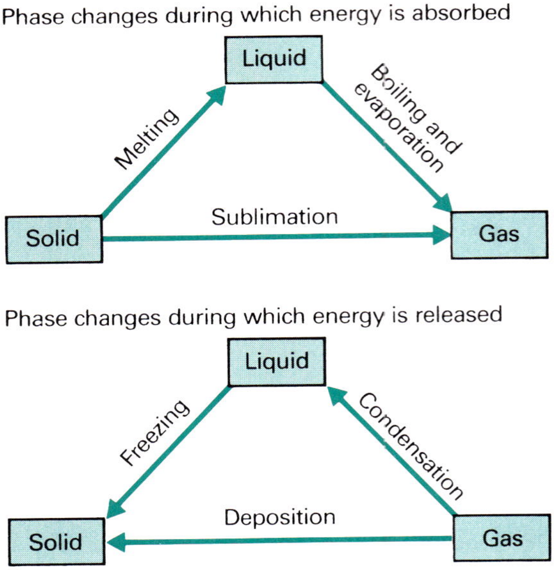

Table 5 Six Possible Phase Changes

Change of Phase	Term Used to Describe Change	Examples
Solid to liquid	Melting	Ice melts to water
Liquid to solid	Freezing	Water freezes to ice
Liquid to gas	Boiling; evaporation	Water boils to steam
Gas to liquid	Condensation	Steam condenses to water
Solid to gas	Sublimation	Solid carbon dioxide ("dry ice") sublimes to a gas without melting
Gas to solid	Deposition	When cooled, iodine gas deposits directly as iodine crystals

Table 6 Temperatures of Phase Changes

Type of Change	Occurs at	For Water	For Iron	For Oxygen
Solid to liquid	Melting point	0°C	1535°C	−218°C
Liquid to solid	Freezing point	0°C	1535°C	−218°C
Liquid to gas	Boiling point	100°C	3000°C	−183°C
Gas to liquid	Condensation point	100°C	3000°C	−183°C

Sample Questions

1. Which of the following materials is considered to be matter?
   (1) electricity
   (2) light
   (3) heat
   (4) air

2. All substances have
   (1) good solubility in water
   (2) densities of 1 g/cm^3 or larger
   (3) strong chemical activity
   (4) unique physical properties

3. Which physical property is *not* true for copper metal?
   (1) has orange-brown color
   (2) is usually in solid phase
   (3) dissolves well in water
   (4) conducts electricity well

4. Material *X* has these physical characteristics: gas; boiling point of −196°C; colorless; no odor. Material *X* might be
   (1) nitrogen
   (2) chlorine
   (3) alcohol
   (4) glass

5. To date, how many elements are known to exist?
   (1) 3
   (2) 96
   (3) 106
   (4) millions

6. How many elements occur commonly on Earth?
   (1) 3
   (2) less than 53
   (3) 96
   (4) 106

7. Iron is an element with the symbol
   (1) I (2) Ir (3) In (4) Fe

8. Every material must contain
   (1) just one element
   (2) at least one element
   (3) at least two elements
   (4) more than two elements

9. At extremely high temperatures, matter can exist in an unusual phase called "plasma." Including plasma, how many phases are possible?
   (1) 107 (2) 2 (3) 3 (4) 4

10. Below are diagrams of the smallest parts of four materials. Which material is the element?

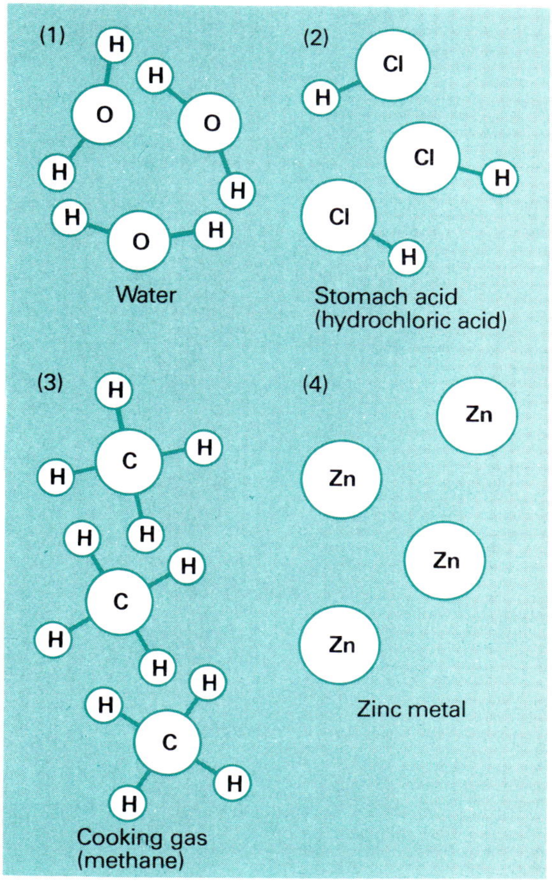

11. The diagram below shows the atom arrangement of methane (cooking gas). Where is the chemical energy of the methane stored?

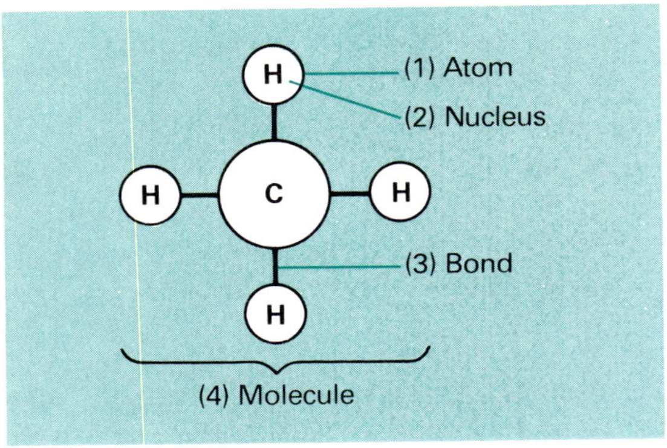

(1) in each atom
(2) in the nucleus (middle) of each atom
(3) in the bonds between atoms
(4) in the motion of the entire molecule

12. In which change is energy absorbed? (In other words, which change requires energy in order to occur?)

(1) Solid to liquid (melting)

(2) Liquid to solid (freezing)

(3) Gas to liquid (condensation)

(4) Gas to solid (deposition)

13. Which phase has both characteristics listed below?
A. Has a definite shape and size.
B. The particles have little freedom to move and little speed.
(1) solid (3) gas
(2) liquid (4) plasma

14. A certain chemical melts at 50°C. What is also true of this chemical?
(1) It freezes at 50°C.
(2) It boils at 50°C.
(3) It condenses at 50°C.
(4) It boils at 100°C.

15. What phase change occurs as water boils?

(1) solid to liquid
(2) solid to gas
(3) liquid to gas
(4) gas to solid

16. A steam burn is even more harmful than a burn from boiling water. This is true because
(1) steam condenses at a temperature greater than 100°C
(2) steam releases energy as it condenses
(3) steam absorbs energy as it condenses
(4) water (at 100°C) has more energy than steam (also at 100°C)

III. CHEMICAL CHANGES

1. Physical and Chemical Changes *(H20, H21, H22)*

Matter can be changed in two ways—physically or chemically. In **physical changes** the *look* of the matter changes, but no new material is made. However, in **chemical changes** the old material disappears and new materials are made.

Examples of Physical Changes Water can change to ice or steam. However, ice and steam are water. The water still remains, even though it looks different. A phase change has occurred. Nothing new was created.

When sugar is mixed with water, it **dissolves** and seems to disappear. However the original water and sugar are still unchanged in the solution. No new material has been produced. If this sugar solution is allowed to evaporate, the original sugar will be left behind unchanged.

No matter how many times a piece of paper is torn or shredded, it still remains paper. If a rock is hammered and crushed into powder, the powdered material is the same stuff that was in the rock. Only its form has changed. Grinding, tearing, and breaking are physical changes.

Examples of Chemical Changes If paper, wood, or sugar are set on fire the original material no longer remains. New materials—smoke, water vapor, ashes, and carbon soot—are produced. These are definitely different from the original material. Burning is a chemical change.

When an iron nail rusts, some of the iron joins with oxygen from the air to make a new material, rust. The same occurs when coal (which is carbon) burns. It combines with oxygen to make a new material, carbon dioxide gas.

If chalk or marble is mixed with a strong acid, it is destroyed. Carbon dioxide gas bubbles out and new materials are formed and left in the acid. When electricity is passed through water, the water is broken apart into its two elements, hydrogen gas and oxygen gas. When new materials form, a chemical change has occurred.

The new materials produced during a chemical change have their own properties. The properties of the original materials can no longer be detected, since the original materials no longer exist. A clear illustration of this occurs when a piece of sodium metal is allowed to react with chlorine gas in a jar (Figure 8–7). Both sodium and chlorine are toxic. The chemical they produce, however, is common table salt.

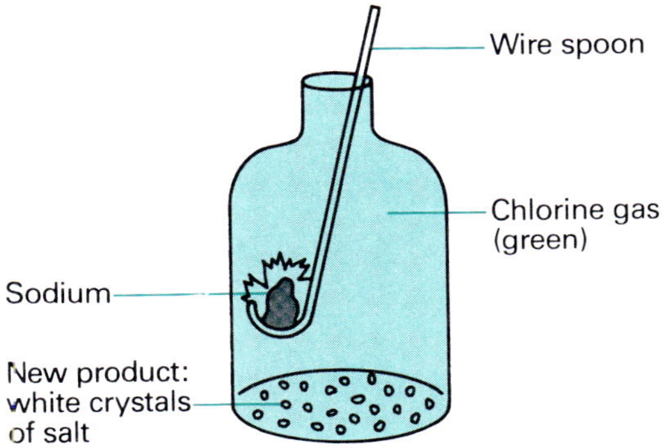

Figure 8–7. Sodium reacting with chlorine gas.

2. Energy and Chemical Changes *(H23, H24)*

A few chemical changes can start by themselves without the addition of energy. For example, as soon as an Alka Seltzer tablet is put into water a reaction occurs that adds gas bubbles and medicine to the water. When it is exposed to air, phosphorus immediately starts to smoke, producing a new material. However, most chemical changes need a little energy to get them started. For example, a piece of wood will burn on its own, but the fire must be first started with a flame. Some chemical changes will not begin until some heat energy, electrical energy, or light energy has been added. The explosion of gasoline in a car engine must be triggered by a spark of electrical energy.

Once a chemical change begins, energy may still be required to keep it going. Or, energy may be released by the reaction.

Chemical Changes That Release Energy

Burning: Energy released as both heat and light

Batteries: Energy released as electrical energy

Fireflies: Energy of chemical reactions in their bodies is released as light

Chemical Changes That Absorb Energy

Cooking: Heat energy is needed; it is absorbed by the food

Photosynthesis: Light energy is absorbed to keep this chemical reaction going in green plants

3. Influencing the Rate of Reactions *(H25, 26)*

The **rate** of a chemical reaction, or its speed, usually increases as the temperature increases. For example, food that is cooked in a pressure-cooker experiences higher than usual temperatures, and so it cooks faster. A usual rule of chemistry is that the rate of a chemical change doubles for each 10°C increase in temperature. If a potato requires 30 minutes of cooking at 100°C, it will need only 15 minutes of cooking at 110°C, because the speed of chemical change is doubled.

Another way to speed up a chemical change is to make the particles of a material smaller. A piece of iron and a lump of sulfur held together will hardly react at all. But if powdered sulfur and specks of iron are mixed, they can be made to react very quickly. A lump of coal or a grain of wheat burns very slowly. But coal dust or wheat powder tossed into a fire will burn so quickly it may explode. Breaking substances into smaller particles allows more particles to meet and react, so the rate of chemical change increases.

Sample Questions

1. The main characteristic of chemical changes is that they
(1) release energy
(2) absorb energy
(3) produce new phases
(4) produce new materials

2. Which one of the following is a chemical change?
(1) phase change
(2) burning
(3) dissolving
(4) crushing

3. Lightning often strikes a tree and sets it burning. What energy facts are illustrated about wood in this situation?
(1) Wood starts burning on its own, and then releases energy.
(2) Wood starts burning on its own, and then absorbs energy.
(3) Wood starts burning with added energy, and then releases energy.
(4) Wood starts burning with added energy, and then continues to absorb energy.

4. Element *X* is white; element *Y* is black. When they combine, what is true of the product?
(1) It must be black.
(2) It must be white.
(3) It must be gray.
(4) It could be red.

5. Element *A* is solid; element *B* is a gas. When they combine, what is true of the product?
(1) It must be a solid.
(2) It must be a liquid.
(3) It must be a gas.
(4) It may be a gas, liquid, or solid.

6. Hydrogen gas and oxygen gas can be mixed in a bottle safely. No reaction will occur. However, a tiny spark or flame will make them combine with violent speed and energy. These facts illustrate that some chemical changes
(1) release energy immediately
(2) absorb energy immediately
(3) must be triggered with a little energy
(4) are difficult to start

7. Which form of zinc metal will react with the acid in the beaker below with the fastest rate? Each zinc sample has the same weight.

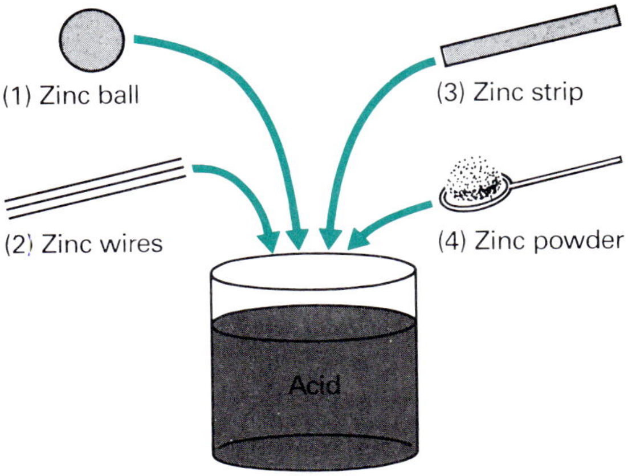

8. A student drops two identical pieces of magnesium into equal amounts of an acid. When magnesium dissolves in acid, it creates bubbles of hydrogen gas. The student changed the temperature of the second acid sample to see what effect temperature had on the speed of the reaction. Here are the results.

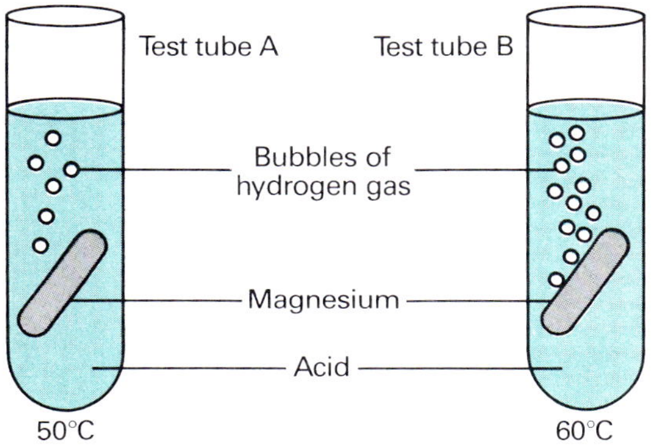

Data Table

Sample	Temperature of the Acid	Time for Magnesium to Fully Dissolve
Test tube A	50°C	40 seconds
Test tube B	60°C	?

What time is expected for test tube B?
(1) 20 seconds
(2) 30 seconds
(3) 40 seconds
(4) 80 seconds

9. Every so often newspapers report the explosion of a corn grain storage bin. The cause of this problem is probably that
(1) corn burns easily
(2) corn dust explodes from a small spark
(3) corn piles gradually get hotter as they are stored
(4) human error causes a fire to start

Issues in Science, Technology, and Society

Better Things Through Chemistry?

Much of the modern world is artificial. Many of the materials that surround us do not occur naturally, but are produced by chemistry. Plastics, nylon and rayon fabric, teflon, vitamins, low-calorie sweeteners, medicines, gasoline, film, paint, and computer chips are but a few materials made or purified by chemistry.

However, we have now come to learn that many such chemicals have harmful effects. When many plastics burn, they release a dangerous, choking gas, making fires even more dangerous. Older types of gasoline and paints had compounds of lead added to them. These lead chemicals have been found to be very poisonous, causing death or mental disabilities. Chemical accidents have caused thousands of deaths and have made millions ill. In the past, a chemical called PCB was used in electrical equipment. It has now been found in rivers, fish, and of course, humans. PCB can cause cancer. A medicine that used to be taken by women to prevent miscarriages (DES) was found to lead to deformed and crippled babies. Some people can even become ill from the chemicals used in certain medicines or added to food to keep it fresh.

INGREDIENTS: WHOLE OAT FLOUR, WHEAT STARCH, SUGAR, SALT, CALCIUM CARBONATE, TRISODIUM PHOSPHATE, VITAMIN C (SODIUM ASCORBATE), IRON (A MINERAL NUTRIENT), A B VITAMIN (NIACIN), VITAMIN A (PALMITATE), VITAMIN B_6 (PYRIDOXINE HYDROCHLORIDE), VITAMIN B_2 (RIBOFLAVIN), VITAMIN B_1 (THIAMIN MONONITRATE), VITAMIN B_{12}, AND VITAMIN D.
PEPPERMINT GUM INGREDIENTS: SORBITOL, GUM BASE, HYDROGENATED GLUCOSE SYRUP, GLYCERIN, NATURAL FLAVOR, SODIUM SACCHARIN (5.6 MG/SERVING).
BUBBLE GUM INGREDIENTS: SORBITOL, GUM BASE, MANNITOL, HYDROGENATED GLUCOSE SYRUP, GLYCERIN, ARTIFICIAL FLAVOR, ARTIFICIAL COLOR, SODIUM SACCHARIN (6.2 MG/SERVING).

A list of ingredients and chemicals in a popular cereal that also had a "gift" of chewing gum inside.

Society has taken action to reduce and prevent these harmful effects of chemistry. New products or chemical processes require an *environmental impact statement* before being approved. Many government, business, and private "watchdog" groups check these statements carefully. Courts have permitted people to sue companies if they are hurt by products discovered to be dangerous. Therefore, chemical companies have become very careful about safety in their methods and products. Companies continually test their products for bad effects on people, animals, and the environment.

This illustrates several facts about science and technology.

- Everyone interacts with the products of science in some way.
- Every science product or process affects the environment in some way.
- Every science or technology product has advantages and disadvantages and provides *benefits and burdens* for people and the environment.
- All products must be examined for short-term and long-term benefits or bad effects.

1. Examine the labels of some food boxes and cans and identify chemicals that have been added to the natural ingredients.
2. Give two examples of modern products or devices that have helped and hurt people or the environment. (Newspaper or magazine articles might be helpful in answering this question.)
3. Is it possible to live today and not interact with any products of science and technology? What would such a life be like?

CHAPTER 9 Energy: Sources and Issues

I. THE NEED FOR ENERGY AND FOSSIL FUELS

1. Energy Sources in Modern Life

The United States today uses energy from three major sources:

1. Fossil fuels, such as coal, oil, and natural gas
2. Moving water, flowing in a stream or through a dam
3. Uranium fuel

In addition to these, many minor sources of energy are used in certain places or are being developed. These include:

4. Burning of trees, plant matter, and animal waste
5. Ocean tides
6. The wind
7. Heat energy trapped inside Earth (geothermal)
8. Sunlight
9. Hydrogen in fusion nuclear reactors

Notice that electricity is not on this list. Electricity is an excellent way of transferring and using energy, but electricity is not a source of energy. Electricity must be made from the *sources* of energy listed.

2. Measuring Energy: Calories and Watts *(I1, I2)*

In order to talk about energy, scientists and the public must be able to measure it. One unit used to measure energy is the **calorie**. Calories are used to measure heat energy and to compare the amount of heat energy in food and fuels. A single calorie is a rather small amount of heat energy. As shown in Figure 9–1, one calorie causes 1 gram of water to increase in temperature only 1°C.

When referring to food energy, the word *Calories* is usually spelled with a capital "C." A food-Calorie is 1000 times bigger than an ordinary calorie. One food-Calorie is actually 1 *kilo*calorie.

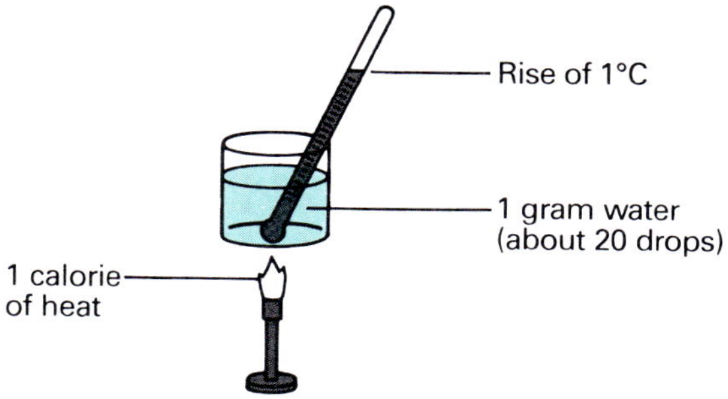

Figure 9–1. Measuring 1 calorie of energy.

Table 1 Energy Required

Action	Energy Needed
Warming 1 g of water by 1°C	1 calorie
Lifting a 1-kg weight up 1 meter	2.3 calories
Walking up stairs	1000 calories
Using a toaster for 1 minute	17,000 calories
Using a 60-watt bulb for 1 hr	51,000 calories
Warming 1 kg of water (a liter) from 0°C to 100°C	100,000 calories
Daily adult requirement	*1,000,000–2,000,000 calories

*Equal to 1000–2000 food-Calories or kilocalories

Table 2 Energy Available

Energy Source		Energy Released
Fuels	Wood	4200 calories per gram
	Coal, alcohol	8000 calories per gram
	Heating oil	10,000 calories per gram
	Gasoline	12,000 calories per gram (10,000,000 cal. per liter)
	Natural gas	14,000 calories per gram (250,000 calories per cubic foot)
Foods	Sugar	**4000 calories per gram (16,000 cal. per teaspoon)
	Cereal	**4000 calories per gram (110,000 cal. per 1-ounce serving)
	Butter	**6000 calories per gram (70,000 cal. in a 1 × 1 × ¼-inch pat)
	Fat	**10,000 calories per gram (280,000 cal. per tablespoon)

Table 1 compares the amounts of energy required for certain actions. Table 2 compares the amounts of energy released by some fuels and foods.

Another unit used to measure energy is the **watt**. Actually, the watt measures the *rate of energy being used*, not merely the amount of energy used. Watts are used to measure and compare how much energy *per second* is used by electrical devices. Table 3 shows the number of watts used by some common household electrical devices.

Table 3 Energy Used by Electrical Devices

Electrical Device	Energy Needed
Flashlight bulb	3 watts
Household light bulbs	25–150 watts
Toaster, television	1200 watts
Air conditioner	1700 watts
Electric heater	up to 2000 watts

3. We Want Energy . . . More Energy *(I3)*

Every year for the past hundreds of years people have increased their demands for energy. As a result, there is a need to find new and better sources of energy. There are several reasons why the need for energy keeps increasing.

Labor-saving Devices Modern lifestyles require machines to a great extent. People use labor-saving devices to do many ordi-

**Divide these values by 1000 to obtain values in food-Calories. Thus, one teaspoon of sugar contains 16,000 calories or 16 food-Calories.

nary tasks. We ride in cars, trains, and planes. Gone are the days of riding horses or walking great distances. People prefer to lift things with motors instead of pulling them up by hand using pulleys. Even food is whipped, ground, and mixed by electrical blenders instead of by hand. All these devices make modern life easier, but they require large amounts of energy.

Luxuries People use many electrical devices for pleasure or convenience. These devices, such as electric blankets, televisions, air conditioners, elevators, stereos, microwave ovens, and amusement park rides, require energy.

Developing Nations Many nations are progressing toward modern life. These developing nations need energy to improve their industries and their home life.

Increasing Population The world population is increasing, increasing the need for energy (see Figure 9–2).

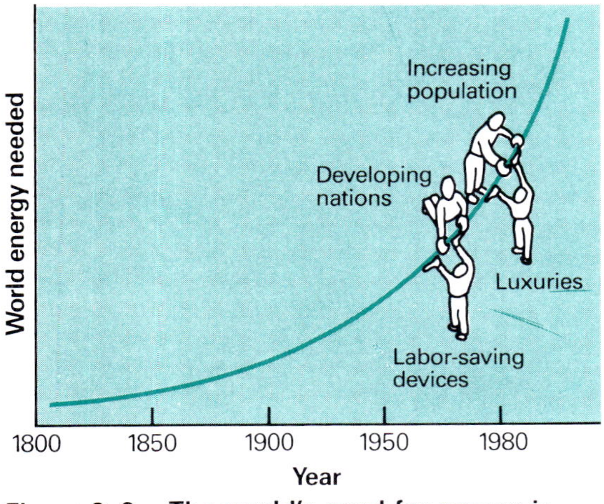

Figure 9–2. The world's need for energy is constantly increasing.

4. Fossil Fuels *(I4, I5, I6, I7, I8, I13, I14)*

There have been plants and animals on Earth for millions of years. When organisms die, their remains disintegrate and decompose into energy-rich materials. Over millions of years, fuels are formed from these materials. Since the fuels originally came from living things, they are called **fossil fuels**. There are three fossil fuels used widely in the United States:

1. coal,
2. oil or petroleum, and
3. natural gas.

Coal is a hard, black, shiny rock made of almost pure carbon. It releases much heat energy as it burns. Coal is used mainly to produce electricity. It is also used to heat homes and to provide energy for industry.

Oil is a thick, black liquid that is a mixture of many materials. These materials are separated from one another in a process known as **fractional distillation**. The oil is boiled and then its vapors are condensed at different temperatures. Gasoline and home heating fuel are two important products that are distilled from oil. Fertilizers, plastics, and some medicines are also made from materials found in oil. Oil contains so many useful things (Figure 9–3) that it is sometimes called "black gold."

Natural gas is taken out of the ground, where it is trapped in rock layers. It is used in homes for heating and cooking and is also used in industry. Natural gas is popular

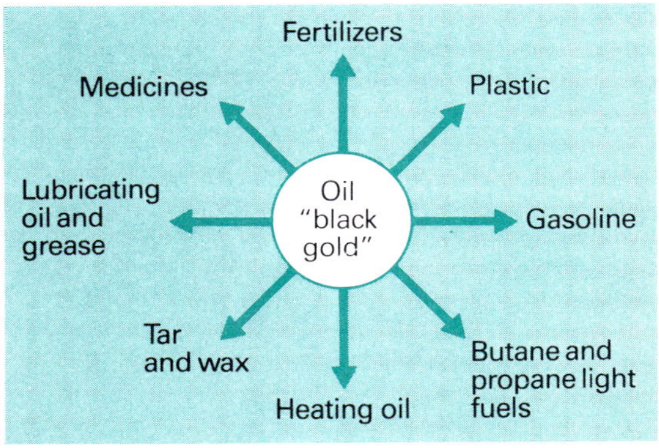

Figure 9–3. Many products are derived from oil.

for home use because it heats easily, quickly, and cleanly. Pure natural gas as it comes from the ground has little odor. A special ingredient is added to it to provide a strong odor so people can detect gas leaks. If there is a strong odor of gas, turn off the gas stove or main gas valve immediately and open a window. Do *not* light a match or create sparks, by using a kitchen appliance, until the smell of gas is gone.

Most of the energy used in the United States today comes from these three fossil fuels. The underground reserves of coal in the United States are much greater than the reserves of oil and natural gas. At this time, however, it is cheaper for the United States to import oil from foreign countries than it is to mine, clean, and use our vast coal reserves. In the future this might not be true.

Science Skill

INTERPRETING GRAPHS

At the right are two graphs—a circle graph ("pie graph") and a bar graph—that show the same data in different ways. Study the graphs and then answer the questions that follow.

1. Which fuel contributes the most energy to the United States?
   (1) coal (3) oil
   (2) nuclear energy (4) natural gas
2. What percentage of the energy used in the United States is provided by natural gas?
   (1) 5% (2) 25% (3) 2% (4) 2.5%
3. What percentage of the energy used in the United States is provided by all the fossil fuels combined?
   (1) 2% (2) 10% (3) 45% (4) 90%
4. What *fraction* of the energy comes from moving water?
   (1) $\frac{1}{20}$ (2) $\frac{1}{4}$ (3) $\frac{1}{5}$ (4) $\frac{9}{10}$
5. Wind energy is one of the "other" sources of energy. What percentage of the energy comes from wind energy?
   (1) between 3–10%
   (2) between 2–3%
   (3) 2%
   (4) less than 2%

Sources of U.S. Energy

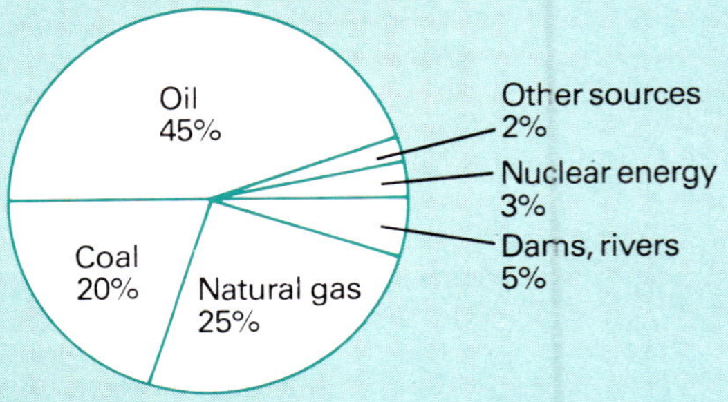

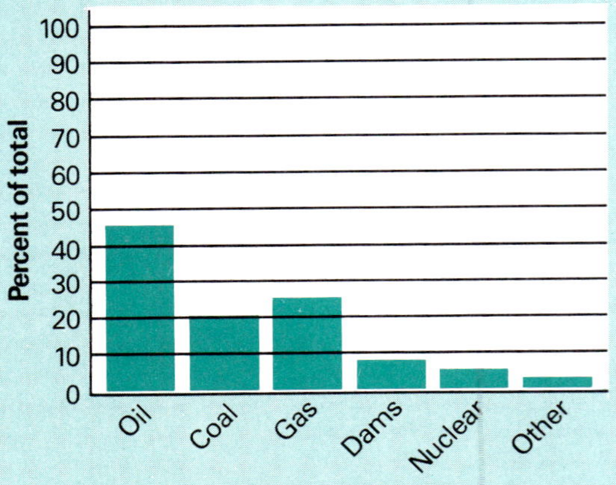

U.S. Energy Sources

Sample Questions

1. Which one of the following pairs of units is used to measure energy?
(1) pounds and kilograms
(2) feet and meters
(3) pounds per square inch and newtons per square meter
(4) calories and watts

2. Which one of the following is not yet a major energy source for the United States?
(1) wind power
(2) fossil fuels
(3) uranium
(4) moving water

3. Which one of the following is not a *source* of energy, but a *product*?
(1) electricity
(2) uranium
(3) fossil fuels
(4) moving water

4. Which graph shows how the need for energy has changed during the past 100 years?

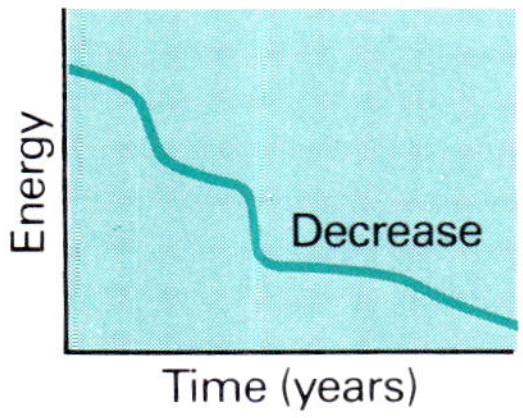

(1)

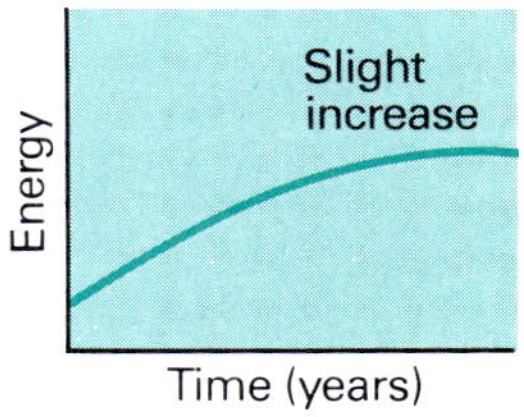

(2)

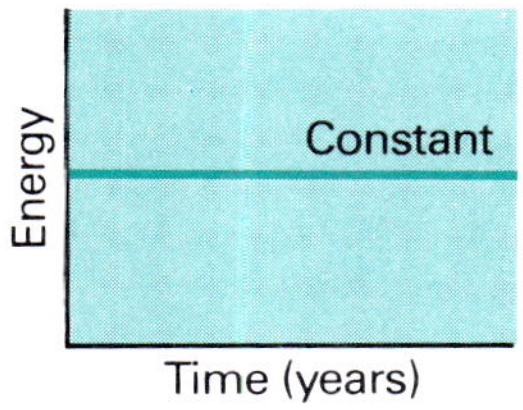

(3)

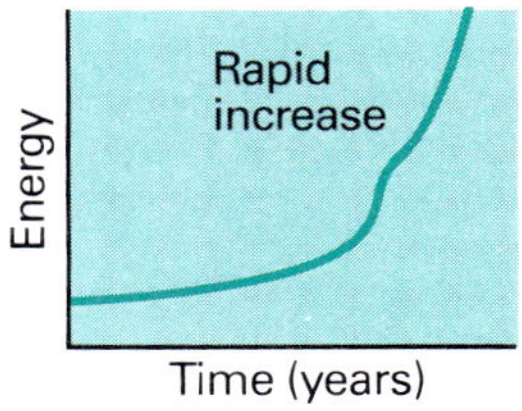

(4)

5. As the demand for energy increases, the need for sources of energy
(1) increases
(2) decreases
(3) remains the same

6. One calorie of heat energy is added to one gram of water at 10°C. What will be the new temperature of the water?
(1) 1°C
(2) 2°C
(3) 9°C
(4) 11°C

7. Two grams of water were heated from 20°C to 21°C. How many calories of heat were needed?
(1) 1 calorie
(2) 2 calories
(3) 40 calories
(4) 42 calories

8. Which electrical device uses the greatest number of watts?
(1) a toaster
(2) a light bulb
(3) an air conditioner
(4) a flashlight

9. Which food provides the most calories per gram?
(1) sugar
(2) cereal
(3) butter
(4) fat

10. Which one is *not* a fossil fuel?
(1) solar energy
(2) oil
(3) natural gas
(4) coal

11. A piece of candy is marked "250 Calories." This means it contains
(1) 250 ordinary calories
(2) 250,000 ordinary calories
(3) 250,000 food-Calories
(4) 0.250 kilocalories

12. Fossil fuels come from
(1) living plants and animals
(2) remains of dead plants and animals
(3) the splitting of atoms
(4) ancient rocks

13. What material is the source of the products shown below?

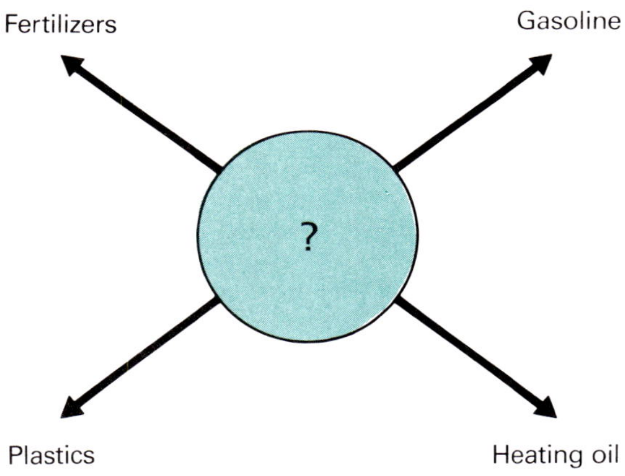

(1) natural gas
(2) coal
(3) oil
(4) plant matter

14. Which material is used mainly to produce electricity?
(1) coal
(2) oil
(3) natural gas
(4) plant matter

15. Of which fuel does the United States have the greatest supply?
(1) coal (3) natural gas
(2) oil (4) plant matter

16. Which fuel does the United States import from foreign countries?
(1) coal (3) natural gas
(2) oil (4) uranium

17. Oil is often shipped in barrels. Below is a diagram illustrating a barrel of oil.

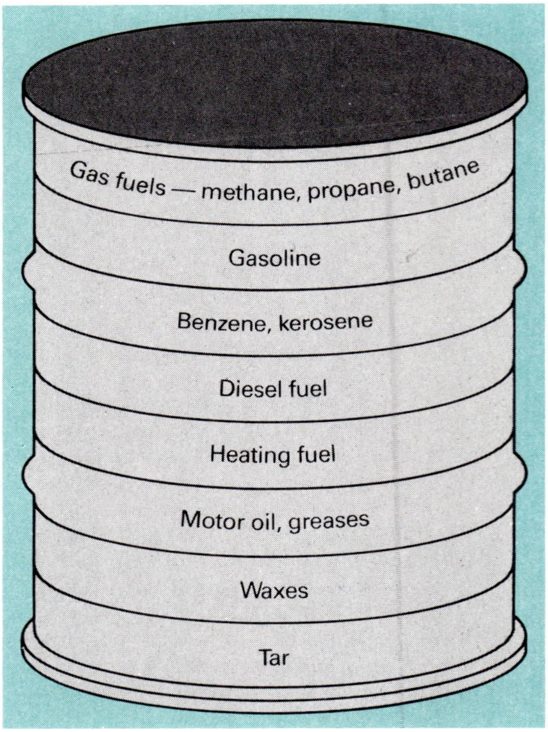

A good title for this diagram might be:
(1) The Many Sources of Oil
(2) The Industries that Use Oil
(3) How Oil Is Shipped
(4) The Materials Within Oil

II. ELECTRICAL ENERGY

1. Moving Water—A Source of Energy *(19)*

As water moves, it carries a lot of kinetic energy. Huge **generators** transform this kinetic energy into electrical energy. A river may flow fast enough to do this task, but usually water is first made to pile up behind large dams. The water is then directed by means of large pipes to flow down to generators located next to the dam (Figure 9–4).

New York State is fortunate to obtain a large portion of its electricity from generators near Niagara Falls. Other states, such as Connecticut and Colorado, put dams along their rivers. The giant Hoover Dam in Nevada is a well-known dam used to provide electricity.

Moving water generates electricity by forcing a turbine—similar to a paddle wheel—to turn. The spinning turbine causes a shaft with a large coil of wires to turn within an electromagnet. As this coil of wires turns in the magnet, electricity is produced (see Figure 9–5).

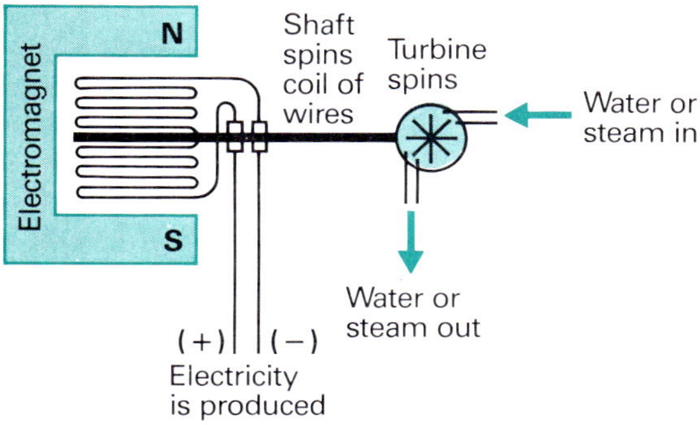

Figure 9–5. How a generator works.

The energy transfer taking place is:

KINETIC ENERGY (in moving water)	→	ELECTRICAL ENERGY (from generator)

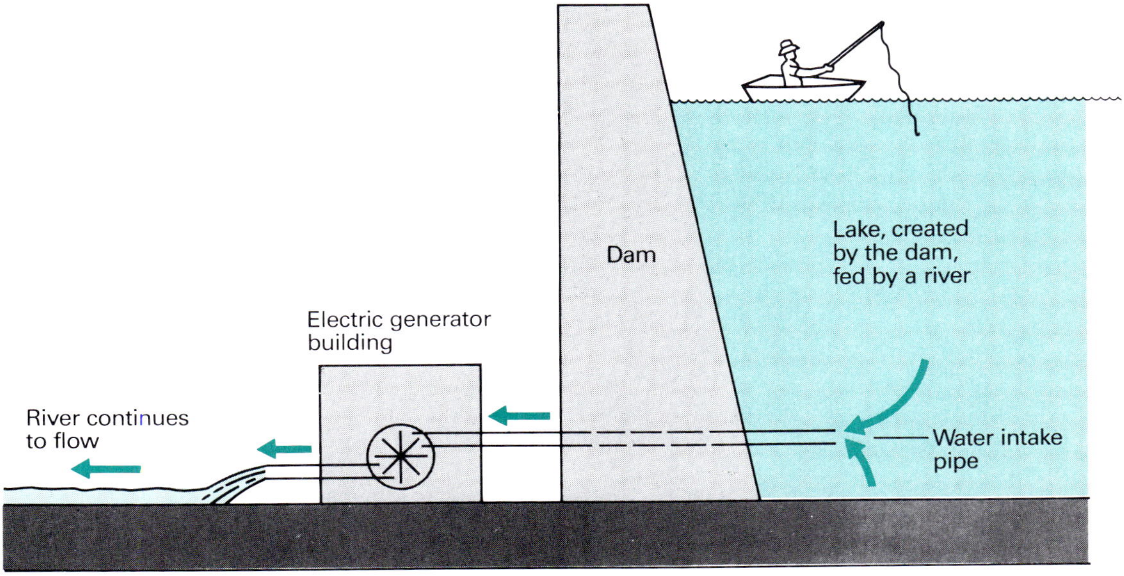

Figure 9–4. The operation of a dam.

2. Electricity Is Essential to Modern Society (I11, I12)

Electricity is everywhere in our lives. It is used to heat and cool buildings, to run machines and appliances, and to provide lighting. Electricity is a clean form of energy. It is easily transmitted through conductors, such as wires made of copper, aluminum, and silver. Through various electrical devices, it can be made to perform a wide variety of tasks.

However, electricity is not itself a source of energy. It must be produced from moving water, fossil fuels, or uranium in nuclear reactors. These sources of energy turn the generators that make the electricity. Without these energy sources, generators would stop and there would be no flow of electricity.

3. Nuclear Energy (I10)

Uranium is the fuel used in nuclear reactors. The nucleus of the uranium atom is unstable. It breaks apart and releases tremendous amounts of heat energy (Figure 9–6). In fact, this release of energy is the same event that occurs in an atomic bomb.

The release of energy from the nucleus is the basis of **nuclear energy**. It is called *nuclear* because the energy is released from the nucleus (the center) of uranium atoms.

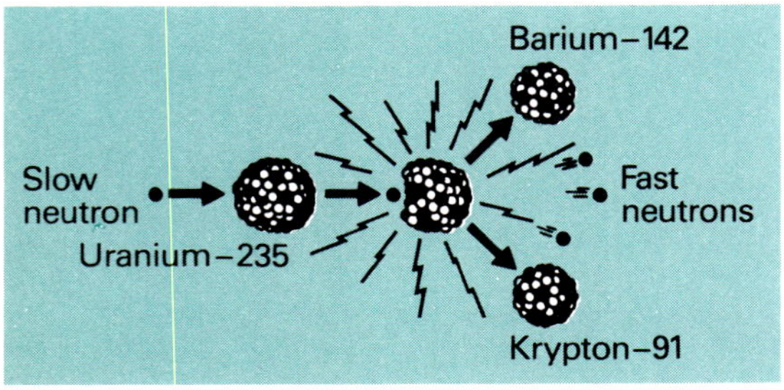

Figure 9–6. When a uranium atom is split, energy is released.

In a nuclear reactor, the heat released from uranium atoms is used to boil water. The water is changed into fast-moving, high-pressure, high-temperature steam. This steam turns turbines to make electricity (Figure 9–7), just as fossil fuels provide energy to turn turbines.

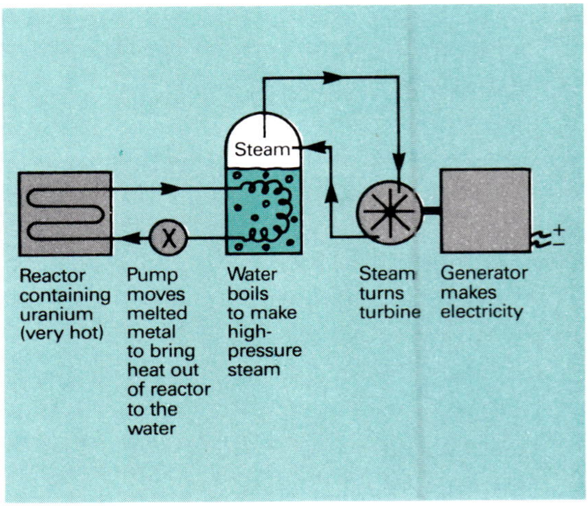

Figure 9–7. The operation of a nuclear reactor.

The energy transformations that occur in a nuclear reactor are:

NUCLEAR ENERGY
(in uranium)
↓
HEAT ENERGY
(boils water)
↓
KINETIC ENERGY
(in steam)
↓
ELECTRICAL ENERGY
(from steam turning turbine)

Science Skill

MEASURING; INTERPRETING

Electric meters tell how much energy has been used by a home or business. They measure electricity in **kilowatt-hours** of energy. Below is a typical set of meter dials. To obtain the correct reading, read the digit toward which the marker points or the last digit it passed.

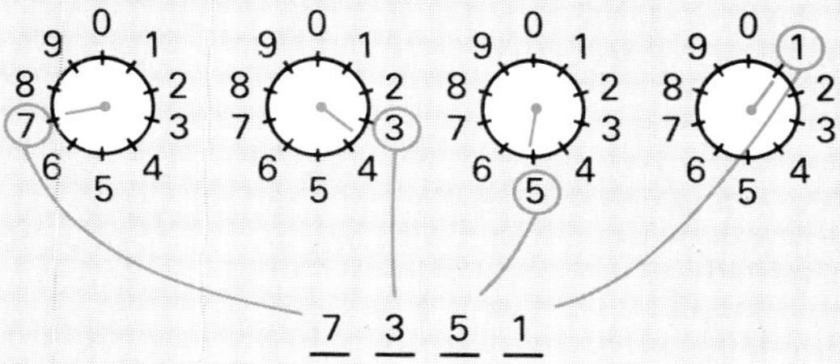

In the example shown, the reading is 7351 kilowatt-hours.

A local electric company uses meter readings to calculate electric bills. Read the meters above at the right and then answer the questions.

On July 1

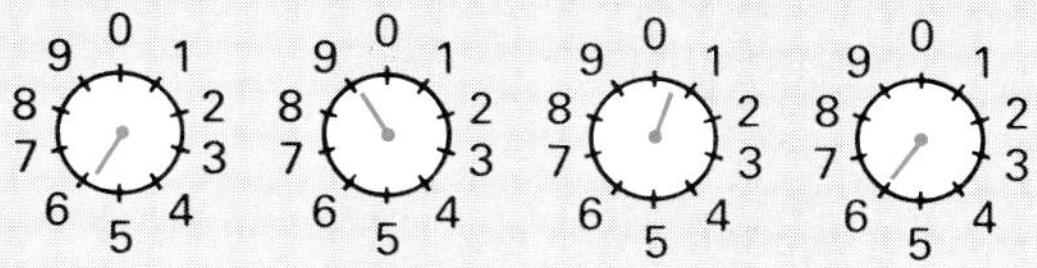

On August 1

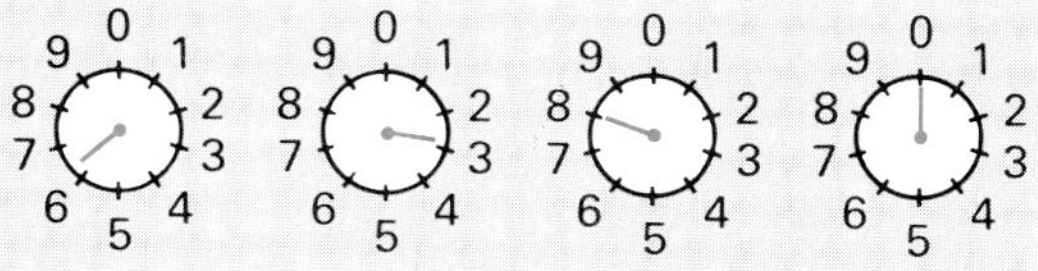

1. What was the reading on July 1?
   (1) 6906 (3) 5906
   (2) 6916 (4) 5916

2. What was the reading on August 1?
   (1) 6380 (3) 7380
   (2) 6280 (4) 7280

3. How many kilowatt-hours of electric energy were used during the month of July? (Subtract the two readings.)
   (1) 1474 (2) 274 (3) 464 (4) 374

4. If the cost of electricity is $0.17 for each kilowatt-hour, what will be the charge for the electricity used during July? (Multiply your answer to question 3 by $0.17.)
   (1) $635.80 (3) $63.58
   (2) $250.58 (4) $46.58

Sample Questions

1. In making electricity, the energy source is used to
(1) provide the needed electrons
(2) turn a turbine
(3) create sparks
(4) conduct the electrical energy

2. The word *nuclear* in nuclear energy indicates that the energy comes from
(1) powerful explosions
(2) chemical reactions
(3) the center of the atoms
(4) radiation

3. The main function of a dam in producing electricity is to
   (1) form a lake for recreation
   (2) prevent flooding after heavy rain
   (3) provide continuous fast-moving water
   (4) create thermoelectric conversion from solar warming

4. Which equation summarizes how moving water and wind produce electricity?
   (1) thermal energy → electrical energy
   (2) electrical energy → magnetic energy
   (3) electrical energy → kinetic energy
   (4) kinetic energy → electrical energy

5. The diagram below shows the steps used in making electricity in a nuclear reactor.

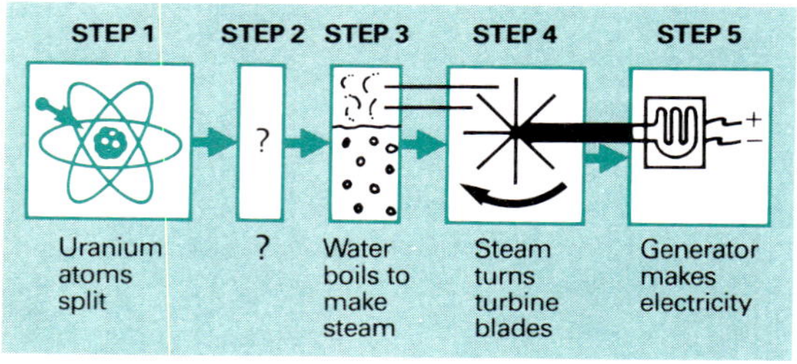

Which is the best description for Step 2?
   (1) Atoms fuse.
   (2) An explosion results.
   (3) Radiation is released.
   (4) Heat is released.

6. Which material is the conductor in ordinary home wires?
   (1) copper (3) plastic
   (2) rubber (4) gold

7. The purpose of fossil fuels in the making of electricity is
   (1) to store electrical energy
   (2) to release electrical energy
   (3) to make steam that turns a turbine
   (4) to make heat that is converted to electricity by thermocouples

8. The fuel used in nuclear reactors is
   (1) oil
   (2) uranium
   (3) coal
   (4) nuclear particles

9. Which statement about electricity is *not* true?
   (1) It is a source of energy.
   (2) It is transmitted by conductors.
   (3) It is essential to modern life.
   (4) It can perform many different tasks.

III. PROBLEMS AND ISSUES OF ENERGY

1. Environmental Pollution

(I15, I16, I17, I18, I19)

Energy sources can bring tremendous social benefits, but they also bring environmental problems. Chief among these problems are air pollution, land pollution, water pollution, thermal pollution, and nuclear energy hazards.

Air Pollution The burning of fossil fuels—coal, oil, natural gas—contributes to **air pollution**. All fossil fuels produce carbon dioxide gas when they are burned. Carbon dioxide gas is not directly harmful to humans and it is used by plants and trees. However, there is evidence of indirect harm. Increased levels of carbon dioxide in the atmosphere are making planet Earth warmer by a few degrees. This warming could eventually cause the ice caps to melt, flooding coastal cities worldwide. The danger is distant but real.

Fossil fuels also present a more immediate air pollution threat. They produce gases such as nitrogen oxides and sulfur dioxide when burned. These gases are irritants to the eyes, lungs, and skin. They also harm trees by making the rain slightly acid. Coal is the biggest culprit in producing these pollutant gases. Coal is far more abundant in the United States than oil. It is not used as much as oil, however, partly because it contributes to air pollution. Scientists are trying to learn how to "clean" the coal of unwanted materials so it will not present problems in the future.

Land Pollution Coal presents still another problem: **land pollution**. Beautiful and productive areas of land must be bulldozed and dug up deeply to obtain the coal. This process is called **mining**. After an area is mined it is left ugly and useless for many years.

The ecology of an area may be changed when dams, pipelines, and electric power lines must be built. Animals and trees may be harmed or eliminated.

Water Pollution Oil and natural gas are trapped underground and are obtained by drilling. During drilling, many spills occur. The problem has worsened since oil companies have begun drilling from offshore platforms. When accidents and oil spills occur, fish and shellfish are harmed and beaches are damaged. In addition, the transportion of oil and natural gas by pipelines and ships has resulted in serious accidents and pollution.

Thermal Pollution **Thermal pollution** occurs when river water is used to cool parts of a reactor or generator. The warmed water is pumped back to the river and raises its temperature. Even a slight temperature increase can trigger changes in the plant and fish life in the river.

Nuclear Energy Hazards Nuclear reactors produce extremely dangerous radioactive waste products. If released into the environment, these wastes could harm or kill millions of people and other living things. These waste materials must regularly be removed, shipped, and buried. Since they remain dangerous for hundreds of years, the dump sites must be guarded. It's no surprise that many communities have voiced resistance (and filed lawsuits) regarding storage and transport of nuclear waste.

2. Conservation *(120)*

Conservation is the saving of natural resources by wise usage. Conservation involves *reducing any waste* of energy. For example, lights should be turned off when they are not being used. Homes should be insulated to reduce the amount of heat lost in the winter. Even wearing warmer clothing in the winter is conservation, since the room temperature can be kept slightly lower. In the summer, conservation means using air conditioning less and fans more. Used bottles and cans can be recycled to make new bottles and cans. Recycling is a form of conservation, since much less energy and materials are needed to recycle containers than to produce new containers.

Conservation also means *improving efficiency*. Industry is looking for new ways of getting more useful energy from fuel and reducing the amount wasted as heat. Car manufacturers have been improving the miles per gallon rating of their cars through new engine design, lighter materials, and streamlining the body shape to reduce wind drag. Inefficient cars get about 8–15 miles to the gallon on the open highway. Efficient cars can get 30 or even 40 miles to the gallon on the highway.

Science Skill

INTERPRETING DIAGRAMS

Below are two diagrams that show where energy is used. They show in picture form data that could be shown in tables or graphs. Using illustrations helps to make the data more interesting. Study the illustrations and then answer the following questions.

1. What percentage of oil is used to make gasoline for cars and trucks?
   (1) 14%
   (2) 40%
   (3) 15%
   (4) 10%

2. If the United States uses 650 million gallons of oil every day, how much is lost or used up during refining?
   (1) 650 gallons
   (2) 6.5 million gallons
   (3) 650,000 gallons
   (4) 65 million gallons

3. Which uses the greatest volume of oil products?
   (1) transportation
   (2) heating
   (3) electricity
   (4) chemical products

4. What is the major use for coal in the United States today?
   (1) electricity
   (2) export
   (3) industry
   (4) home use

5. What percentage of coal mined in the United States is used within the United States?
   (1) 10%
   (2) 64%
   (3) 26%
   (4) 90%

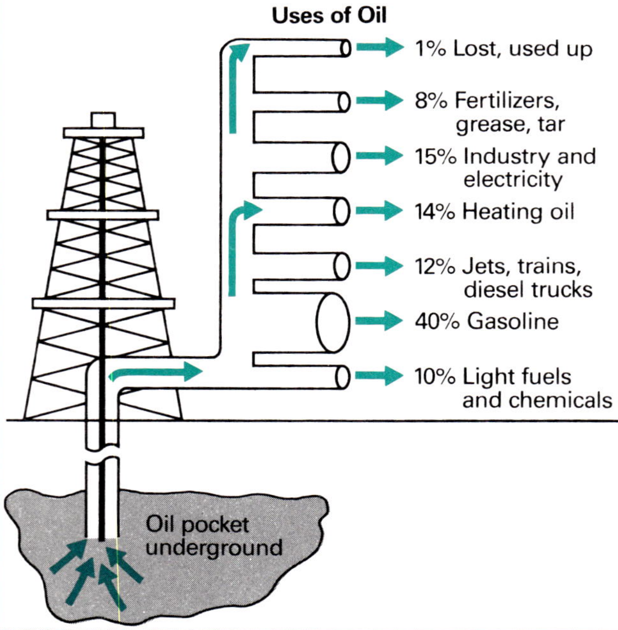

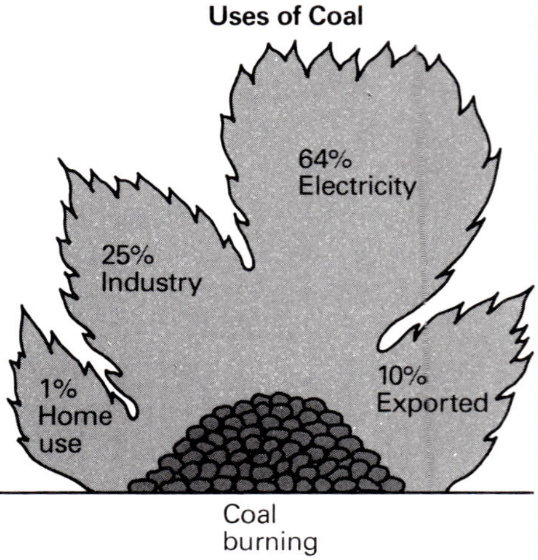

3. Renewable Resources

(I21, I22, I26, I27, I28)

Renewable resources are resources that are replaced ("renewed") by nature in a relatively short period of time. Moving water, wind, sunshine, and plants are examples of renewable sources of energy. Much research and public interest in the United States is focused on how to use more renewable sources of energy.

For example, plant matter and animal wastes can be burned to produce heat. They can also be converted into fuels, such as methane gas and "gasohol." People are performing experiments in order to design better wind generators. These new machines use large propellers to convert the wind's kinetic energy into electrical energy. But such machines sitting on mountaintops or in open fields are not attractive to look at. They also don't work when the wind is light. This illustrates a fact about any source of energy: there are advantages and disadvantages associated with its use.

Nonrenewable resources are those that are not being replaced. Fossil fuels and uranium are prime examples of nonrenewable resources. Once used, they're gone.

4. The Sun as an Energy Source *(I23, I24, I25)*

The sun is the primary source of all energy on Earth. Almost every source of energy can be traced back to the sun.

Plants and trees grow using the sun's energy during photosynthesis.

Fossil fuels come directly from plants, or indirectly from animals that ate plants. These ancient plants began the food chain by capturing the sun's energy through photosynthesis.

The wind is caused by the sun's heating effects on the atmosphere.

Moving water is caused by the processes of evaporation, condensation, and precipitation. The sun is responsible for the evaporation of water from oceans and the ground. The water vapor condenses and forms clouds. The clouds bring rain, which feed streams and rivers. Without the sun's energy, rivers and dams would be dry and unable to generate electricity.

The sun's energy can also be captured directly and used to provide heat and hot water for homes, offices, and factories (see Figure 9–8). Many people and businesses use solar heating systems to do just that.

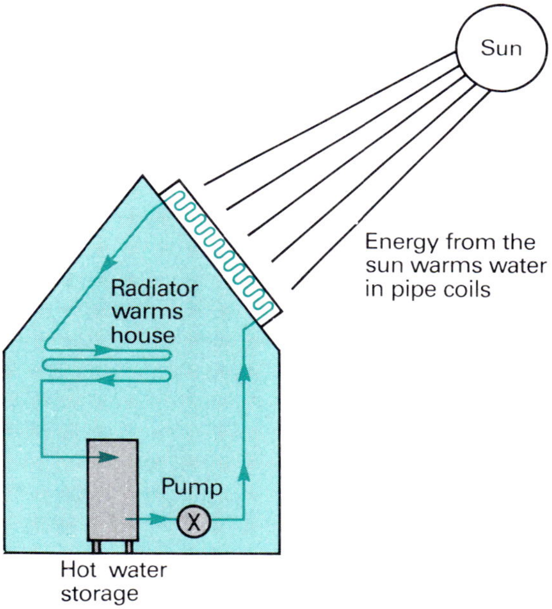

Figure 9–8. A home solar heating system.

Technology has also made it possible to convert solar energy (sunlight) directly into electricity with a solar cell. Solar cells are used to charge batteries for electric cars, to operate cameras and calculators, and to operate spacecraft. Someday people may put solar-cell panels on buildings and homes to supplement the electricity obtained from power companies.

Sample Questions

1. Energy sources always bring benefits and problems. The major environmental problems of energy are
   (1) pollution and hazards
   (2) high prices and shortages
   (3) easy living and waste
   (4) overuse and loss of resources

2. The burning of fossil fuels contributes mainly to
   (1) thermal pollution
   (2) radiation hazards
   (3) air pollution
   (4) land pollution

3. Water pollution is usually associated with finding and transporting
   (1) uranium
   (2) coal
   (3) oil
   (4) natural gas

4. Nuclear waste is
   (1) easy to get rid of
   (2) very dangerous
   (3) radioactive for a short time
   (4) no longer a controversial issue

5. What do the following energy sources—sunshine, plants, wind, and water—have in common?
   (1) They are major energy sources in the United States today.
   (2) They make better electricity than fossil fuels.
   (3) They are always available for use.
   (4) They are renewable.

6. The illustration below shows people carrying signs in a rally.

   Of what does this rally appear to be in favor?
   (1) world peace
   (2) equal rights
   (3) nuclear energy
   (4) energy conservation

7. Which one of the following indicates improved efficiency in newer cars?
   (1) increased miles per gallon
   (2) lower prices for the car
   (3) extra options
   (4) larger gas tank

8. The construction of dams, pipelines, and electric power lines can
   (1) harm animal and plant life in an area
   (2) make electricity too expensive
   (3) cause radiation to increase
   (4) improve energy efficiency

9. At different speeds a car uses its gasoline with different efficiencies. The graph below shows the miles per gallon that a car gets at different speeds.

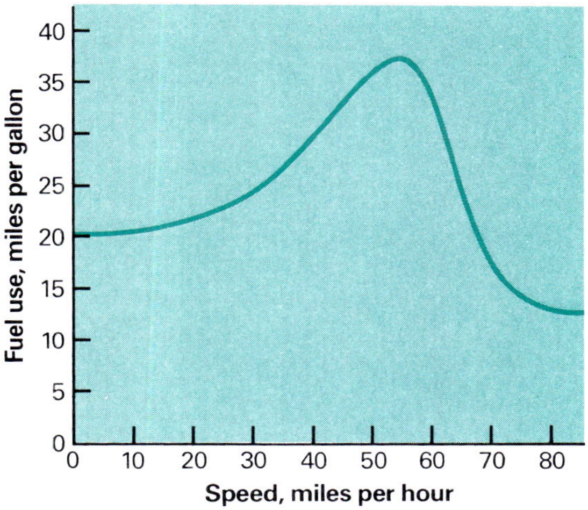

What speed is best for getting the best use of this car's fuel?
(1) 20 miles per hour
(2) 45 miles per hour
(3) 55 miles per hour
(4) 70 miles per hour

10. Which is a nonrenewable energy resource?
(1) wind
(2) sunshine
(3) moving water
(4) uranium

11. Almost every energy source in the world can be traced back to energy from
(1) radioactivity
(2) kinetic energy
(3) living or dead organisms
(4) the sun

12. Sunlight can be changed directly into electrical energy using a
(1) generator
(2) reactor
(3) solar heating system
(4) solar cell

13. New fuels, such as gasohol for cars, are being made from
(1) plant matter
(2) geothermal lava
(3) oil
(4) plutonium

14. Electricity can be generated using the ocean tides to turn turbines. Tides are a free, renewable source of energy. Unfortunately, the tides come and go at full speed only 50% of each day. Also, the construction of generators that use tidal power interrupts fish breeding in those areas.

The above information illustrates the fact that

(1) any energy source has advantages and disadvantages
(2) tidal energy is not useful
(3) the disadvantages of tidal energy outweigh its advantages
(4) renewable resources are not as good as nonrenewable resources

Nuclear Energy—Pros and Cons

Pro The proponents of nuclear energy see it as a source of endless and cheap energy. Just one kilogram of purified uranium fuel gives energy equal to more than 2.8 million kilograms of coal and more than 24,000 liters of oil. The United States has a rich supply of uranium ore, enough for hundreds of years to come. Therefore, nuclear energy can help the United States become "energy independent."

Some reactors produce the element plutonium as part of the waste materials. This plutonium can be removed, purified, and used as a fuel. The uranium fuel is thereby used twice! Reactors that produce plutonium are called *breeders,* since they breed more fuel. The efficiency of a nuclear reactor (about 35%) is a little better than fossil fuel generators for making electricity. So far, the safety record of nuclear reactors is better than fossil fuel generating plants. Besides, the entire nuclear industry is carefully monitored by the public and government agencies.

Con The opponents of nuclear energy emphasize its dangers and costs. A nuclear reactor operates at very high temperatures (several thousands of degrees Celsius) and at fast speeds. This combination almost guarantees that accidents will happen. Controlling the splitting of uranium atoms is a very complex process, which can easily fail. The explosive energy that would be released in an accident could kill thousands of people. Furthermore, the gases and other materials released during a nuclear accident could harm or eventually kill millions more due to radiation.

The waste products produced by a nuclear reactor must be removed every year or two. They are then transported and buried deep under the ground. During transportation there is added opportunity for spills and accidents. After operating for 30–40 years, the reactor must be torn down and sealed.

Because of the expense of uranium purification, safe design, and meeting complicated regulations, the cost of electricity from nuclear reactors is high. It will never be as cheap as safer fossil fuels. Nuclear energy is not worth the cost or the risk.

1. Prepare for a group debate or presentation on nuclear energy. Obtain additional materials to support your case. You may even wish to survey people on their attitudes about nuclear energy.
2. What is your opinion on nuclear energy? Which one argument is most convincing for you?

Pros	Cons
Fuel is inexpensive	Complicated design makes power plants expensive
The U.S. has an abundant supply of uranium ore	Nuclear power plants have the potential to kill many people in a nuclear accident
Mining uranium is much safer than mining coal	When the plant reaches the end of its useful life, it must be sealed for hundreds of years; this procedure is costly and carries the risk of nuclear problems far into the future
Nuclear power plants are more efficient than fossil fuel plants	Disposal of nuclear wastes provides opportunity for accidents

CHAPTER 10 Science, Technology, and Society

I. THE RELATIONSHIP OF SCIENCE AND TECHNOLOGY

1. Science and Technology Defined *(J1, J2)*

Science solves problems in order to understand the natural world. Science seeks to know what the world is made of, what forces exist in the world, what laws control events, and how the world "works." For example, scientists classify organisms in order to understand how they are alike or different. They investigate the chemicals in acid rain and have developed the theory of atoms to explain how matter behaves.

Technology solves problems in order to improve the lives of people and advance society. Technology does this by combining scientific knowledge with other resources—such as industry, finance, construction, machines, and marketing—to develop products and processes that benefit people. Technology is applied, practical science. For example, technology has developed vaccines, artificial legs, jet airplanes, rockets, and computers. Technology is the work of engineers, technologists, and craftspeople such as machinists and carpenters.

Table 1 provides illustrations that contrast science and technology.

Table 1 Comparison of Science and Technology

Questions Asked by Science	Questions Asked by Technology
What are the structures of bacteria and viruses?	How can we control the growth of bacteria and viruses? What can be done to eliminate or use them?
What factors create weather conditions? Can temperature and pressure graphs be used to predict local weather?	How can we make better forecasts that people, farmers, and businesses can depend on? How might computers be used to help make 24-hour and 48-hour predictions?
What occurs when certain fibers burn? How might the burning be reduced by altering the molecules or additives in the fiber?	How can fabrics be treated and prepared to make them fire-resistant? What special techniques are needed to weave such materials into safe clothing and draperies, especially for children?

In summary, *science seeks to gain new knowledge; technology seeks to apply existing knowledge.*

2. Science and Technology Help Each Other *(J3)*

Science and technology advance one another. Scientific advances help people to invent or improve technological devices. Table 2 lists some ways in which science has helped technology.

On the other hand, advanced technological devices help scientists probe more deeply into their studies. Table 3 lists some ways in which technology has helped science.

Another way of showing the interaction of science and technology is illustrated in Figure 10–1.

Table 2 Science Helping Technology

Science	→	Technology
Optics (study of light)	→	Telescopes and microscopes
Electronics, chemistry, and mathematics	→	Development of computers and supercomputers
Atomic theory and other physics concepts	→	Nuclear energy for weapons, electricity, and medicine
Studies in cell biology and genetics	→	Genetic engineering in which traits of living things are modified
Space sciences and electromagnetic theory	→	Satellite communications systems

Table 3 Technology Helping Science

Technology	→	Science
Computers	→	Help chemists solve equations and discover new patterns from their data
Electron microscopes	→	Help biologists see how tiny organisms and cell parts work
Nuclear reactors and accelerators	→	Help physicists smash particles in order to discover what atoms are made of
Radar and jet airplanes	→	Help earth scientists obtain immediate data about temperature, pressure, humidity, and other weather factors
Advanced telescopes	→	Help astronomers better understand stars, galaxies, and the universe

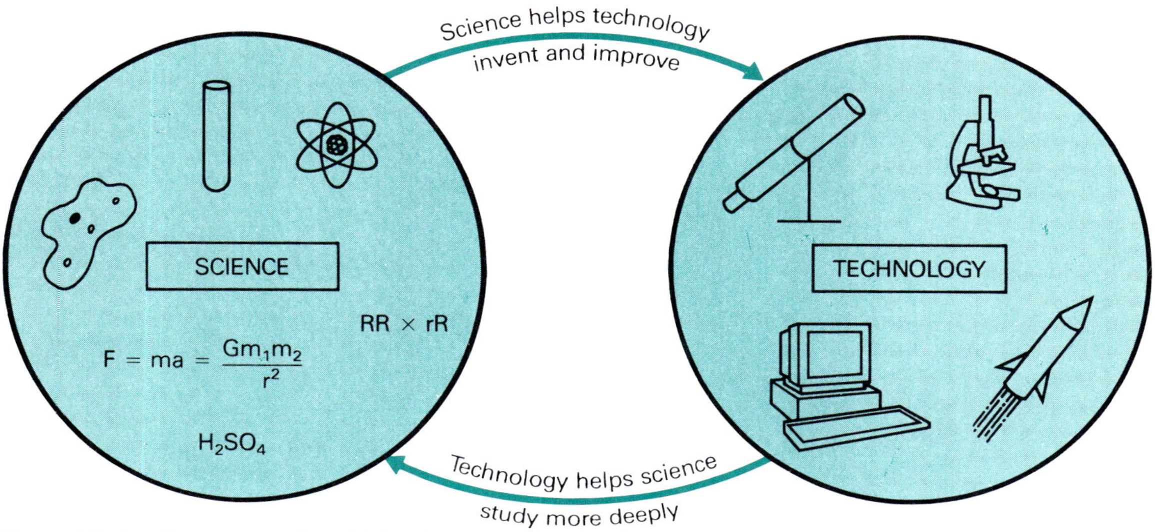

Figure 10–1. Some ways in which science and technology interact.

3. Technology Impacts Everyone and Everything

(J6, J7)

Everyone is affected by technology in many ways. Alarm clocks, refrigerators, credit cards, televisions, cars, street lights, and tools are a few examples of technology in ordinary life. Some technologies, such as microscopes, telescopes, telephones, thermometers, and radar, help people extend human abilities. Some technologies, such as eyeglasses, contact lenses, hearing aids, artificial limbs, calculators, and electronic recorders, help people overcome weaknesses. Even a ballpoint pen is an example of technology. This book is made possible by the technologies of typewriters and printing presses.

In addition, the environment around people is affected by technology. Artificial lighting has completely changed the activities of people after dark. It has changed the concept of time—time for sleep, time for work, time for recreation. Automobiles and planes have changed the concepts of distance and travel. They have widened our environment. Television brings the world into homes as part of our environment. Lawnmowers and shovels make small adjustments to local surroundings. Bulldozers, tractors, dams, chain saws, and dynamite can make great changes to an area.

Many technologies improve the environment. Unfortunately, many technologies hurt the environment. Technologies that hurt the environment include the following:

- Phosphate detergents destroy lakes.
- Sewage treatment plants can pollute rivers and oceans.
- Mining for coal and other ores can ruin the land.
- Smoke from cars and factories pollutes the air we breathe and makes rain slightly acid, causing damage to forests.
- A dam creates a lake that may cover miles of land and even small towns.

Science Skill

RECORDING DATA

In any investigation, thought must be given to what facts must be collected and how they should be recorded. Observations and data must be recorded in an organized, neat manner so they will be understood correctly when analyzed later.

Survey 20–30 friends on how many television sets they have at home. (Or do this for any other technology, such as the number of radios, cars, clocks and watches, or typewriters they own.) First prepare a frequency table, as shown below, that lists all the possible replies you may obtain. As you take the survey, make a little line (called a "tally mark") next to the reply you get from each friend. When the survey is over, add up the tally marks for each reply. This is called the *frequency* of that reply. For example, if you have these tally marks —𝍸///— listed next to reply 2, that means eight people said they had two television sets at home.

Data Table

A	B	C
Number of Televisions — Possible Replies	**Tally Column**	**Frequency**
0		
1		
2		
3		
4		
5		
6		
7		
8		
	Total Surveyed	

It is possible to use this frequency table for further analysis. For each line across, multiply the *Number of Televisions* by the frequency obtained. If you add up all of these multiplications, you will obtain the total number of televisions owned by all the people you surveyed.

A ×	C =	D
Number of Televisions	**Frequency**	**Total Televisions**
1		
2		
3		
4		
5		
6		
7		
8		

Finally, if the grand total of televisions is divided by the total number of people you surveyed, then an average number of televisions per person can be obtained.

Here is one set of data from a survey.

Data Table

A	B	C	D
Number of Televisions — Possible Replies	**Tally Column**	**Frequency**	**Total Televisions (A × C)**
0	//	2	0
1	𝍸 𝍸 //	12	12
2	𝍸 //	7	14
3	𝍸	5	15
4	///	3	12
	Totals	29	53

Results

Total number of people surveyed = 29

Total number of televisions owned = 53

Average number of televisions per person $= \frac{53}{29} = 1.8$

4. *Technology as a System*

(J4, J5)

In a **system** several independent parts work together to produce a result. The parts of any system perform certain roles, such as the following:

Input—the starting materials or starting signals

Comparison/Control—decision whether or not to take any action

Processing—the taking of some action

Output—the results from the action

Feedback—further decision and additional actions

As shown in Figure 10–2, automatic control of a room's temperature during cold weather is a system—different technologies must act together.

It is more convenient to show these parts in a flow diagram (Figure 10–3).

Figure 10–2. A system for controlling the temperature of a room.

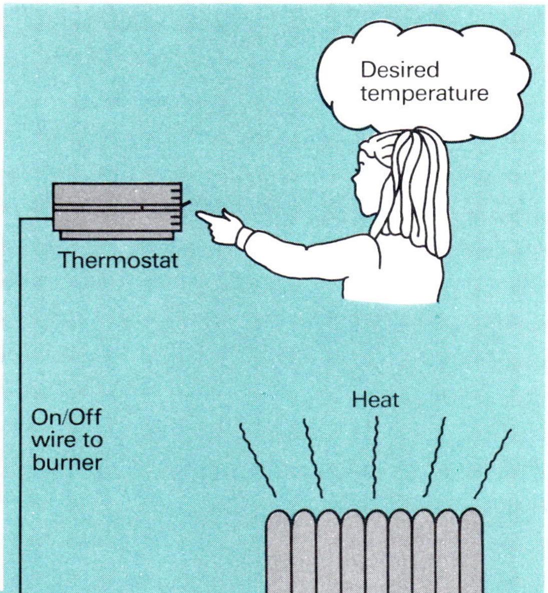

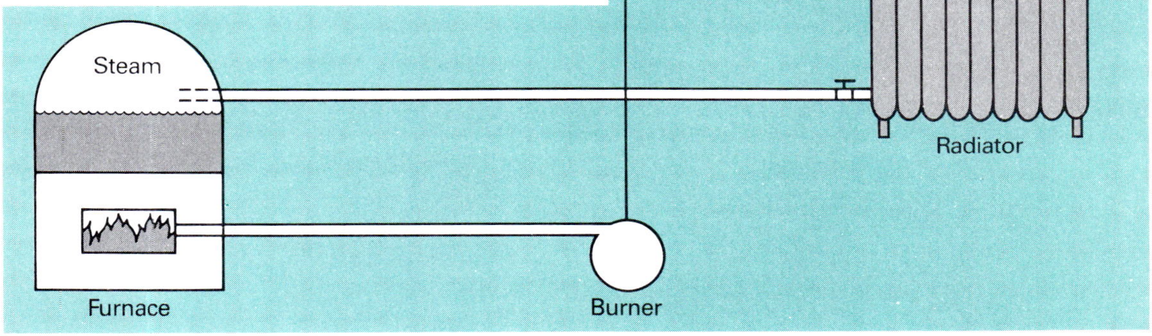

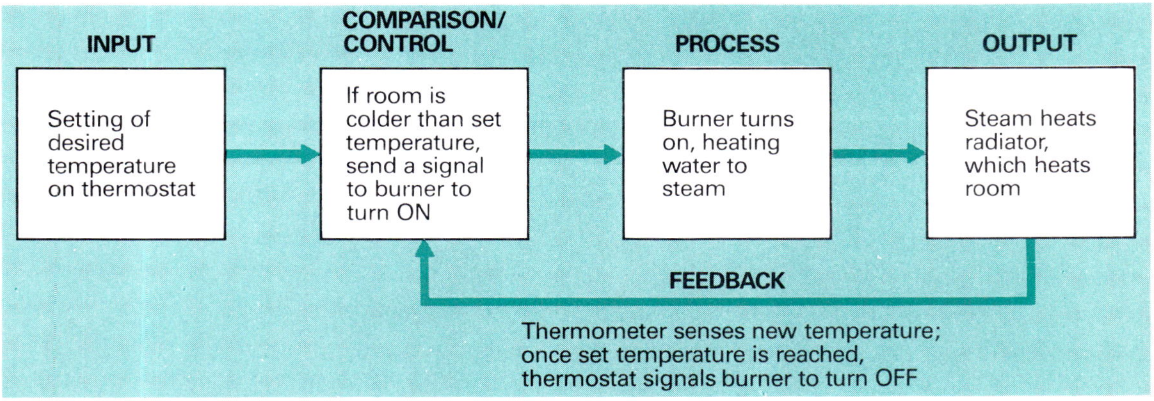

Figure 10–3. Flow diagram for a temperature control system.

Figure 10–4. Systems analysis for driving a car.

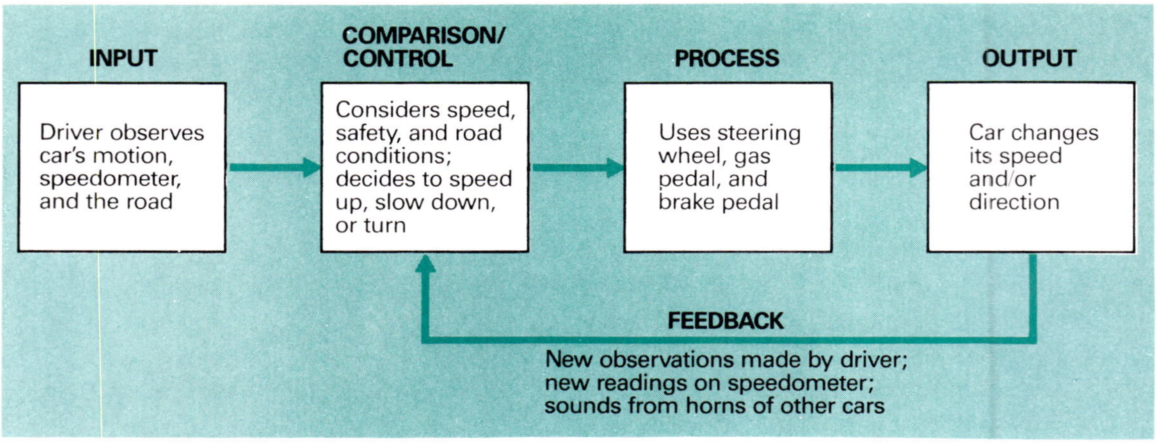

Figure 10–4 shows a similar systems analysis for the act of driving a car.

The system approach is one way to view complex technologies. Another way to view complex technologies is to list the various subparts or subsystems that they incorporate.

System: A Telephone Network

Subsystems:
- Dial
- Receiver and ear speaker
- Individual and trunk lines
- Line amplifiers
- Touch-tone or pulse interpreter
- Switching box
- Local or long-distance facilities
- Error message recordings
- Ring or busy-signal generators
- Bell

System: A Skyscraper

Subsystems:
- Management and rental agents
- Custodians
- Electrical systems
- Elevators
- Water and plumbing systems
- Telephone network
- Heating, cooling, and ventilation systems

System: A Car

Subsystems:
- Engine
- Cooling system
- Exhaust system
- Instrumentation
- Battery, generator, electrical system
- Power train—shaft, gears, axles
- Heater and air conditioner
- Lubrication pumps
- Braking system

Sample Questions

1. Which one of the following is the best example of technology?
   (1) C.B. (citizen's band) radios for cars and boats
   (2) exploring how atoms are put together
   (3) equations for the "big bang" theory of the origin of the universe
   (4) classifying differences between normal and cancerous cells

2. Which one of the following is vital to science but not to technology?
   (1) theories
   (2) products
   (3) devices
   (4) processes

3. Three of the statements below are important goals of technology; one is the chief goal of science. Which one represents the goal of science?
   (1) to develop useful products
   (2) to solve some of the problems of society
   (3) to understand how nature works and what laws exist in nature
   (4) to meet the special needs of individuals who are handicapped

4. Every technological device
   (1) is more expensive than the device it replaces
   (2) affects the environment in some way
   (3) is immediately accepted by the public
   (4) makes a serious impact on society

5. A new type of telescope has been built that uses electronics to "see" the stars by the radio signals they emit. This has helped astronomers classify stars better and learn more about the life of a star. Which principle is best illustrated in this example?
   (1) Every technology has advantages and disadvantages.
   (2) Some technologies can be viewed as a system.
   (3) Every technology affects the environment in some way.
   (4) Science and technology help to advance one another.

6. As shown below, getting a desired program on the television can be analyzed as a system.

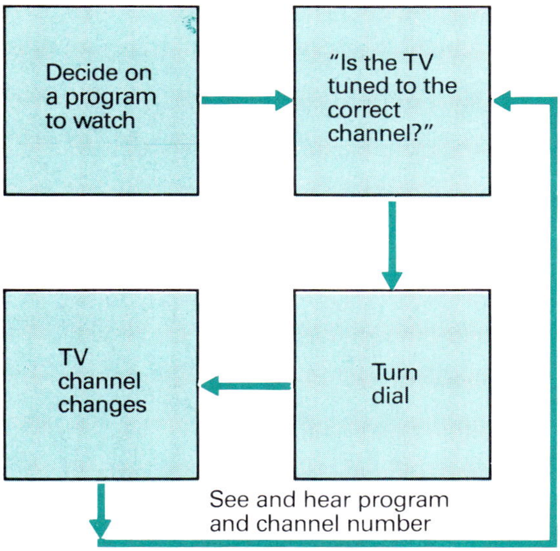

   In this example, what step represents processing?
   (1) deciding on a program to watch
   (2) deciding if the television is turned to the correct channel
   (3) turning the dial
   (4) seeing and hearing the television

7. The diagram below shows standard aspects of a system.

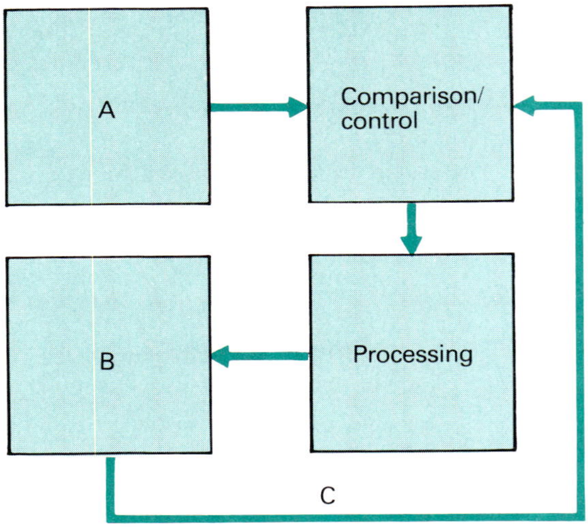

In correct order, the names for parts A, B, and C are
(1) feedback, output, input
(2) input, feedback, output
(3) input, output, feedback
(4) output, input, feedback

8. Which is an illustration that science can produce new and better technologies?
(1) The study of lasers led to the compact disc.
(2) Powerful magnets led physicists to find quarks inside atoms.
(3) Electron microscopes led biologists to uncover parts of bacteria.
(4) Radar was used to learn about and map the planet Venus.

9. People interact with technology every day. Which of the following technologies probably affects the greatest number of people each day?
(1) purification of drinking water
(2) airport radar
(3) telephone answering machines
(4) radiation diagnosis and treatment

10. As shown below, learning new words can be analyzed as a system.

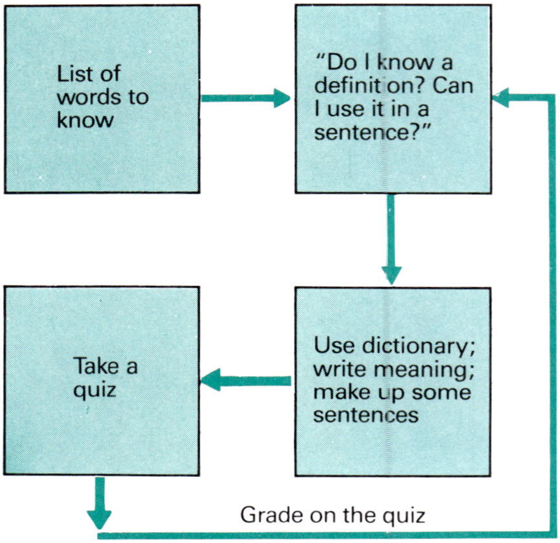

The part called "Grade on the quiz" can be thought of as
(1) input
(2) feedback
(3) processing
(4) comparison and control

11. A computer is a complex technological device made of simpler devices. Which of the following is *not* a part of a computer itself (not part of its "hardware")?
(1) its calculating and memory chip
(2) its keyboard
(3) the output devices, such as printer and T.V./monitor
(4) the data typed in about a problem to be solved

II. INTERACTIONS WITH SOCIETY

1. Effects of Science and Technology on Society

(J8, J9, J14)

A change in science, technology, or society often affects the other two.

The Industrial Revolution that took place in the late 1800s saw a tremendous burst of technology in industry. This new technology—machines, gasoline engines, factories—made tremendous changes in the simpler farm society that preceded it. The automobile had a revolutionary impact on society during the period 1920–1950. Roads were built, travel became possible for ordinary families, hotels developed, and oil companies prospered.

Today, television and computers have also changed society. They affect how people spend free time, get their news, do their banking, organize their schools, and conduct business. Even shopping can now be done using television and computers. Our society is very different due to these two technologies alone.

When technology fails, society suffers. A computer malfunction can create financial problems for individuals and businesses. When traffic lights go out or go off their proper timing, traffic jams are created. A major electrical blackout has an immediate effect upon society.

Generally, however, technology has improved the standard of living of people and changed their lifestyles in positive ways. Consider some of these positive changes.

- Americans work fewer hours per week and have more leisure time than in the 1800s.
- We are healthier and live longer.
- Diseases such as tuberculosis, smallpox, and polio have been completely or nearly eradicated.
- Households today have fewer people, and people tend to live farther away from their relatives.
- Television and music have enriched and widened our lives.

Finally, people have increased choices in their lives because of the products of technology. We have much variety and many options regarding food, entertainment, use of leisure time, transportation, learning, and careers. This variety has roots in technology.

2. Society's Effect on Science and Technology *(J8, J12)*

Often the reverse process occurs: society affects technology. For example, for a number of years automobiles were being made more powerful and faster, obtaining speeds of 100 miles per hour and greater. This trend could have continued. However, society decided to "Live With 55." This gave a message to automobile engineers—they should design for safety, convenience, and efficiency but no longer for speed. Automobile technology took a new direction.

Biologists know how to develop new strains of bacteria and other organisms. They have experimented with small modifications in human reproduction. But society, through laws and government agencies, has prohibited or restricted certain research and development in these areas. The dangers from mistakes in biology are just too serious to permit free experimentation. Society can affect science.

A symbol has been created to express the fact that science, technology, and society interact. As shown in Figure 10–5, three intersecting circles represent the separate concerns of science, technology, and society. In some places two circles overlap. For example, the area of overlap between the science circle and the society circle indicates those issues in pure science that influence or are influenced by society. In the center of the symbol is an area that is part of all three circles. This central area represents issues that directly affect science, technology, and society—such as stopping the deadly AIDS virus or finding ways to reduce pollution.

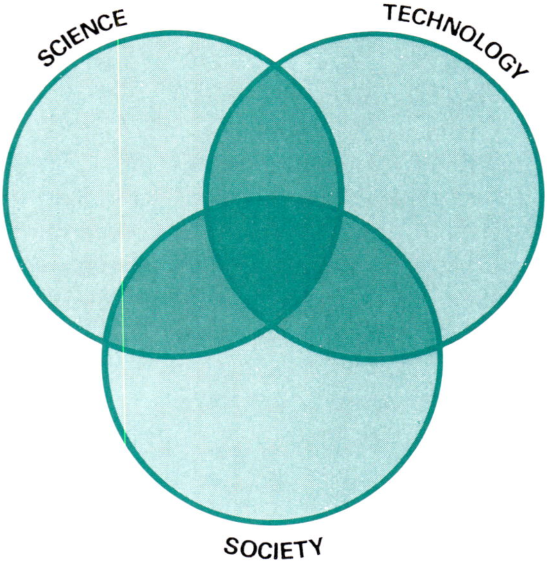

Figure 10–5. Science, technology, and society are not independent of each other.

Attitudes can affect the use of a technological product. For years, front-wheel drive cars were popular only in Europe. That is changing now, as more American cars are being sold with front-wheel drive. We in the United States are suspicious of tofu, a food made from soybeans and used all over Asia. In Asia people have little trust in food technologies that produce hot dogs and processed breakfast cereals. In the mid-1970s American passengers did not think it important to be able to cross the Atlantic Ocean in two hours instead of five hours. This attitude killed further research and development on the SST (Super Sonic Transport), a plane that could fly 2500 miles per hour.

Topographic maps give detailed information about land areas. They result from many technologies—from the radar and photographic surveys taken from airplanes to the precise multicolored printing of the maps. In the United States topographic maps are easily available from the government or from private stores. In many other countries, however, topographic maps are regarded as subversive. They are seen as providing opportunities to plan revolutions. This attitude seems strange to us, yet it affects the mapmaking technologies available in such nations.

3. Business, Industry, and Employment *(J10)*

There are several ways in which technology affects business and industry.

New Practices New technologies may change old practices in industry and business. A computer may replace a filing system or inventory books. Conference telephone calls can do away with group meetings. Bank transactions can now be carried out over telephone lines using small computers rather than in person or by mail. Robots can replace people who perform dreary tasks—such as work on automobile assembly lines—or dangerous tasks.

New Products Often the new technologies themselves create new businesses and industries. The use of video cassette recorders has caused video stores to spring up all over. The expanding use of computers has resulted in the formation of new software companies to provide the computer programs.

Sometimes new technologies cause some older businesses and products to become obsolete. For example, the use of calculators did away with slide rules. Fiberglass and foam insulation did away with cancer-producing asbestos insulation. Automobiles did away with the horse and buggy, and diesel engines took over from steam locomotives.

New Skills Changes in business can affect job tasks and employment. Many people find themselves unneeded when new technologies arise. These people must either learn new skills within their job or leave for some new career. Office workers must often learn to use word processors even though they were originally hired as typists. Government and industry leaders have recognized the need for *retraining* of workers in some occupations and have joined to pay for retraining courses. Robots may replace workers from an assembly line plant, but other people will be needed to fix and operate the robots. When radios became solid state, modular, and inexpensive, they weren't worth fixing. Radio repairmen had to learn to repair televisions, stereos, and videocassette recorders. Medical technicians need continuous retraining for new equipment such as NMR and CAT scanners.

In summary, with respect to employment, technology may

1. require workers to learn new skills on the job;
2. cause some jobs to be eliminated; or
3. open up new jobs.

4. Solving Society's Problems *(J11)*

Many of society's problems may be solved some day by science and technology. On the other hand, many problems are due to human behavior, to natural disasters, to political differences, or to a lack of resources. Technology can't do much about these. Technology may help, but technology can't solve society's problems alone. Big problems such as world hunger, nuclear war, pollution, and overpopulation, can be solved by changing habits, by government, and by new attitudes – not simply by new technology.

5. Global Effects *(J13)*

A technological device or process in one country may have an international or global effect. Nuclear radiation, pollution, and acid rain don't stay within national boundaries. Accidents can spill over to several countries. For example, in the 1950s and 1960s the United States and the Soviet Union experimented with above-ground nuclear testing. The radiation fallout from these tests spread across the entire globe. For this reason, both countries have since agreed to only test underground.

Japan has made excellent progress in a number of fields, including advanced computers, automobiles, and the use of robots. The competition from Japan has forced American industries to improve their technology.

Many technologies bring the world together. International telephones, satellite television, trade in technologies and energy sources, export and import of food and minerals – all of these involve technologies that require cooperation among nations. A famine or earthquake is seen on television worldwide.

Result: money and other forms of support begin to flow immediately to help the affected people.

The world faces global problems also. The increasing amounts of carbon dioxide in the air may cause Earth to become slightly warmer. This warming would cause ice caps at the poles to melt, raising ocean levels and flooding coastal cities everywhere. The United Nations has asked for worldwide cooperation to solve this threat.

Finally, the threat of nuclear war affects the entire world. This is a terrible technology with fearful consequences for the whole planet, not just for the warring nations.

Sample Questions

1. Improvements in raising crops and animals and the use of high-tech farm machines have reduced the number of farmers in the United States. Many small farms have disappeared. This is an illustration of how
(1) society affects technology
(2) society affects science
(3) technology affects society
(4) technology affects science

2. President John F. Kennedy decided it was important that the United States be the first nation to land on the moon. Billions of dollars and thousands of engineers invented technologies to carry out this goal. This is an example of technology being affected by
(1) science
(2) society
(3) basic human needs
(4) the profit motive

3. What new business was made possible by the development of video cassette recorders?
(1) television repair
(2) stereo compact discs
(3) cable television
(4) videotape rentals

4. The use of electric refrigerators put ice-cutters and ice deliverers out of work. This shows that technology
(1) has terrible disadvantages
(2) harms society
(3) changes employment opportunities
(4) changes basic human needs

5. Which statement about technology and employment is *not* true?
(1) Technology makes some jobs obsolete.
(2) Technology creates new jobs.
(3) Technology sometimes makes job retraining necessary.
(4) Technology has no effect on business and employment.

6. Which statement about science and technology is most correct?
(1) They can solve any problem if given enough time.
(2) They are not involved with society's problems.
(3) They are part of the problem, not the solution.
(4) They cannot solve society's problems alone.

7. In many supermarkets special fluorescent lights are used in the vegetable department. These lights give the vegetables a dark unnatural color. However, Americans prefer these darker colors and associate them with freshness. This is an example of technology being used to
(1) deceive people
(2) make people healthier
(3) keep food fresher
(4) satisfy society's attitudes

8. Below is a diagram of a television program from country *A* being beamed via satellites to country *B*.

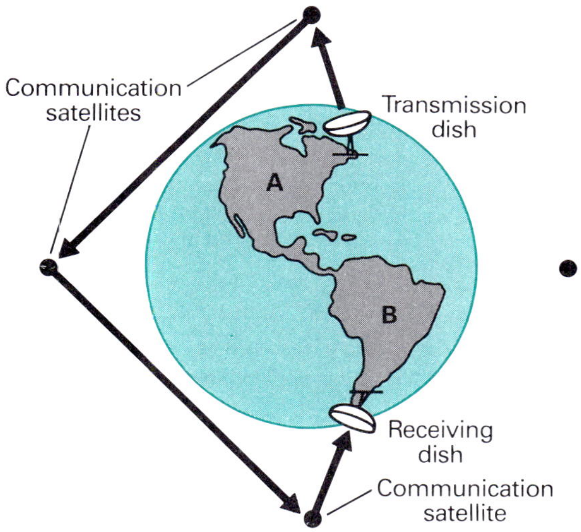

This illustrates the *general principle* that technology
(1) is used for communication
(2) has international and global effects
(3) will make everyone speak one language
(4) isolates countries from one another

9. Which one of the following is an example of society affecting science?
(1) finding that matter is composed of atoms
(2) the law that energy is never lost as it changes forms
(3) establishing the law of gravity
(4) regulations for experiments on living things

10. Which of the following problems will science and technology be able to solve without help from society?
(1) eliminating hunger from the world
(2) ensuring that nuclear war won't happen
(3) controlling overpopulation
(4) building a better mousetrap

11. Which of the following social attitudes has a great effect on technology?
(1) Americans do not like warm milk or warm milk products.
(2) The American word *elevator* and the British word *lift* refer to the same device.
(3) Asians like very spicy foods.
(4) *July 11, 1987* is abbreviated *7/11/87* in the United States but *11/7/87* in many other countries.

12. Which one of the following technologies has enabled consumers to make wiser choices regarding food quality?
(1) variety of package sizes
(2) nutritional information on food labels
(3) variety in coffee products
(4) computer scanning labels for faster, more accurate checkout

III. MAKING DECISIONS ABOUT TECHNOLOGY

1. Benefits and Burdens

(J15, J16)

Every technological device or process has **benefits**, or advantages, and **burdens**, or disadvantages, for people and the environment. Some examples of benefits and burdens are illustrated in Figure 10–6.

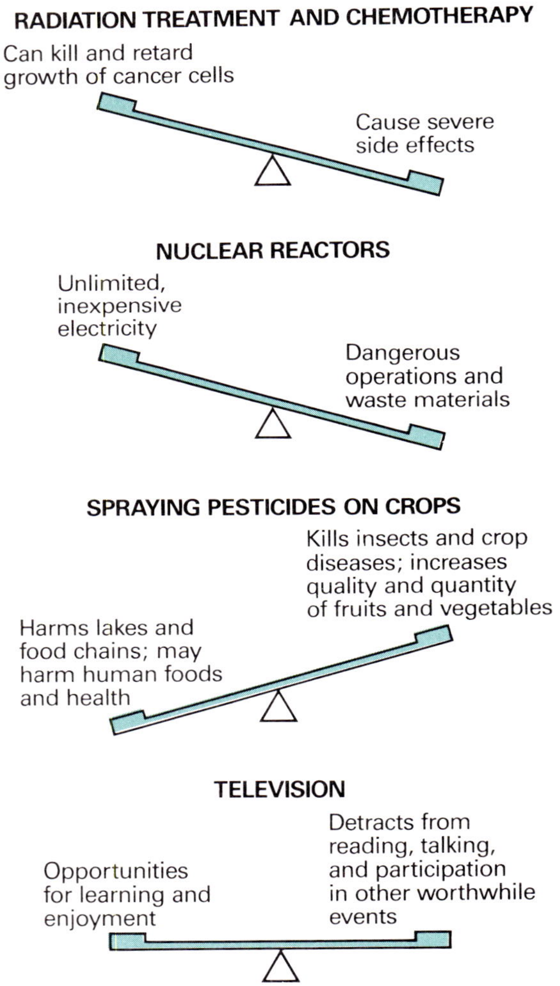

Figure 10–6. Benefits and burdens of some technologies.

As these see-saw illustrations suggest, the advantages and disadvantages of each device or process may or may not balance. Technological devices and processes ought to be judged by their advantages and disadvantages.

Sometimes the public responds to the pluses and minuses of a technology by buying more or less of a product, by protest meetings, by court action, or by writing letters. For example, a few years ago a new drug taken by women was found to increase the chance of miscarriages and deformed babies. Letters, protests, Congressional hearings, and lawsuits quickly pulled that drug off store shelves. Recently health and exercise clubs have started using high-tech exercise machines in pleasant rooms. This technology has proven very popular. Many people find that the use of such machines has advantages, even though a few people have been harmed by overuse or improper use of this technology.

Private and governmental groups also assess the advantages and disadvantages of new technologies. Underwriters Laboratories, specialized magazines, insurance companies, the Better Business Bureau, the Occupational Safety and Health Administration of the United States Department of Labor, state legislatures, and state committees are examples. They are called "watchdog" groups. For example, some states, including New York, have decided that the advantages of recycling cans and bottles are very convincing. To encourage people to recycle, a refundable deposit has been placed on every can or bottle sold.

2. Short-term and Long-term Considerations *(J17, J18)*

When a new technology is adopted it is important to collect data on its effects on people, the environment, and future generations. For example, some insecticides are used because they have good short-term effects—they kill insects that destroy plants. However, new data suggests that these chemicals eventually are washed into lakes and rivers where they harm fish. Some amounts of the insecticides pass into fish and eventually are eaten by humans. If the long-term effects of the insecticides are found to be harmful to humans, the insecticides will be banned.

Safety belts are the opposite case. Many people find them a nuisance. Some believe safety belts are unsafe because they prevent speedy exit from the car in an emergency. In other words, safety belts have some short-term burdens or disadvantages. However, data over many years suggests that in the long run safety belts save lives. The long-term benefits or advantages to society have convinced lawmakers to require the wearing of safety belts in many states, including New York.

Will the United States become a nuclear energy country? The answer to that question must await the studies now being made on the long-term effects of nuclear energy. Will the safety record, the operating problems, and the need for disposal of radioactive wastes cause the United States to fear the long-term consequences of nuclear energy? Or, will these problems be seen as manageable? Years of data will be required. For now, however, no *new* nuclear reactors are being planned until the present ones are fully evaluated.

3. Deciding about Technology and Making Trade-offs *(J19, J20)*

If the disadvantages of a technological device outweigh its advantages, the device may be rejected. However, if future modifications reduce or remove the disadvantages, then the device may be accepted again. For example, the pesticide DDT was once used widely in the United States to control insects on crops. It was found to have a big disadvantage: it can cause cancer and genetic defects. It was accepted, then banned.

Early-model computers were not accepted well. They were complicated, difficult to use, had limited memory, and often came with poorly written and highly technical instructions. These disadvantages reduced any interest by the public and small businesses in computers.

Eventually, computers were made "user friendly." They were given simple keyboards, easy instructions, and even provided the user with feedback about errors. Increased memory made the newer computers very powerful as well. Within a few years computers were accepted again for home and business use, and are now very popular.

Windmills used to perform simple tasks, such as grinding corn to make corn meal. They became obsolete. Now engineers are redesigning wind devices to make them turn generators to produce electricity efficiently.

When planners make decisions about complex technologies, they often must make compromises. Some burdens must be accepted in order to get the benefits. Such compromises are called **trade-offs**.

For example, NASA officials know that it is impossible to have a spaceship that is 100% safe. The cost to build it would be too high. The time needed to design such a spaceship would be very long. It would never get off the ground. Some trade-offs on safety items must be made. The demand for adequate safety must be balanced against the need for working within a fixed budget and keeping to a reasonable schedule.

A heavier car is usually safer and more

Science Skill

PROBLEM SOLVING

A model is a picture or an understanding that tries to explain the results of an investigation. The model that describes how science and technology work to solve problems is called the *problem-solving model* or the *scientific method*.

Chapter 11 deals with the steps of the scientific method in detail. However, here is an overview of a model for problem-solving.

Defining the Problem to be Solved	
EXPERIENCES ↓	Some observation is made.
DISCREPANCIES ↓	These are the differences and inconsistencies between what is observed and what was expected. Often what we observe and experience doesn't "fit" with what we expected or believed previously. This is a discrepancy.
QUESTIONS	Once discrepancies are found, questions automatically begin. Well-formed questions are vital to problem solving. Good questions define what problem must be solved and what research is needed.

Notice the experiences, discrepancies, and questions found in the following examples.

1. A student notices that her eyeglasses need to be repaired. However, no replacement screw is available. How else might the glasses be held together temporarily? Where should she look to find a person who can fix the glasses permanently?
2. A car is found to get 20 miles per gallon of gasoline. The estimated rate in the manufacturer's advertisement is 28 miles per gallon. Under what conditions was the manufacturer's estimate

comfortable than a lighter car. But heavier cars cost more and get fewer miles per gallon than lighter cars. After doing comparison shopping, a purchaser must make some trade-offs or compromises in order to decide which car to buy.

Vaccines help children resist some diseases, such as whooping cough. However, these vaccines can cause serious side effects in a small percentage of children. Society is trading off the possible ill effects in a few for the general health of the many.

made? Who might be able to explain the reason for the difference? How might the car be compared with other cars to see if this is a real problem or a false problem? What would be the effect of using higher-octane gasoline and adding 3 more pounds per square inch of air pressure to the tires?

Once the problem has been defined, it is solved using the problem-solving model below. This is further discussed in Chapter 11.

Using the Problem-Solving Model

PLANNING ↓	An investigation is planned to answer the key problem.
OBTAINING DATA ↓	Information is gathered that may relate to the problem. This data may be qualitative (word descriptions) or quantitative (numbers and measurements).
ORGANIZING DATA ↓	Tables and graphs are made that present some pattern in the data or organize it clearly.
ANALYZING DATA ↓	Mathematical trends, equations, and deeper patterns are uncovered within the data. Cause-and-effect relationships and other inferences are suggested. Specific conclusions from the investigation are made.
GENERALIZING ↓	Conclusions are used to suggest larger, more general conclusions about the problem and the investigation. In science such general conclusions are often called theories or laws.
DECISION MAKING	Choices are made clearer as a result of the investigation. A decision is taken to help attack the problem or to wait and do further study on the problem.

Sample Questions

1. Two-cycle engines are small and are very simple to operate and fix. They are used in lawn mowers, motor bikes, small boats, and snowmobiles. Lubrication oil is mixed directly with the gasoline. This makes the exhaust fumes smoky and smelly.

   The above information provides an example that technological devices
   (1) have advantages and disadvantages
   (2) must always harm the environment
   (3) are safer when they are smaller
   (4) are better when they are smaller

2. What might be a disadvantage of a telephone answering machine?
   (1) People can leave messages if no one is at home.
   (2) An important activity need not be interrupted by the phone.
   (3) Playback of messages is possible by a phone away from home.
   (4) It suggests that an apartment or house is empty and unprotected.

3. What might be a disadvantage of small, compact cars?
   (1) miles per gallon
   (2) safety in an accident
   (3) cost
   (4) maneuvering and parking

4. In building nuclear reactors for electricity, a compromise is necessary between
   (1) military and civilian purposes
   (2) energy output and safety
   (3) research and development
   (4) profits and price

5. Fluorocarbon chemicals have been used for years in refrigerators and spray cans (aerosols). Recently, scientists have discovered that fluorocarbon chemicals are depleting the ozone gas layer that surrounds Earth. This ozone layer shields living things from cancer-causing ultraviolet rays from the sun. The United Nations has asked countries to reduce or ban the use of fluorocarbons.

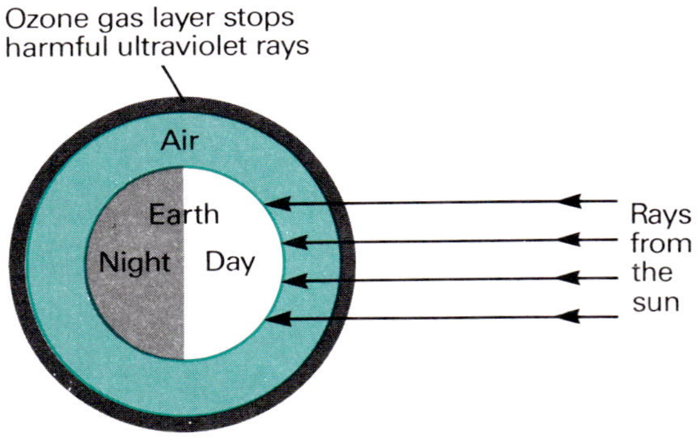

   The above is an example of a technology that may be
   (1) bad in the short term, but good in the long term
   (2) terminated if its disadvantages outweigh its advantages
   (3) considered as only one nation's problem
   (4) continued, no matter what the consequences are

6. What possible long-term consequence of artificial sweeteners must be given top priority by researchers?
(1) convenience for diabetics who can't eat sugar
(2) effectiveness for people on a diet
(3) increased risk of cancer
(4) impact upon the sugar industry

7. What burden does cushioning packages with synthetic materials—like styrofoam—bring with its benefits?
(1) fresher foods
(2) protection from tampering
(3) indestructible waste
(4) less shipping damages

8. In the 1970s one fad in technology was quadraphonic sound. Four speakers gave a "surround sound": left, right, front, and rear. Suddenly the fad died. People (and sound experts) began to realize that human ears can't easily tell front from rear sounds. "Quad" systems just didn't give any special hearing pleasure.

This is an example of a technological process that was short-lived because
(1) its disadvantages outweigh its advantages
(2) it was too costly
(3) it had bad long-term consequences
(4) it was based on good science

9. Some people become drowsy or get headaches from allergy pills. Yet they are willing to tolerate these side effects in order to stop the sneezing, itching eyes, and congestion caused by allergies. This is an example of
(1) technology (in the pills) solving all problems
(2) an environmental impact of technology
(3) modifying technology to make it better
(4) a trade-off between benefits and burdens

10. Personal computers became popular again after they were redesigned to make them easier to use and faster. Microwave ovens were rejected, then accepted again once the problem of radiation leakage was overcome. These examples illustrate that
(1) people judge technology only by its advantages
(2) people judge technology only by its disadvantages
(3) modifications can reduce or eliminate disadvantages
(4) technology must always improve with time

11. Which is *not* important in deciding whether a technology is good or bad?
(1) its advantages and disadvantages
(2) its short- and long-term consequences
(3) how it is used by people
(4) the science principles that make it work

CHAPTER 11 Science Skills

I. PLANNING AND DESIGNING AN EXPERIMENT

1. The Scientific Method

Suppose a group of scientists is working to solve a problem. First they need background information, or knowledge. Then they must carefully define the problem they wish to solve. In order to solve the problem, they must carefully plan the steps they will follow. The **scientific method** is a series of steps used by scientists in solving problems. The steps of the scientific method are listed below and explained in this chapter.

Steps of the Scientific Method

Making an *observation*
Defining a *problem*
Developing a *hypothesis* (an *explanation*)
Designing an *experiment* with *controls*
Carrying out an experiment
Getting *results* (*qualitative* and *quantitative*)
Recording results using *data tables* and *graphs*
Making *conclusions*
Validating or *discarding* the hypothesis under investigation
Formulating new questions based on findings

2. Making Observations and Defining a Problem (1.1)

Scientists carefully observe the world around them. They use their observations as a springboard for asking questions or defining **problems.** Listed below are three **observations** that scientists have made.

A. *People who eat foods high in fat face greater risks of getting heart disease.*

B. *Plants placed on a windowsill bend toward the sun.*

C. *Monkeys placed in an overcrowded cage become overactive.*

Below are three **questions** scientists have asked about the observations listed above.

A. *How do foods high in fat affect the human body?*

B. *What causes plants to bend toward the sun?*

C. *What effect does overcrowding have on the life activities of a monkey?*

3. *Developing a Hypothesis to be Tested in an Investigation* *(1.3)*

Once a problem has been defined, scientists think of a possible solution or answer. To put it another way, they develop a temporary explanation for their observations. They call this explanation a **hypothesis**, or educated guess. The hypothesis is based on knowledge and common sense.

To test the accuracy of the hypothesis, experiments are carried out. Below are three hypotheses developed by scientists to solve the questions listed above.

A. *Perhaps fat deposits clog the blood vessels, blocking the flow of blood to the heart.*

B. *Perhaps unequal amounts of a chemical growth substance in different parts of the stem cause a plant to bend toward the sun. (As shown in Figure 11–1, perhaps the presence of more growth substance on the shady side causes this side to grow more, thereby turning the plant to the sun.)*

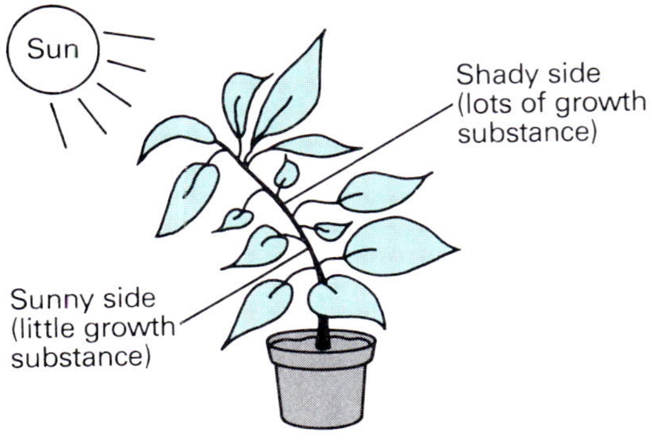

Figure 11–1. A plant bending toward sunlight.

C. *Perhaps blood pressure, heart rate, and respiratory rate increase when monkeys are placed in an overcrowded cage.*

4. *Designing an Observation or Measurement Procedure* *(1.2, 1.4)*

To be accepted as true, a hypothesis must be demonstrated. To do this, scientists perform experiments.

Scientists must carefully design their experiments before they can be carried out. Scientists must decide what they are looking for, the observations they plan to make, the measurements they must take, the procedures and techniques they must use, and the instruments they will need. They use their knowledge and experience to predict the outcome of the experiment.

Below are some experimental designs planned to test the three hypotheses listed above.

A. *Some laboratory animals will be fed a high-fat diet. Then their blood vessels will be surgically removed and examined for fat deposits. The fat deposits will be measured using the proper instruments.*

B. *Biochemical tests will be done on plants that have bent toward the sun to determine the amounts of growth substance in the dark and light side of the stem.*

C. *Medical tests will be performed on monkeys living in overcrowded cages. A stethoscope will be used to measure heartbeat. A sphygmomanometer will be used to measure blood pressure. The number of breaths per minute of the monkeys will also be recorded.*

5. *Designing a Controlled Experiment* *(1.5)*

Something is missing from the experimental designs (procedures) just described.

What is missing is a comparison called a control. In a properly designed experiment, two experiments must be set—the **control** part and the **experimental** part. The experimental and control parts differ in only one condition. This one condition is called the **variable.** After both experiments are done, a comparison is made.

Below are some controlled experiments designed to test the three hypotheses previously listed.

A. *To determine whether people who eat food high in fat face greater risks of getting heart disease, scientists would have to experiment with two groups of people: the experimental group and the control group. For many years the experimental group would be fed a high-fat diet while the control group would be fed a low-fat diet. A comparison would be made of the number of people in each group who developed heart disease.*

B. *To determine whether different amounts of a growth chemical in the stem cause a plant to bend toward the light, scientists would have to experiment with two different groups of plants: an experimental group and a control group. One group (the control) would be placed in an area where light beamed in all directions. The other group (the experimental) would be placed in an area where light shone from only one direction. All other conditions, including the amount of water, carbon dioxide, temperature, etc., would be the same for each group. A comparison would be made to see if only those plants exposed to the single beam of light bent toward the light, and if they had different amounts of the plant growth substance on the lighted and shaded parts of the stem.*

C. *To determine whether monkeys living in an overcrowded cage become overactive, scientists would have to experiment with two different groups of monkeys. Each group would be of the same species, sex, age, and weight. One group would be placed in a cage large enough to house them comfortably (control). The other group would be placed in a small, overcrowded cage (experimental). A comparison would be made to see if the monkeys in the small cage became overactive.*

Sample Questions

1–2. Questions 1–2 refer to the following experiment. *A student planned an experiment on the growth of tomato plants. She grew tomato plants in four pots. Each pot was placed in its own incubator. The incubators were kept at different temperatures; all other conditions remained the same. The heights of the tomato plants in each pot were recorded after two weeks.*

1. What is the student's hypothesis?

(1) The amount of water affects the growth rate of tomato plants.
(2) Growth rate is affected by the temperature.
(3) Growth rate is affected by the amount of fertilizer used.
(4) Growth rate is affected by the amount of light in each incubator.

2. The variable in this experiment is

(1) food
(2) moisture
(3) light
(4) temperature

3. Which one of the following questions can be best researched by a scientist?
(1) Does smoking cause lung cancer?
(2) Does money make people happy?
(3) Is it fair to use animals in scientific research?
(4) Do traffic jams make drivers angry?

4. A control is needed in an experiment to
(1) make a comparison
(2) make the experiment more complex
(3) give scientists a clue
(4) make the experiment more interesting

5. An educated guess about what might occur in an experiment is called
(1) a problem
(2) a hypothesis
(3) a result
(4) a conclusion

6. A science student wants to determine which of the following will help her car get more miles per gallon.
A. A higher grade of gasoline
B. A better type of engine oil
C. A carburetor adjustment
D. More air pressure in the tires
To determine the effect of each of these upon her car's performance she should
(1) change one item at a time and observe its effect
(2) change two items each time and observe their effects
(3) change three items each time and observe their effects
(4) change all four items at the same time and observe their combined effect

7. A student wants to find out if a potato cooked at 400°F would cook twice as fast as an identical potato cooked at 200°F. This is an example of
(1) a research question
(2) an experimental design
(3) a conclusion
(4) a law of science

8. What would be the best way to determine which brand of paper towels has the greatest "wet strength"?
(1) comparing T.V. advertisements that demonstrate wet strength
(2) tearing different brands of towels when they are wet to feel which seems strongest
(3) adding known weights to a saucer placed on a wet paper towel until the towel breaks
(4) conducting a survey of consumers, professional cooks, and restaurant staff people

9. In an experiment to study how crowding affects hostility among monkeys in a zoo, what would be the most scientific way to measure their level of hostility?
(1) Observe them and note if they seem to be angry.
(2) Interview zoo officials and staff.
(3) Train the monkeys to indicate whether they are angry, sad, satisfied, or happy.
(4) Determine the average number of screeches or fights per minute during a few hours of observation.

10. A controlled experiment is one that
(1) is performed very carefully according to the plan
(2) compares an experimental group with a control group
(3) leads to a clear, definite conclusion
(4) uses electrical and mechanical control devices

II. PERFORMING THE EXPERIMENT

1. Making Accurate Observations *(2.1a, 2.1b)*

After an experiment is designed, it must be carried out accurately and safely. This involves a number of steps, beginning with accurate observations.

Scientists are trained to make accurate **observations.** They may use their senses (sight, hearing, touch, smell, and taste) to learn about the world around them. They may also use instruments such as microscopes, telescopes, and X-rays to help them see more than they could see with the unaided eye.

Scientists must observe things as they are, not as they think they are or want them to be. To illustrate this point, think of what happens at the scene of an accident as a group of witnesses give their own interpretations when they are asked what happened.

Another example of the importance of careful observation is shown by the lines in Figure 11–2. Which looks longer – A or B?

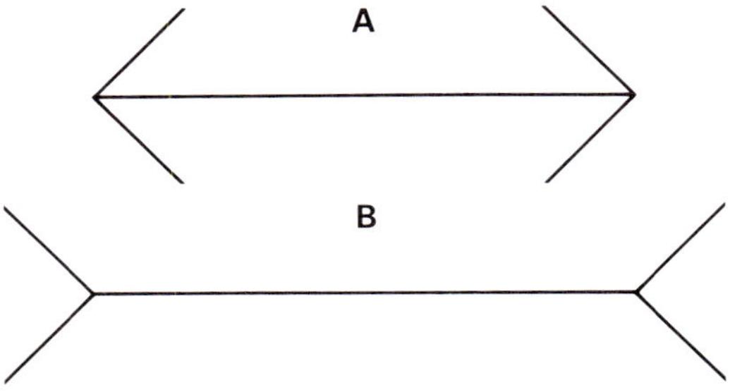

Figure 11–2. Which line is longer?

Now measure each line with a ruler to find out which is longer. Were you surprised to learn that they are both the same length?

Are the blood vessels of people who eat a high-fat diet really clogged with fat material? Are monkeys in overcrowded cages really overactive? It is often difficult to observe what really is. In order to be successful, scientists must be able to make accurate observations.

There are two kinds of observations: qualitative and quantitative. **Qualitative observations** provide a general word description. For example, the statement, "The monkeys in an overcrowded cage are overactive," is a qualitative observation. On the other hand, **quantitative observations** provide an exact value or measured quantity. For example, the statement, "The average heartbeat of the monkeys in an overcrowded cage is 150 beats per minute," is a quantitative observation.

2. Taking Accurate Measurements *(2.1b)*

Making accurate quantitative observations (taking measurements) requires the use of measuring instruments. For example, to determine the height of a plant, a ruler is used. To determine the mass of a rock, a balance is used.

Metric Ruler A metric ruler is used to measure length or distance. One meter contains 100 centimeters. One centimeter contains 10 millimeters. Figure 11–3 shows a metric ruler. How many millimeters and centimeters does it contain? How tall is the plant in millimeters?

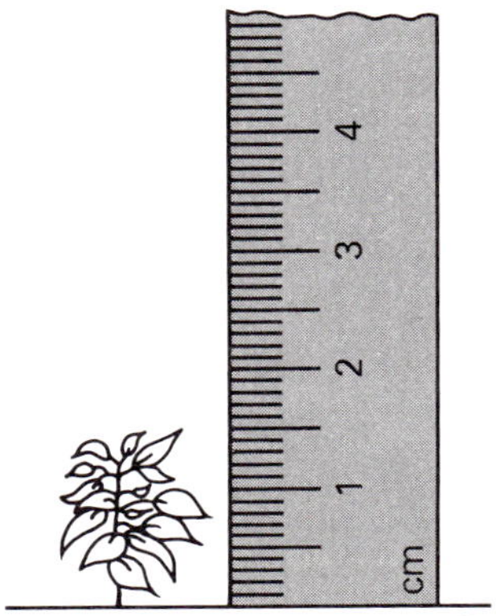

Figure 11–3. How tall is the plant?

Thermometer A thermometer is used to measure temperature. Look at the thermometer in Figure 11–4. Compare the two temperature scales. Notice that the scale on the Celsius side contains 100 equal units while the scale on the Fahrenheit side contains 212 equal units. The Celsius scale is the one used by scientists. What temperature reading (in °C and °F) is shown on the thermometer in the illustration?

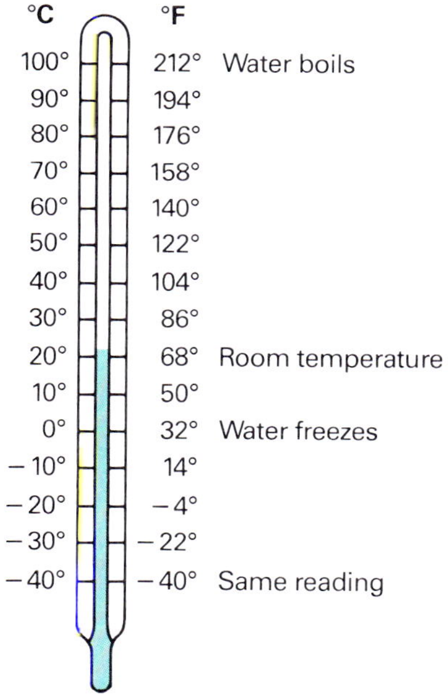

Figure 11–4. Comparison of the Celsius and Fahrenheit temperature scales.

Graduated Cylinder A graduated cylinder is used to measure the volume of a liquid. The volume of a liquid is measured in metric units called *liters*. One liter contains 1000 milliliters, or 1000 cubic centimeters (1 mL = 1 cm^3). Look at the graduated cylinder in Figure 11–5. How many milliliters of liquid can it hold when completely filled? How many milliliters is it holding in the illustration? To find out, notice the curved surface, or **meniscus.** The volume of most liquids is measured at eye level at the bottom of the meniscus.

Figure 11–5. How to read a graduated cylinder.

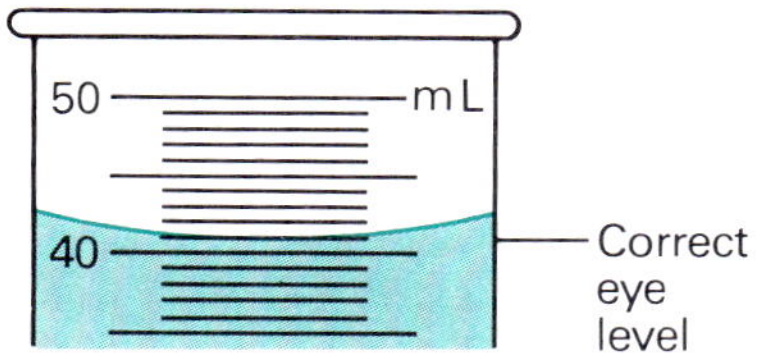

Balance A balance is used to measure the mass of a substance. Mass is measured in metric units called *grams*. One gram contains 1000 milligrams. Look at the balance in Figure 11–6. What is the mass of the rock on the balance? To find out, look at both scales.

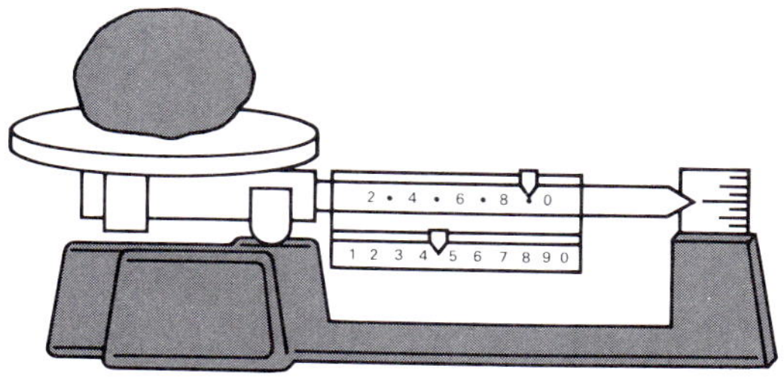

Figure 11–6. A laboratory balance.

Other Equipment Figure 11–7 shows some other pieces of equipment used by scientists in their experiments. How many are you familiar with?

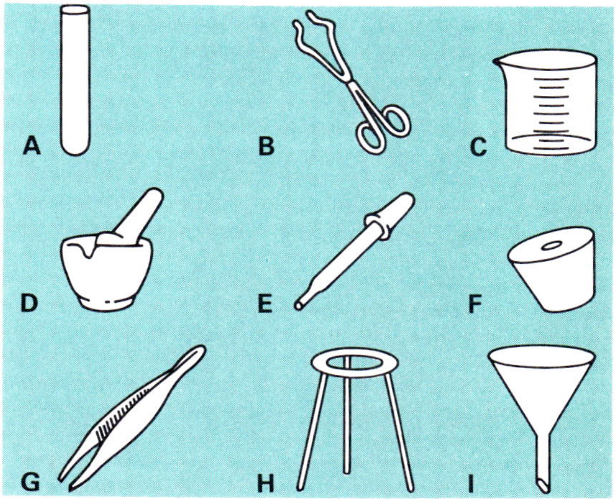

Figure 11–7. Laboratory equipment: (A) test tube, (B) tongs, (C) beaker, (D) mortar and pestle, (E) eye dropper, (F) rubber stopper, (G) tweezers, (H) tripod, (I) funnel.

To do the experiments discussed earlier in this chapter, scientists could use some of the following instruments:

A. *The metric ruler could be used to measure the thickness of fat deposits in the walls of blood vessels. The fatty deposits could be scraped off and weighed using a balance.*

B. *The growth hormone could be extracted in solution from the stem of a plant and placed in a graduated cylinder to measure its volume.*

C. *A stethoscope could be used to measure the heartbeat of the monkeys. A sphygmomanometer could be used to measure blood pressure.*

3. Recording Observations and Measurements with Precision *(2.3)*

As an experiment is performed, the scientist records a description of the observations made. The scientist also records, in an organized manner, important data on a **data table** or a **graph**.

Figure 11–8 shows some data collected on the heights and weights of four girls. Notice that the data can be placed in either a data table or graph.

What kinds of data would be collected and recorded as the three experiments discussed throughout this chapter are performed? Some examples are listed below.

A. *An increase in the thickness of the fat deposits in the walls of the blood vessels over time; the number of individuals getting heart disease over time*

B. *The mass and volume of the growth substance extracted from the sunny and shady sides of the stem; the angle of bend of the plant stem toward the sunlight*

C. *The average blood pressure and rate of heart beat of the monkeys in the crowded and uncrowded cages; the change in average blood pressure of the monkeys in both cages over time*

Girl	Height (cm)	Weight (kg)
1	100	30
2	115	35
3	130	40
4	145	55

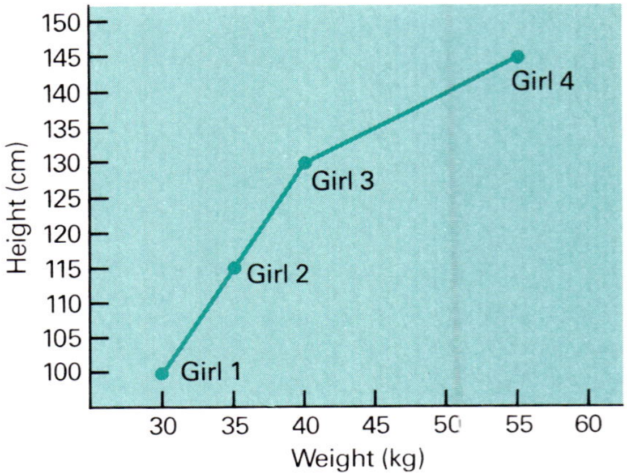

Figure 11–8. The same data can be recorded in more than one way.

4. Performing Numeric Calculations *(2.4)*

Sometimes numeric calculations must be performed during an experiment. For example, in the monkey experiment scientists might want to calculate the average heart rate of the monkeys in each cage. To calculate average heart rate, the pulse of every monkey in the cage would have to be taken and totaled. Then the sum of the heart rates of all the monkeys would have to be divided by the number of monkeys in the cage in order to calculate the average heart rate.

Suppose scientists need to identify an unknown mineral. To help them identify the mineral, they might want to calculate its density. In order to calculate density they need to use a balance to find the mineral's mass and a graduated cylinder containing water to determine its volume. The formula $D = M/V$ is used to find density. For example, suppose the mass of the unknown mineral is 1129.1 g and its volume is 58.5 cm^3. Using the formula $D = M/V$, the density is 1129.1 g ÷ 58.5 cm^3 or 19.3 g/cm^3, the density of gold. Scientists can conclude that the unknown mineral is gold.

5. Making Decisions about Experimental Technique *(2.5)*

What should scientists study? On what investigations should large sums of money be spent? Which experimental method would provide the best results? Which kinds of instruments would be best suited for collecting the data? How should the data be collected, and in what form?

Scientists are constantly faced with making decisions like these. Good scientists need to be able to make the right decisions. If they make the wrong decisions, they should be flexible enough to make new decisions and repeat their work.

6. Manipulating Instruments Safely *(2.2)*

Scientists must follow safe laboratory procedures at all times. Here are some safety suggestions to follow when working in a laboratory.

1. Know the proper way to handle chemicals and equipment.
2. Do not use broken or crushed equipment or glassware.
3. Do not play around in the lab.
4. Report any injury to yourself or others, no matter how minor, to the laboratory supervisor or teacher.
5. Wear safety goggles when mixing chemicals and when heating materials.
6. Exercise great care when heating things over a flame.
7. Do not wear loose clothing or dangling jewelry in the laboratory, and keep long hair tied back when doing an experiment.
8. Never taste or inhale unknown or unidentified chemicals.
9. Wear a lab apron and gloves when directed to do so.
10. Know the location of fire blankets and fire extinguishers.
11. Learn the techniques for smelling a chemical if it is necessary to do so.
12. Always carry lab materials correctly and carefully.
13. Know how to handle lab materials safely and correctly when performing an experiment.
14. When in doubt about proper safety procedures, do not hesitate to ask the lab supervisor or teacher.

Sample Questions

1. A scientist needs to know the volume of a cage used to house laboratory animals. The cage measures 100 cm long, 75 cm wide, and 25 cm high. What is its volume? To calculate the volume, use the formula $V = l$ (length) $\times$ w (width) $\times$ h (height).
   (1) 250,000 cm^3 (3) 187,500 cm^3
   (2) 750,000 cm^3 (4) 100,000 cm^3

2. A scientist wishes to determine how effective a vaccine is in protecting mice against a contagious disease. Which experimental procedure should this scientist use?
   (1) Expose 100 mice to the disease and then vaccinate all of them.
   (2) Give vaccinations to 50 of the 100 mice and then expose all 100 to the disease.
   (3) Give vaccinations to 100 mice and then expose all of them to the disease.
   (4) Vaccinate 50 of the 100 mice and then expose only the 50 vaccinated mice to the disease.

3. A student is studying how pressure affects the temperature at which water boils. He guesses that as the pressure increases, the temperature at which water boils also increases. How could he test his guess?
   (1) Boil water samples at different pressures and then calcuate how much evaporation occurs.
   (2) Boil water samples at different pressures and record the boiling temperatures for each.
   (3) Boil water samples in pots of different volumes and record the boiling temperature for each.

4. A student wants to shorten the ripening time for squash plants. He predicts that the more water the seedlings receive, the faster they will develop fruit. To test this prediction he should
   (1) vary the amount of water given to 10 squash plants and record the time it takes for fruit to develop on each
   (2) vary the amount of water and sunlight received by 10 squash plants and record the time it takes for fruit to develop on each
   (3) keep constant the amount of water given to the 10 squash plants and record the number of fruit each plant has after 6 weeks
   (4) vary the amount of water given to 10 squash plants and measure the height of each after 20 days

5. Which procedure is not safe to perform in a laboratory?
   (1) tasting a chemical to identify it as an acid or base
   (2) wearing safety goggles when mixing acids and bases
   (3) heating a dilute acid slowly under the direct supervision of the teacher
   (4) reporting an injury to the teacher immediately after it occurs

6. It is important to measure accurately in an experiment because measurements are
   (1) often incorrect
   (2) easily changed
   (3) used to test a prediction
   (4) easily discarded

7. A scientist wishes to identify an unknown mineral by finding its density. Its mass is 10 grams and its volume is 2 cm^3. What is its density? (Use the formula D = M/V.)

(1) 0.2 g/cm^3 (3) 12 g/cm^3
(2) 5 g/cm^3 (4) 20 g/cm^3

8. Which piece of equipment is most appropriate for measuring specific amounts of liquid?

(1) triple-beam balance
(2) beaker
(3) flask
(4) graduated cylinder

9. A solid metal brick measures 4.0 cm × 3.0 cm × 2.0 cm and has a mass of 72 g. What is the density of this metal?

Volume = length × width × height

$$\text{Density} = \frac{\text{Mass}}{\text{Volume}}$$

(1) 0.33 g/cm^3
(2) 8.0 g/cm^3
(3) 3.0 g/cm^3
(4) 24 g/cm^3

10. A student grew five tomato plants. She counted the total number of tomatoes on all five plants at the end of each two-week period for ten weeks. Her results are shown in the data table below.

Data Table

Time after Planting (weeks)	Number of Tomatoes
2	5
4	12
6	26
8	27
10	32

Which graph best describes her results?

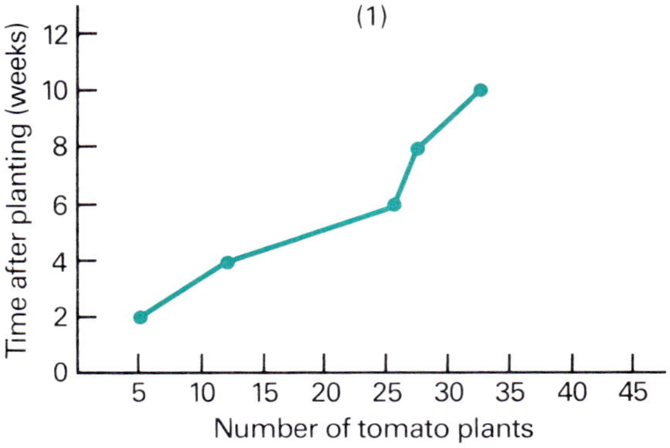

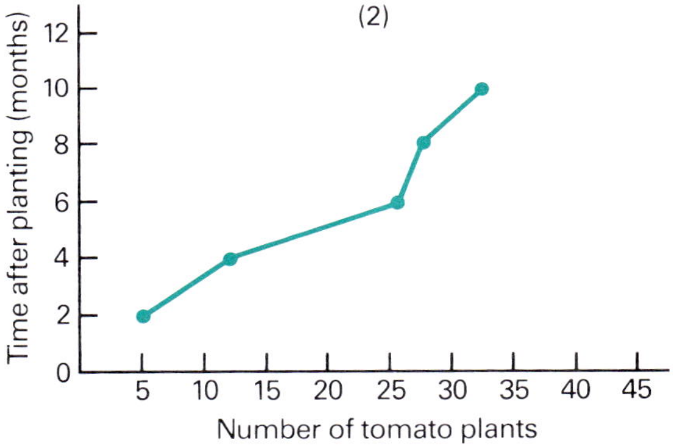

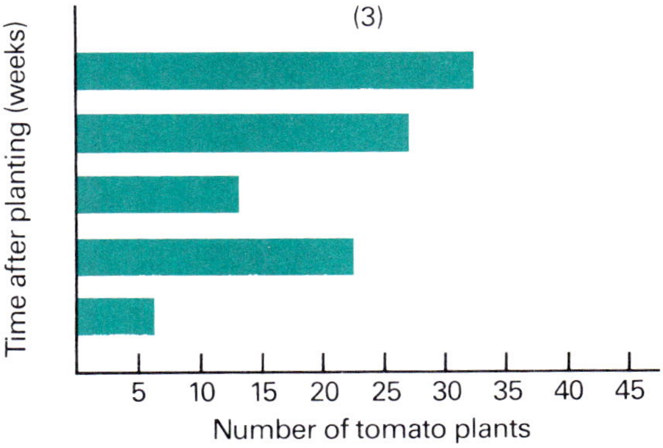

11. Which one of the following is a qualitative measurement?

(1) mass, g
(2) temperature, °C
(3) speed, km/hr
(4) color

III. INTERPRETING THE EXPERIMENT

1. *Reorganizing the Data into Table Form* *(3.1a)*

Once an experiment is completed, its raw results may need to be reorganized into a more meaningful table of data. For example, suppose a student desires to find the mass of different volumes of a certain liquid by using a graduated cylinder. Figure 11–9 shows the student's raw data.

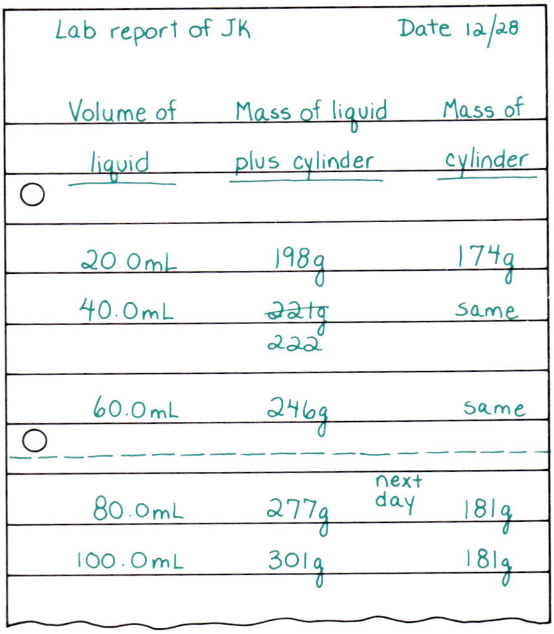

Figure 11–9. The student's raw data, as recorded in a laboratory notebook.

The student realizes that the mass of the liquid plus the cylinder is not very important. What matters is the mass of the liquid alone. The student adjusts the data by subtracting the mass of the cylinder, and then types up the data in more organized form. Table 1 shows the organized data.

Table 1 Student's Data Table

Volume of Liquid (mL)	Mass of Liquid (g)
20.0	24.0
40.0	48.0
60.0	72.0
80.0	96.0
100.0	120.0

The completed data table now presents the important facts in a clear manner.

2. *Graphing the Data* *(3.1b)*

"A picture is worth a thousand words." A graph, like a picture, is also an excellent way to present data that has been collected. Figure 11–10 shows a properly constructed graph of the data in Table 1.

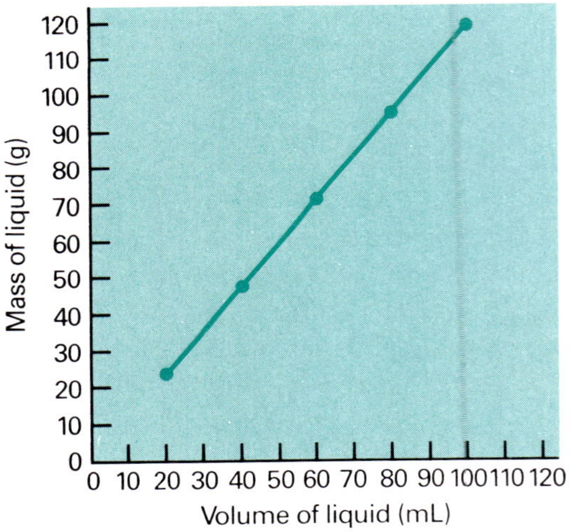

Figure 11–10. Mass vs. volume data for a liquid.

A number of factors must be considered in drawing a graph. Figure 11–11 illustrates some of the points to consider in making any graph.

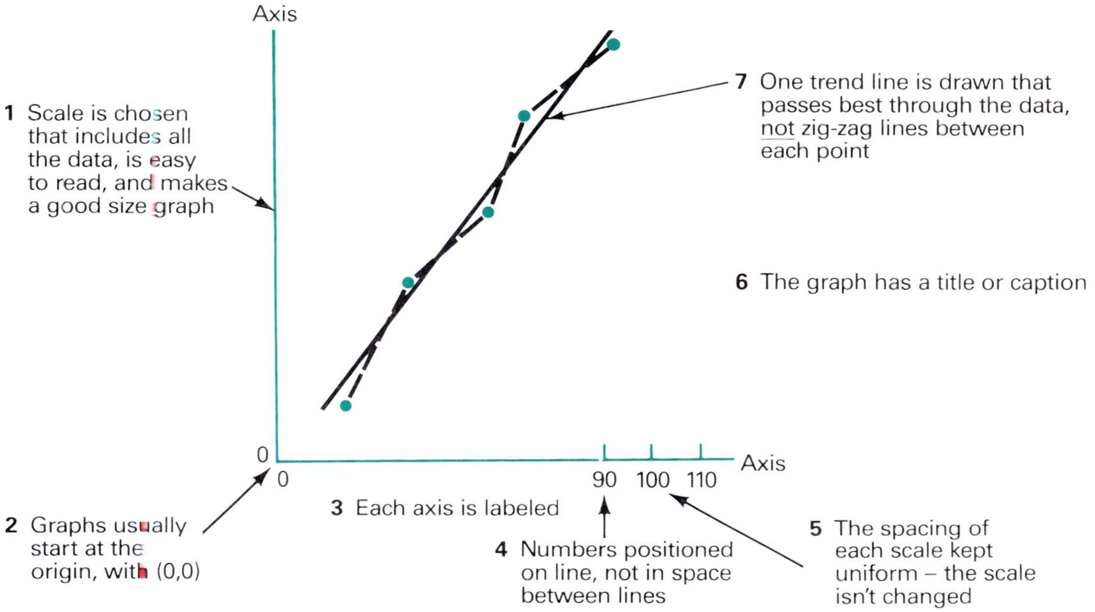

Figure 11–11. Good graphing technique.

3. Determining Relationships from the Data *(3.2a, 3.2b)*

By studying the data or graph it may be possible to note certain trends or relationships. A **qualitative relationship** describes *in words* a trend that has been noted. A **quantitative relationship** describes *by numbers or equations* the trend observed in the data. For example, here are some possible relationships that can be obtained from the experiment discussed above.

Some Qualitative Relationships (1) The mass, in g, is always larger than the volume, in mL. (2) As the volume increases, the mass also increases.

Some Quantitative Relationships (1) If the volume is doubled, the mass is also doubled. If the volume is tripled, the mass is also tripled. If the volume is multiplied by five, the mass is also multiplied by five. (2) If the mass is divided by the volume, the same ratio is obtained in each case.

$$\frac{24\text{ g}}{20\text{ mL}} = 1.2\text{ g/mL}$$

$$\frac{48\text{ g}}{40\text{ mL}} = 1.2\text{ g/mL}$$

$$\frac{72\text{ g}}{60\text{ mL}} = 1.2\text{ g/mL}$$

$$\frac{96\text{ g}}{80\text{ mL}} = 1.2\text{ g/mL}$$

$$\frac{120\text{ g}}{100\text{ mL}} = 1.2\text{ g/mL}$$

$$\frac{\text{Mass}}{\text{Volume}} = \text{a constant ratio}$$

(3) Another way to express this relationship is to say that the mass in g = 1.2 × the volume in mL. (4) As shown in Figure 11–12, the graph permits us to predict values that are *between* the values taken in the experiment and also values that are *outside* the range of values in the experiment. Using the graph we can make predictions like

these: A volume of 70.0 mL of this liquid would have a mass close to 84 or 85 g; a volume of 10.0 mL of this liquid would have a mass of about 12 or 13 g.

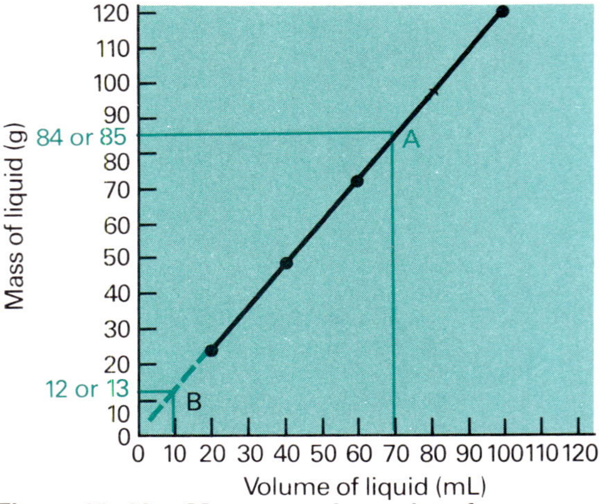

Figure 11–12. Mass vs. volume data for a liquid. (A) Predicting a value *between* data points; (B) predicting a value *beyond* data points.

4. Assessing the Experiment

(3.3, 3.4, 3.5)

The experiment and data are always reviewed after the experiment is completed. Scientists try to determine how accurate the data are, whether limitations or errors were present in the experiment, and if any procedures ought to be redone.

5. Interpreting the Data *(3.6a)*

The results of a laboratory experiment or any other type of research are often presented in tables, graphs, or diagrams. The following examples illustrate how scientists might present data on the ten leading causes of death in the United States in 1900 and 1980. Each example stresses a different aspect of the data, as illustrated in the questions that follow each example.

Data in Table Form Table 2 shows how the data on causes of death might be presented in a table.

Questions that could be asked based on Table 2 include the following:

1. How have the number and the ranking of deaths by accidents changed from 1900 to 1980? (Sample answer) The number of deaths due to accidents increased from 75 to 95 deaths per 100,000 population. It moved from seventh place to third place.

2. How many deaths per 100,000 population occurred in 1900 due to the top five causes of death combined? (Sample answer) 215 + 185 + 140 + 130 + 110 = 780.

3. What diseases from 1900 had disappeared by 1980? What diseases have been added to the 1980 listing?

4. If the population of the United States in 1980 was 200 million, how many people died of cancer in that year? (Sample answer)

$$\text{Total deaths due to cancer} = \frac{185}{100{,}000} \times 200{,}000{,}000 = 185 \times 200 = 37{,}000$$

5. Which six causes of death were among the top ten killers in both 1900 and 1980? Which three causes of death were among the top five killers in both 1900 and 1980?

Data in a Bar Graph Figure 11–13 shows how the data on causes of death could be presented in a bar graph.

Questions that could be asked based on this bar graph include the following:

1. For which diseases did the death rate increase over the period 1900–1980? By approximately how much did the death rates increase? (Sample answer) Heart disease – more than doubled; cancer – nearly tripled; accidents – increased slightly

Table 2 Ten Leading Causes of Death in the U.S., 1900 and 1980

Cause of Death	Deaths Per 100,000 Population		Ranking	
	1900	1980	1900	1980
Pneumonia & influenza	215	40	1	5
Tuberculosis	185	—	2	—
Diarrhea	140	—	3	—
Heart disease	130	340	4	1
Stroke	110	85	5	4
Kidney disease	85	—	6	—
Accidents	75	95	7	3
Cancer	65	185	8	2
Senility	55	—	9	—
Diphtheria	40	—	10	—
Diabetes	—	35	—	6
Liver disease	—	30	—	7
Artery disease	—	25	—	8
Suicide	—	20	—	9
Homicide		15	—	10
Totals	**1100**	**870**		

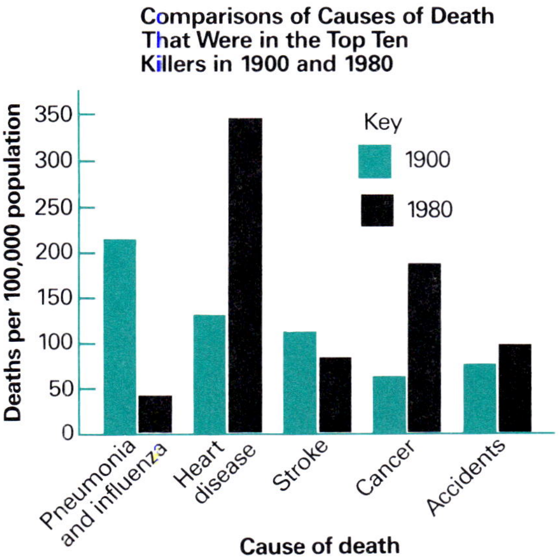

Figure 11–13. Data on causes of death, in bar graph form.

2. For which diseases did the death rate decrease over the period 1900–1980? By approximately how much did each of these decrease?

3. In 1980, how many more times deadly than cancer was heart disease? (Compare the heights of the bars.)

4. For which of the diseases has the death rate shown the greatest change (either increase or decrease) from 1900 to 1980?

5. What were the death rates for pneumonia and influenza in 1900 and 1980, according to this bar graph? (Sample answer) 1900 – about 210 to 220 per 100,000, depending on how the scale is read; 1980 – about 40 per 100,000

Data In a Line Graph Figure 11–14 shows how the data on causes of death could be presented in a line graph.

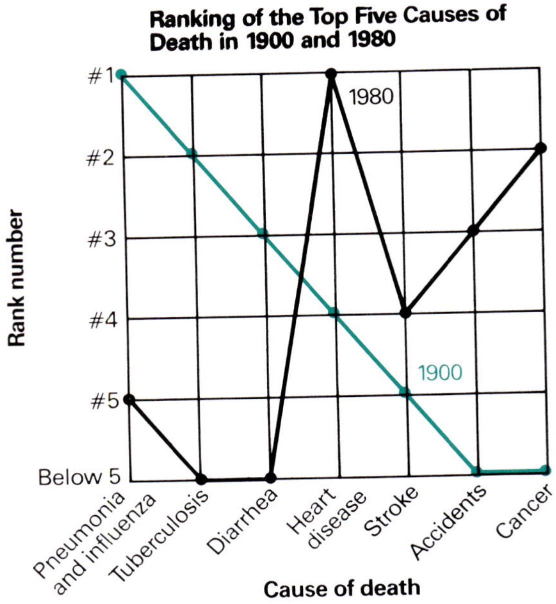

Figure 11–14. Data on causes of death, in line graph form.

Questions that could be asked based on this line graph include the following:

1. What diseases were the #1 cause of death in 1900 and 1980? (Sample answer) 1900 – pneumonia and influenza; 1980 – heart disease
2. Which disease went from being ranked below fifth place in 1900 to being in second place in 1980? Which disease went from second place in 1900 to being ranked below fifth place in 1980?
3. Which disease changed the least in rank between 1900 and 1980?
4. What were the top five killers in 1980, in order of importance?
5. According to the line graph, how did the ranking of accidents as a cause of death change between 1900 and 1980? (Sample answer) In 1900, accidents ranked below #5; in 1980, accidents ranked #3.

Data in Circle Graphs Figure 11–15 shows how the data on causes of death could be presented in circle graphs.

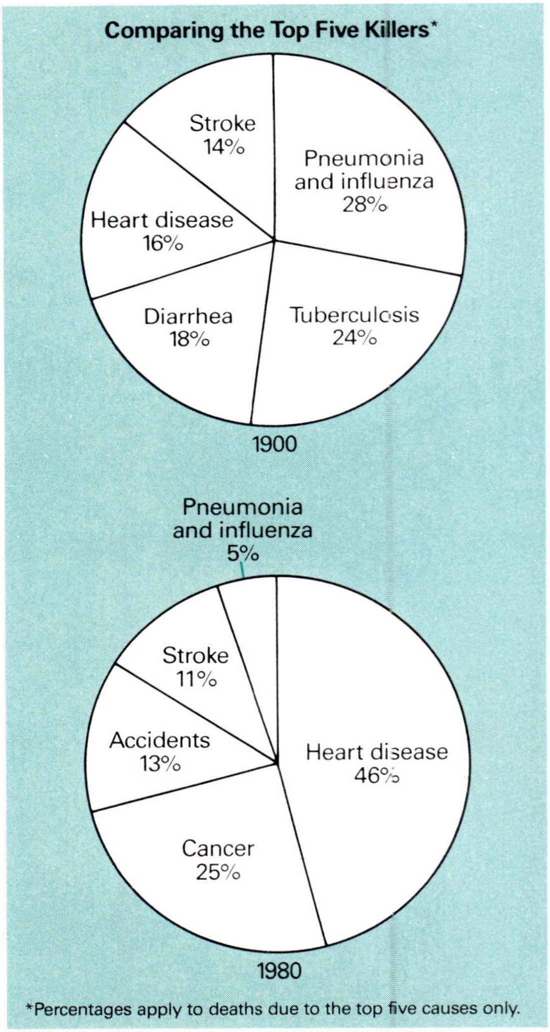

Figure 11–15. Data on causes of death, in circle graph form.

Questions that could be asked based on the circle graphs include the following:

1. What percentage of deaths (due to the top five causes) were caused by strokes in 1900 and 1980? (Sample answer) 1900 – 14%; 1980 – 11%
2. What percentage of deaths (due to the top five causes) were caused by pneumonia and influenza in 1900 and 1980?
3. Which cause of death almost tripled in percentage from 1900 to 1980?
4. In 1980, what percentage of deaths were due to the top two causes combined? (Sample answer) 46% + 25% = 71%
5. How do circle graphs help to convey the importance of each component they contain?

Data in Picture Graphs There are many types of picture graphs. Some, like the one in Figure 11–16, use small symbols to represent a unit amount. Some use a clever drawing of an object to show percentages. For example, a tree might be drawn with parts shaded to show the percentages of trees preserved in forests, used for paper products, used for lumber, and used for fuel. An oil barrel is often drawn to show percentages that go into different products or to show the nations that supply oil.

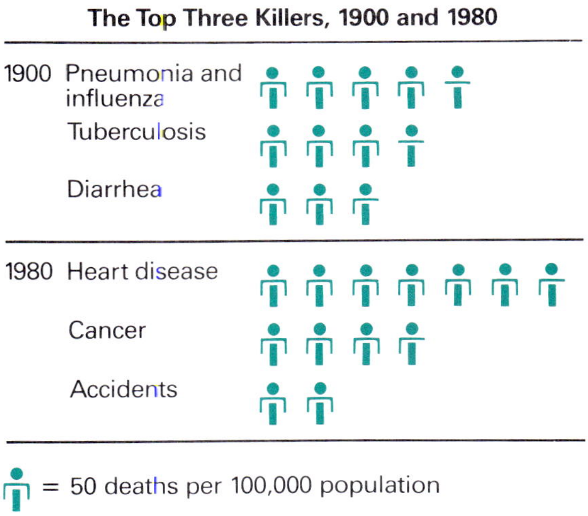

Figure 11–16. Data on causes of death, in picture graph form.

Questions that could be asked based on this picture graph include the following:

1. What was the death rate due to diarrhea in 1900? (Sample answer) The picture graph shows two *full* body symbols and one *partial* body symbol. This means the death rate was more than 100 but less than 150 deaths per 100,000 population, or about 130 per 100,000.
2. What were the death rates in 1980 for the three causes of death given in the picture graph?
3. Suppose disease *X* and disease *Y* have death rates of 250 and 75 per 100,000 population, respectively. If these death rates were drawn with the body symbol used in Figure 11–16, how many full and partial body symbols would be needed for each disease?

6. Explaining a Relationship Using a Model *(3.6b)*

Once a pattern or relationship has been discovered in an experiment, the scientist tries to explain why such results were obtained. To do this a model is suggested. A **model** is a picture or explanation of what might be happening. Models are not directly observable in the experiment but are reasoned out and suggested after some thought about the experiment's results.

For example, suppose a student uses a light meter, as shown in Figure 11–17, to find out how a light's brightness changes with distance.

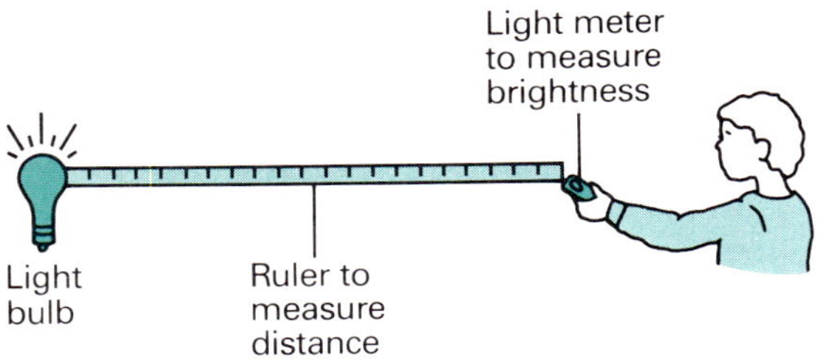

Figure 11–17. Student measuring brightness with a light meter.

The student's results are shown below in Table 3.

Table 3 Student Results with Light Meter

Distance from Light (meters)	Brightness (on light meter)
1	36
2	9.0
3	4.0

The student notes the following relationship: *As the distance from the light was increased, the brightness decreased very rapidly.* What model would explain why a light's brightness decreases rapidly with even a small change in distance? The accepted model for this result, shown in Figure 11–18, assumes that light rays leave the bulb in straight lines. As the light rays spread out they shine upon larger areas, so the brightness of the light decreases. Because the areas grow rapidly, the brightness must decrease rapidly with greater distances.

Here are other examples of models that explain results of an experiment.

Result: Chemical changes go twice as fast for every 10°C rise in temperature.

Model: A higher temperature means atoms are moving faster, so when they collide they have more energy. This higher collision energy increases the rate at which the materials will react (Figure 11–19).

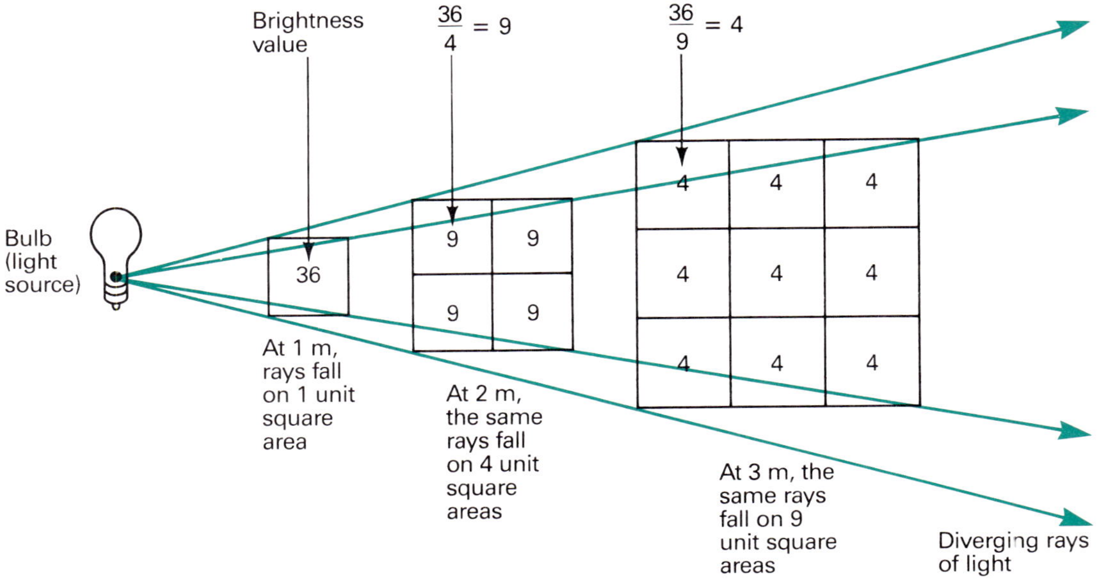

Figure 11–18. A model to explain how brightness decreases with distance.

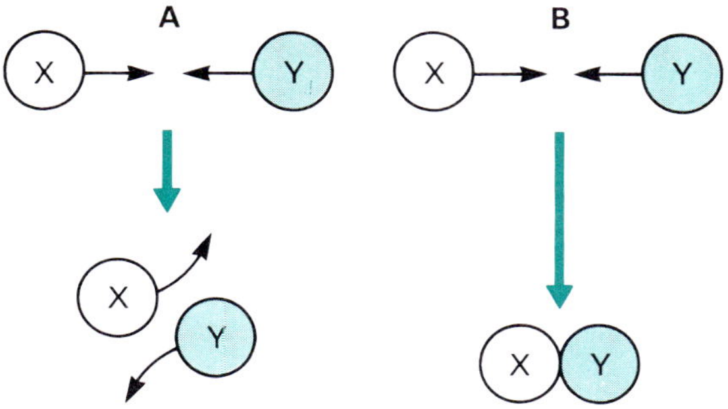

Figure 11–19. A model to explain the effect of temperature on the rate of chemical change. (A) At lower temperatures, materials X and Y don't collide with enough energy to join. (B) At higher temperatures, X and Y collide with greater speeds and energies, allowing them to join.

Result: In biology many chemicals will only join if a third material, called an enzyme, is present.

Model: The enzyme first attaches the two chemicals to itself. Once both are attached to the enzyme, the two chemicals join with each other. The enzyme is no longer necessary to keep them together. This is called the "Lock and Key" model of an enzyme (Figure 11–20).

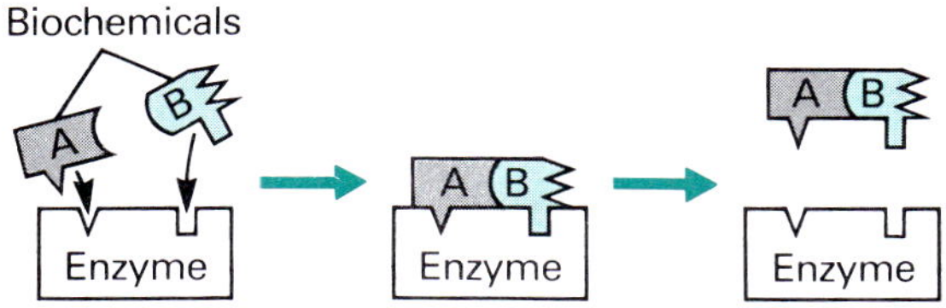

Figure 11–20. "Lock and Key" model for enzyme action.

7. *Further Investigations* *(3.7)*

From the results of an investigation, new questions or problems always arise. An entire new round of experiments may now be planned.

8. *Making Predictions* *(3.8)*

The real test of whether the conclusions or models drawn from an experiment are true is if they can make correct predictions. For example, astronomers used the theory of gravitation to predict the changing positions of the planet Uranus. However, Uranus was found to be delayed from these predictions. Suggestions were made that another planet, not yet discovered, might be pulling on Uranus and causing this delay. Sure enough, a new planet, Neptune, was discovered precisely where it would cause this delaying action on Uranus' orbit. Pluto was also discovered by the same logic. These successful predictions helped to verify the theory of gravitation.

Here is an example of how predictions can be made based on an experiment. Suppose a student hangs masses of various sizes on a spring and then measures the length of the spring, as shown in Figure 11–21.

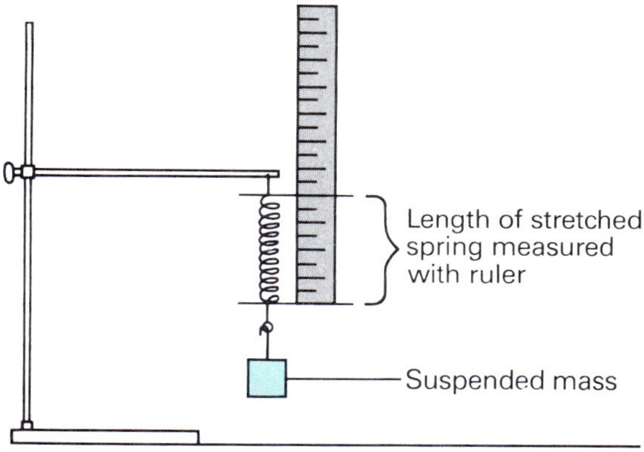

Figure 11–21. Student setup for measuring the length of a stretched spring.

The student obtains the data shown in Table 4.

Table 4 Student Data

Suspended Mass (g)	Length of Spring (cm)
100	7.0
200	8.0
300	9.0
400	10.0

Questions that could be asked based on the student's data include the following:

1. What *qualitative* relationship appears in the data? (Answer) As the mass increases, the length of the spring also increases.

2. What *quantitative* relationship appears in the data? (Answer) Each increase of 100 grams causes the length to increase by 1.0 cm.

3. Make a graph of the data. (Answer) See Figure 11–22.

4. What spring lengths might be predicted for masses of 500 g and 250 g? (Answer) 500 g—a length of 11.0 cm; 250 g—a length of 8.5 cm

5. What masses might stretch the spring to lengths of 12.0 cm and 7.5 cm? (Answer) 12.0 cm—a mass of 600 g; 7.5 cm—a mass of 150 g

6. Is it legitimate to extend this trend far beyond the values measured in the experiment? Can a length for 1000 g or 5000 g be predicted? (Answer) No, predictions beyond the measured data can be made only for values that are not too far beyond the measured values. In this case, as larger masses are added there is no guarantee that the same pattern (a 1.0 cm stretch for each additional 100 g) will continue. Furthermore, there must come a point at which the spring will break.

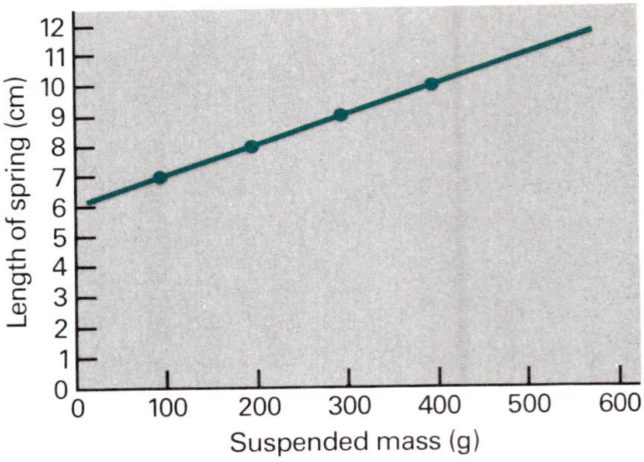

Figure 11–22. Graph of student data, showing suspended mass vs. length of spring.

Sample Questions

1–2. Base your answers to questions 1 and 2 on the information and data table.

A student was studying the relationship between different amounts of substance X and the height of bean plants. She started with six groups, each of which contained the same number of bean plants with identical heights. Conditions were kept the same, except that each group was watered with a different amount of substance X for a period of two weeks. She recorded the amount of substance X used in watering each group of plants and the average height for each group of plants.

Data Table

Group	Amount of Substance *X* Added (mL)	
Group A	6 mL	32.3 cm
Group B	0 mL	28.7 cm
Group C	2 mL	29.4 cm
Group D	8 mL	37.1 cm
Group E	4 mL	31.5 cm
Group F	10 mL	30.7 cm

1. How should the third column in the data table be labeled?
(1) Height of Bean Plants (meters)
(2) Height of Bean Plants (centimeters)
(3) Weight of Bean Plants (grams)
(4) Weight of Bean Plants (milligrams)

2. From the data table it can be concluded that
(1) the greater the amount of substance *X* added, the greater the rate of growth of the bean plants
(2) bean plants grow best when given 10 mL of substance *X* at each watering
(3) the smaller the amount of substance *X* added, the greater the rate of growth of the bean plants
(4) bean plants grow best when given 8 mL of substance *X* at each watering

3–4. Base your answers to questions 3 and 4 on the information in the data table, which shows a summary of high and low temperatures in a town in New York State during one week in April.

Data Table

Day	High Temperature (°F)	Low Temperature (°F)
1	48	40
2	68	46
3	62	42
4	66	30
5	70	40
6	54	48
7	52	34

3. The lowest temperature recorded for the week was on day
(1) 2 (3) 4
(2) 3 (4) 5

4. Freezing temperatures may have occurred on day
(1) 2 (3) 4
(2) 3 (4) 5

5. Identical amounts of boiling water (at 100°C) are poured into two cans that are identical except for their color. Can *A* is painted white outside; can *B* is painted black outside. The temperature of each can is taken every minute for a total of 60 minutes. The room temperature is 20°C. The results are shown in the graph below.

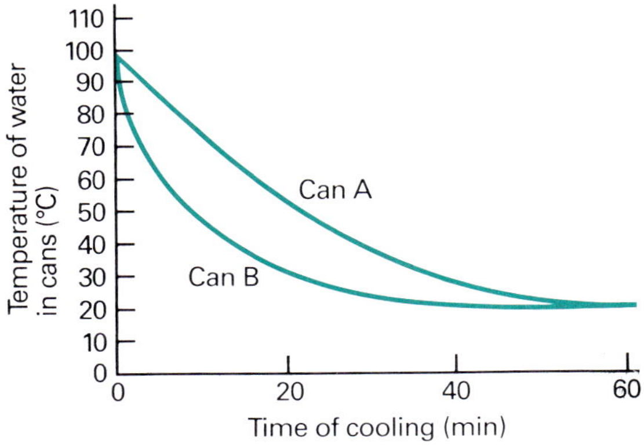

What conclusion is possible from this experiment?
(1) Since the starting and ending temperatures are the same, there is no difference between the cans
(2) The black can permits faster cooling.
(3) Water in a black can will always be colder than water in a white can.
(4) The white can seems to add heat energy into the water.

6. The graph below was developed as the result of an investigation on amounts of bacteria of three identical cultures grown at different temperatures. Which conclusion might be correctly drawn from this graph?

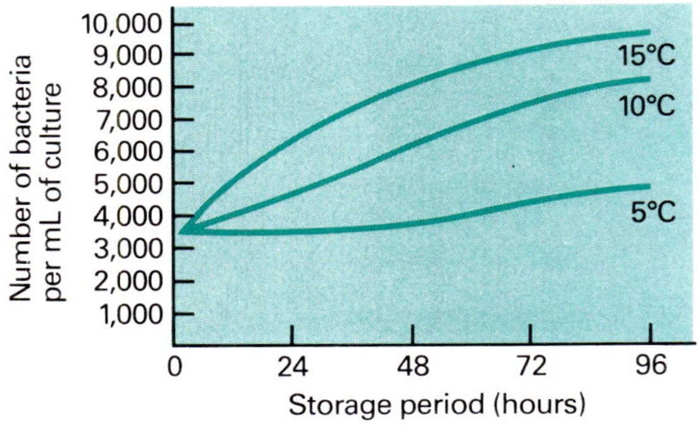

(1) The culture contains no bacteria.
(2) Refrigeration slows down bacterial reproduction.
(3) Temperature is unrelated to the bacteria reproduction rate.
(4) Bacteria cannot grow at a temperature of 5°C.

7–9. Base your answers to questions 7–9 on the information, illustration, and data table that follow.

In engineering labs a compression test is given to solid cylinders of various metals. Tremendous forces squeeze the metal, causing it to compress.

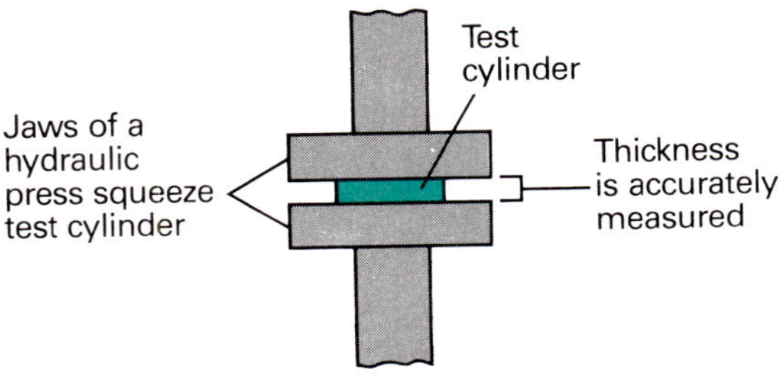

Data for One Sample

Force Applied (tons)	Thickness (mm)
0	352
2	346
4	340
6	334
8	328

7. Which of the following is a *quantitative* relationship in the data?
(1) The test cylinders should all be identical in size.
(2) As compression force increases, the thickness decreases.
(3) At some higher force, the cylinder will melt or collapse.
(4) Each 2-ton increase in force causes a 6-mm decrease in thickness.

8. What thickness can be predicted for 5 tons?
(1) 331 mm
(2) 334 mm
(3) 337 mm
(4) 343 mm

9. Which statement is *not* justified from analysis of the data?
(1) As compression force increases, thickness decreases.
(2) A model to explain the data is that force squeezes the atoms together.
(3) At 10 tons of force, the thickness would be 322 mm.
(4) Predicting a thickness for 200 tons is reasonable.

Issues in Science, Technology, and Society

The Population Boom

In 1961 the magazine *Population Bulletin* published an article by Glenn D. Everett entitled "One Man's Family." In his research on large families, Mr. Everett had come across an Amish farmer in Ohio who had 410 living descendants when he died at age 95. The following table presents facts from the article. Tables and graphs are not appropriate in stories, poetry, and magazine articles that try to convey the "human interest" side of a story. However, they are appropriate in presenting and analyzing the bare facts of a story.

The Miller Family

Generation	Number of People	Number Alive When Mr. Miller Died
#1—Mr. and Mrs. Miller	2	0
#2—Their children	7	5
#3—Their grandchildren	63	61
#4—Their great-grand-children	341	338
#5—Their great-great-grandchildren	6	6
Totals	419	410

Two of Mr. Miller's children died before reaching middle age. All six great-great-grandchildren were born in the last year of his life. This was the largest complete family found in America in 1960.

These figures show the fast-multiplying effect when families have many children, as the Amish people do. They also show that science and technology, through improved medical treatment and nutrition, can affect society. Notice how the survival rate to age 40 increased from generation 2 to generation 3. Contrast these rates to those from hundreds of years ago when the survival rate to age 40 was less than 50 percent.

Generation	Survival Rate to Age 40
#2	5 out of 7, or 71%
#3	61 out of 63, or 97%

Yet there is a dark side to this story. More people means less land and less living space. As Mr. Miller put it, "Where will they all find farms?"

Crowded conditions can produce violence, social instability, and a reduced standard of living. Mass starvation and miserable living conditions are common in some parts of the world today. Such conditions will spread if action is not taken.

Science and technology will be a part of the solution. New sources of food and energy and new housing arrangements are being developed. Technology cannot handle this problem alone, however. Society will have to work together with technology to solve the problems accompanying the population boom.

1. Make a graph of number of people vs. generation for the first four generations. Extend this graph to predict the number of offspring for generation #5.
2. How are science and technology involved with the story of the Miller Family?
3. Make a similar analysis of your own family or the families of your friends. Do you find the same trends as in the Miller data?

RCT Test-Taking Strategies

PREPARING FOR A TEST

Before you take a test, you need to get ready in two ways. First, you need to review the ideas and information that you expect the test to cover. That is what chapters 1–11 of this book have helped you to do. Next, you need to find out as much as you can about what kinds of questions are on the test. For example, does the test include multiple-choice questions? problems? essays?

Once you know what kinds of questions are on the test, you can use strategies that will help you answer the questions. A **strategy** is a way of thinking about a question so that you can use everything you know in choosing or writing your answer.

FINDING OUT ABOUT THE RCT IN SCIENCE

The RCT in Science has 70 questions, almost all of which are multiple choice. In a **multiple-choice question,** you are asked to pick the correct answer—or the best answer—from four choices. This part of the book will help you learn strategies for answering the kinds of multiple-choice questions that make up the RCT in Science.

More than 50 percent of the questions on the RCT in Science require **understanding of concepts** or **recall of information.** These questions look like this:

57. Seventy-eight percent (78%) of air consists of
(1) carbon dioxide
(2) oxygen
(3) boron
(4) nitrogen

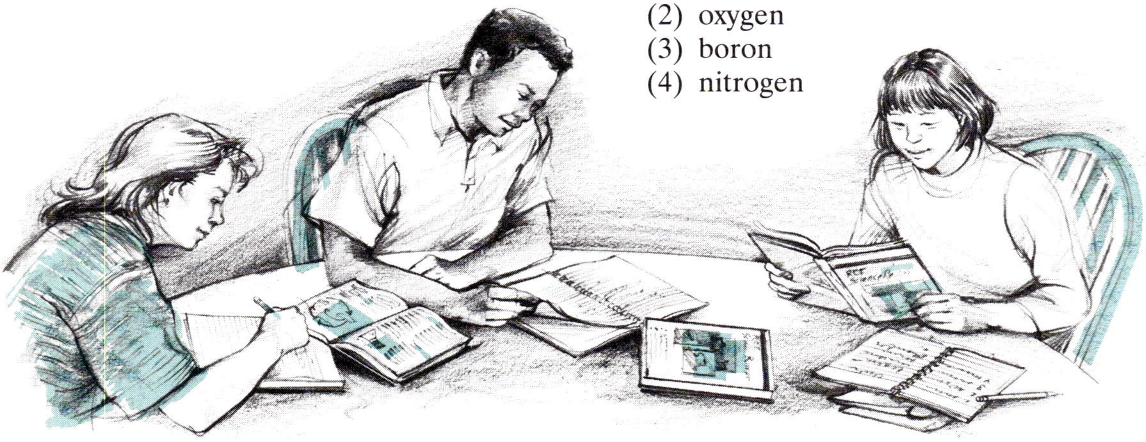

In this kind of question, you need to pick the correct answer from the four choices.

About 20 percent of the questions on the RCT in Science are based on **diagrams.** In this kind of question, you need to understand the diagram and then use it to help you answer the question.

Another 20 percent of the questions are based on **data tables** and **graphs.** You work on these questions in the same way as those with diagrams: first understand the table or graph, and then use that information to answer the question.

STRATEGIES FOR ANSWERING ANY TYPE OF MULTIPLE-CHOICE QUESTION

Four strategies for answering multiple-choice questions are described. As you go along, try out each strategy on the practice questions. Answers to all the practice questions are on page 227.

Strategy #1

Read the question carefully. *Before* you read the choices, try to think of the correct answer.

Practice Question 1: Which process changes a liquid to a gas?

Write your answer on a separate piece of paper. Then compare your answer with the four choices. Find the choice that best matches your answer.

(1) freezing
(2) boiling
(3) condensing
(4) melting

The correct answer is (2) boiling. This strategy helps you use what you already know as you answer the question. If your answer matches one of the choices given, it is likely to be correct.

Use Strategy #1 again on practice questions 2 and 3.

Practice Question 2: Objects fall to Earth's surface because of Earth's

Write your answer on a separate piece of paper. Then compare your answer with the four choices.

(1) rotation
(2) orbit around the sun
(3) gravity
(4) position in the galaxy

Practice Question 3: Electrical devices are grounded so they will be

Write your answer on a separate piece of paper. Then compare your answer with the four choices.

(1) attached securely to the incoming current
(2) more efficient
(3) more reliable in a thunderstorm
(4) safer for people to use

Strategy #2

Read *all four* choices before you decide which one is correct. Sometimes one choice is partially correct, while another one may be completely correct.

Use Strategy #2 in combination with Strategy #1. First read the question and try to think of the correct answer. Then read all the choices and decide which one is correct.

Practice Question 4: Neurons are

Write your answer on a separate piece of paper. Then be sure to read all four choices.

(1) in the brain
(2) always acting separately from the spinal cord

(3) parts of the sense organs
(4) the cells that make up the nervous system

The correct answer is (4). However, notice that choice (1) is a true statement also. Choice (4) is the correct answer because it gives more complete information. If you stopped at choice (1) and did not read all four choices, you might have picked choice (1) as the answer.

Use Strategies #1 and #2 on practice question 5.

Practice Question 5: A fish has gills for breathing under water. These structures are

Write your answer on a separate piece of paper. Then be sure to read all four choices.

(1) a response to stimuli
(2) parts of the fish
(3) known as adaptations
(4) dormant

Strategy #3

Narrow down the choices before you answer the question. Sometimes you can figure out that some of the choices are wrong, even if you are not sure at first which is the correct answer. Use what you know about the questions to help you find the incorrect answer(s). Also look for clues in the question itself.

Using Strategy #3, you eliminate the choices that you know are wrong. When you have decided that a choice is incorrect, draw a line through its number in your test booklet. When you have crossed out all the answers you know are wrong, make the best guess you can from the remaining choices.

To see how Strategy #3 works, read practice question 6 and the paragraphs that follow it. Then apply this strategy to practice questions 7, 8, and 9.

Practice Question 6: The apparent motion of the stars in the night sky is caused by

(1) the rotation of Earth on its axis
(2) the fact that the sun is the "parent" of Earth
(3) the revolution of Earth around the sun
(4) the movement of the stars in circles around Earth

Suppose you have read this question and don't know at first which choice is correct. You can still arrive at an answer. Probably you know that the word *apparent* does not mean "parent." So you can cross out choice (2), because it doesn't relate to the question. Also, you probably know that the stars do not move in circles around Earth. So you can cross out choice (4).

This leaves only choices (1) and (3). If you know what *rotation* means (turning on its own axis), you know that choice (1) is correct. Even if you don't know what *rotation* means, narrowing down the choices lets you guess from only two possibilities rather than four. So your chance of guessing the right answer is twice as good!

Practice Question 7: You are the pilot of a small plane. At the airport in Elmira, you cannot take off if the wind speed on the runway is over 40 knots. The instrument that provides this information is

Write your answer on a separate piece of paper. Then be sure to read all four choices. Decide which choices are incorrect.

(1) the barometer
(2) the anemometer
(3) the wind vane
(4) the wet-and-dry-bulb thermometer

Cross out the choices that you know are wrong. Then choose the correct answer.

Practice Question 8: Oiling the wheel bearings of a bicycle helps to

Write your answer on a separate piece of paper. Then be sure to read all four choices. Decide which choices are incorrect.

(1) increase the energy available
(2) reduce friction
(3) change the direction of the force
(4) transform the bicycle into a pulley

Cross out the choices that you know are wrong. Then choose the correct answer.

Practice Question 9: The rate of a chemical reaction usually increases

Write your answer on a separate piece of paper. Then be sure to read all four choices. Decide which choices are incorrect.

(1) as time goes on
(2) as more elements are added to the reaction
(3) as it gets heavier
(4) as the temperature increases

Cross out the choices that you know are wrong. Then choose the correct answer.

Strategy #4

Try to narrow down the choices first. When you eliminate even one choice and then guess, you increase the chances of your guess being correct. But if you can't narrow down the choices at all, *just guess!* There is no penalty for guessing incorrectly on the RCT in Science. So you have one chance in four of guessing correctly.

Remember

Strategy #1: Read the question carefully and try to think of the correct answer before you read the choices. Compare your answer with the four choices and find the choice that best matches your answer.
Strategy #2: Be sure to read all four choices before you decide which one is correct.
Strategy #3: Narrow down the choices before you answer the question. Try to eliminate the choices you know are wrong.
Strategy #4: If you can't narrow down the choices at all, just guess!

ANSWERING QUESTIONS BASED ON DIAGRAMS

When a question includes a diagram or picture, it usually gives the information needed to get the correct answer. With this kind of question, follow these two steps.

Step 1: First look carefully at the diagram or picture. Ask yourself: What is this diagram about? What does this diagram tell me?

Look at the Science Skill "Interpreting Diagrams" on page 81 of this book. It gives an example of a diagram and questions you might ask yourself to help you understand the diagram.

Now look at Figure A below and practice step 1. On a separate piece of paper, write your answers to the two questions: What is Figure A about? What does Figure A tell me?

Step 2: Read the question carefully, and follow strategies 1–4 for answering multiple-choice questions.

Practice Question 10: During the event shown in Figure A, the moon's shadow

(1) is larger than Earth
(2) is the same size as Earth
(3) is smaller than Earth
(4) can be larger or smaller than Earth

In step 1, you should have written answers similar to these: The diagram shows Earth, the sun, and the moon. The moon is between Earth and the sun, and the moon's shadow is falling on Earth. The diagram must show an eclipse. Since the moon is blocking out the sun from a part of Earth's surface, it shows an eclipse of the sun.

Following strategies 1–4, you arrive at the correct answer, (3).

Now use steps 1 and 2 to answer practice questions 11–13.

Practice Question 11: Currently the weather in City A is warm and clear. According to the diagram, what will happen to City A's weather soon?

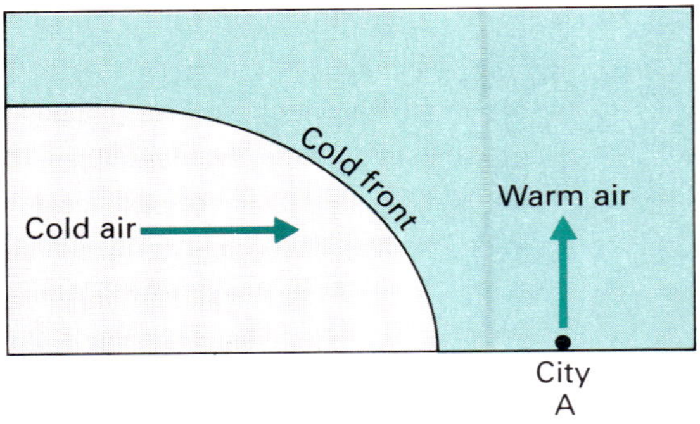

On a separate piece of paper, answer these questions: What is the diagram about? What does this diagram tell me? Then write the correct answer if you know it.

(1) It will become cooler and rainy.
(2) It will get hot.
(3) There will be no change.
(4) It will be the beginning of winter.

Figure A

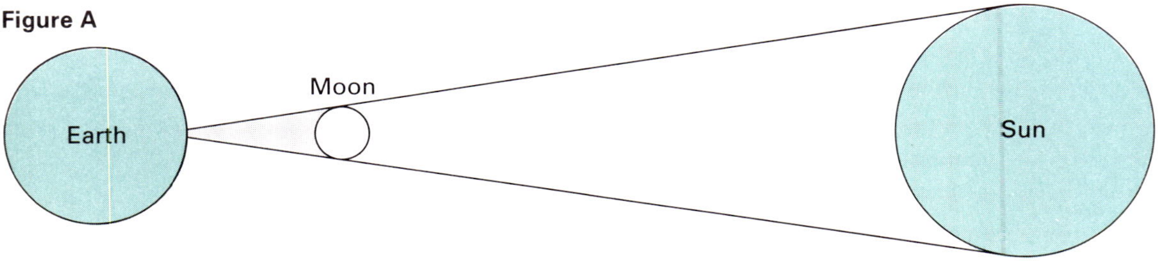

Practice Question 12: The diagram shows a metal spoon in a pot of boiling water. Why is the spoon hot?

On a separate piece of paper, answer these questions: What is this diagram about? What does this diagram tell me? Then write the correct answer if you know it.

(1) Metal is an insulator.
(2) Heat energy is the rapid movement of the particles in the water.
(3) Heat flows from the water into the metal.
(4) Heat expands the metal spoon.

Practice Question 13: In the food chain shown, what role do the decomposers play?

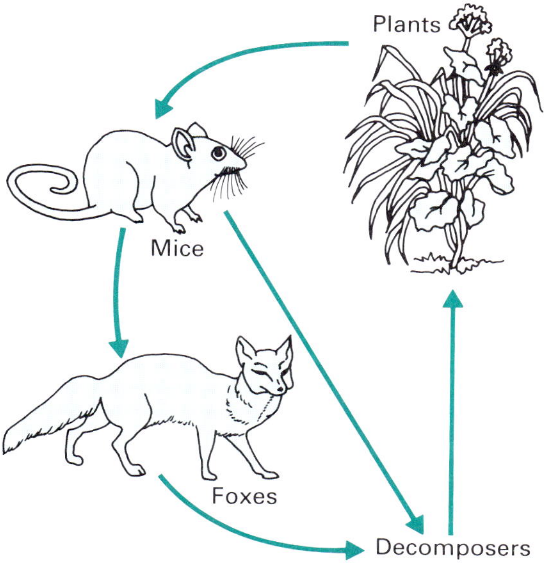

On a separate piece of paper, answer these questions: What is this diagram about? What does this diagram tell me? Then write the correct answer if you know it.

(1) The decomposers produce food for the plants.
(2) The decomposers break down the remains of dead organisms and organic wastes.
(3) The decomposers feed the soil.
(4) The decomposers play no role in this food chain.

Remember

To answer questions based on diagrams, follow these steps.

Step 1: First look carefully at the diagram or picture. Ask yourself: What is this diagram about? What does this diagram tell me?

Step 2: Read the question carefully, and follow strategies 1–4 for answering multiple-choice questions.

ANSWERING QUESTIONS BASED ON DATA TABLES

A data table uses rows and columns to present information in a condensed way. The kinds of information given are usually listed as **column heads** across the top row of the table. The subjects of the table are usually listed in the left-hand column.

For example, the table below contains facts about three dairy products. The dairy products are listed in the left-hand column.

Nutritional Facts About Three Dairy Products

Food	Calcium (% RDA)	Calories	Protein	Fat
Yogurt (1 cup)	35	150	9g	7g
Lowfat milk (1 cup)	35	110	10g	2g
Chocolate milk (1 cup)	30	230	8g	9g

Read the table by following these steps.

1. Read the title at the top of the table. It tells you what the table is about.
2. Read the list of subjects in the left-hand column. In this table, there are three subjects: yogurt, lowfat milk, and chocolate milk.
3. Read the categories of data given as column heads across the top of the table. In this table, there are five categories: food, calcium, calories, protein, and fat.
4. Read the information given for the first subject, going across the table from left to right. Refer back to the top row of categories each time you move to a new column. Be sure to note whether the table shows amount, percentage, or some other measure.
5. Repeat step 4 for each subject in the left-hand column.
6. Evaluate the data in the table by choosing the first category in the top row and reading down the column. Become aware of the differences among the data for each subject. Then do the same for the other categories in the top row of the table.

When a question is based on a data table, the data table usually gives you the information you need to get the correct answer. To answer questions based on data tables, follow these steps.

Step 1: Quickly read the data table, following the procedure you just learned.

Step 2: Use the strategies you have learned for multiple-choice questions to help you answer the question.

Step 3: Look back at the data table as needed to find the correct answer.

Use steps 1–3 to answer practice questions 14–19.

Practice Question 14: Base your answer to this question on the data table entitled "Nutritional Facts About Three Dairy Products."
For a person who wants to have a low-fat and high-protein diet, which food would be the best choice?

If you know the correct answer, write it on a separate piece of paper.

(1) yogurt
(2) chocolate milk
(3) lowfat milk
(4) none of the above

The question asks about two categories in the table: protein and fat. To find the correct answer in the table, look at the protein and fat information for each food. Yogurt has more protein than fat, so it is a possibility. Chocolate milk has more fat than protein, so you would eliminate it as a possible answer. Lowfat milk has more protein than fat, so it is another possible answer.

When you compare the data for your two possible answers, yogurt and lowfat milk, you see that lowfat milk is higher in protein and lower in fat than yogurt. So you know the correct answer must be (3) lowfat milk.

Practice Question 15: Base your answer to this question on the data table entitled "Nutritional Facts About Three Dairy Products."

If you drank three cups of lowfat milk, what percentage of your RDA of calcium would you consume?

If you know the correct answer, write it on a separate piece of paper.

(1) 100%
(2) 110%
(3) 90%
(4) 105%

Practice Question 16: The table at the right shows causes of death in the United States in 1900 and 1980.

For which disease did the death rate decrease the most from 1900 to 1980?

If you know the correct answer, write it on a separate piece of paper.

(1) pneumonia and influenza
(2) diarrhea
(3) stroke
(4) diabetes

Causes of Death in the U.S., 1900 and 1980

Cause of Death	Deaths Per 100,000 Population	
	1900	1980
Pneumonia and influenza	215	40
Diarrhea	140	—
Heart disease	130	340
Stroke	110	85
Accidents	75	95
Cancer	65	185
Liver disease	—	30

Practice Question 17: Base your answer to this question on the data table entitled "Causes of Death in the U.S., 1900 and 1980."

Which cause of death nearly tripled over this 80-year period?

If you know the correct answer, write it on a separate piece of paper.

(1) pneumonia and influenza
(2) cancer
(3) accidents
(4) heart disease

Practice Question 18: The table shows the speeds of sound and light through different substances.

Speeds of Sound and Light

Medium	Speed of Sound *(miles/sec)*	Speed of Light *(miles/sec)*
Water	0.9	138,000
Air	0.2	186,000

According to the table, through which medium does light travel most quickly?

If you know the correct answer, write it on a separate piece of paper.

(1) sound
(2) water
(3) air
(4) solids

Practice Question 19: Base your answer to this question on the table entitled "Speeds of Sound and Light."

About how many times faster does sound travel through water than through air?

If you know the correct answer, write it on a separate piece of paper.

(1) 10 times faster
(2) 138,000 times faster
(3) 3 times faster
(4) 4.5 times faster

Remember

To answer questions based on data tables, follow these steps.

Step 1: Quickly read the data table, following the procedure you just learned.

Step 2: Use the strategies you have learned for multiple-choice questions to help you answer the question.

Step 3. Look back at the data table as needed to find the correct answer.

ANSWERING QUESTIONS BASED ON GRAPHS

A graph is a "tool" for showing relationships among data. The RCT in Science has questions based on three different types of graphs: bar graphs, line graphs, and circle graphs. If you need to review the various types of graphs, refer to pages 202–207 of this book.

When a question is based on a graph, the graph usually contains the information you need to get the correct answer. To answer questions based on graphs, follow these steps.

Step 1: Read the graph and answer these two questions: *What is this graph about? What does this graph show me?*

Step 2: Use the strategies you have learned for multiple-choice questions to help you answer the question.

Step 3: Look back at the graph as needed to find the correct answer.

Use steps 1–3 to answer practice questions 20–25.

Practice Question 20: Base your answer to this question on the graph below.

First read the graph and answer these two questions: What is this graph about? What does this graph show me? Then read the question and use your multiple-choice strategies.

Which planet is about ten times farther from the sun than Earth?

If you know the correct answer, write it on a separate piece of paper.

(1) Venus
(2) Uranus
(3) Saturn
(4) Neptune

Distance from Sun as Compared to Earth's Distance from Sun

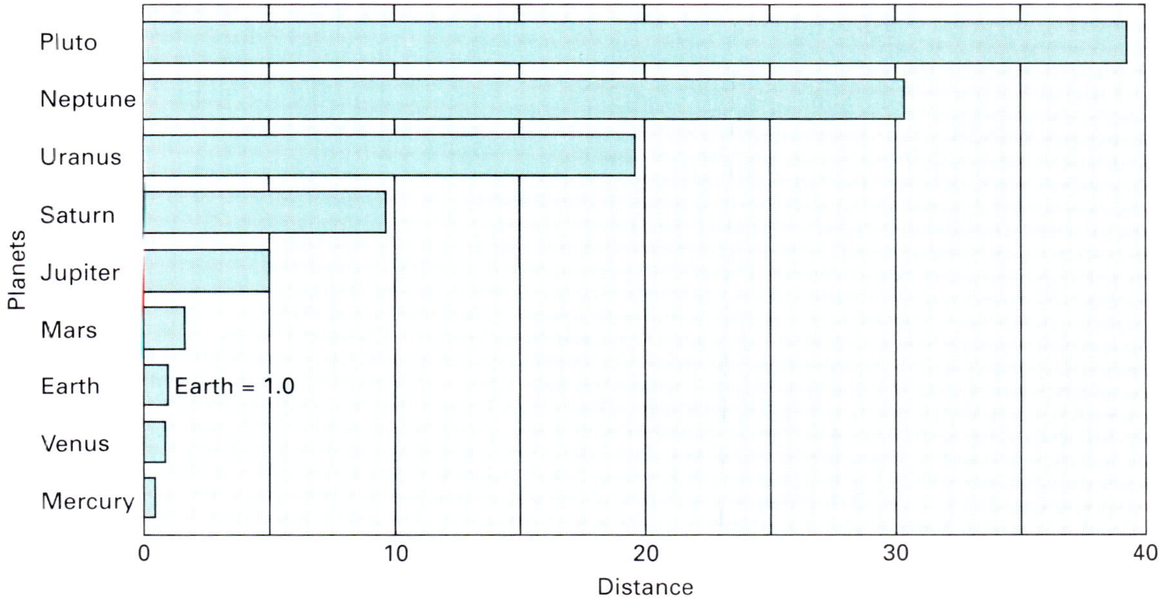

Practice Question 21: Base your answer to this question on the graph entitled "Distance from Sun as Compared to Earth's Distance from Sun."

How many times farther from the sun is Pluto than Earth?

If you know the correct answer, write it on a separate piece of paper.

(1) 39
(2) 40
(3) 41
(4) 34

Practice Question 22: Base your answer to this question on the graph below.

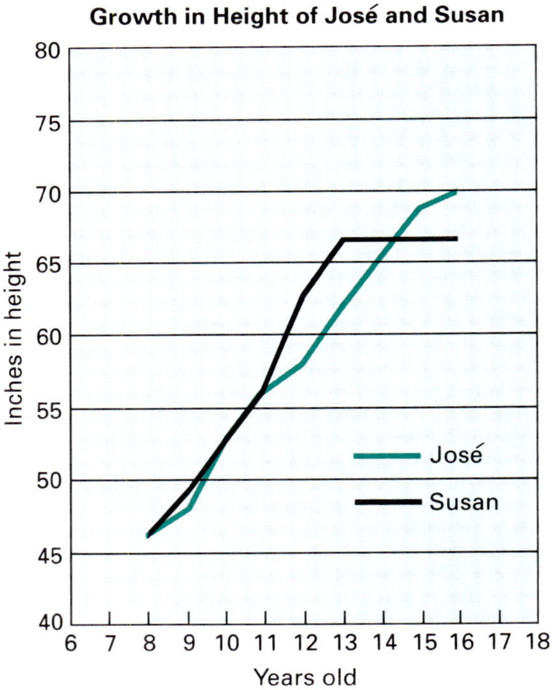

First read the graph and answer these two questions: What is this graph about? What does this graph show me? Then read the question and use your multiple-choice strategies.

At what ages was Susan taller than José?

If you know the correct answer, write it on a separate piece of paper.

(1) 12 and 13
(2) 12, 13, and 14
(3) 12
(4) 13 and 14

Practice Question 23: Base your answer to this question on the graph entitled "Growth in Height of José and Susan."

At what age did Susan reach her full height?

If you know the correct answer, write it on a separate piece of paper.

(1) 11
(2) 13
(3) 15
(4) 18

Practice Question 24: Base your answer to this question on the graph below.

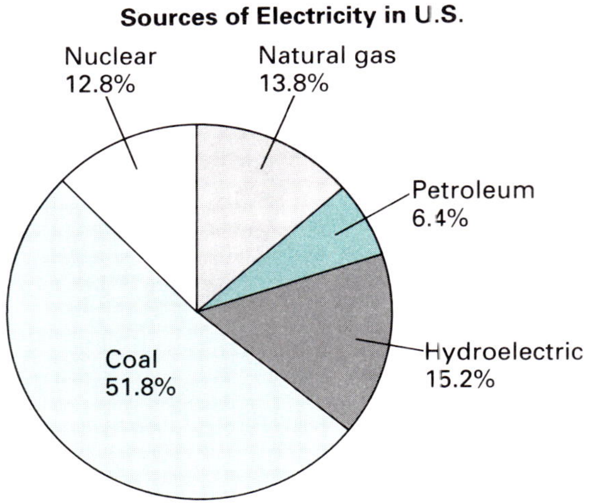

First read the graph and answer these two questions: What is this graph about? What does this graph show me? Then read the question and use your multiple-choice strategies.

Which source of electric energy contributed more than all of the others combined?

If you know the correct answer, write it on a separate piece of paper.

(1) gas
(2) nuclear
(3) hydro
(4) coal

Practice Question 25: Base your answer to this question on the graph entitled "Sources of Electricity in U.S."

Which source of electricity contributes about half as much as nuclear?

If you know the correct answer, write it on a separate piece of paper.

(1) gas
(2) petroleum
(3) hydro
(4) coal

Remember

To answer questions based on graphs, follow these steps.
Step 1: Read the graph and answer these two questions: *What is this graph about? What does this graph show me?*
Step 2: Use the strategies you have learned for multiple-choice questions to help you answer the question.
Step 3. Look back at the graph as needed to find the correct answer.

PREPARING FOR THE RCT IN SCIENCE

Here are three tips that will help you get ready for the RCT in Science. You will also find them useful in preparing for other tests.

Spread Your Studying Over Several Days

It is better to study three or four times for an hour each on different days than to study for three or four hours the night before the test. Most people remember more when their studying is spaced out over several days. So, if you plan to spend four hours studying for the RCT in Science, spend an hour a day over four days rather than four hours the night before the test. Also, each time you study, look back at some material you have already covered as well as looking at new material.

Review Your Strategies

The night before the test, review your strategies for answering multiple-choice questions. Be sure to go over all the strategies, so you can use them all when you take the RCT in Science. These strategies will help you use all of the ideas and data that you know.

Get a Good Night's Sleep

On the night before the test, get a good night's sleep. And be sure not to skip meals. If the test is in the morning, be sure to eat breakfast. If the test is in the afternoon, be sure to eat lunch.

You have probably heard this before, and maybe you think it is foolish, but sleeping enough and eating correctly really do make a big difference. If you are tired or hungry, you won't be able to concentrate as well on the test.

TAKING THE RCT IN SCIENCE

Remember as you take the test that the RCT in Science does not have a time limit. Don't feel that you need to rush to get through it. You will want to work at a steady pace, but don't feel that you have to hurry.

When you come to a question for which you do not know the answer, narrow down the choices and make the best guess you can. If you can't narrow down the choices at all, mark the question and come back to it when you have answered all of the other questions. Sometimes you will remember something during the test that will help you.

If you still can't narrow down the choices in any way after you have come back to a question, just guess. You have a 25 percent chance of guessing correctly, and there is no penalty on the RCT for an incorrect answer.

ANSWERS TO PRACTICE QUESTIONS

1. (2) The process in which a liquid changes to a gas is boiling.
2. (3) Gravity is the force that causes objects to fall to Earth's surface.
3. (4) Grounding causes electricity to be drained to the ground.
4. (4) The cells that make up the nervous system are neurons.
5. (3) Gills are an adaptation enabling fish to breathe under water.
6. (1)
7. (2) An anemometer measures wind speed. A barometer measures atmospheric pressure; a wind vane shows wind direction; the wet-and-dry-bulb thermometer is used to determine relative humidity.
8. (2) Oil is used to reduce friction in the bearings.
9. (4) Most reactions go at a faster rate if the temperature is increased. The rate of a reaction stays the same over time, although the reaction progresses as time goes by. Adding other elements does not affect reaction rate. Answer (3) is meaningless.
10. (3)
11. (1) The diagram shows an advancing cold front. Rain usually accompanies the arrival of a front.
12. (3) Only choice 3 provides an answer to the question. Choices 2 and 4 have nothing to do with the question asked. If choice 1 were true, heat would not flow into the spoon.
13. (1) Choice 2 is true; it is a definition of "decomposers." However, it does not answer the question. According to the arrows on the food chain, choice 4 is incorrect and choice 1 is correct.
14. (3)
15. (4) Find the percentage of RDA of calcium in lowfat milk in the table (35% per cup). Then multiply by 3 to obtain the correct answer.
16. (1) Pneumonia and influenza showed a decrease of 215 − 40, or 175 fewer deaths per 100,000. For diarrhea the difference was 140 fewer and for stroke it was 25 fewer. Diabetes is not listed in the table.
17. (2) Deaths due to pneumonia and influenza declined, deaths due to accidents increased slightly, and deaths due to heart disease increased about $2\frac{1}{2}$ times.
18. (3) According to the table, the speed of light in air is 186,000 miles/sec, and in water it is 138,000 miles/sec. The speed of light in solids is not shown. Sound is not a medium.
19. (4) To find the answer, divide 0.9 by 0.2. Sound travels 4.5 times faster through water than through air.
20. (3) According to the graph, Venus is closer to the sun than Earth. Uranus is almost 20 times farther from the sun, and Neptune is about 30 times farther from the sun.
21. (1) Choice 3 cannot be correct because it would be off the graph. In order for choice 2 to be correct, the bar for Pluto would have to extend all the way to the edge of the graph. Choice 4 seems to apply to Neptune, not Pluto.
22. (1) Look for the places on the graph where Susan's line is above José's.
23. (2) Susan's height seems to have leveled off after age 13.
24. (4) Since coal contributed 51.8%, it must be the correct answer.
25. (2) Nuclear contributes 12.8%. Half of that amount would be 6.4%, which is the amount contributed by petroleum.

Glossary

absorption: The weakening of light as it passes through a substance.

acid test: A test in which a few drops of hydrochloric acid are placed on a mineral sample to see whether the mineral contains carbonates.

adaptation: A structure or pattern of behavior that helps an organism to survive in its environment.

air mass: A large body of air that has the same temperature, pressure, and humidity throughout.

air pollutants: Harmful substances added to the air by human activities.

air pollution: The addition of harmful substances to the atmosphere.

air pressure: The force with which air presses down on Earth.

allergy: An abnormal sensitivity to certain substances in the environment.

altitude: The height of a place above sea level.

apparent motion: A movement that does not really occur but that appears to occur because of one's viewpoint.

arteries: Thick, muscular blood vessels that carry oxygen-rich blood from the heart to all parts of the body.

asexual reproduction: Reproduction in which a new individual forms from a single parent.

atom: The smallest particle of any element.

axis: An imaginary line through Earth's center around which Earth turns.

bedrock: Unbroken solid rock.

benefit: An advantage to society of a technology or device.

biological succession: The process by which new communities are established in an area after an ecosystem is destroyed or disturbed.

biological weathering: The breaking down of rock by plants and animals.

blood: A liquid tissue, composed of several different types of cells, that transports digested food, water, and oxygen to the cells of the body and transports carbon dioxide and other wastes from the cells.

brain: The part of the central nervous system, located in the skull, that interprets sensory impulses and coordinates and controls body activities.

breastbone: A bone in the top of the chest to which the ribs are attached.

bronchi: Two large branches of the windpipe that carry air to the lungs.

burden: A disadvantage to society of a technology or device.

calorie: A unit used to measure heat energy.

capillaries: Tiny blood vessels that surround the body tissues and permit the exchange of materials between the blood and the body cells.

cartilage: A flexible tissue that cushions the bones and provides flexibility.

cell: The unit of structure and function in an organism.

cellular respiration: The release of energy from food that takes place in the cells. The food combines with oxygen and energy is released. Carbon dioxide and water are produced as waste products of cellular respiration.

chemical bond: The link that holds atoms together.

chemical change: A change in which a new material is produced.

chemical digestion: The process during which the nutrients in food are changed into a form that can be absorbed into the bloodstream.

chemical weathering: The breaking down of rock due to changes in its chemical composition.

chemistry: The study of what the world is made from.

circuit: The path electricity takes as it flows.

cleavage: The property of a mineral to break in definite directions along smooth surfaces or faces.

climate: The general weather of a place over a long period of time.

cloud: A large mass of tiny condensed water drops.

coal: A hard black rock, made from almost pure carbon, that is burned to produce energy.

cold front: The boundary that forms when a cold air mass moves into a warm air mass.

community: All the different populations of living things interacting in any given area.

compound: A combination of elements.

condensation: The change of phase from gas (vapor) to liquid.

conductor: A material that permits electricity to pass very well.

conservation: The saving of materials and energy by wise usage.

consumer: An organism that obtains energy from the food it eats. Animals are consumers.

continental shelf: The section of the ocean bottom that slopes gently away from the shore.

continental slope: A steeper portion of the ocean bottom that connects the continental shelf with the ocean floor.

control part: The portion of an experiment in which the experimental variable is *not* changed.

crystal form: A geometric or crystalline mineral shape that is determined by the internal arrangement of the atoms making up the mineral.

data: Individual facts or pieces of information.

decomposer: An organism that breaks down organic wastes and the remains of dead organisms.

degree: The unit used to measure temperature.

density: The mass of a substance divided by its volume.

dew point: The temperature at which water vapor starts condensing into water.

dissolve: To enter into solution.

doldrums: The area around the equator where there is very little wind.

earthquake: A sudden movement in Earth's crust.

ecosystem: All the living and nonliving things in the environment.

efficiency: The amount of energy given out by a machine divided by the amount of energy put in. An efficient machine loses very little energy.

electrical energy: The energy carried by moving electrons.

electricity: The flow of large numbers of electrons.

electromagnetic waves: A family of waves that includes radio and television waves, microwaves, infrared waves, visible light, ultraviolet waves, X-rays, gamma rays, and others.

element: One of the 106 substances from which all other substances are made.

ellipse: An oval shape, somewhat like that of an egg or football.

energy: The ability to do work.

environment: All the living and nonliving things in an organism's surroundings that affect the way the organism lives and acts.

erosion: The process by which rock material is carried away.

esophagus: A tube that connects the mouth with the stomach.

evaporation: The change of phase from liquid to gas (vapor).

excretion: The process by which wastes are removed from the cells into the blood and eventually from the body.

experimental part: The portion of an experiment in which a single variable is changed.

fault: A crack in Earth's crust along which movement has occurred.

feces: Solid human wastes.

flammable: Capable of burning easily.

folding: The process by which rocks are squeezed into folds.

food chain: The flow of energy among organisms.

fossil: The remains or imprint of an ancient animal or plant.

fossil fuel: A fuel formed from the remains of once-living things. Coal, oil, and natural gas are fossil fuels.

fractional distillation: The process by which the various materials in oil are separated from each other by boiling.

fracture: An irregular break in a mineral.

friction: The rubbing of one surface against another. Friction causes energy to be lost as heat and results in a decrease in efficiency.

front: The boundary between two air masses.

galaxy: A large group of stars. The sun is in the Milky Way galaxy.

gametes: Reproductive cells (sperm and egg).

generator: A device that produces electricity.

glacier: A large, slowly-moving mass of snow and ice.

grounding: The connecting of a wire from a machine to a metal object that is in contact with the ground. Any excess electricity is conducted harmlessly to the ground.

ground water: Water in the soil and rock.

habitat: The environment in which an organism lives.

hardness: The ability of a mineral to resist scratching.

heart: An organ made of muscle tissue that pumps blood to all parts of the body.

heat energy: Energy caused by the movement and collision of the particles in a material.

high: An area of high air pressure.

hormones: Chemicals secreted by the endocrine glands directly into the bloodstream. Hormones are transported by the blood to other organs where they produce their effects.

humidity: The amount of water vapor in the air.

hypothesis: A temporary explanation.

igneous rock: A rock that formed from cooled and hardened magma.

index fossil: The fossil of an organism that existed for only a short period of time and was relatively abundant.

insulator: A material that does not permit electricity to pass.

inversion: A condition that occurs when the air at the surface is cooler than the air above it.

involuntary muscles: Muscles that cannot be consciously controlled. The cardiac muscle, which is responsible for the heart's pumping action, is an involuntary muscle.

joints: Places in the skeleton where bones are connected to each other.

kidneys: A pair of organs that filter water, urea, minerals, and other wastes from the blood.

kinetic energy: Energy of motion.

land pollution: Damage done to the land by the activities of people.

large intestine: Organ through which indigestible materials pass on their way out of the body. Water is reabsorbed from these indigestible materials into the bloodstream.

latitude: The measure of a place's distance north or south of the equator.

lens: A piece of glass that has been ground to a special shape in order to bend light passing through it.

ligaments: Connective tissue that connects bones to bones at joints.

light-year: The distance light can travel in one year.

limbs: The arms and legs.

locomotion: The movement of the entire body.

loudness: The strength of sound vibrations.

low: An area of low air pressure.

lungs: Two spongy organs made of air sacs. In the lungs, oxygen passes from the air sacs into the capillaries, and carbon dioxide moves from the capillaries into the air sacs.

luster: The way the surface of a mineral reflects light.

lymph: A fluid that bathes the body cells.

lymph vessels: Tiny vessels that surround all the body tissues and bathe the body cells with fluid.

machine: A device that transfers mechanical energy from one object to another.

magma: Hot, molten rock lying beneath Earth's surface.

mammary glands: The breasts, which produce milk that nourishes the offspring.

mass: The amount of matter in an object.

matter: Anything that takes up space and has mass.

medium: The substance through which sound waves and other waves travel.

meiosis: A kind of cell division that reduces the number of chromosomes in half, forming sperm or egg cells.

meniscus: The curved surface of a liquid in a container.

metamorphic rock: Rock formed from igneous or sedimentary rock that has been subjected to extreme heat, pressure, and/or chemical action.

meteor: The flash in the sky caused by a chunk of rock falling through the atmosphere.

meteorite: A piece of rock from space that passes through the atmosphere and lands on the ground.

meteorologist: A scientist who studies the weather.

microorganism: An organism that is too small to be seen with the unaided eye.

microscope: An instrument used to magnify tiny objects.

mineral: A solid inorganic substance with definite physical and chemical properties.

mining: The process by which resources such as coal are removed from the ground.

mitosis: A kind of cell division that results in the reproduction of new cells.

model: A picture or explanation used to understand the pattern found in a set of facts.

muscles: Tissue that expands and contracts to move the joints and some organs.

natural contaminants: Harmful substances added to the air by natural happenings, such as volcanoes and forest fires.

natural gas: A fossil fuel that is trapped in rock layers.

neurons: The cells that make up the nervous system.

nonrenewable resources: Resources that cannot be replenished.

nuclear energy: Energy released from the center (nucleus) of an atom.

nutrients: Substances in food that provide energy and the materials for growth and repair.

observation: Something that can be directly seen or measured.

ocean floor: The bottom of the ocean, that stretches from continent to continent.

orbit: The path an object follows as it moves in space.

organ: A group of tissues working together to do a special job.

organism: A living thing.

organ system: A group of organs working together to perform a specific function.

ovaries: Two organs of the female reproductive system that produce eggs.

oviducts: Two tubes through which eggs travel from the ovaries to the uterus.

pathogens: Harmful microorganisms, including some bacteria, viruses, fungi, and protozoa.

phase: (1) One of the three forms – solid, liquid, or gas – that matter may take. (2) The apparent change in the shape of the moon as seen from Earth.

photosynthesis: The process by which green plants make food. In the presence of light energy, carbon dioxide and water combine during photosynthesis to produce food and oxygen.

physical change: A change in which the look of the matter changes, but not what it is made from. Examples of physical changes include changes of phase, grinding, tearing, breaking, and dissolving.

physical digestion: The process of breaking food into smaller pieces.

physical weathering: The breaking of rock into smaller pieces.

plain: A broad, flat region of undisturbed sedimentary rock with little variation in elevation.

plateau: An area of undisturbed sedimentary rocks that sits at a high altitude.

plate tectonics: The theory that Earth's crust is broken into a number of blocks, or plates, that move about.

potential energy: Stored energy, or energy of position.

precipitation: Condensed water that falls from the sky. Rain, snow, sleet, and hail are the four kinds of precipitation.

prevailing winds: Winds that always blow in the same direction, forming the pattern of Earth's winds.

problem: A question for which scientists seek an answer.

producers: Organisms that make food. Green plants are producers.

qualitative: A description of observed facts using words alone.

quantitative: A description of observed facts using measured quantities.

radiation: (1) Invisible particles given out by radioactive materials. (2) The movement of energy in the form of waves.

radioactive dating: A method of finding the actual age of a rock, which uses radioactive decay rates.

reflection: The return (bouncing) of light from a surface it strikes.

reflex: An automatic, inborn response to a stimulus.

renewable resources: Resources, such as soil, forests, and water, that can be replenished.

reproduction: The process by which living things make more of their own kind.

respiration: The process by which oxygen is taken in and carbon dioxide is released.

response: The reaction to a stimulus.

revolution: The movement of one object around another object, for example, the movement of Earth around the sun.

ribs: Curved bones that surround and protect the heart and lungs.

rock: A naturally-occurring solid substance made of one or more minerals.

rock cycle: The interrelationship among the three types of rock. Any type can change to any other type.

rotation: Turning or spinning around an axis.

science: The study of the natural world.

scientific method: A series of steps used by scientists in solving problems.

sedimentary rock: Rock that formed from fragments cemented together under pressure.

sense organs: Organs that are adapted to receive stimuli. The sense organs include the eyes, ears, nose, taste buds, and receptors in the skin.

sexual reproduction: Reproduction that requires two parents.

simple machines: The basic parts of all complex machines. Levers, pulleys, inclined planes, screws, and gears are simple machines.

skin: The organ that covers and protects the body. Sweat glands in the skin excrete wastes such as water, salts, and nitrogenous substances.

skull: A group of flat bones that surround and protect the brain.

small intestine: Organ in which digestion is completed. The end products of digestion are absorbed from the small intestine into the bloodstream.

soil: A combination of finely broken up bedrock and organic matter in which plants grow.

solar system: Our sun, with its planets and their moons.

sound: A form of energy produced by vibrating objects.

sperm ducts: Tiny tubes that carry sperm cells away from the testes.

spinal column: The backbone.

spinal cord: The part of the central nervous

system that is located within the spinal column.

stimulus: A change in the environment that causes an organism to react.

stomach: Digestive organ in which chemical digestion begins.

streak: The color of a powdered mineral.

system: Independent parts working together to produce a result.

technology: Applied, practical science.

temperate: A climate that has warm summers, cold winters, and precipitation throughout the year.

tendons: Tissue that connects muscles to bones.

testes: Two organs of the male reproductive system that produce sperm cells.

thermal pollution: An increase in the temperature of a lake or stream that may damage plant and fish life.

thunderstorm: A violent local rainstorm accompanied by lightning.

tides: The continuously changing level of the ocean, caused by the pull of the moon on the ocean waters.

tissue: A group of similar cells working together to do the same job.

tornado: A violent, funnel-shaped wind.

toxic: Poisonous.

trachea: The windpipe.

trade-off: A compromise, in which some disadvantages are accepted in order to gain advantages.

transmission: The passing of light through a substance.

trenches: The deepest valleys in the ocean floor.

uranium: A radioactive element that provides fuel for nuclear reactors.

uterus: A muscular organ in which the developing offspring is protected and nourished.

vapors: Fumes, gas, or odors given off by a substance.

variable: The single condition that is changed, or varied, in an experiment.

veins: Blood vessels that carry oxygen-poor blood back to the heart.

volcano: A mountain formed from molten rock that comes up from beneath the surface.

voluntary muscles: Muscles that are consciously controlled.

warm front: The boundary that forms when a warm air mass moves into a cold air mass.

water table: The level below which the soil and rock are saturated with ground water.

water vapor: Water in the gaseous state.

watt: A unit used to measure the rate (per second) of electrical energy being used.

weather: The condition of the atmosphere at a particular place and time.

weathering: The process by which rocks crumble and decay.

wind: Moving air.

wind belts: The patterns made by the prevailing winds.

work: A force moving an object over a distance.

zygote: The single cell formed when an egg is fertilized by a sperm. The zygote undergoes repeated cell divisions to become an organism of many cells.

Index

Practice Tests

Practice Test 1

1. The diagram below represents a food chain in a pond. Which of the organisms is the *producer*?

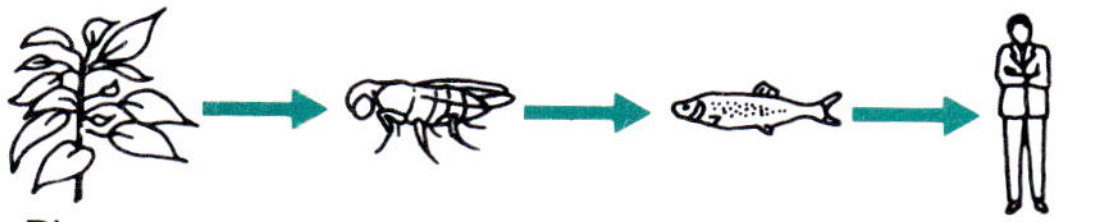

(1) plant (3) fish
(2) insect (4) human

2. Which organism releases oxygen to the atmosphere?
(1) mushroom (3) maple tree
(2) cow (4) bullfrog

3. Organisms that live in the desert save water. This is an example of
(1) a response to a stimulus
(2) an adaptation for survival
(3) recycling materials
(4) balance in an ecosystem

4. Some bacteria use dead organisms and wastes of living organisms for food. As a result, these bacteria
(1) recycle materials in the ecosystem
(2) produce their own food
(3) store their waste products
(4) disturb the balance of nature

5. Which represents a way in which humans have harmed their environment?
(1) adding natural fertilizer to the soil
(2) spraying crops with insecticide
(3) rotating crops
(4) planting seedlings to create new forests

6. To which human body system does the heart belong?
(1) respiratory
(2) circulatory
(3) excretory
(4) digestive

7. Which two systems play the major role in coordinating and controlling body activities?
(1) circulatory and digestive systems
(2) respiratory and nervous systems
(3) skeletal and muscular systems
(4) endocrine and nervous systems

8. The presence of blood capillaries in organs such as the lungs, small intestine, and kidneys provides for
(1) the exchange of materials between the body organs and the blood
(2) the transport of digested food to these organs
(3) the transport of oxygen to these organs
(4) all of the above

9. Which organ is a part of the female reproductive system?
(1) sperm duct (3) testes
(2) oviduct (4) gallbladder

10. Which system distributes hormones to the cells of the body?
(1) digestive
(2) circulatory
(3) reproductive
(4) excretory

11. Which type of diseases are caused by microscopic organisms that can be transmitted from one individual to another?
(1) noninfectious diseases
(2) infectious diseases
(3) allergies
(4) hormonal diseases

12. Milk is pasteurized in order to
(1) improve taste
(2) increase fat content
(3) control microorganisms
(4) remove radioactive substances

13. All of the following are functions of cells *except*
(1) they carry impulses
(2) they excrete wastes
(3) they release energy
(4) they contain a nucleus

14. The diagram below represents an animal cell observed under a microscope.

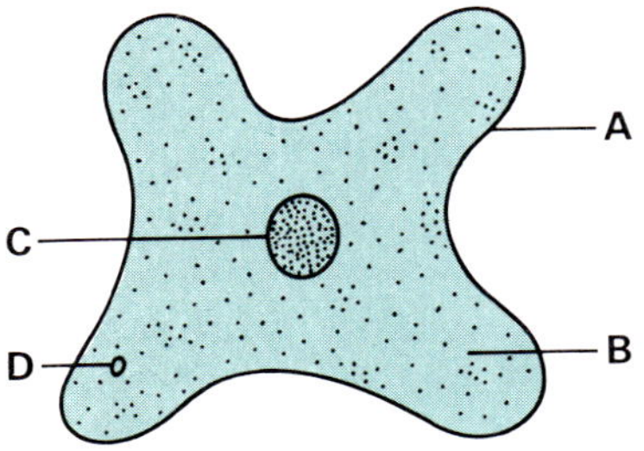

Which cell structure controls the activities of the cell?
(1) A (2) B (3) C (4) D

15. Humans have damaged the quality of the environment by
(1) introducing industrial pollutants that cause disease
(2) conserving natural resources
(3) building sewage treatment plants
(4) controlling the spread of infectious diseases

16. Soil contains humus, which is
(1) organic matter
(2) oxygen gas
(3) water molecules
(4) nitrogen molecules

17. Weathering and erosion are driven largely by the
(1) human species
(2) water cycle and gravity
(3) animals living on land
(4) interactions of all living things

18. One example of a process that builds up Earth's surface is
(1) weathering
(2) erosion
(3) evaporation
(4) volcanism

19. The soil in the diagram below may move from location *A* to location *B* due to a process called

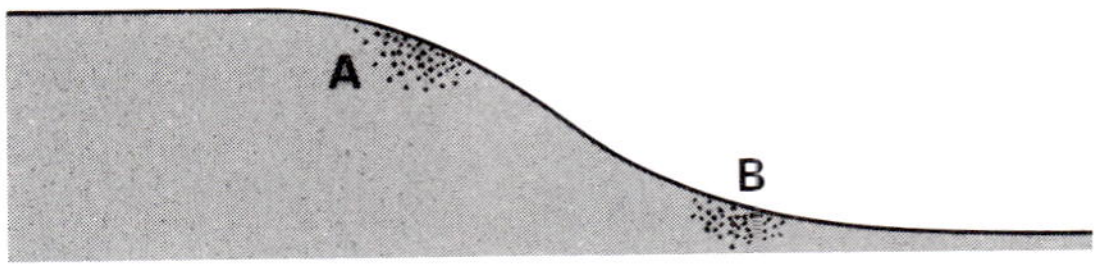

(1) folding
(2) erosion
(3) condensation
(4) weathering

20. The processes of folding and faulting originate from
(1) volcanic activity
(2) crustal plate movements
(3) weathering and erosion
(4) glacial activity

21. The diagram below shows the direction of movement of a cold front into location *A*.

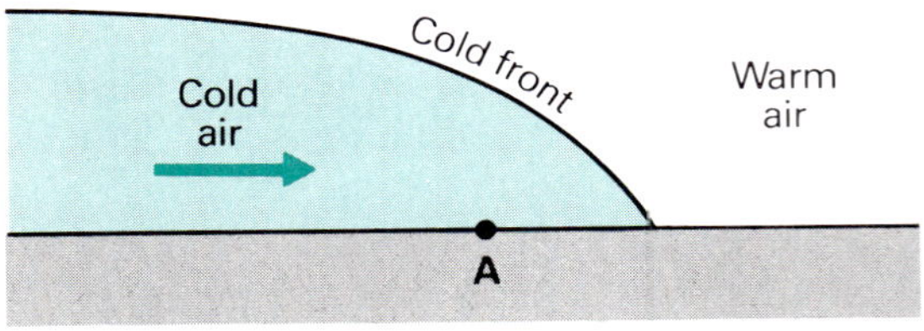

The cold front may bring
(1) an increase in humidity
(2) a decrease in humidity
(3) an increase in temperature
(4) a tropical air mass

22. A student noticed water droplets on the grass one morning, even though it had not rained. What is the best explanation for this?
(1) Water vapor from the air condensed on the grass.
(2) Some of the water from beneath the ground came to the surface.

(3) Hydrogen and oxygen in the air chemically combined to form water.
(4) The garden hose leaked water during the night.

23. The processes of evaporation, condensation, and precipitation are part of a cycle called the
(1) rock cycle
(2) reproductive cycle
(3) water cycle
(4) tidal cycle

24. Which statement about air is true?
(1) Cold air is less dense than warm air.
(2) Cold air is more dense than warm air.
(3) Cold air can hold more water vapor than warm air.
(4) Cold air is lighter than warm air.

25. The primary source of energy in the atmosphere is the
(1) moon
(2) sun
(3) Earth
(4) ocean

26. The daily motions of the sun, moon, and stars across the sky can be explained by
(1) their actual motion in space
(2) Earth's rotation
(3) Earth's revolution
(4) the tilt of Earth's axis

27. In the diagram below, the moon is positioned between the sun and Earth.

What phase of the moon results from this alignment?
(1) new moon
(2) crescent moon
(3) half moon
(4) full moon

28. The diagram below shows Earth revolving around the sun.

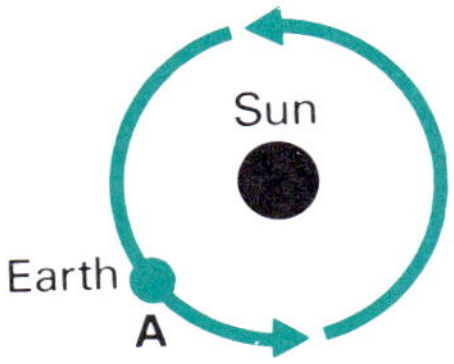

How long does it take for Earth to travel from location *A* around the sun and back to location *A* again?
(1) one day
(2) one week
(3) one month
(4) one year

29. The diagram below shows the alignment of the sun, Earth, and moon on a certain day. At what places on Earth will there be high tides?

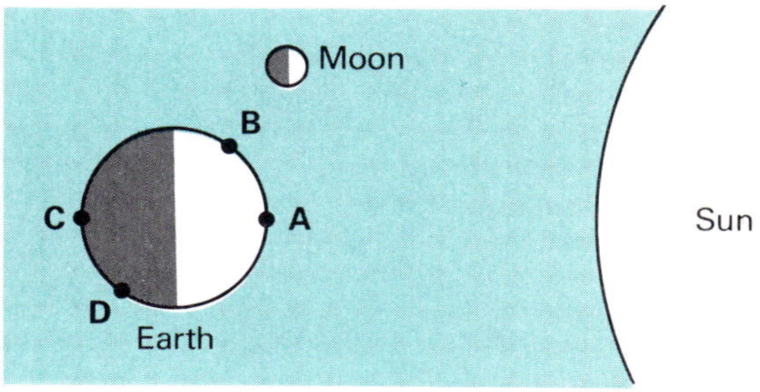

(1) location *A* alone
(2) locations *A* and *C*
(3) location *B* alone
(4) locations *B* and *D*

30. What is unique about the third planet from the sun?
(1) It rotates fastest of all the planets.
(2) It revolves fastest of all the planets.
(3) It appears to be the only planet that supports life.
(4) It is the only planet with any atmosphere.

31. In the diagram below, the object is lifted from the ground and placed at level *A*. Which statement about this action is NOT true?

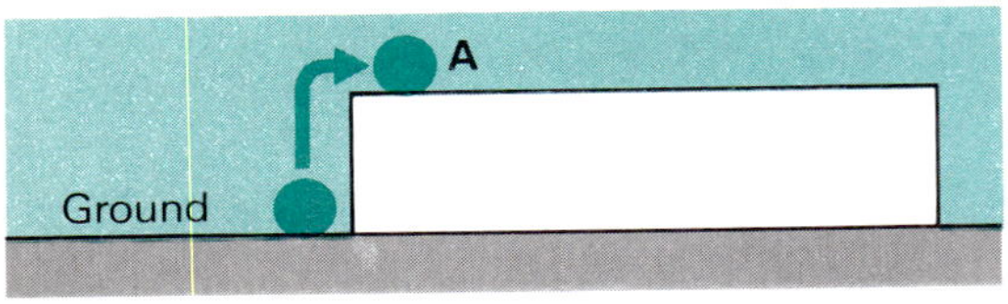

(1) The object has greater potential energy after it is lifted.
(2) Work was done during the lifting.
(3) Energy was required to do the lifting.
(4) The kinetic energy of the object is greater after it is lifted.

32. Which of the following contains the most kinetic energy?
(1) a four-ton water tank sitting on the roof of a tall building
(2) a battery
(3) a person jogging
(4) a pound of uranium fuel

33. Which one of the following is most likely to cause damage to hearing?
(1) loud sounds
(2) sounds so soft they strain one's hearing
(3) very high-pitched musical notes
(4) complete silence

34. The person in the diagram below is using pulleys to lift an object. The total work given to the object is 70 units. How much work does the person use in pulling on the rope?

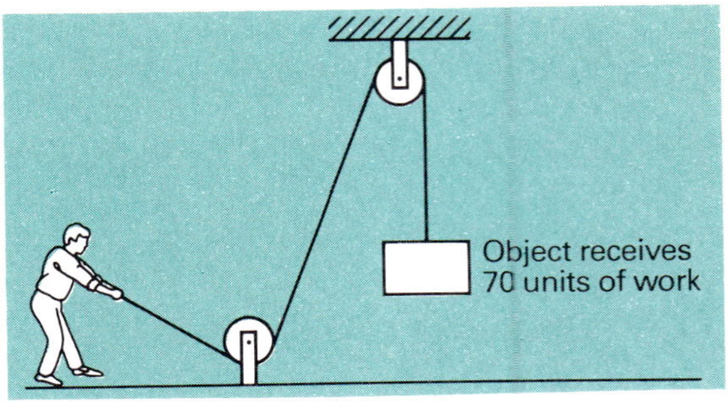

(1) much less than 70 units of work
(2) slightly less than 70 units of work
(3) exactly 70 units of work
(4) more than 70 units of work

35. The equipment illustrated below is an air thermometer. Even a brief touch of a warm hand on the flask with the air causes the colored water to be pushed down.

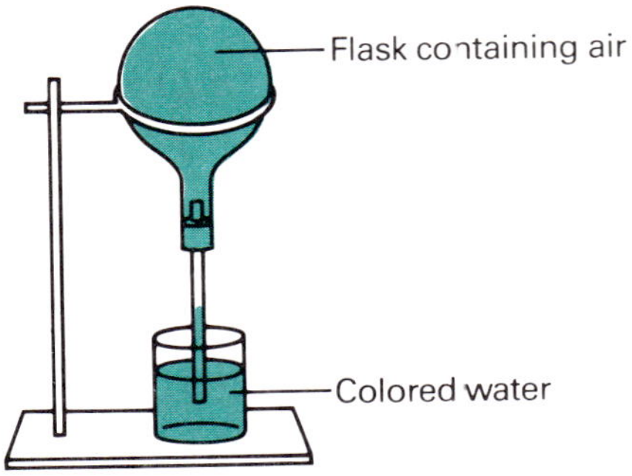

This illustrates that
(1) air, like all materials, expands when heated
(2) water contracts when heated
(3) touching creates a pressure on the glass, the air, and the water
(4) water is repelled by heat

36. Which one of the following is considered to be matter?
(1) electricity
(2) sound
(3) magnetism
(4) air

37. Flammable liquids such as cleaners and paint removers should be used
(1) in ventilated places without flames
(2) only in dim light
(3) in solutions diluted with water
(4) when they are chilled below room temperature

38. The diagram below shows one molecule of a certain chemical.

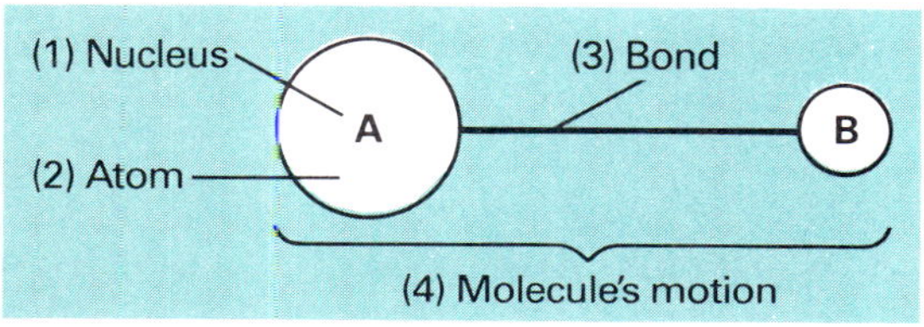

Where is the chemical energy stored in this molecule?
(1) in the nucleus of each atom
(2) in the separate atoms
(3) in the bond between the atoms
(4) in the molecule's kinetic motion

39. Chemicals *A* and *B* are both safe. They are neither toxic nor flammable. When combined, they produce chemical *C*. What can be predicted about chemical *C*?
(1) It must be safe.
(2) It must be unsafe.
(3) Cannot be predicted.

40. Which one of the following illustrates a chemical change?

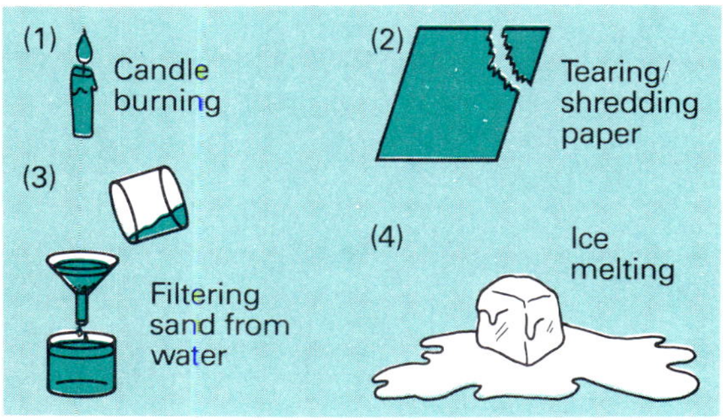

41. What information given on food labels tells the energy content of the food?
(1) the list of ingredients
(2) the percentages it supplies of daily needs for vitamins and minerals
(3) the calories per serving
(4) the number of grams of fats, carbohydrates, and fiber per serving

42. What can be concluded from a study of the bar graph below?

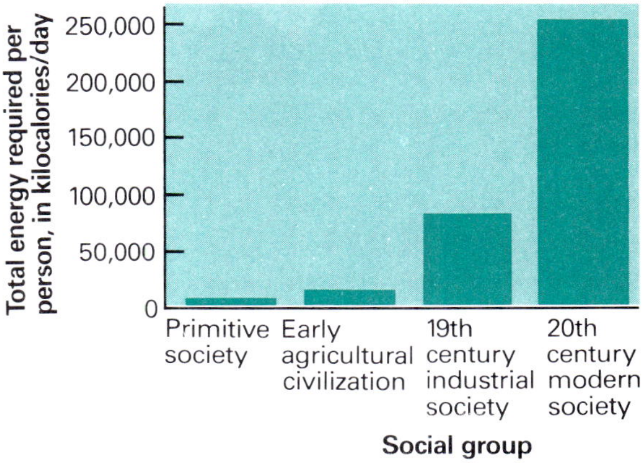

(1) Energy will always be available to meet growing demands.
(2) Individuals eat richer and greater quantities of foods now than in the past.
(3) Individuals today are working fewer hours and with less effort than in the past.
(4) People's energy needs have increased over time.

43. Electricity may be produced from various energy sources, including uranium, coal, moving water, and wind. Which of the following is true about using these sources to make electricity?
(1) Steam must first be made from each energy source.
(2) A generator is turned in each case.

(3) Electricity is drawn directly out of each energy source.
(4) These sources have about equal use in the United States today.

44. According to the graph below, what percentage of electricity comes from renewable resources?

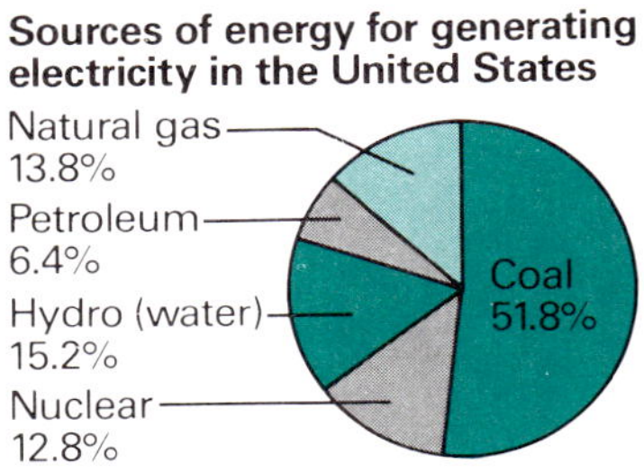

(1) 15.2% (3) 72.0%
(2) 28.0% (4) 100%

45. What would be the best title for the diagram below?

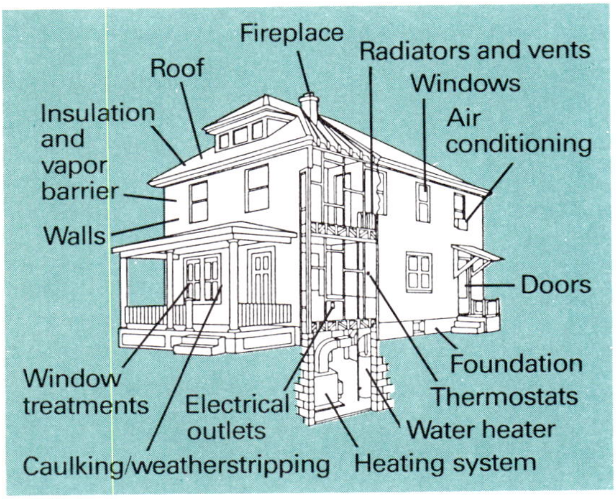

(1) Locations Where Heat Energy Escapes
(2) Wasteful Aspects of Modern Homes
(3) Sources of Home Pollutants
(4) Targets for Energy Conservation

46. Science has established the principle that heat kills bacteria. What technology applies this principle?

(1) microwave ovens
(2) the electron microscope
(3) the growing of yogurt bacteria
(4) the pasteurization of milk

47. Biologists use high-speed cameras and rapidly flashing (strobe) lights to make slow-motion movies of animal actions that can't normally be observed by people. This example best illustrates
(1) science advancing technology
(2) technology advancing science
(3) society shaping technology and science
(4) technology and science shaping society

48. Below are newspaper headlines from four consecutive days. What do they illustrate about technology?

(1) Science discoveries help to advance technology.
(2) Every technological device or process affects the environment in some way.
(3) Technology has improved the standard of living.
(4) Technological devices are systems of subparts working together.

49. During the 1940s and 1950s, most families had at least one member who worked in some part of the automobile industry. Today the same thing can be said about the computer industry. This illustrates that
(1) technology affects business and employment opportunities
(2) if a technological device has too many disadvantages, it may be rejected
(3) a technological device is judged by short-term and long-term results
(4) science and technology alone cannot solve society's problems

50. Which technology has short-term burdens but long-term benefits?
(1) automobile safety belts
(2) "cool-tasting" menthol cigarettes
(3) farm pesticides
(4) nuclear weapons

51. What is the length of the object represented in the diagram below?

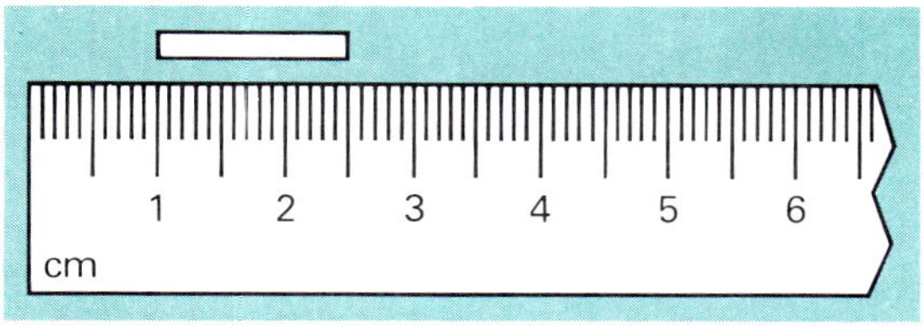

(1) 1.0 cm (3) 1.5 cm
(2) 2.0 cm (4) 2.5 cm

52. The graph below shows temperature readings taken in Albany on July 29.

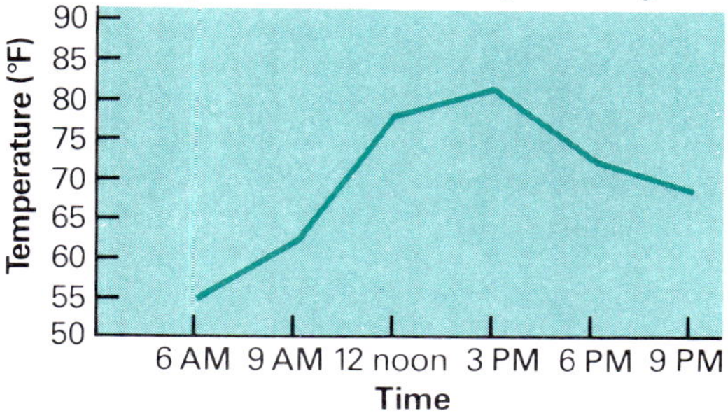

What was the temperature reading at 6:00 P.M.?
(1) 55°F (3) 72°F
(2) 62°F (4) 81°F

53. A student experiments with a simple pendulum as shown below.

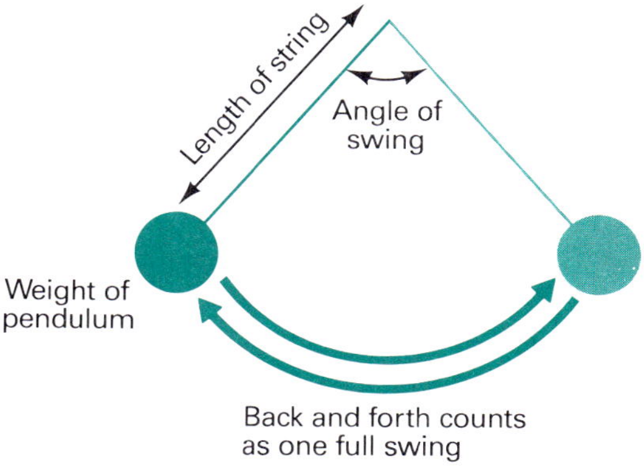

The student's data are shown below.

Data Table

Length of String (cm)	Number of Swings in 60 Seconds
20	67
40	47
80	33

Which of the following questions does this experiment seem to be exploring?
(1) What is the effect of a pendulum's weight on the rate at which it swings?
(2) What is the effect of a pendulum's angle of swing on the rate at which it swings?
(3) What is the effect of a pendulum's length on the rate at which it swings?
(4) What is the effect of the amount of time a pendulum is swung on the length of the pendulum?

54. Two girls of about the same weight, height, and age are to be compared for their body responses to exercise. One girl is athletic; the other is not. After putting them through a series of exercises, what measure might be taken to compare how each of them responds to the exercises?

(1) Check their blood pressure and heart rate.
(2) Obtain their scores on a brief I.Q. test.
(3) Ask them how they liked the exercises and how they feel.
(4) Observe whether or not they seem to be equally tired.

55. An empty cylinder has a mass of 250 grams. After 50 mL of a certain liquid have been poured into it, the mass of the cylinder plus the liquid is 290 grams. What is the density of the liquid?

$$\text{density} = \frac{\text{mass of liquid alone (g)}}{\text{volume of liquid (mL)}}$$

(1) 0.80 g/mL (3) 5.0 g/mL
(2) 1.25 g/mL (4) 5.8 g/mL

56. The data below show how electric current increases when the strength of the electric source is increased. The measurements were taken on a single piece of wire.

Electric Strength (Voltage)	Electric Current (Amps)
1	20
2	40
3	60
4	80
5	100

Which one of the following graphs is best prepared for plotting these data?

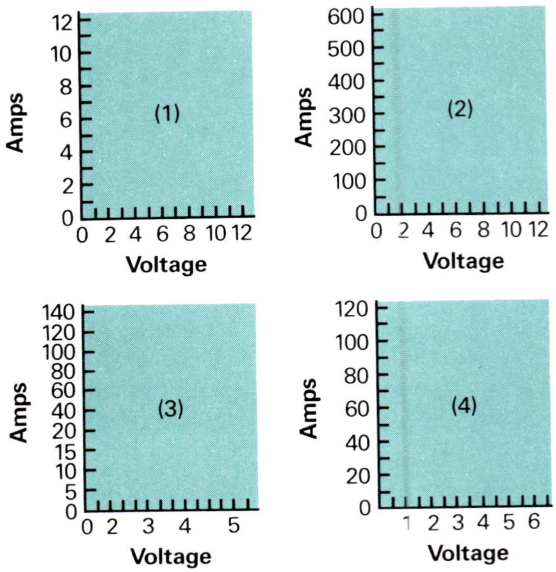

57. The following data were taken from a well drilled 8 km deep into Earth's crust. The figures suggest that the deeper parts of Earth are rather hot.

Depth, km	Temperature, °C
0	15
1	52
2	88
3	120
4	151
5	179
6	206
7	232
8	257

Study the pattern of change in the temperature data. What temperature value might be predicted for a depth of 9 km?
(1) 233°C (2) 281°C (3) 310°C
(4) The temperature cannot be reasonably predicted, since 9 km is too far past the range of data taken.

58–60. Base your answers to questions 58–60 on the experiment described below.
A student used 2 groups of 100 carrot seeds to test for the effects of different temperatures on the growth of seeds. One group was kept at a temperature of 20°C and the other at 10°C. All of the other conditions were kept the same. The student observed the carrots and recorded his data in the table below.

Data Table

Day of Observation	Total Number of Seeds that Grew	
	10°C	20°C
7	0	5
10	20	35
15	40	70
20	45	80
25	45	80

58. According to this experiment, what is the difference in the number of seeds that had grown at the two temperatures on day ten?
(1) 15
(2) 20
(3) 30
(4) 35

59. Which is a correct conclusion based on the data gathered from this experiment?
(1) The experiment was a failure, since not all of the carrot seeds grew.
(2) Fewer seeds grew at a temperature of 20°C than at 10°C.
(3) More seeds grew at a temperature of 20°C than at 10°C.
(4) At a temperature of 20°C, no seeds grew before the seventh day.

60. Which is the variable in this experiment?
(1) light
(2) water
(3) carbon dioxide
(4) temperature

Answers to Practice Test 1

1. (1) Plants produce their own food through photosynthesis; therefore, they are called producers.
2. (3) During photosynthesis, green plants release O_2 to the atmosphere.
3. (2) Organisms have structures and/or behavior patterns that enable them to survive in a particular environment. For example, desert cacti conserve water; polar bears have thick white fur for warmth and protection.
4. (1) Bacteria live off dead organisms. They decompose the dead organisms and as a result recycle (return) minerals to the soil.
5. (2) When people use insecticide sprays such as DDT, they contaminate the soil and the crops that grow there. When these crops are eaten by animals (including humans), the insecticides can interfere with normal body functions.
6. (2) The heart is part of the circulatory system.
7. (4) The endocrine and nervous systems keep all the other systems of the body in touch with one another. They control body activities, including the reproductive cycle, digestion, respiration, and locomotion, to name just a few.
8. (4) Materials are exchanged between the body organs and the blood through capillaries. Capillaries bring nutrients and oxygen to cells and carry wastes away from the cells. Capillaries provide large surface areas for the exchange of materials between the blood and the cells.
9. (2) The oviduct is a tube that carries the egg from the ovary to the uterus. Fertilization may occur in the oviduct if sperm cells are present.
10. (2) Hormones travel from their source (the endocrine glands) through the circulatory system to target organs, where the hormones express their effects.
11. (2) Infectious diseases are caused by microscopic organisms such as bacteria and viruses. They may be spread through the air, water, food, or by direct contact.
12. (3) Pasteurization is the process of heating milk to retard the growth of microorganisms.
13. (4) The nucleus is a structure within a cell. A function is an activity, such as carrying impulses, excreting wastes, or releasing energy.
14. (3) Part *C* is the nucleus. The nucleus controls the activities of all the other parts of the cell. For example, it controls the production of enzymes that regulate all the chemical activities in the mitochondria, ribosomes, chloroplasts, and so forth.
15. (1) Industrial pollutants, such as asbestos, sulfur dioxide, hydrogen sulfide, etc., have damaged the environment. These pollutants have had negative effects on living things.
16. (1) Humus is the remains of dead organisms and the wastes of living organisms.
17. (2) The water cycle produces water in streams and ground water, both of which remove and transport rock fragments. The force of gravity carries rock fragments from location to location.
18. (4) Volcanism is the eruption of molten rock (magma) from volcanoes. Mountains and plateaus have been formed by the buildup of materials from erupting volcanoes.
19. (2) Erosion is the removal and transport of rock fragments at Earth's surface. The water cycle and gravity are the major driving forces of erosion. Glaciers and wind also cause erosion.

20. (2) Movements of crustal plates (toward each other, away from each other, alongside each other) cause folding and faulting.
21. (2) Cold air can hold less moisture than warm air. The amount of moisture in the air is called humidity.
22. (1) The ground cools at night when the temperature falls. The air next to the ground cools as the ground cools. The cooled air cannot hold as much water vapor as it did when it was warm. This causes the water vapor to condense, forming droplets on the grass.
23. (3) During the water cycle, water evaporates from bodies of water (oceans, lakes, and ponds). As the air carrying the water vapor rises it cools, causing the water vapor to condense and form clouds. When clouds become filled with water vapor, precipitation (rain, sleet, snow, or hail) may occur.
24. (2) Cold air is more dense (heavier) than warm air. This is because molecules in air move faster and farther apart as the air is heated, leaving less matter (fewer molecules) in a given space.
25. (2) The sun provides heat and light energy to Earth. The sun warms Earth's surface, causing the warming of the air above the surface. The sun provides plants with light energy for photosynthesis.
26. (2) Earth's rotation makes the objects in the sky look as though they are moving across the sky. That is not their actual motion in space, however. Earth's revolution causes one year to pass and the tilt of Earth's axis is the cause of the seasons.
27. (1) The unlighted side of the moon faces Earth's lighted side. It is not possible to see the moon in this position, since it is in the bright sky close to the sun. This phase, when the moon is not visible, is called *new moon*.
28. (4) From location *A* around the sun and back is one complete revolution, which takes a year. A day is one rotation (spin) of Earth on its axis. A week has no meaning in astronomy—it is merely seven days. A month is about the time needed for the moon to revolve around Earth and go through all its phases.
29. (4) Since the moon is closer than the sun, it pulls more on Earth's waters. There will be a high tide on the side of Earth facing the moon and on the side directly opposite as well.
30. (3) The third planet is Earth, which seems to be the only planet in our solar system that can support life. Jupiter rotates fastest (8 hours); Mercury revolves fastest (88 days). Most planets have some atmosphere, although of a different composition from Earth's atmosphere.
31. (4) Kinetic energy requires motion. The object isn't moving when it is on the ground or at position *A*. Lifting requires work, which in turn requires energy. The energy put in during lifting is "hidden" in the object as increased potential energy at location *A*.
32. (3) Kinetic energy exists only when an object is moving. The water tank on a roof has potential energy; a battery contains stored electrical energy; uranium contains nuclear energy.
33. (1) Loud sounds (heard over a long period of time) lead to ear damage.
34. (4) The work put *in* to a machine is always more than the work given *out* by the machine. Seventy units were given to the object lifted; additional units of energy go to friction in the rope and pulleys.
35. (1) The air in the flask is slightly warmed when the flask is touched. As a result it expands, thereby pushing down the colored water in the tube.
36. (4) Matter has weight and occupies space. Air is matter because it has weight and it certainly requires space. Electricity, sound, and magnetism are forms of

energy, not matter.

37. (1) Flammable liquids burn easily and give off explosive vapors; therefore, they are used in places with adequate ventilation and no flames.

38. (3) A bond is the link that joins atoms together. Chemical energy is stored in bonds.

39. (3) The product of any chemical reaction has its own properties, which cannot be predicted from the properties of the original materials.

40. (1) When a candle burns, wax turns to carbon dioxide gas and water. New materials are formed. This is the chief characteristic of a chemical change. The other changes shown are merely physical changes.

41. (3) Calories are a measure of energy.

42. (4) The graph shows that the total energy needs of each person have increased to 250,000 kilocalories per day. It does not show that energy will always be available, nor does it state anything about food or work.

43. (2) Electricity is made by turning a generator. Uranium and coal *are* used to make heat or steam to turn generators. However, moving water and wind turn the generators directly. Coal is the main energy source for electricity; wind is only a tiny source.

44. (1) Only hydroelectric power is a renewable resource; the others are nonrenewable.

45. (4) The diagram shows places in a typical home where improvements in energy conservation can be made. Walls, windows, doors, and the roof can be insulated; thermostats can be set to lower temperatures; air conditioners can be used less; radiators and vents can be cleaned. Not all parts of the diagram are places where heat escapes, or where there are sources of pollution.

46. (4) Milk is pasteurized by being heated under pressure to kill bacteria. In producing yogurt, bacteria are not killed but are encouraged to grow.

47. (2) The cameras and strobe lights are aspects of technology. This is technology advancing science.

48. (2) The headlines indicate that certain industries and automobiles are creating pollution that is not being blown away by the wind. Instead, a dangerous cloud of smog is forming. Here technology is affecting the environment.

49. (1) As technology changes, employment patterns must also change. The other choices are true statements, but they don't relate to the job changes mentioned in the question.

50. (1) Not many people enjoy fastening their safety belts. They are a nuisance, but only for a few seconds. In the long term they save lives. Cigarettes have long-term burdens on health; pesticides have a short-term benefit but long-term risks; nuclear weapons are dangerous burdens.

51. (3) The object extends from the 1-cm mark to the 2.5-cm mark. The difference between these two marks is 1.5 cm, which is the length of the object.

52. (3) The line on the graph indicates that the 6:00 P.M. temperature reading was 72°F.

53. (3) The data table indicates that as the length of the pendulum was changed the swinging rate changed also. This must be the research question. The pendulum's weight and angle of swing are not part of the recorded data.

54. (1) Blood pressure and heart rate are quantitative measurements that will properly compare the results of exercise. An I.Q. test does not measure response to exercise. Asking the girls how they feel or observing them will provide qualitative responses that may not be correct.

55. (1) Mass of liquid = 290 − 250 = 40 g.

$$\text{Density} = \frac{40\text{ g}}{50\text{ mL}} = 0.80\text{ g/mL}$$

56. (4) The scales in graph 4 cover the needed ranges: from 1 to 5 volts and from 20 to 100 amps. The graph will nicely fill the space. Graph 1 will not permit the amps to be plotted. Graph 2 has scales of inappropriate size; the graph will occupy only a small part of the space. Graph 3 has uneven scales.

57. (2) The temperature increases for each kilometer of depth, but each increase is slightly less than the previous increase. The increase from 7 to 8 km was +25°C, so a +24°C increase is in keeping with this trend. Choice 1 would be a reversal of the pattern; choice 3 would be a larger increase than expected. Both are possible, but are not suggested by the trend of the data. Predicting to 20 km or 100 km would be unreasonable; predicting to 9 km is not unreasonable.

58. (1) The data table shows that on day ten 20 carrot seeds grew at 10°C and 35 carrot seeds grew at 20°C. The difference is 15.

59. (3) The data table shows that at the end of each time period more seeds had grown at a temperature of 20°C than at 10°C.

60. (4) A variable in an experiment is the condition that changes. In this experiment, the seeds were grown at two different temperatures. All the other conditions were the same.

Practice Test 2

1. Frogs feed on insects. Based on this statement, to which feeding group do frogs belong?
(1) producers (3) decomposers
(2) consumers (4) parasites

2. During respiration, animals
(1) produce food
(2) release carbon dioxide (CO_2)
(3) capture light
(4) release oxygen (O_2)

3. Green plants provide food for humans through the process of
(1) respiration (3) photosynthesis
(2) excretion (4) digestion

4. The diagram below represents a food web.

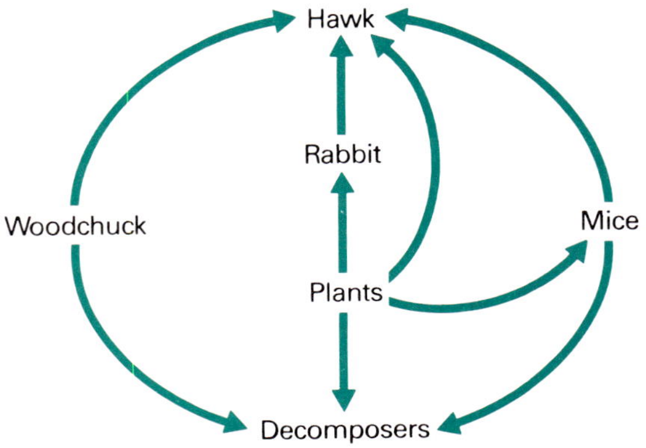

Which statement concerning the interaction among the organisms in the food web is true?
(1) The rabbits, mice, and woodchuck feed on the hawk.
(2) If all the hawks in the area disappeared, the number of rabbits would probably increase.
(3) Elements are recycled due mainly to the activities of plants.
(4) Rabbits feed on plants and mice.

5. The diagram below shows the series of changes a frog goes through during reproduction and development.

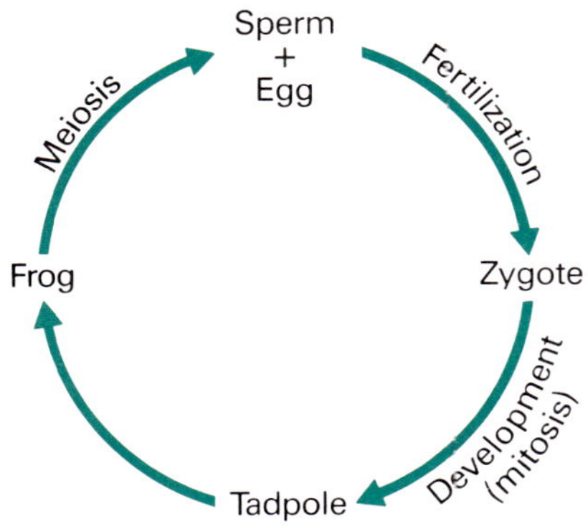

This diagram is an example of a(n)
(1) life style
(2) life cycle
(3) natural balance
(4) evolutionary change

6. Digested food is carried to all the cells of the human body by the
(1) nerves
(2) muscles
(3) bones
(4) blood

7. Which pair of organs have similar functions?
(1) heart and stomach
(2) brain and kidney
(3) esophagus and oviduct
(4) skin and kidney

8. Which human body system contains the trachea, bronchi, and lungs?
(1) respiratory
(2) circulatory
(3) reproductive
(4) digestive

9. Undigested and indigestible materials make up
(1) urine (3) feces
(2) bile (4) blood

10. The process in which oxygen is used to release energy from digested foods is called
(1) cellular respiration
(2) photosynthesis
(3) excretion
(4) chemical digestion

11. Some industrial pollutants have been identified as causes of cancer. One example of such an industrial pollutant is
(1) pollen (3) asbestos
(2) bacteria (4) mold

12. Which statement concerning sexual reproduction is *false*?
(1) It leads to variations in future generations.
(2) It involves two parents.
(3) It produces offspring identical to the parents.
(4) It results when two cells fuse to form one zygote.

13. A few bacteria are placed in a growing dish. After several hours, thousands of bacteria are present. Which life function is responsible for this occurrence?
(1) digestion (3) reproduction
(2) egestion (4) respiration

14. Osteoporosis is a bone disorder caused by the lack of calcium in the diet. Osteoporosis is an example of a(n)
(1) disease caused by bacteria
(2) disease caused by a virus
(3) infectious disease
(4) deficiency disease

15. Vaccinations are given to prevent the spread of
(1) noninfectious diseases
(2) infectious diseases
(3) allergies
(4) cancer

16. Hot, molten rock beneath Earth's surface is called
(1) lava
(2) magma
(3) igneous
(4) basalt

17. Which are the three main agents of erosion?
(1) running water, wind, and glaciers
(2) animals, plants, and microorganisms
(3) the sun, moon, and planets
(4) air, rocks, and sand

18. Which type of weathering is illustrated below?

(1) chemical
(2) physical
(3) biological
(4) human

19. Mountains are built as a result of which two processes?
(1) folding and faulting
(2) condensation and precipitation
(3) weathering and erosion
(4) the water cycle and the force of gravity

20. In which type of rock are fossils found?
(1) igneous
(2) metamorphic
(3) sedimentary
(4) molten

21. The table below shows relative humidity readings for a city in New York State for five consecutive days.

Day	Relative Humidity
1	35%
2	40%
3	50%
4	75%
5	95%

From the data it might be concluded that
(1) a cold front is moving into the area
(2) a continental polar air mass has arrived
(3) the area is under the influence of a maritime tropical air mass
(4) humidity will continue to increase for the next five days

22. The data table below shows selected average monthly temperatures for a city in the United States.

Month	Temperature (°F)
January	21°
March	39°
June	75°
September	69°
November	43°

The city is probably located in
(1) southern California
(2) northern New York State
(3) North Carolina
(4) New Mexico

23. Which type of air mass brings very cold weather to New York State in winter?
(1) continental polar
(2) maritime polar
(3) continental tropical
(4) maritime tropical

24. As a direct result of which one of the following processes do clouds, fog, and dew form?
(1) evaporation (3) condensation
(2) precipitation (4) sublimation

25. A low-pressure area forms in the Caribbean Sea in September. It carries very high winds and torrential rains. This kind of storm is most likely the beginning of a
(1) thunderstorm (3) winter storm
(2) tornado (4) hurricane

26. On the diagram of Earth below, which location can have several weeks of continuous daylight?

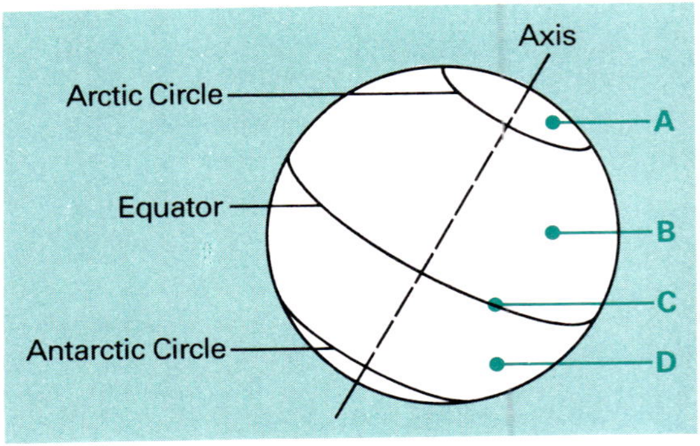

(1) location *A* (3) location *C*
(2) location *B* (4) location *D*

27. The table below shows some information gathered from a newspaper.

Day	Time of Sunrise	Time of Sunset
Yesterday	5:59 A.M.	6:01 P.M.
Today	6:00 A.M.	6:00 P.M.
Tomorrow	6:01 A.M.	5:59 P.M.

What is the date of this newspaper?
(1) December 22
(2) March 21
(3) June 21
(4) September 22

28. How much of the moon's surface is lighted by the sun?
(1) The amount varies night by night.
(2) 24%
(3) 50%
(4) 100%

29. If Earth's axis were *not* tilted, which of the following would result?
(1) Life would not exist.
(2) Seasons would not occur.
(3) Day and night would not occur.
(4) Tides would not exist.

30. A meteor is caused by
(1) a star that has fallen from its position
(2) a rock from space burning in the air
(3) an atmospheric electrical discharge
(4) a tiny satellite circling Earth

31. In the experiment shown below, a small mass is released and makes an indentation in the clay. The experiment is repeated with a larger mass. The second mass makes a deeper indentation in the clay. What principle is illustrated by this experiment?

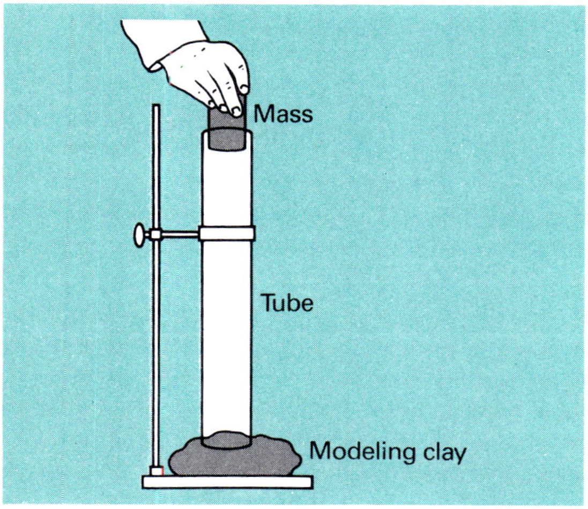

(1) Objects with greater mass fall faster.
(2) With greater potential energy, more work can be done.
(3) Clay is not compressible.
(4) Heat energy results from most energy changes.

32. Which of the following energy transformations occurs in a toaster?
(1) electrical → chemical
(2) electrical → heat
(3) chemical → electrical
(4) magnetic → heat

33. All of the illustrations below show applications of the same simple machine. What simple machine is represented by these tools?

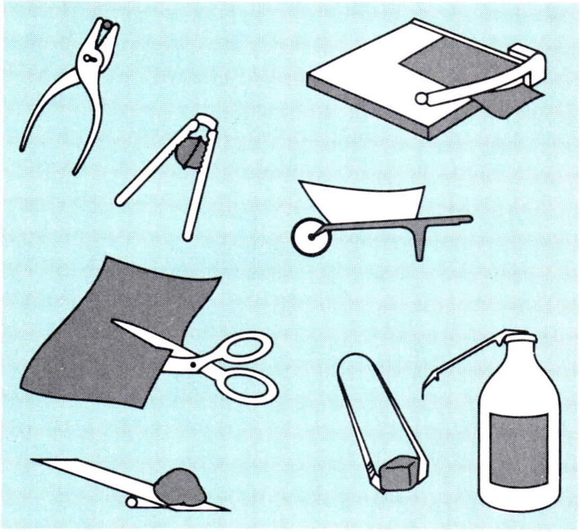

(1) inclined plane
(2) lever
(3) pulley
(4) gear and screw

34. Which form of electromagnetic waves is used for both communications and cooking?
(1) radio/T.V.
(2) X-rays
(3) ultraviolet light
(4) microwaves

35. The illustration below shows the electrified rail of a subway train, sometimes called the "third rail." The third rail is held above the ground by insulating supports. Which material could *not* be used for these supports?

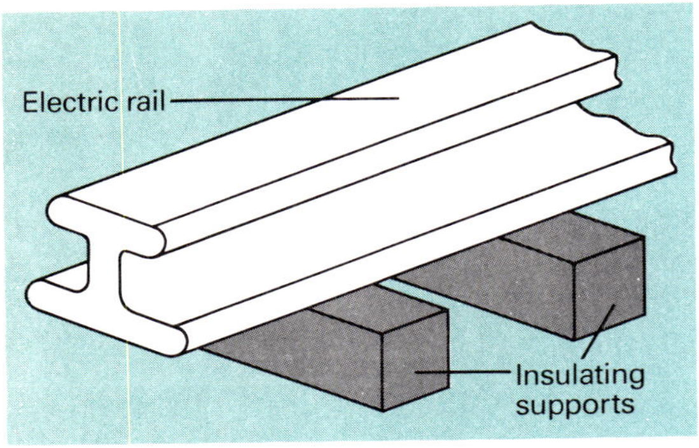

(1) steel
(2) rubber
(3) wood
(4) glass/ceramic

36. The three factors illustrated below all tend to

(1) prevent chemical change from occurring
(2) increase reaction rates
(3) promote physical change, not chemical change
(4) increase the total amount of material produced by a reaction

37. Mixing chemicals in the laboratory or at home without instructions is
(1) potentially dangerous
(2) permissible in small amounts
(3) part of good experimentation
(4) suggested for science projects

38. All substances are made from one or more
(1) compounds
(2) mixtures
(3) components
(4) elements

39. In which example of chemical change shown below is energy *absorbed*, not released?

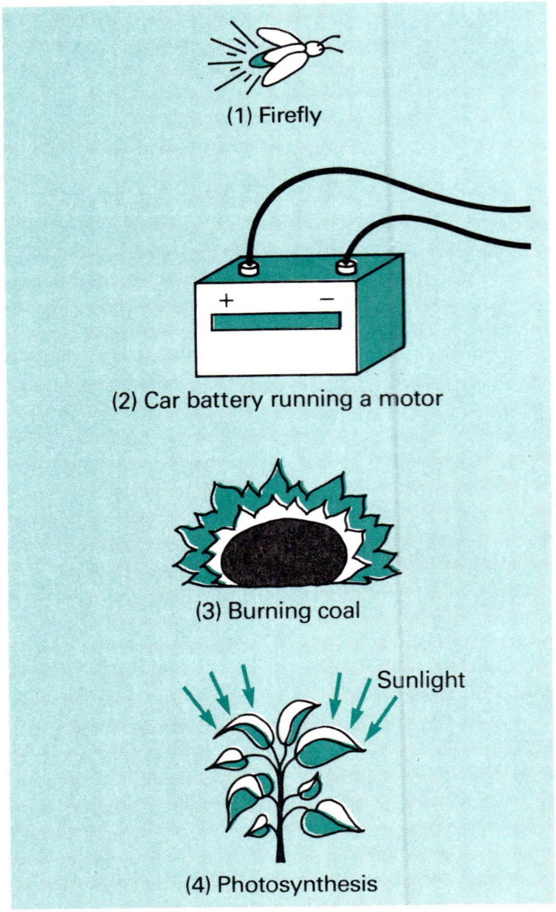

40. In which of the phase changes illustrated below is energy *released*?

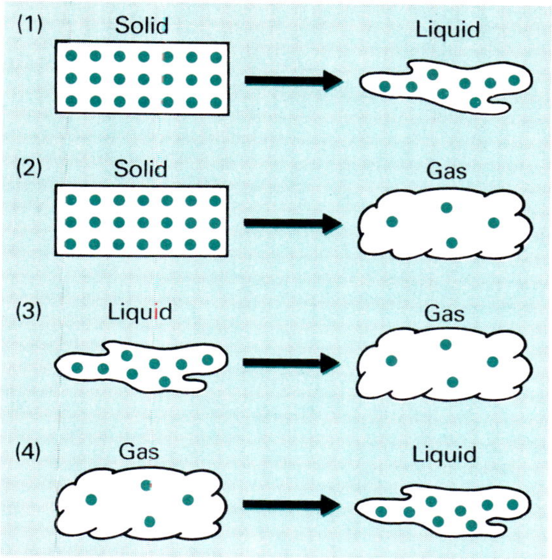

41. Which of the following is a fossil fuel?
(1) natural gas
(2) geothermal sources
(3) uranium
(4) any of the renewable energy resources

42. A light bulb is rated at 60 watts, a toaster at 1200 watts. Compared to the light bulb, the toaster uses
(1) more total energy
(2) more energy per second when turned on
(3) less total energy
(4) less energy per second when turned on

43. Which of the following statements about coal is *not* true?
(1) Coal is the leading source of energy in the United States today.
(2) Coal reserves in the United States are very abundant and can supply our energy needs for the next century.
(3) The burning of coal contributes greatly to air pollution.
(4) Coal mining contributes to land pollution and ecological destruction.

44. According to the graph below, what percentage of electricity used in the United States is generated from fossil fuels?

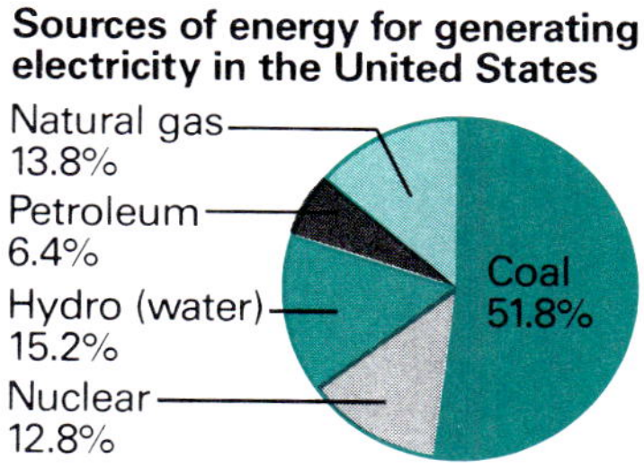

(1) 6.4%
(2) 51.8%
(3) 72.0%
(4) 84.8%

45. A disadvantage of solar energy is that it
(1) is renewable
(2) varies with time and place
(3) does not produce pollution
(4) can be collected with simple technologies

46. What scientific principle is the basis for the light bulb?
(1) Substances expand when heated and contract when cooled.
(2) Molecules and crystals have natural vibrations.
(3) Sufficient electricity makes a wire hot enough to glow.
(4) Light energy can be converted directly into electrical energy.

47. The compressor, motor, and fan are parts of an air conditioner. Which part of the air conditioning *system* do these devices represent?
(1) input and control
(2) processing
(3) output
(4) feedback

48. Below are listed some aspects of campaigning for President of the United States in 1888 and 1988.

1888	1988
Political songs Individual supporters make speeches for the candidate Citizens hold discussions with politicians on issues and attitudes Candidates must look good for a brief stopover by train	T.V./radio commercials Candidates fly by jet to three rallies every day Computerized telephone polls are used to get reactions from the public Candidates must look good for T.V. cameras at debates and interviews

These comparisons are examples of how technology
(1) changes society
(2) is changed by society
(3) advances science
(4) is shaped by people's attitudes

49. Which technological product has the greatest international effect?
(1) microwave ovens
(2) microwave communication via satellite
(3) spray-can paints
(4) plastic surgery

50. The illustration above at the right shows two ways of obtaining coal—strip mining and underground mining. Strip mining leads to land pollution and destruction of the local environment. Therefore, one coal company decides to use the underground method, even though this decision means that costs and safety problems will increase.

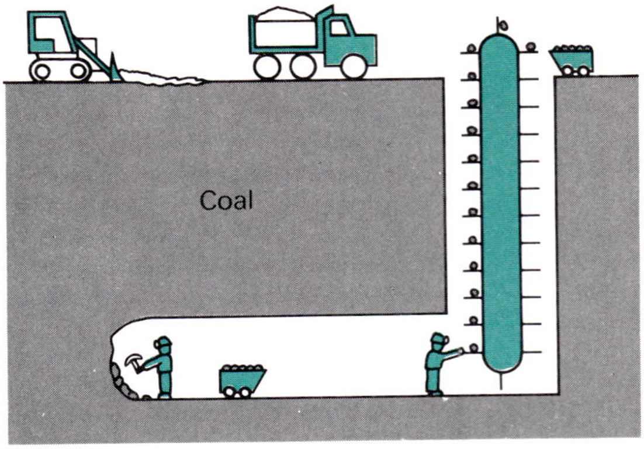

This decision illustrates
(1) that technology influences science
(2) the interaction of society with science
(3) short-term consequences
(4) trade-offs

51. To answer the question "Does more sugar dissolve in hot water than in cold water?" a student stirs packets of sugar into two glasses of water, one hot and one cold. What research design will make this a *controlled* experiment?
(1) Use equal amounts of water in each glass and equal-sized packets of sugar.
(2) Make one glass exactly 40°C and the other exactly 80°C.
(3) Stir with a glass rod.
(4) Record carefully the total number of packets used.

52. A scientist mixes two chemicals at a particular temperature. A gas is released, collected, and studied. Which one of the following would be a *qualitative* measurement in such an experiment?
(1) the smell of the gas (sweet, sharp, etc.)
(2) the temperature of the reaction
(3) the calculated density of the gas
(4) the amounts and strengths of the two chemicals

53. The illustration below shows a liquid being heated in a small test tube.

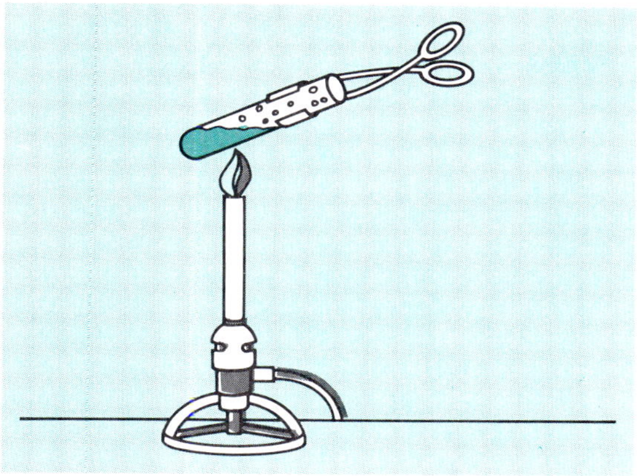

Which of the following procedures is *not* suggested if the liquid is to be heated safely?

(1) Wear safety goggles and a lab apron.
(2) Point the mouth of the tube away from people, in case liquid spurts out.
(3) Boil vigorously, with the flame held at one spot only.
(4) Use tongs or a test tube holder while heating the liquid.

54. Which organism should be placed at position *X* on the food web below to best complete the food web?

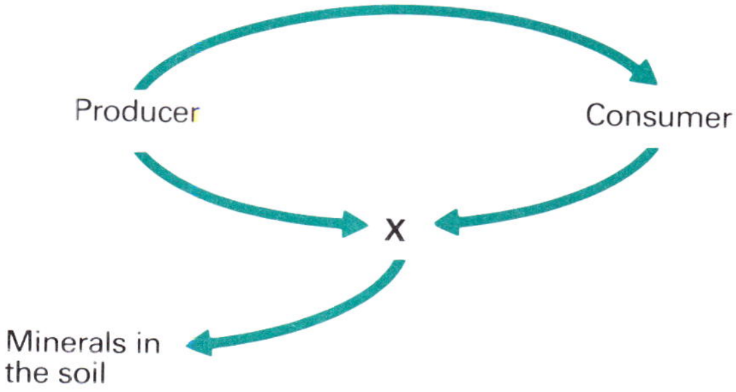

(1) green plant (3) virus
(2) cow (4) decomposer

55. The table below shows data on coal use in the United States in 1975.

Purpose	Amount of Coal Used (millions of tons)
Homes	6
Export	60
Industry	150
Electricity	384
Total	**600**

Which of the following circle graphs correctly shows the percentages of coal used for each purpose?

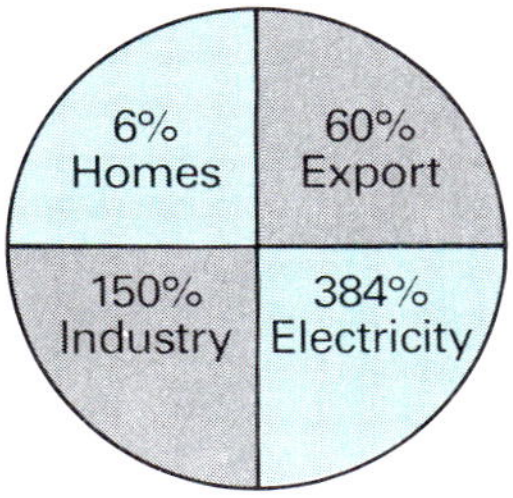

(1)

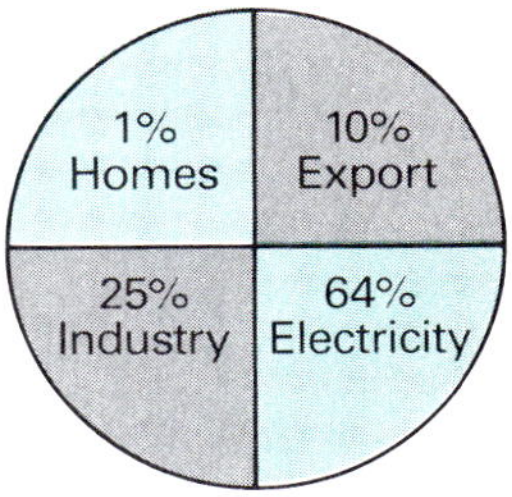

(2)

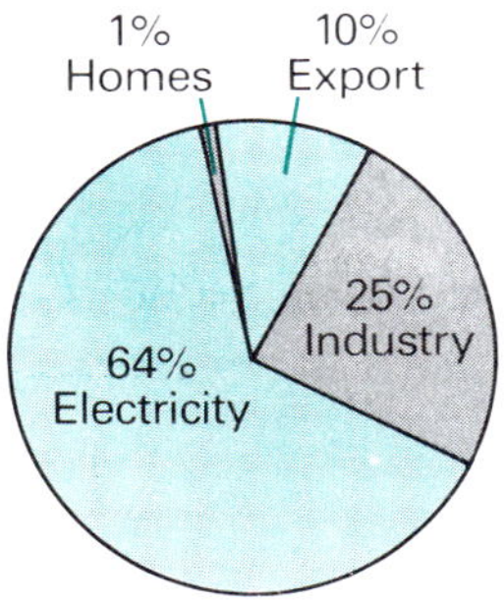

(3)

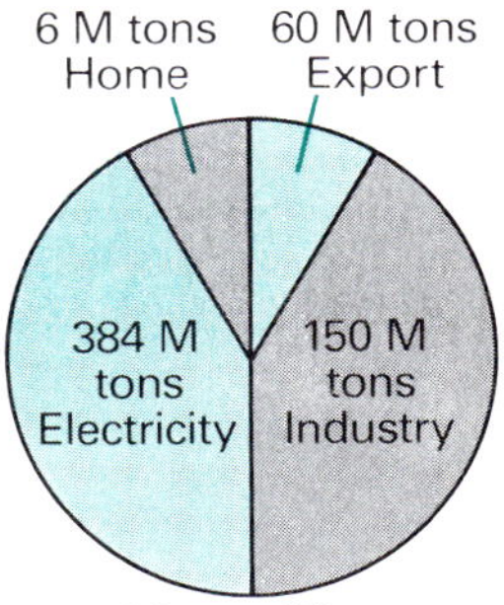

M = million

(4)

56. Suppose 200 units of work were put into a pulley to lift an object. The work given out by the pulley was reduced by 50 units due to friction. What was the efficiency of this pulley?

$$\text{Efficiency } (\%) = \frac{\text{Work out}}{\text{Work in}} \times 100$$

(1) 25% (3) 133%
(2) 75% (4) 400%

57. The illustration below represents a portion of a graduated cylinder containing water.

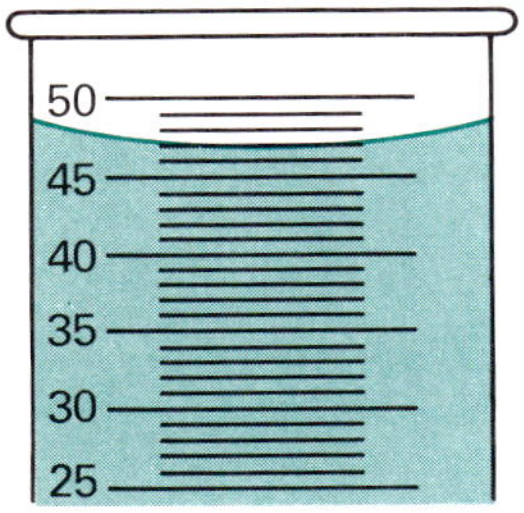

What is the total volume of water in this cylinder?

(1) 45.2 mL (3) 47.5 mL
(2) 47.0 mL (4) 48.0 mL

58. The illustration below shows the depth of the ocean floor at various locations.

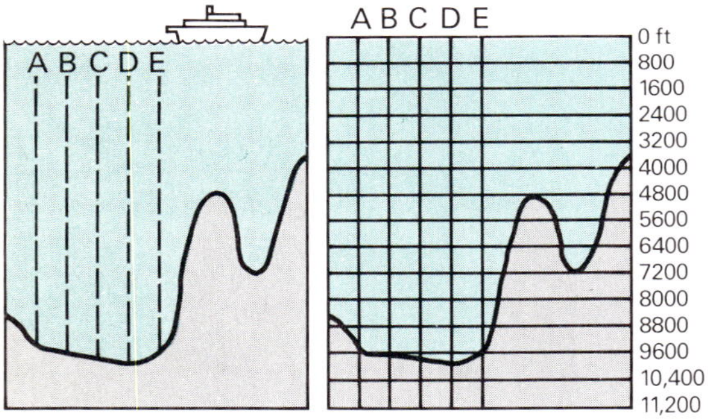

How deep is the ocean floor at location *A?*

(1) 8800 ft (3) 10,400 ft
(2) 9600 ft (4) 11,200 ft

59–60. Base your answers to questions 59 and 60 on the experiment described below.

A student wanted to find out whether temperature affects the growth of the bacteria E. coli. *She grew* E. coli *in three different petri dishes, all of the same size and containing the same amount and type of food. She placed the first petri dish in an incubator at 0°C, the second at 30°C, and the third at 45°C. After one week she counted the number of colonies of* E. coli *in each of the three petri dishes.*

59. The variable in this experiment was
(1) the type of food
(2) the amount of food
(3) the temperature at which the bacteria were grown
(4) the size of the petri dishes used to grow the bacteria

60. What hypothesis was the student testing?
(1) Temperature affects the growth of *E. coli*.
(2) The amount of space affects the growth of *E. coli*.
(3) Temperature affects the growth of all species of bacteria.
(4) Light affects the growth of all species of bacteria.

Practice Test 3

1. Human beings inhale oxygen and exhale carbon dioxide. This is just one example of the way humans
(1) exchange materials with their environment
(2) satisfy their nutritional needs
(3) adapt to their environment
(4) respond to stimuli

2. Green plants are called producers because they can
(1) manufacture carbon dioxide
(2) make their own food
(3) release energy in the form of light
(4) change chemical energy to electrical energy

3. The diagram below is an example of a(n)

insects→frog→snake

(1) food chain
(2) ecosystem
(3) biome
(4) life cycle

4. In the summer of 1988 fires destroyed some forests in Yellowstone National Park. To encourage tourists to continue to visit, park officials have advertised the park as *Nature's Laboratory: A Place to Watch the World Remake Itself*. Which of the following terms do biologists use to express the changes that may take place in this burned forest ecosystem?
(1) succession
(2) evolution
(3) adaptation
(4) regeneration

5. What nutrient group is missing from the cereal whose label is shown below?

NUTRITION INFORMATION

SERVING SIZE: 1.4 OZ. (1 OZ. WHEAT FLAKES WITH 0.4 OZ. RAISINS; 39.4 g, ABOUT ⅔ CUP)

SERVINGS PER PACKAGE: 10

	CEREAL & RAISINS	WITH ½ CUP VITAMINS A & D SKIM MILK
CALORIES	130	170*
PROTEIN	3 g	7 g
CARBOHYDRATE	32 g	38 g
FAT	0 g	0 g*
CHOLESTEROL	0 mg	0 mg*
SODIUM	170 mg	230 mg
POTASSIUM	170 mg	370 mg
PERCENTAGE OF U.S. RDA		
PROTEIN	4	15
VITAMIN A	25	30
VITAMIN C	**	2
THIAMIN	25	30
RIBOFLAVIN	25	35
NIACIN	25	25
CALCIUM	**	15
IRON	6	6
VITAMIN D	10	25
VITAMIN E	25	25
VITAMIN B_6	25	25
FOLIC ACID	25	25
VITAMIN B_{12}	25	35
PHOSPHORUS	10	20
MAGNESIUM	8	10
ZINC	25	30
COPPER	6	8

(1) carbohydrate
(2) fat
(3) minerals
(4) vitamins

6. The illustrations below show two geranium plants. Plant A received water containing dissolved minerals for 4 weeks. Plant B received water without minerals for this same time period.

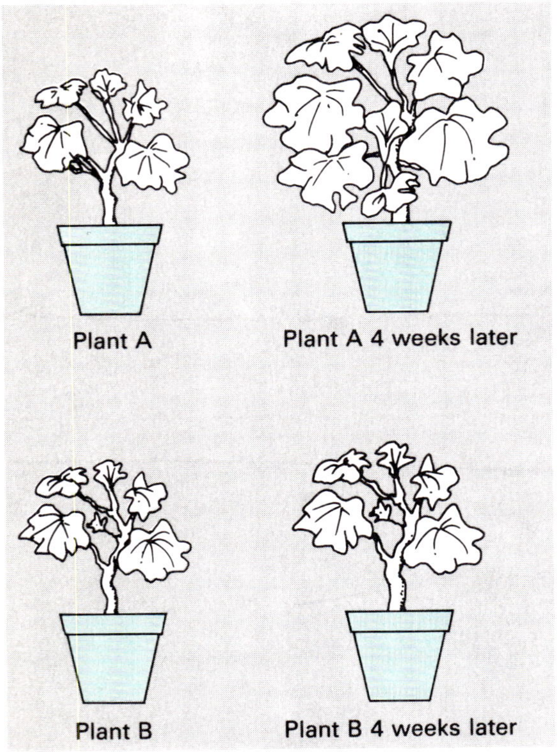

Based on the diagrams, which conclusion can be drawn concerning the growth of these plants?
(1) Minerals slow the rate of growth of geranium plants.
(2) Minerals increase the rate of growth of geranium plants.
(3) Minerals have no effect on the rate of growth of geranium plants.
(4) Geranium plants will grow only if minerals are dissolved in the water they receive.

7. Which one of the human body organs shown at the right above is the place where respiratory gases are exchanged?

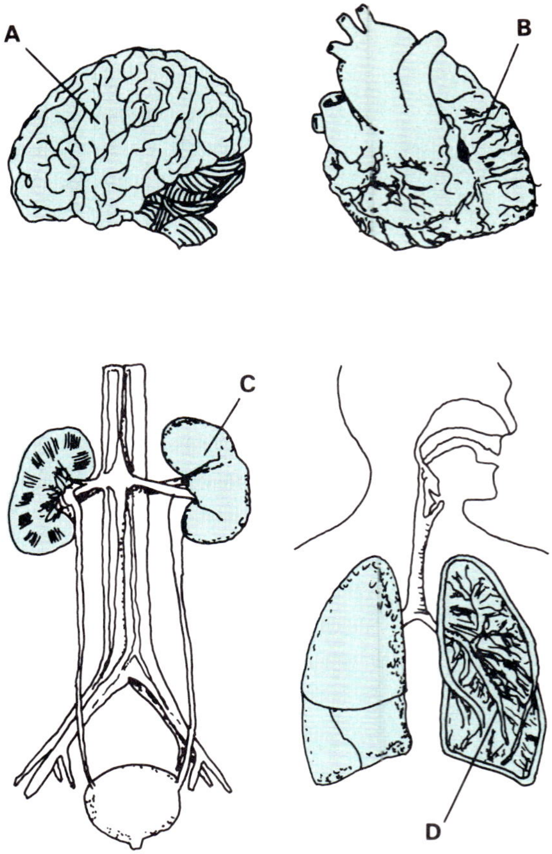

(1) organ A
(2) organ B
(3) organ C
(4) organ D

8. Which human body system consists of the skin, lungs, kidneys, and liver?
(1) circulatory system
(2) respiratory system
(3) excretory system
(4) skeletal system

9. Which two human systems work together to move the parts of the body?
(1) skeletal and muscular systems
(2) excretory and endocrine systems
(3) nervous and circulatory systems
(4) skeletal and reproductive systems

10. Through which part of the human digestive system do feces move before being eliminated by the body?

(1) part A (3) part C
(2) part B (4) part D

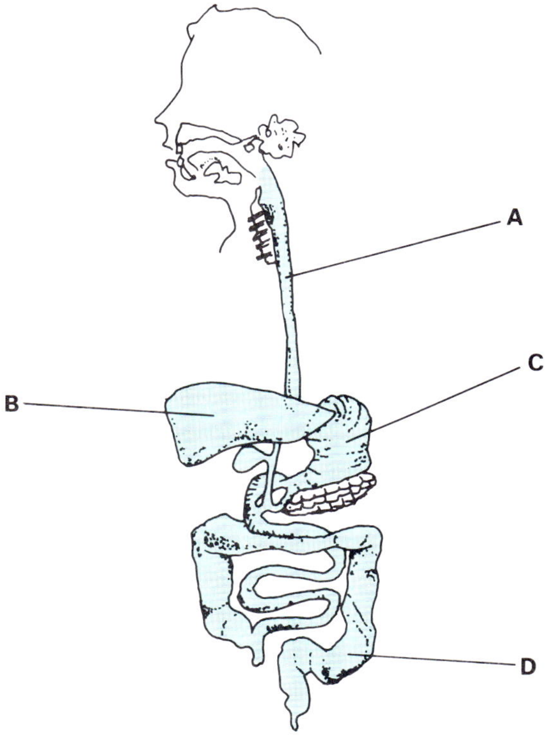

11. After food is digested, it is immediately absorbed into which of the following human body systems?
(1) muscular system
(2) skeletal system
(3) circulatory system
(4) nervous system

12. Which statement below correctly describes the role of the human endocrine system?
(1) It distributes food and oxygen to all parts of the body.
(2) It stores excretory wastes.
(3) Its glands secrete hormones.
(4) Its organs help to digest food.

13. Neurons, nerves, and the spinal cord are structures found in the human body. They are most closely associated with which of the following activities?
(1) the response to stimuli
(2) the storage of cellular wastes
(3) the breakdown of foods
(4) the exchange of oxygen and carbon dioxide gas

14–15. Base your answers to questions 14 and 15 on the diagram below and your knowledge of biology.

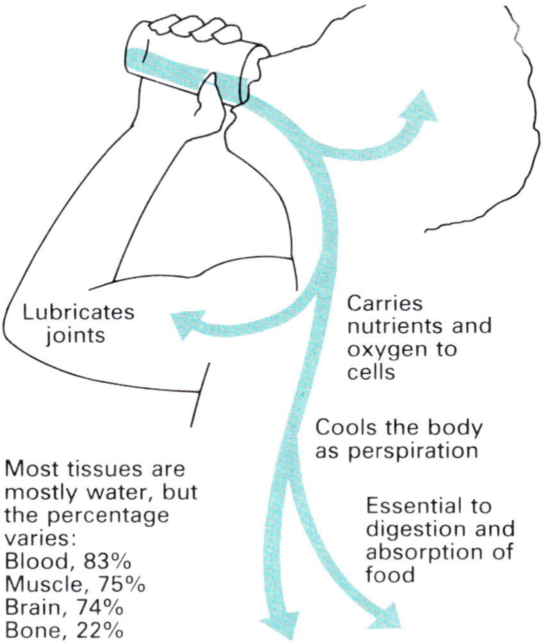

14. Of the tissues listed below, which one contains the greatest percentage of its weight in water?
(1) brain (3) muscle
(2) bone (4) blood

15. Water is required in the human body for various reasons. However, water does *not*
(1) carry nutrients and oxygen
(2) aid in the digestion and absorption of food
(3) contain vitamins and minerals needed for good health
(4) help to cool the body through the process of perspiration

16. An example of a noninfectious disease is
(1) the common cold
(2) AIDS
(3) flu
(4) cancer

17. Which statement is true of an infectious disease?
(1) It spreads from one individual to the next.
(2) It is caused by being exposed to too much sunlight.
(3) It is caused by eating the wrong kinds of foods.
(4) It results from a shortage of oxygen in the cells of the body.

18. A scientist found a mineral in a field. The mineral's mass was 10 grams and its volume was 2 cubic centimeters. The table below, which shows the density of some minerals, helped the scientist identify the mineral.

Mineral	Density (g/cm^3)
quartz	2.6
talc	2.8
pyrite	5.0
cinnabar	8.1
gold	19.3

Which mineral was it?
(1) quartz
(2) talc
(3) pyrite
(4) gold

19–20. Base your answers to questions 19 and 20 on the weather map shown below.

Today's High Temperatures and Precipitation

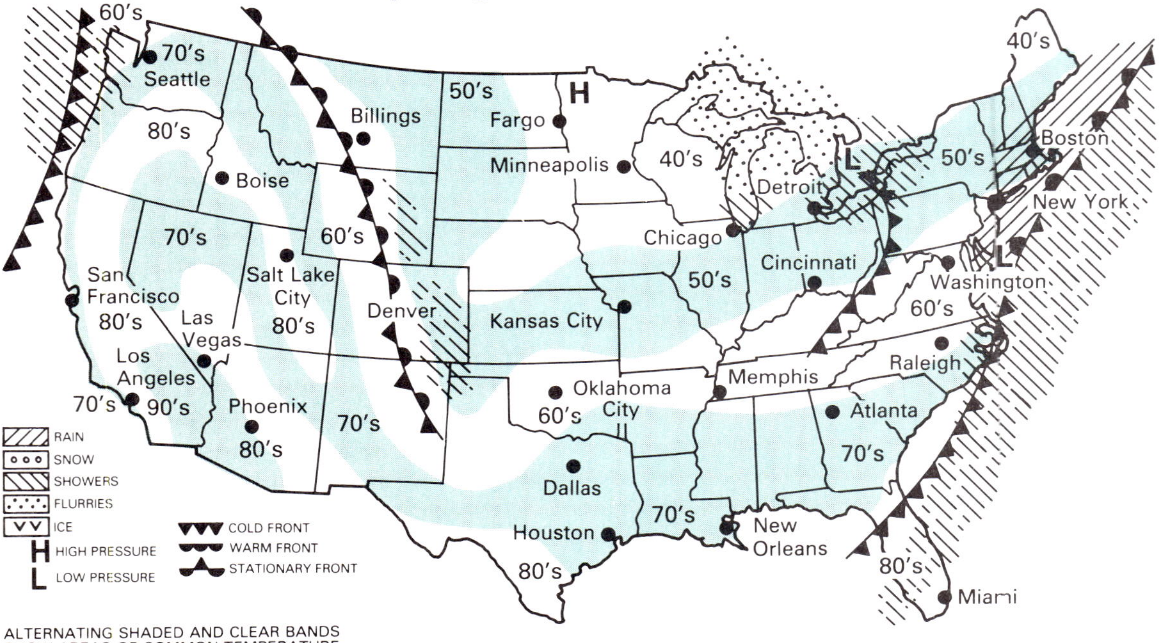

ALTERNATING SHADED AND CLEAR BANDS SHOW AREAS OF COMMON TEMPERATURE.

19. Which area in the United States reported the highest temperature?
(1) northwest (3) northeast
(2) southwest (4) southeast

20. The rain that is falling along the eastern seaboard was probably due to the passing of a(n)
(1) cold front (3) hurricane
(2) warm front (4) earthquake

21. The diagram below represents what cycle?

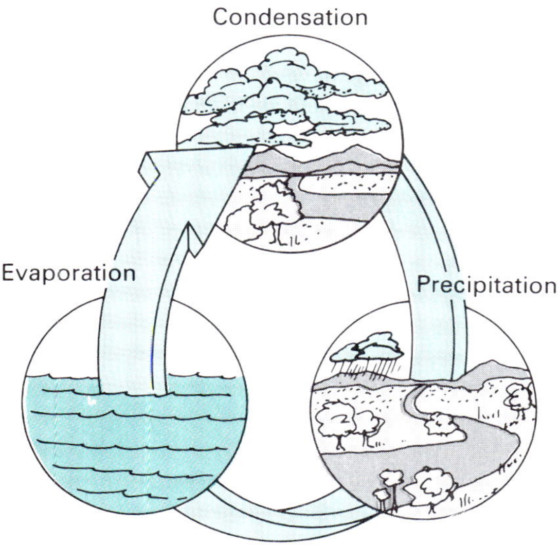

(1) life cycle (3) carbon cycle
(2) water cycle (4) nitrogen cycle

22. Which one of the following statements concerning air is correct?
(1) Warm air is more dense than cold air.
(2) The lower the temperature, the more water air can hold.
(3) When air cools, it can hold less water vapor.
(4) High pressure areas cause the major storm systems in the United States.

23. On a certain day, the air over Syracuse held only one half of the water vapor it could absorb. The relative humidity of the air was
(1) 25%
(2) 50%
(3) 75%
(4) 100%

24. The diagram below shows a cold front as it approaches Town A. As this cold front passes over town A, the weather will probably become

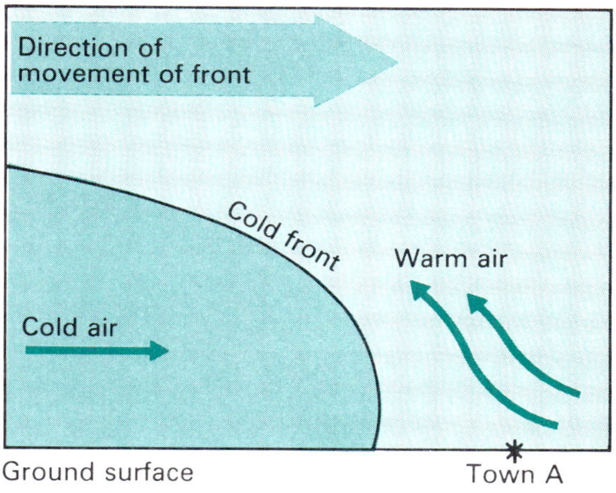

(1) warm and rainy
(2) cool and dry
(3) warm and dry
(4) cool and rainy

25. The following weather changes were reported in a certain area: The temperature dropped 20 degrees centigrade in 7 hours. In that time, the air pressure increased from 96 millibars to 1020 millibars. The sudden changes in the weather were probably due to the passing of a
(1) warm front
(2) cold front
(3) tropical storm
(4) tropical air mass

26. The illustration below shows the water level in a graduated cylinder before and after a rock sample was placed in it.

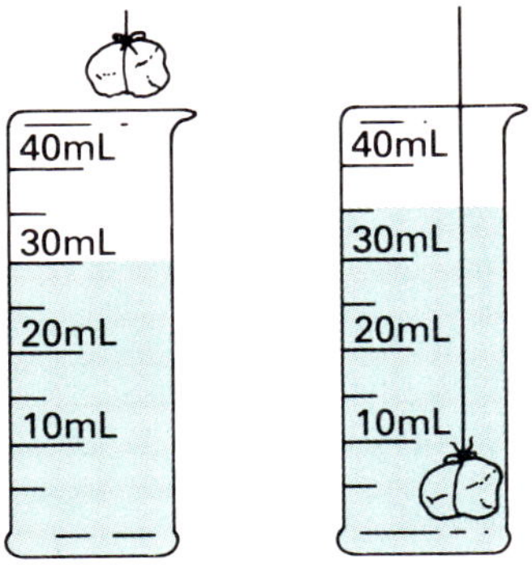

What is the volume of the rock?

(1) 5 ml
(2) 10 ml
(3) 20 ml
(4) 25 ml

27. Which one of the following processes results in the wearing away of the earth's surface?

(1) folding
(2) faulting
(3) weathering and erosion
(4) volcanic eruptions

28. The diagram below represents some layers of sedimentary rock. In which layer would the oldest fossils probably be found?

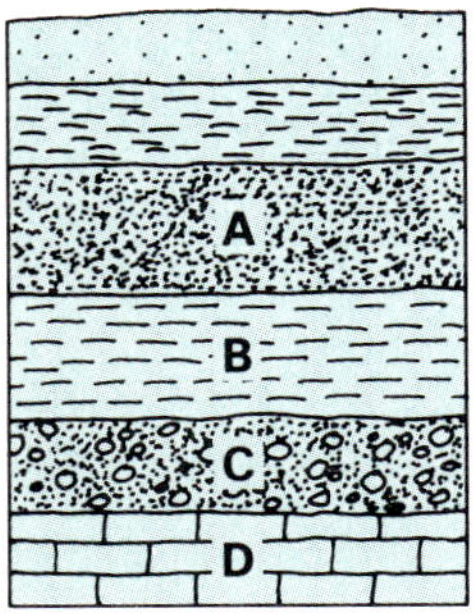

(1) layer A
(2) layer B
(3) layer C
(4) layer D

29. A student set up the demonstration above right to show one process that wears away the surface of the earth.

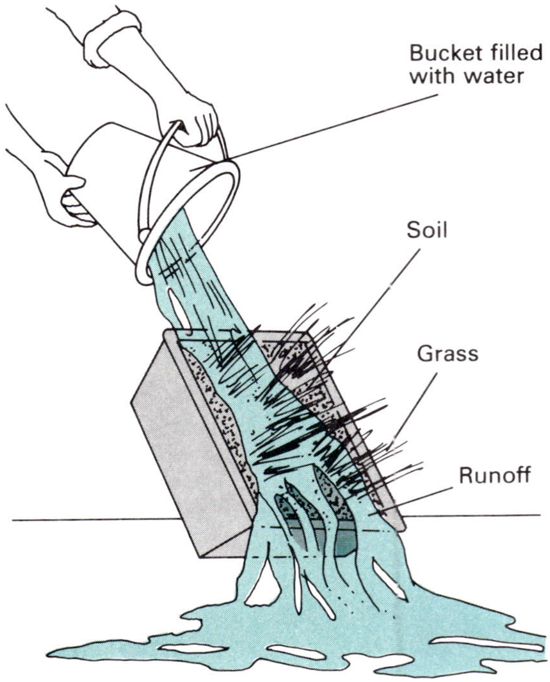

The process the student wanted to demonstrate is

(1) vulcanism
(2) folding
(3) faulting
(4) erosion

30. The following statements appeared in a newspaper article on nuclear power plants:

A. *Radiation leakage from a nuclear power plant may cause mutations in living things.*

B. *The use of nuclear power, unlike the use of coal for energy, adds little carbon dioxide to the atmosphere. Therefore, using nuclear power is not one of the factors that has caused the recent rise in the temperature of the earth's atmosphere.*

These two statements reflect which one of the following ideas about technology.

(1) Technology solves all our problems.
(2) Technology impacts only negatively upon our environment.

(3) Technology must be improved.
(4) Technology offers both benefits and burdens.

31–33. Base your answers to questions 31–33 on the information provided below.

A scientist wanted to see if a certain type of bacterial cell, bacterium X, needed light to grow. She placed equal amounts of bacterium X cells into two test tubes: test tube A and test tube B. Each test tube contained the same types and amounts of nutrients. After adding bacterium X to each tube, she placed test tube A in the light. She placed test tube B in the dark. After 24 hours she observed both test tubes. Test tube A had turned cloudy, indicating that the bacteria had grown. Test tube B remained clear, indicating that the bacteria in that test tube had not grown.

31. What is the variable in this experiment?
(1) temperature
(2) light
(3) type of bacteria
(4) size of the test tubes

32. What conclusion can be made from this experiment?
(1) Temperature affects the growth of bacterium X.
(2) Moisture affects the growth of bacterium X.
(3) Light is needed for the growth of bacterium X.
(4) Bacterium X grows best in a large-sized test tube.

33. Which one of the following changes indicated that bacterium X had grown?
(1) Bubbles of CO_2 gas appeared in test tube A.
(2) Bubbles of O_2 gas apeared in test tube B.
(3) The contents of test tube A turned cloudy.
(4) The contents of test tube A remained clear.

34. The graph below compares the height and weight of 4 girls. Based on the information in the graph, which of the following is true?

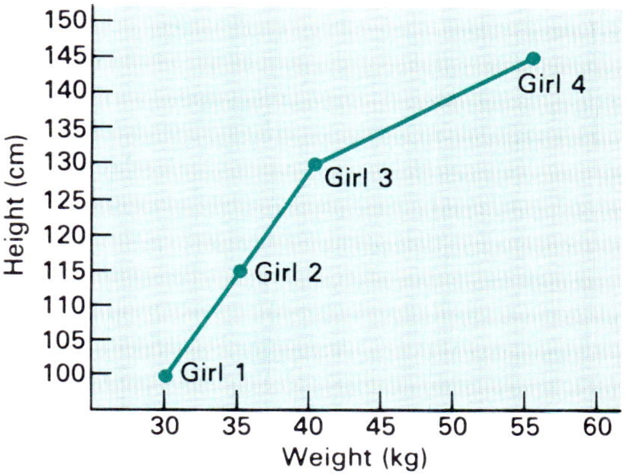

(1) Girl 4 is shorter than girl 3.
(2) Girl 3 weighs more than girl 4.
(3) The tallest girl weighs the most.
(4) The girl who weighs 35 kg is 130 cm tall.

35. How tall is the plant shown below?

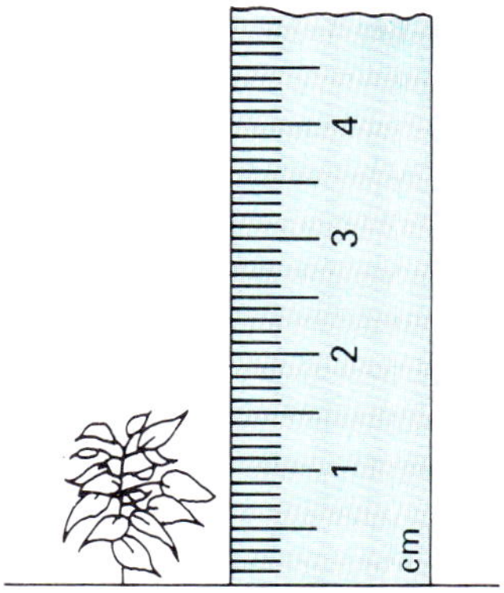

(1) 1.5 mm
(2) 15 cm
(3) 15 mm
(4) .15 cm

36. A calendar shows the following moon phase diagrams for the month of November.

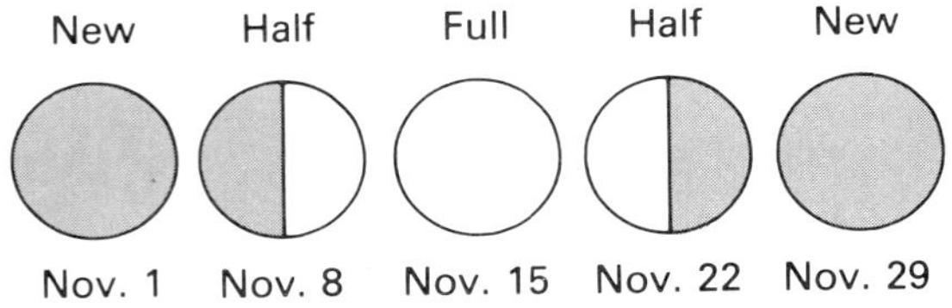

On what date will the moon appear as shown below?

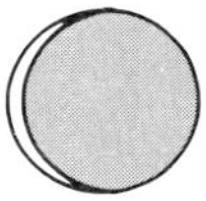

(1) November 2 (3) November 28
(2) November 16 (4) November 30

37. Which one of the following objects shines by its own light rather than by reflected light?
(1) a star
(2) the moon
(3) the inner planets
(4) the outer planets

38. How many rotations does Earth make during one revolution around the Sun?
(1) 1 (3) 24
(2) 12 (4) 365.25

39. About how many times does the Moon revolve around the Earth during the course of one year?
(1) 1 (3) 24
(2) 12 (4) 365.25

40. Comets are glowing objects that appear like a streak in the sky for a short while. Some comets return. Halley's comet returns after an exact number of years. These are the years in which Halley's comet has been seen in modern times: 1682, 1758, 1834, 1910, and 1986. From the pattern of these dates, when can we expect to see Halley's comet again?
(1) 2000 (3) 2076
(2) 2062 (4) 2086

41. Which diagram shows the position of Earth when it is winter in the northern hemisphere?

(1)

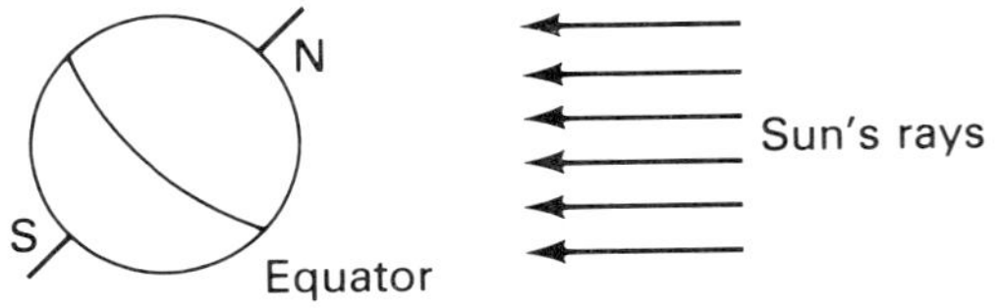

(2)

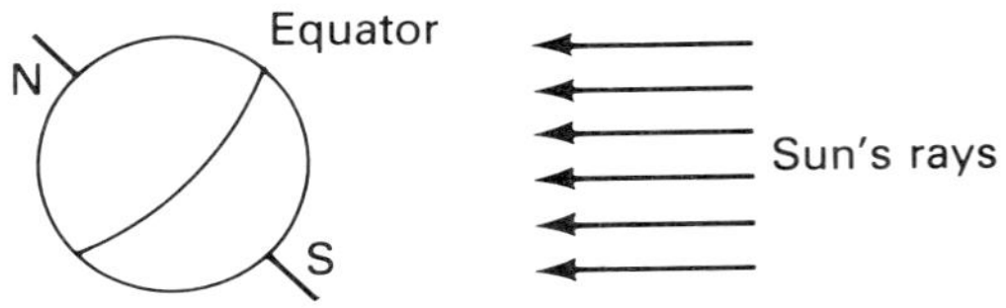

(3)

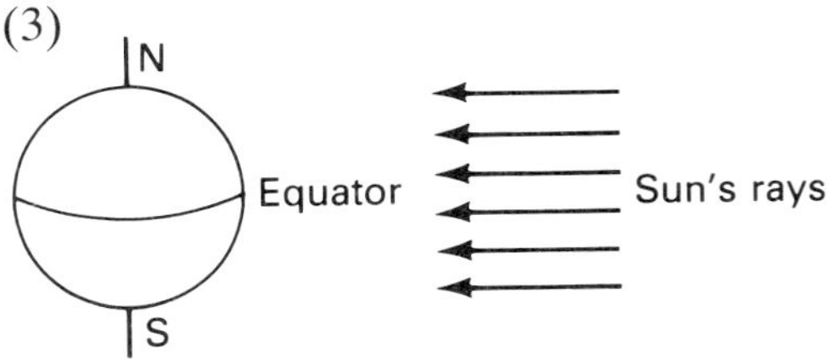

(4)

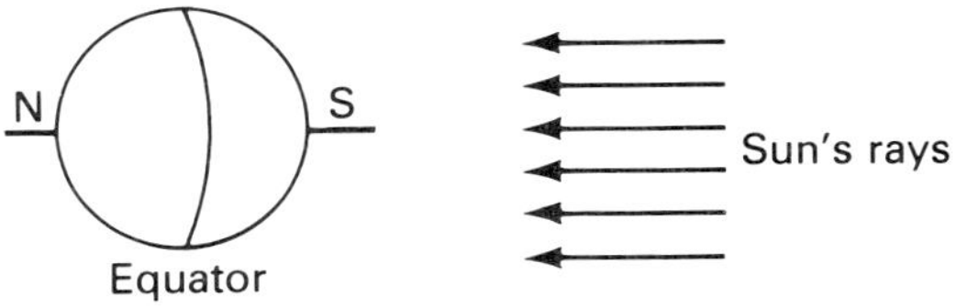

42. A bowling ball rolling down an alley towards the bowling pins contains mainly
(1) chemical energy
(2) gravitational potential energy
(3) magnetic potential energy
(4) kinetic energy

43. A solar powered calculator does not need batteries. What energy change occurs when the calculator is being used?

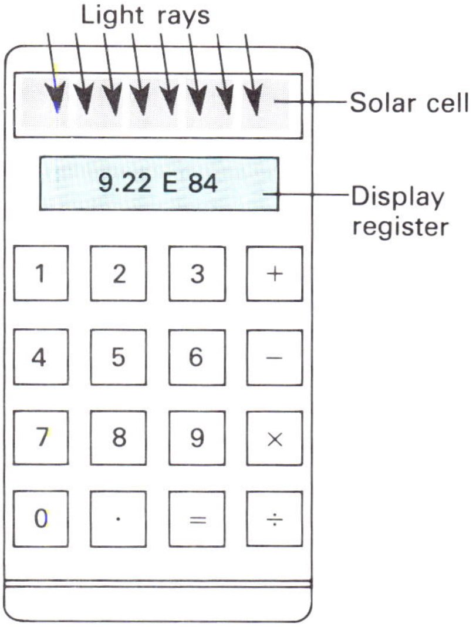

(1) Chemical energy becomes electrical energy.
(2) Electrical energy becomes chemical energy.
(3) Light energy becomes electrical energy.
(4) Light energy becomes nuclear energy.

44. Which of the following is *not* a lever?

(1) hammer removing a nail

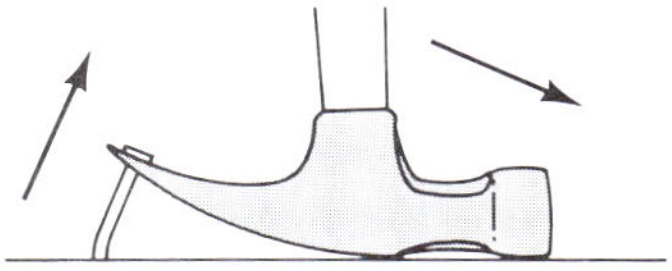

(2) ramp

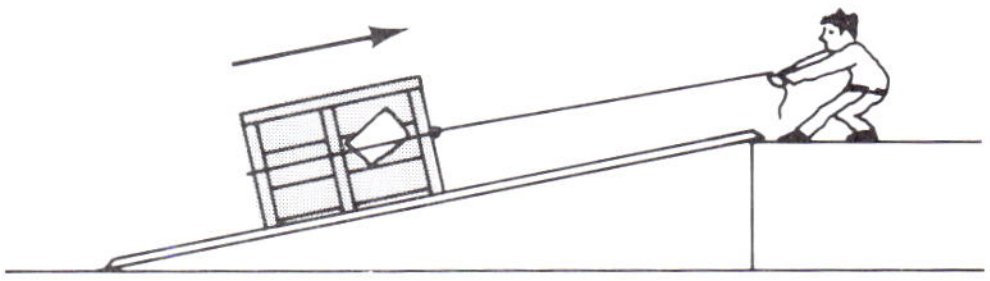

(3) nutcracker

(4) row-boat oar

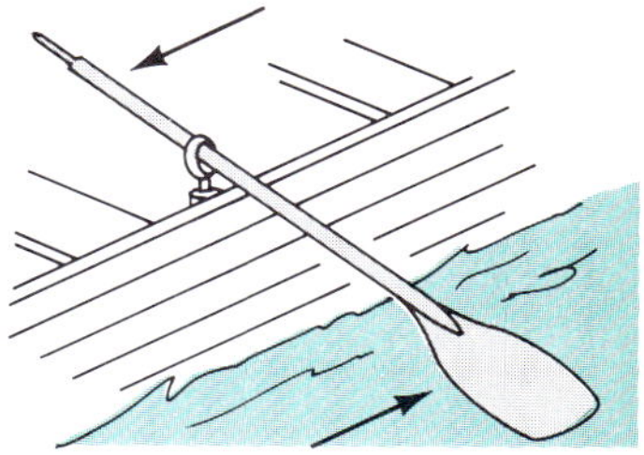

45. Examine the graph below.

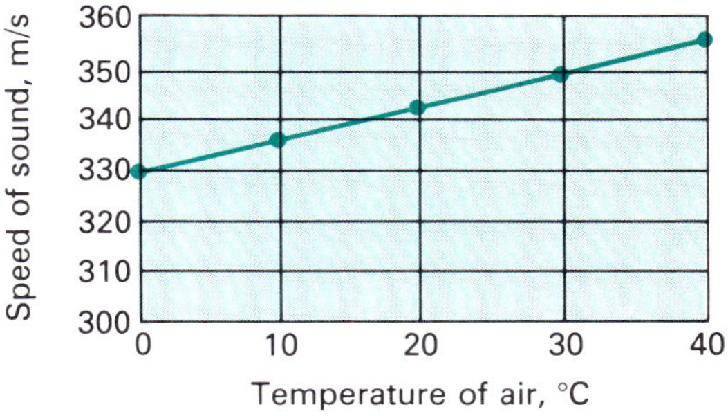

What is indicated about the speed of sound?
(1) It is a fixed constant.
(2) It increases with the density of the medium.
(3) It increases with an increase in temperature.
(4) It decreases with an increase in temperature.

46. A certain type of glass has the following qualities:

Transmission–Low
Reflection–Medium
Absorption–High

This type of glass would be best suited for
(1) camera lenses
(2) windows
(3) mirrors
(4) sunglasses

47. Many restaurants post this sign:

WARNING: MICROWAVE OVENS IN USE

What is this warning based upon?
(1) Microwave ovens are dangerously hot.
(2) Strong sound waves can damage human ears.
(3) Radioactivity can lead to cancer.
(4) Electromagnetic waves have some harmful effects.

48–50. Base your answers to questions 48–50 on the information and graph below.

The volume occupied by exactly 1,000 grams of water was carefully measured at various temperatures by a scientist. His results are shown in the graph.

VOLUME-TEMPERATURE CHANGES IN 1000g OF LIQUID WATER

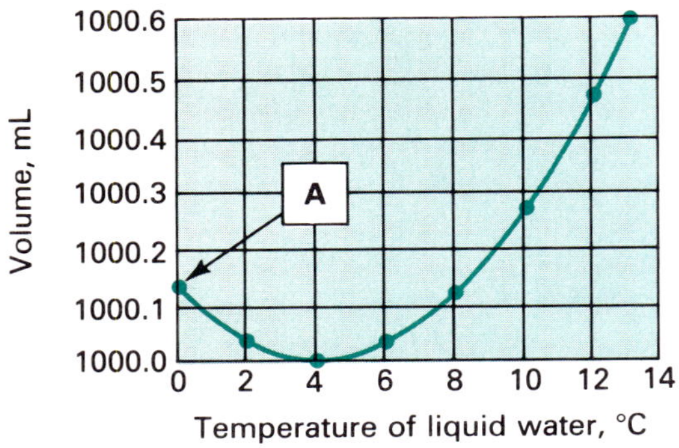

48. At what temperature does the 1,000 g of water occupy the smallest volume? (This will also be the temperature when it has the greatest density.)
(1) at 0°C
(2) at 2°C
(3) at 4°C
(4) at 8°C

49. Look at the graph above. At what temperature does water behave like all other materials in its volume change with temperature?
(1) below 0°C
(2) above 0°C
(3) between 0°C and 4°C
(4) above 4°C

50. In the graph, Point A is the volume of liquid water at 0°C. Once the water freezes, the volume of ice formed expands to 1090 mL. Which choice below shows the correct calculation of the density of the ice formed after all 1,000 g of water freezes, using the formula

$$\text{Density} = \frac{\text{Mass}}{\text{Volume}}.$$

(1) $\text{Density} = \frac{1000\text{ g}}{1000.00\text{ mL}} = 1{,}000\frac{\text{g}}{\text{mL}}$

(2) $\text{Density} = \frac{1000\text{ g}}{1090\text{ mL}} = 0.917\frac{\text{g}}{\text{mL}}$

(3) $\text{Density} = \frac{1000\text{ g}}{1000.13\text{ mL}} = 0.9999\frac{\text{g}}{\text{mL}}$

(4) $\text{Density} = \frac{1090\text{ mL}}{1000\text{ g}} = 1.09\frac{\text{g}}{\text{mL}}$

51. Most new electrical outlets have three slots, as shown in the illustration below.

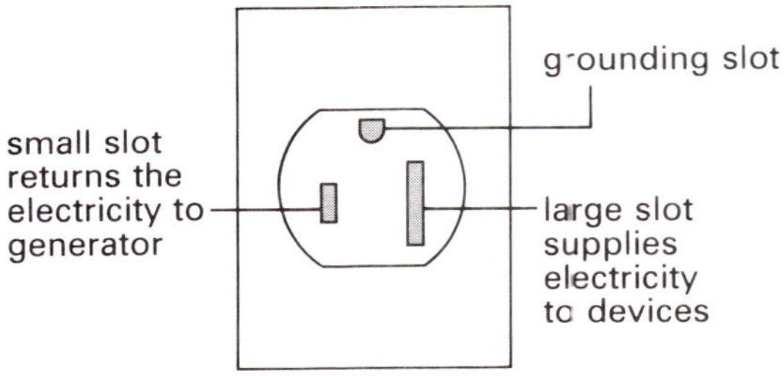

The grounding slot (and grounding wire) are important for
(1) increasing the conduction of electricity
(2) providing more electrical energy
(3) completing the electrical circuit
(4) protection against electric shock

52. Which step must a student take before pouring a flammable liquid in the lab?
(1) close the windows
(2) turn on the water in the sink
(3) turn off all flames
(4) turn off the electricity

53–54. Base your answers to questions 53 and 54 on the two graphs below.

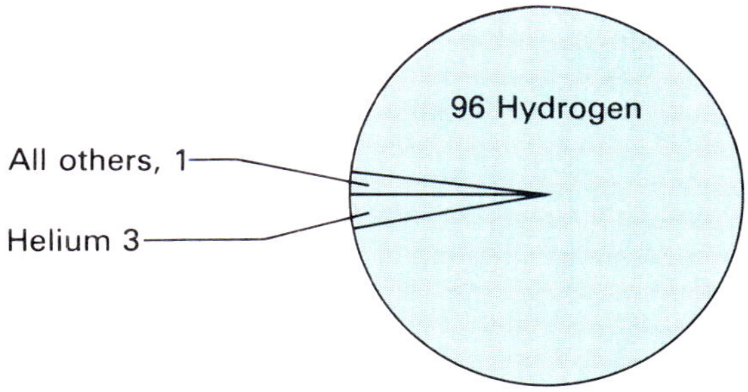

Percentage (by weight) of the elements in the entire universe

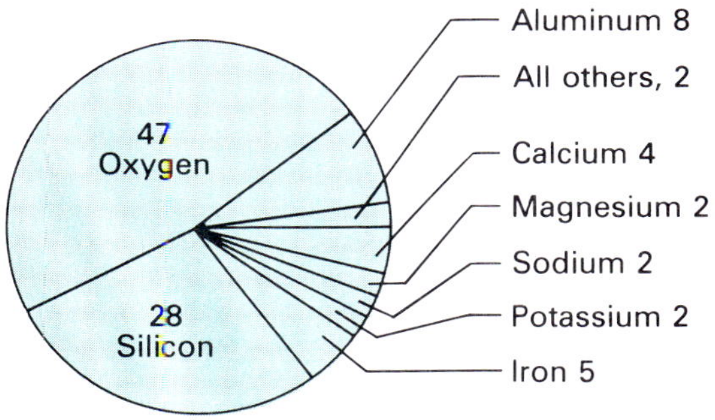

Percentage (by weight) of the elements in the earth's crust

53. What is the most abundant element (by weight) in the earth's crust?
(1) hydrogen
(2) oxygen
(3) silicon
(4) none of these

54. The most abundant element in the universe is what percentage of the earth's crust?
(1) Less than 2%
(2) 2%
(3) 47%
(4) 96%

55. A student examines some chemicals using the checklist shown below.

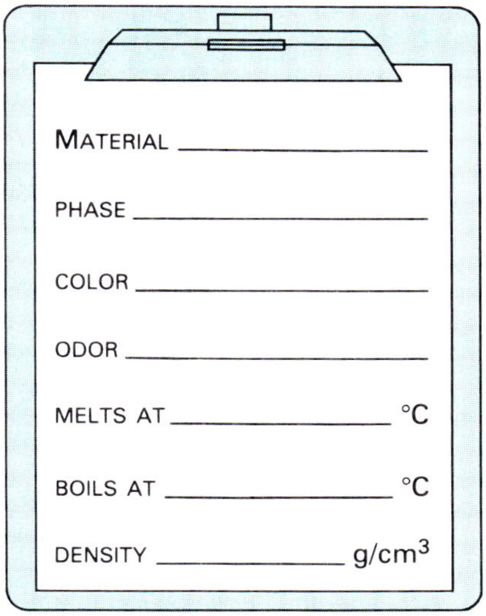

The purpose of this examination is to determine the chemicals'
(1) bonding energies
(2) physical properties
(3) chemical properties
(4) chemical composition (elements that make up the chemical)

56. Water becomes ice in a refrigerator because
(1) heat energy is put into the water
(2) heat energy is removed from the water
(3) cold energy is put into the water
(4) water molecules are made to move faster and spread apart

57. Oxygen and nitrogen are non-toxic gases. When they combine in a chemical change, the new material produced
(1) *must* be non-toxic
(2) *must* be a gas
(3) can never be non-toxic or a gas
(4) might be toxic

58. The technical information label on an air conditioner is reproduced below.

120 VOLTS, 5.0 AMPS (MAXIMUM)
60 HZ (CYCLES PER SEC. CURRENT)
600 WATTS UL
75% EFFICIENCY TESTED
85 LBS. MODEL 6-23-AF/45

Which number reveals the rate of electrical energy needed to make the air conditioner run?

(1) 5.0 amps (3) 120 volts
(2) 75% efficiency (4) 600 watts

59. Here is a copy of an electric company bill. A bill tells how much electrical energy was used during a month, and what the total cost is, including taxes.

EDISON ELECTRIC COMPANY BILL

Meter reading on Feb. 1 3850
Meter reading on Feb. 28 ..4050

Total energy used.................200 units*
Price.....................................$0.20 for each unit

Total cost = energy used × price ....$

Add state and city taxes ......$ 3.00
Amount due..........................$ ______

PLEASE PAY BY MARCH 15. DO NOT SEND CASH. MAKE CHECKS PAYABLE TO EDISON ELECTRIC CO. ENCLOSE THIS BILL.

* Obtained by subtracting the two meter readings. Each energy unit is called a kilowatt-hour.

What will the "amount due" be for this bill?

(1) $3.20 (3) $81.00
(2) $43.00 (4) $203.00

60. River water, tides, wood from trees, and the wind are all energy sources that can be used to generate electricity. What do these sources have in common?

(1) They are the major sources of energy in the United States today.
(2) They are renewable.
(3) They are very harmful to the environment.
(4) They are examples of fossil fuels.

61–62. Base your answers to questions 61 and 62 on the two graphs below.

ECONOMIC GROWTH RATES OF THE TOP FOUR INDUSTRIAL NATIONS

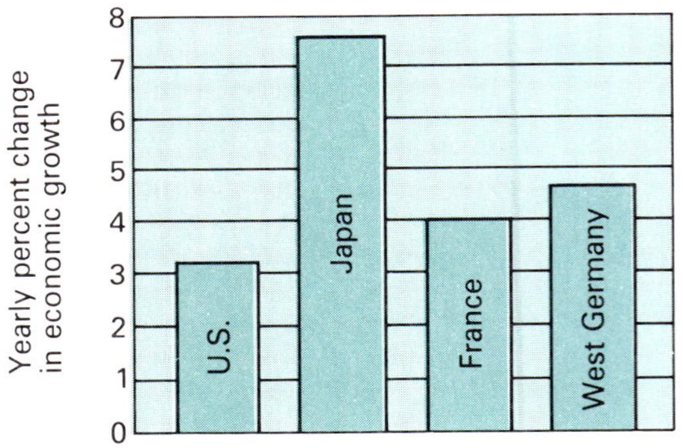

Average yearly rates for 1950–1985

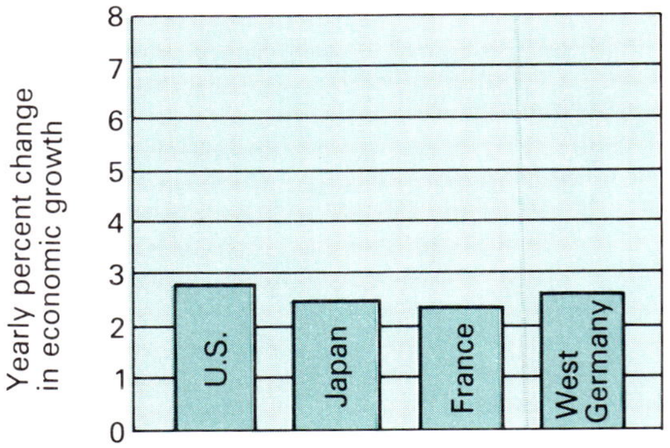

Rates for 1986 alone

61. What was the *difference* between the average yearly economic growth rates of Japan and the United States for 1950–1985?

(1) 3.1% (3) 7.4%
(2) 4.3% (4) 0.2%

62. Which statement regarding economic growth in 1986 is true, as compared to 1950–1985?

(1) Japan decreased and the U.S. increased growth.
(2) Japan and the U.S. increased growth.
(3) The four industrial nations were still very different in growth rate.
(4) All four industrial nations decreased in their growth rate.

63. The following conclusion is from a *Scientific American* study of June 1988:

"U.S. economic growth can be enhanced by improving workers' skills, supporting research, and encouraging technological innovation."

Which statement below best explains this conclusion?

(1) Competition among nations hurts technology and business.
(2) Technology can solve all of the problems of society.
(3) The United States can easily grow with its present science and technology.
(4) Science and technology affect jobs, business, and industry.

64. The diagram below illustrates the steps involved when a person calls someone from phone A to phone B.

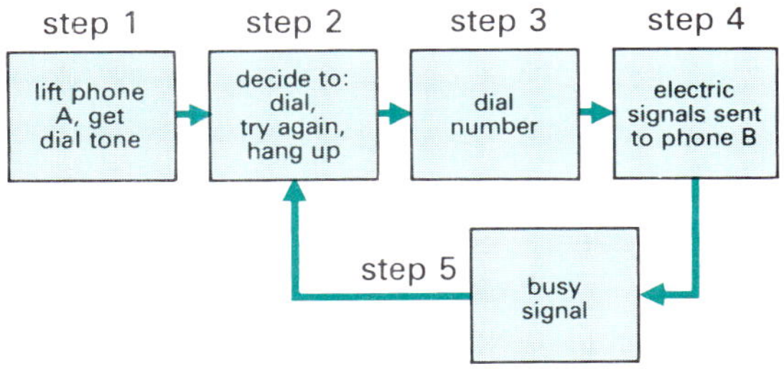

In this system what does step 4 represent?

(1) input control
(2) process
(3) output
(4) feedback

65–67. Base your answers to questions 65–67 on the diagram and information below. The diagram shows what is printed on the side of a milk carton. Shelf life is the time milk will remain fresh at various temperatures.

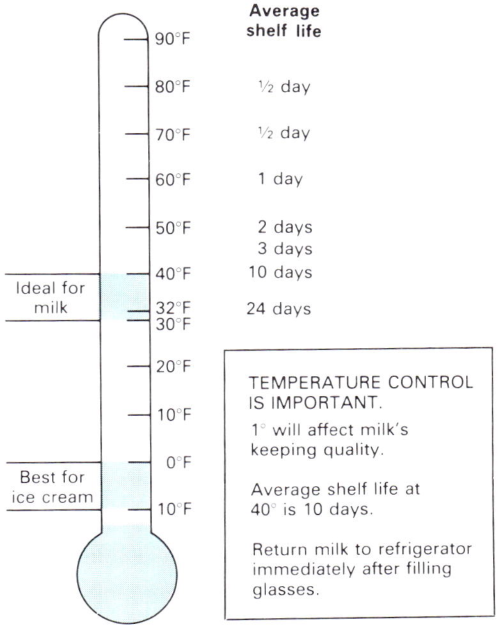

65. Which temperature is best for storing ice cream?

(1) 32°F
(2) 5°F
(3) 5°F below zero
(4) 32°F below zero

66. Milk is left out on a table where the room temperature is 75°F. How long will it stay fresh enough to drink?

(1) just 1 hour
(2) about ½ a day
(3) 1 day
(4) 2 days

67. What general conclusion can be made from the information above?
(1) Milk's freshness slowly decreases at higher temperatures.
(2) Milk's freshness rapidly decreases at higher temperatures.
(3) Milk and water freeze near 32°F.
(4) Frozen milk at 30°F can last for three weeks.

68. Below is a pressure gauge testing the air pressure in a car's tire. The unit "psi" is an abbreviation for pounds per square inch.

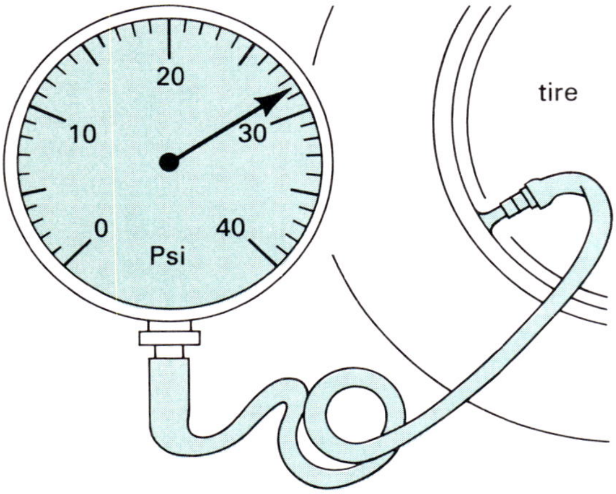

What pressure does the pointer indicate on the scale?
(1) 20.8 psi
(2) 20.85 psi
(3) 28.5 psi
(4) 31.5 psi

69–70. Base your answers to questions 69 and 70 on the information below and at the right above.

A car test driver wants to find out how fast a car can speed up. Starting from a complete stop, she gives full power to the car. Her assistant looks at the speedometer and records the speed after every second that passes. The results are found in the table below.

Time, in seconds	Speed, in km/hr
0 (Start)	0
1	15
2	30
3	45
4	60
5	75
6	75
7	75
8	75

69. Plot these data on the grid below. Complete the graph by connecting the data points with straight lines.

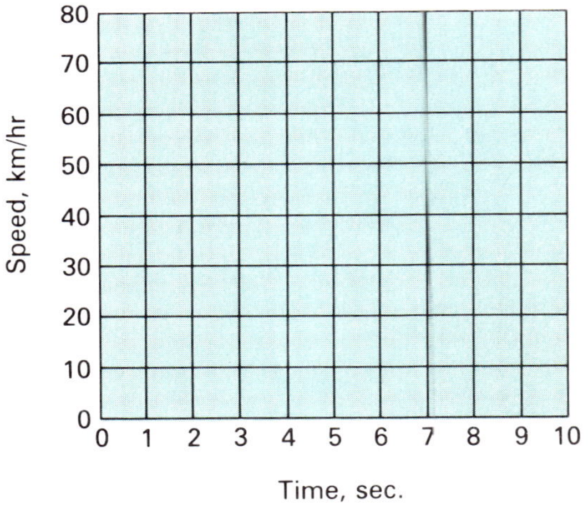

70. Which statement is true about the car's motion after 5 seconds?
(1) It continued to speed up.
(2) It stopped.
(3) It began to slow down.
(4) It remained at constant speed.

Practice Test 4

1. The graph below shows the number of times per minute a goldfish's gill cover opens. What is the best prediction for how many times per minute the gill opens at a temperature of 23°C?

Number of Times Gill Cover Opens at Different Temperatures

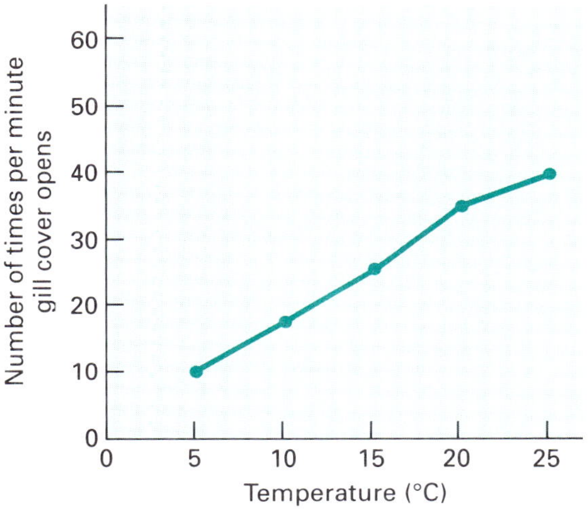

(1) 20
(2) 30
(3) 37
(4) 52

2. Which characteristic of living things is illustrated by the picture below?

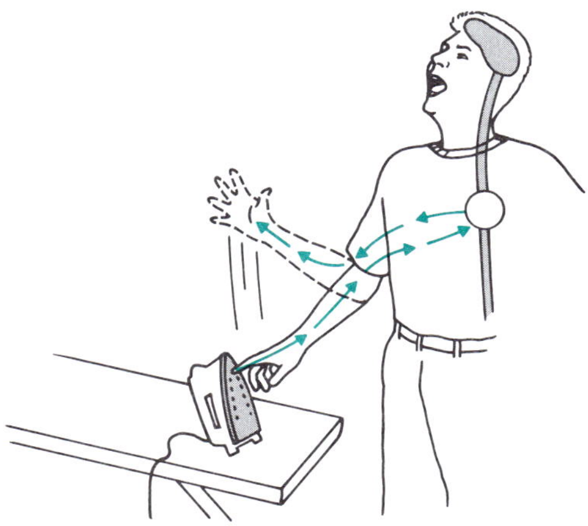

(1) ability to release energy from food
(2) ability to respond to stimuli
(3) ability to grow and develop
(4) ability to use light and heat energy

3. Which one of these statements is true for animals?
(1) They carry on photosynthesis.
(2) They are producers.
(3) They are consumers.
(4) They use light energy and carbon dioxide to produce their own food.

4–5. Base your answers to questions 4 and 5 on the information below. The table shows the percentages of three gases in air inhaled and exhaled by humans.

Gas	% in Inhaled Air	% in Exhaled Air
CO_2	0.04%	5.60%
O_2	21.00%	14.00%
N_2	78.00%	78.00%

4. One conclusion that can be drawn from the table is that to carry on life activities humans
(1) use oxygen and release carbon dioxide
(2) use carbon dioxide and release oxygen
(3) use nitrogen in larger amounts than the other gases
(4) use neither oxygen nor carbon dioxide

5. According to the table, inhaled air contains
(1) 14.00% O_2, 0.04% CO_2, and 78.00% N_2

(2) 21.00% O_2, 0.04% CO_2, and 78.00% N_2
(3) 21.00% O_2, 5.60% CO_2, and 78.00% N_2
(4) 14.00% O_2, 5.60% CO_2, and 78.00% N_2

6. The pyramid of the food groups, shown below, was designed by nutritionists. It suggests that humans should limit their intake of which one of the following nutrient groups?

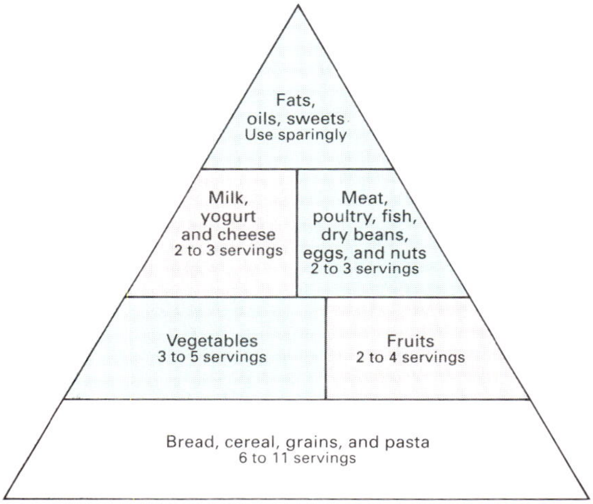

(1) carbohydrates
(2) fats
(3) proteins
(4) water

7. What is shown by the diagram below of the life cycle of a moth?

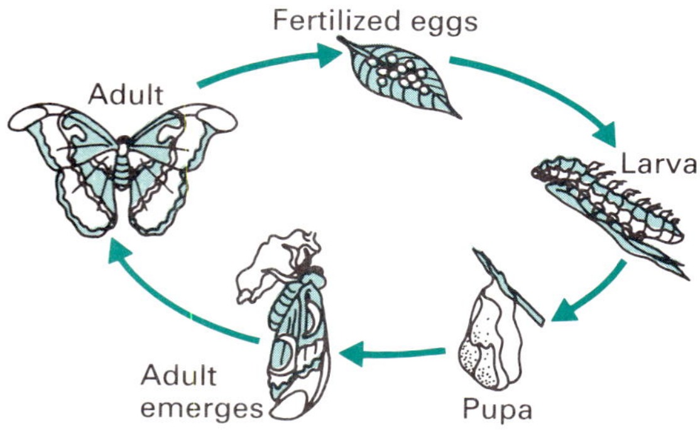

(1) An organism depends on other organisms for food.
(2) The pupa is the youngest stage in a moth's development.
(3) A moth's egg hatches into a mature adult.
(4) A developing moth passes through a series of changes before becoming an adult.

8–9. Base your answers to questions 8 and 9 on the information and data table below.

A student wanted to test how the amount of a new plant food affects the average height of geranium plants. He started with five sets, each containing ten geranium plants. Each plant was 1 centimeter in height. He gave each set of ten plants a different amount of plant food each day for one month. All other conditions, such as the amount of water, sunlight, and temperature, were kept constant. After one month the student measured each geranium plant in each set and then calculated the average height of the plants in each set. The results of his experiment are shown in the data table below.

Amount of Plant Food (g)	Average Height (cm)
1	3
3	5
5	7
7	9
9	6

8. Use the data in the table to construct a line graph on a grid like the one shown on the next page. Mark the location of each point with an X and connect the points with a line.

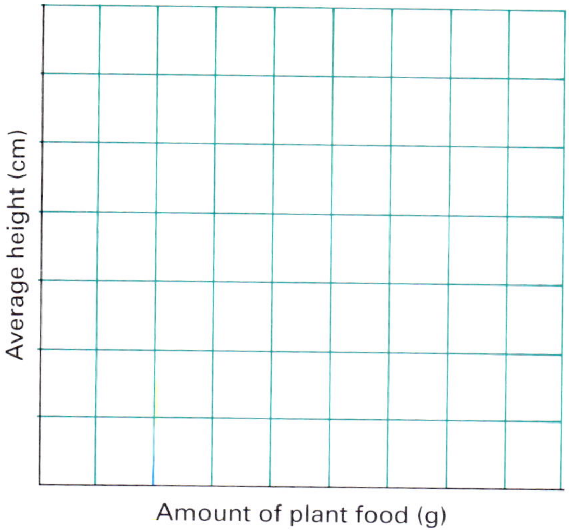

9. Which represents the variable in this experiment?
(1) amount of water used
(2) amount of plant food used
(3) type of plant food used
(4) amount of sunlight provided

10. Which term below best completes the following sentence?
The skull is to the skeletal system as the brain is to the ______________.
(1) digestive system
(2) muscular system
(3) reproductive system
(4) nervous system

11. Which organ system removes wastes from the blood and eventually from the body?
(1) skeletal system
(2) muscular system
(3) endocrine system
(4) excretory system

12. Which list of human body parts is organized from simple to complex?
(1) organs, organ systems, tissues, cells
(2) cells, tissues, organs, organ systems
(3) tissues, organ systems, organs, cells
(4) organ systems, tissues, cells, organs

13. As a result of a life activity called cellular respiration,
(1) solid wastes are eliminated from the body
(2) food is digested and absorbed into the blood stream
(3) energy is released from digested food within the body's cells
(4) nutrients are transported to all the cells

14. Which human organ system consists of hormone-secreting glands?
(1) digestive system
(2) muscular system
(3) excretory system
(4) endocrine system

15. Which one of the following organs contains involuntary muscles?
(1) arm
(2) leg
(3) heart
(4) skin

16. Which one of the following organs does *not* help control the water and mineral balance of the body?
(1) lung
(2) kidney
(3) ovary
(4) skin

17–19. Base your answers to questions 17–19 on the information below and the data table on the next page.

A student performed an experiment to determine the effects of temperature on the growth of bacteria A. To do this experiment, she first used a sterilized inoculating needle to spread bacteria A on six petri dishes. Then she placed each petri dish in its own incubator. The temperature in each incubator was different. Her results are shown in the table on the next page.

Temperature (°C)	Number of Colonies of Bacteria A
5	0
10	2
15	6
25	12
50	8
70	1

17. According to the data, at which temperature did bacteria A grow best?
(1) 10°C
(2) 15°C
(3) 25°C
(4) 70°C

18. At what temperature did the number of colonies of bacteria A begin to decline?
(1) 10°C
(2) 15°C
(3) 25°C
(4) 50°C

19. Based on the above experiment, a scientist can conclude that at temperatures above 25°C
(1) the rate of growth of bacteria A is reduced
(2) the rate of growth of bacteria A is stimulated
(3) all types of bacteria are destroyed
(4) colonies of bacteria A are destroyed

20. Bacteria in the human digestive system assist in digestion of food. This is one example to show that some microorganisms
(1) harm other organisms
(2) cause infectious diseases
(3) help other organisms
(4) cause noninfectious diseases

21–22. Base your answers to questions 21 and 22 on the graph below.

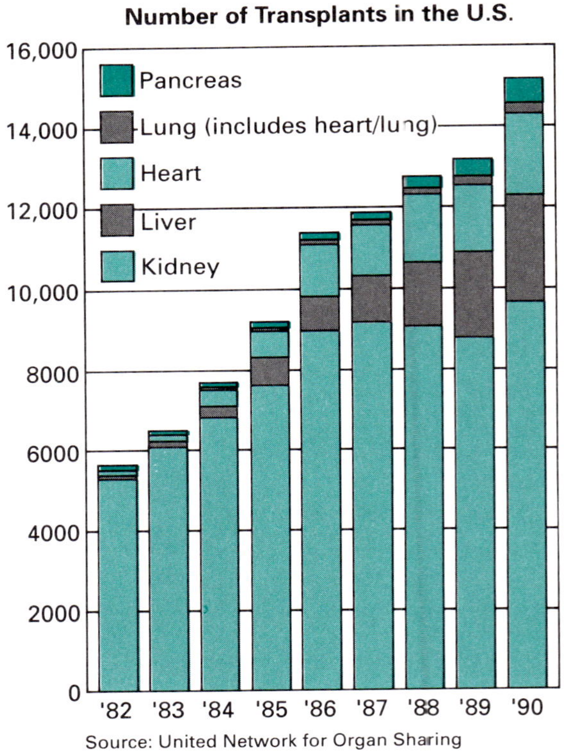

21. Which organ was transplanted most often during this time period?
(1) liver
(2) heart
(3) lung
(4) kidney

22. In 1990 about how many heart transplants were done?
(1) 1000
(2) 2000
(3) 9800
(4) 14,200

23. Milk is pasteurized in order to
(1) remove salt
(2) remove calcium
(3) destroy pathogens
(4) improve taste

24–25. Base your answers to questions 24 and 25 on the information and illustration below.

While on a field trip with her science class, a student used a hammer to break off a piece of rock from the side of a cliff. Her notes are shown next to the illustration below.

24. From this sketch it can be concluded that the rock was probably
(1) sedimentary rock
(2) igneous rock
(3) metamorphic rock
(4) none of the above

25. Which statement concerning the rock in the sketch is correct?
(1) It was formed under the ocean.
(2) It was formed in the desert.
(3) It formed from lava from a volcano.
(4) It formed as the result of an earthquake.

26. What conclusion about South America and Africa is suggested by the diagram below?

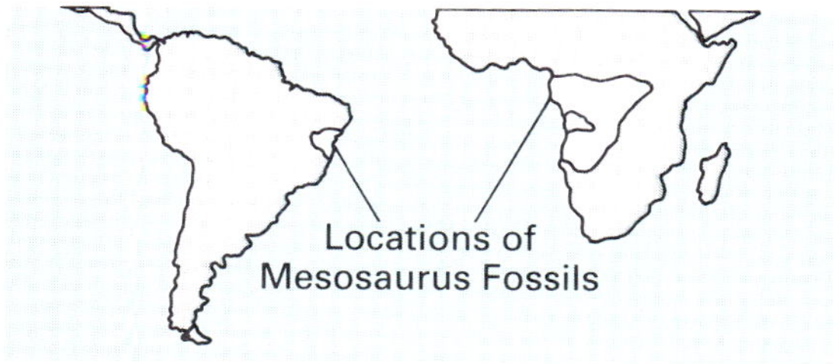

(1) They formed from similar kinds of rock.
(2) They formed from the deposits of glaciers.
(3) They were once joined together.
(4) They were once under water.

27. Earth's mountains form as a result of which of the following activities?
(1) weathering and erosion of Earth's surface
(2) evaporation, condensation, and precipitation
(3) freezing and thawing
(4) folding, faulting, and volcanic eruptions

28. Which of the following statements regarding Earth's surface features is *not* true?
(1) Earth's crust is made of rocks.
(2) Soil and rock fragments are formed by the breaking down of bedrock.
(3) Folding and faulting are caused by crustal plate movements.
(4) The floor of the ocean is smooth and flat.

29. Which cross-sectional diagram represents folding of Earth's crust?

(1)

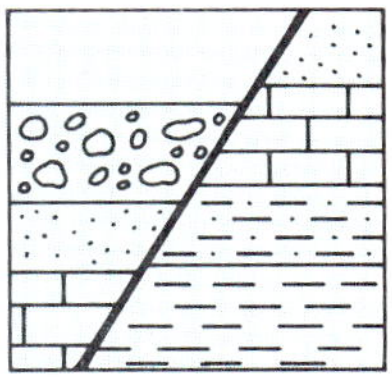
(3)

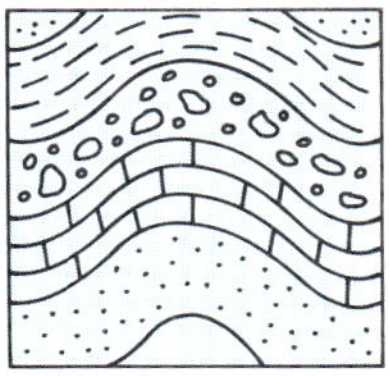
(2)

(4)

(1) diagram 1
(2) diagram 2
(3) diagram 3
(4) diagram 4

30. Based on the information in the chart below, which statement is true?

	Nuclear Power	Fossil Fuel Power
Pros	Nonpolluting; derived from plentiful uranium; reactors and waste disposal are increasingly safe	Fuels (coal, oil, and gas) are abundant; technology is well understood
Cons	Fuel and waste are highly radioactive	Produces greenhouse gases and other pollutants in large quantities
Comments	A potentially vast energy source; hugely oversold at first, now struggling to make a comeback	Increasing environmental costs of hydrocarbon fuels have become the strongest argument against them

(1) Technology creates benefits and burdens.
(2) Technology always creates problems for people.
(3) Nuclear power is safe and should be used.
(4) Nuclear power is dangerous and should not be used.

31. The table gives information about the amount of precipitation at a location in New York State during one July.

Precipitation	
Total yesterday	0.17 in.
Record for this date	3.47 in. (1980)
Total for this July	4.55 in.
Normal amount for July	3.77 in.

Which of the following statements is true for the month shown?
(1) More than the normal amount of rain fell.
(2) Less than the average amount of rain fell.
(3) 3.77 inches of rain fell.
(4) 0.17 inches of rain fell.

32. The map below shows the percentage of normal precipitation for parts of the United States from January 1 to July 28, 1991. In which section of the United States did less than the normal amount of precipitation fall during this period?

Percentage of Normal Precipitation

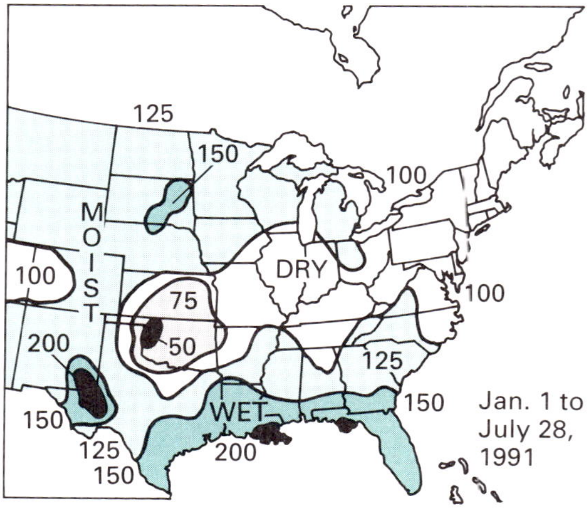

(1) entire midwest
(2) entire southeast
(3) most of the northeast
(4) most of the northwest

33. The graph below shows the average temperature in five cities in New York State during the month of April. What is the average temperature in New York City during the month of April?

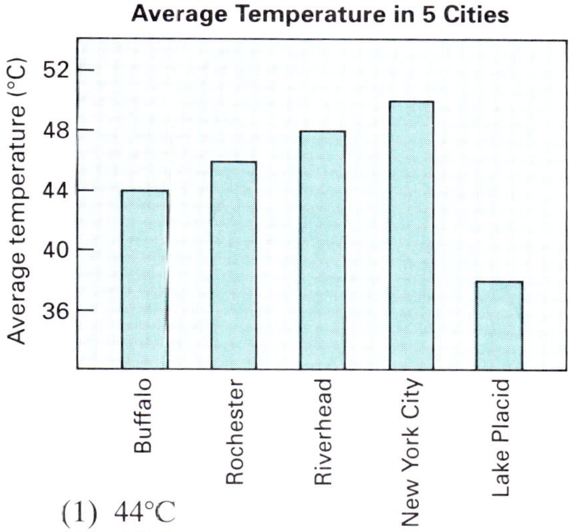

(1) 44°C
(2) 45°C
(3) 48°C
(4) 50°C

34. The diagram below shows an advancing warm front.

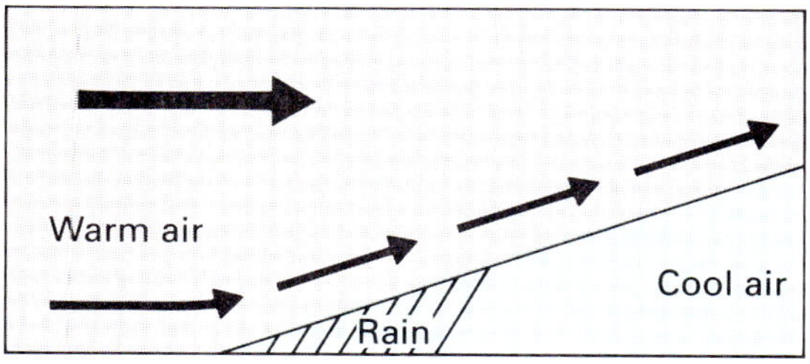

The rain results from the
(1) condensation of water vapor as the cold air rises
(2) condensation of water vapor as the warm air rises
(3) increase in the wind speed as the cold air moves along the ground
(4) decrease in wind speed as the warm air slides over the cold air

35. The diagram below shows the path of a hurricane along the eastern part of the United States.

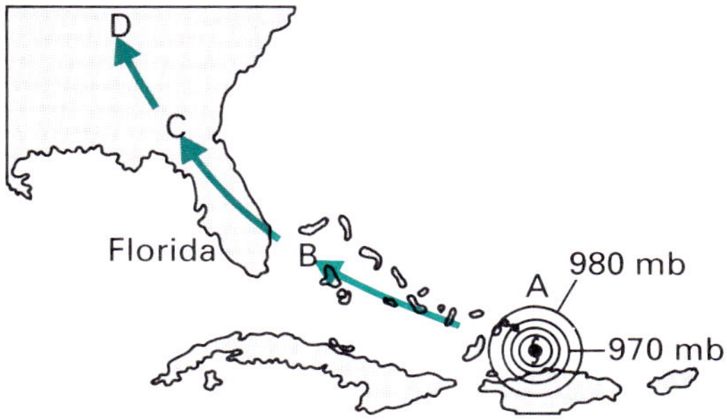

Which of the following statements about the hurricane is correct?
(1) It originated over Florida.
(2) It moved in a southeast direction.
(3) The atmospheric pressure in the center of the hurricane is less than 960 mb.
(4) The atmospheric pressure in the center of the hurricane is more than 980 mb.

36–37. Base your answers to questions 36 and 37 on the diagram below. The diagram shows the path of the sun during various days of the year as seen by students in the United States. The students made these observations facing south.

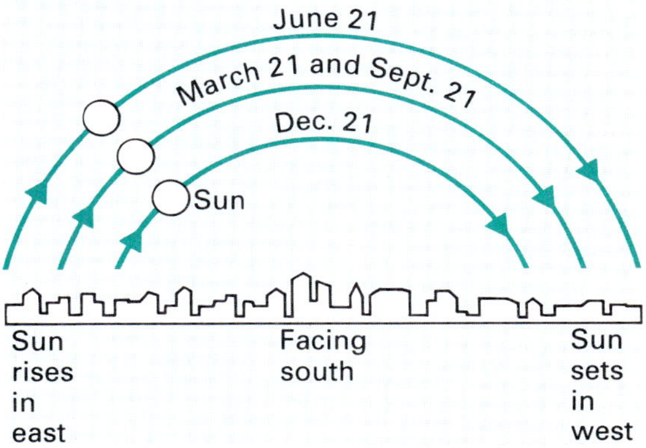

36. The sun stays out for the shortest number of hours when it is lowest in the sky. This occurs on
(1) March 21
(2) June 21
(3) September 21
(4) December 21

37. The sun rises in the east and sets in the west. This occurs because
(1) the sun revolves around Earth from east to west
(2) the sun revolves around Earth from west to east
(3) Earth rotates from east to west
(4) Earth rotates from west to east

38. Earth is slightly closer to the sun on what date?
(1) March 21
(2) June 21
(3) September 21
(4) December 21

39. The table below gives the tides during one day at one place by the ocean.

Tide	Time
High	4:00 A.M.
Low	10:20 A.M.
High	4:40 P.M.
Low	?

At about what time will the next low tide occur?
(1) 4:00 A.M.
(2) 10:40 P.M.
(3) 11:00 P.M.
(4) 12:00 midnight

40. Which of the following names the objects from smallest to largest?
(1) moon, Earth, sun, galaxy
(2) moon, sun, Earth, galaxy
(3) Earth, sun, galaxy, moon
(4) galaxy, moon, sun, Earth

41. One day equals 24 hours. The length of one day is determined by
(1) Earth spinning once on its axis
(2) the tilt of Earth's axis
(3) Earth going once around the sun
(4) the moon going once around Earth

42. A meteor is a
(1) star that falls from its place
(2) fast-moving planet
(3) flash of light in the sky caused when a rock from space burns as it enters the atmosphere
(4) reflection of the sun's light

43. Which energy change causes an electric motor to turn?
(1) chemical to heat
(2) electrical to mechanical
(3) electrical to light
(4) magnetic to sound

44. Which of the following is a form of matter?
(1) elements
(2) electricity
(3) heat
(4) light

45. Which part of a microscope magnifies the objects being observed?
(1) lens
(2) light source
(3) mirror
(4) cover slip

46. The diagram below shows the length of the same nail at various temperatures.

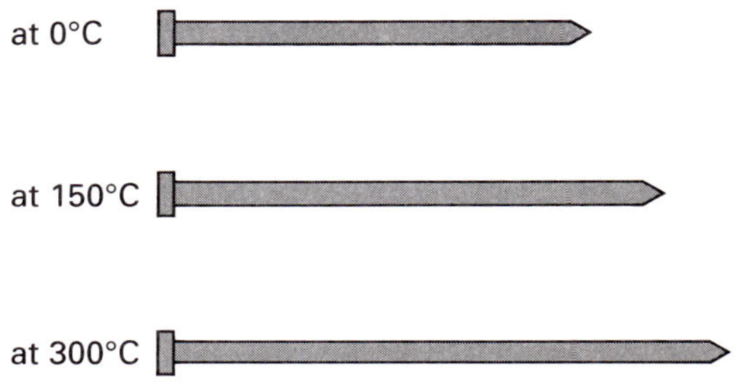

What rule is illustrated by this diagram?
(1) Most materials contract when heated.
(2) Most materials expand when cooled.
(3) Most materials expand when heated.
(4) Most materials are not affected by heating.

47. An unopened can or bottle of soda will crack if it is left in a freezer for several hours. This occurs because
(1) the can or bottle shrinks in the cold
(2) the can or bottle expands in the cold
(3) water shrinks as it freezes
(4) water expands as it freezes

48. It is unwise to stay in bright sunshine without shade, protective clothing, or some sun-block cream, because the skin can be damaged by certain rays in the sunlight. What rays in sunlight are dangerous to skin?
(1) infrared
(2) visible light
(3) ultraviolet
(4) X-rays

49. The diagram below shows four birds. Two are on the ground and two are above the ground.

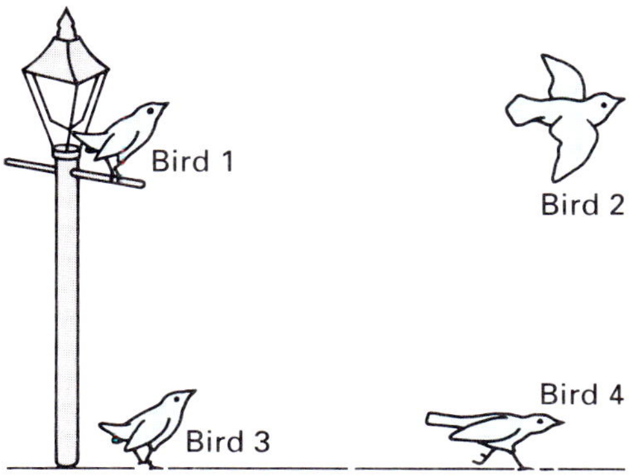

Which bird has both kinetic energy and potential energy above the ground?
(1) Bird 1 (3) Bird 3
(2) Bird 2 (4) Bird 4

50. What is produced when air is made to vibrate rapidly?
(1) sound (2) light
(3) electricity
(4) nuclear radiation

51. A student is instructed to heat water until it is at 35°C. At which marking on the thermometer below should the student stop heating the water?

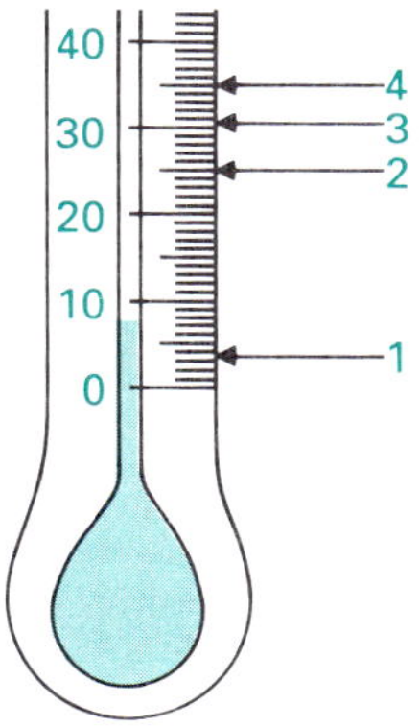

(1) 1 (3) 3
(2) 2 (4) 4

52. A wool sweater is worn during cold days because wool is a good heat insulator. Heat insulators work because they
(1) prevent cold energy from entering the body
(2) prevent heat energy from leaving the body
(3) make heat energy
(4) remove heat energy

53. A car is stuck in snow. Its wheels keep spinning and slipping. One way to get the car to move is to put sand or ashes under the tires. This works because there is now an increase in
(1) energy (3) friction
(2) weight (4) lubrication

54. The diagrams below show light rays striking several types of surfaces. Which diagram shows light being refracted?

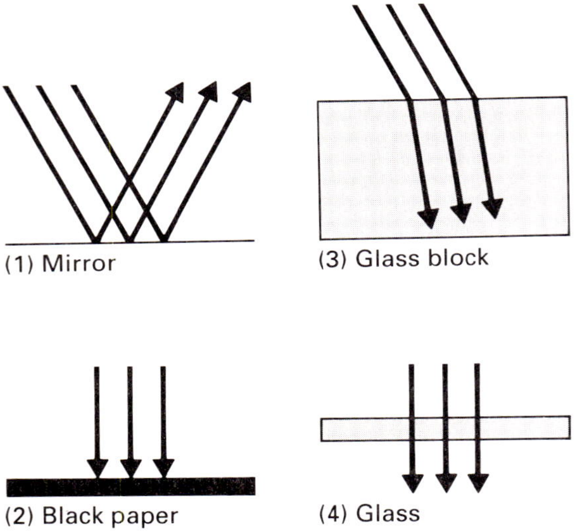

(1) 1
(2) 2
(3) 3
(4) 4

55–56. Base your answers to questions 55 and 56 on the graph below.

Temperature and State of a Material Being Heated

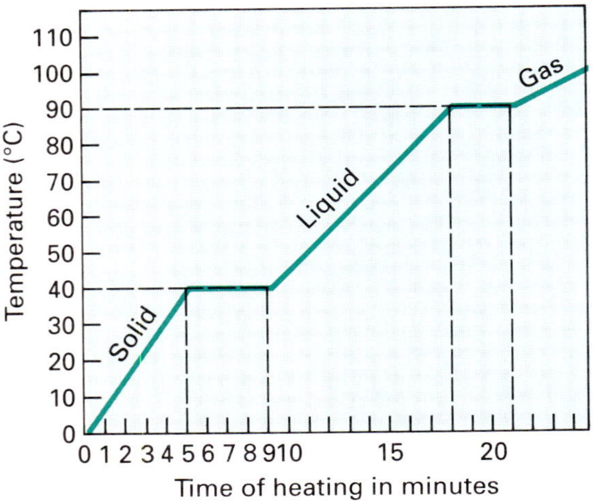

55. What happens to the temperature as heat is added to the material between the 5-minute time and the 9-minute time?
(1) Temperature decreases.
(2) Temperature increases.
(3) Temperature fluctuates.
(4) Temperature remains constant.

56. The melting point of this material is
(1) 0°C
(2) 5°C
(3) 40°C
(4) 90°C

57. What warning usually appears on *pressurized* cans of hair spray, body deodorant, and whipped cream for desserts?
(1) TOXIC
(2) FLAMMABLE
(3) KEEP AWAY FROM HIGH HEAT
(4) all of the above

58. Which statement is correct?
(1) Atoms join by a chemical bond.
(2) Atoms are made of molecules.
(3) Elements are made of compounds.
(4) An atom's electrons are in its nucleus.

59. Which of the following is a chemical change?
(1) burning a match
(2) breaking a match into pieces
(3) dissolving sugar in water
(4) boiling water into steam

60. Use the information in the diagram and table to calculate the density of the liquid in the graduated cylinder.

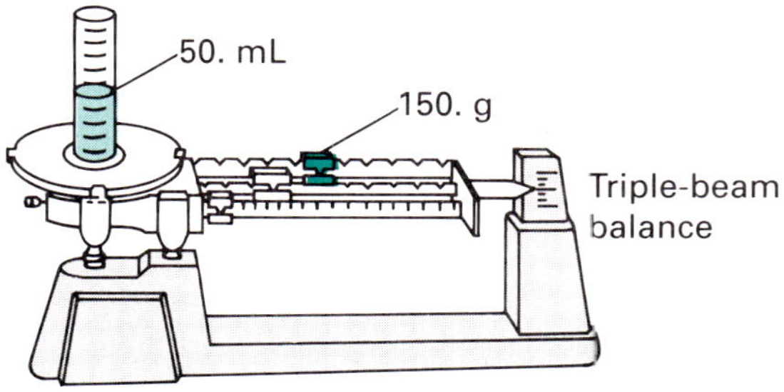

Volume of Liquid	Mass of Liquid Plus Cylinder	Mass of Empty Cylinder
50. mL	150. g	100. g

The density of the liquid (in g/mL) is
(1) 1.0 (3) 3.0
(2) 2.0 (4) 50.0

61. The graph below shows the solubility of three chemicals in water at temperatures between 0°C and 100°C.

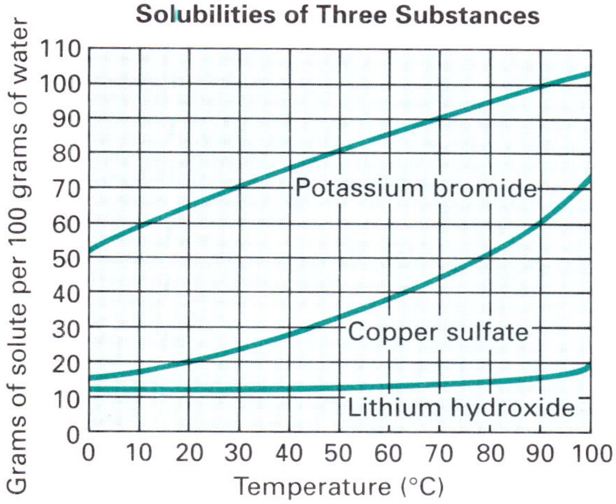

According to the graph, what is the maximum amount of copper sulfate that can dissolve in 100 grams of water at 50°C?
(1) 13 grams (3) 77 grams
(2) 35 grams (4) 80 grams

62–63. Base your answers to questions 62 and 63 on the diagrams below and at the top of the next column, which show how oil and coal are used in the United States.

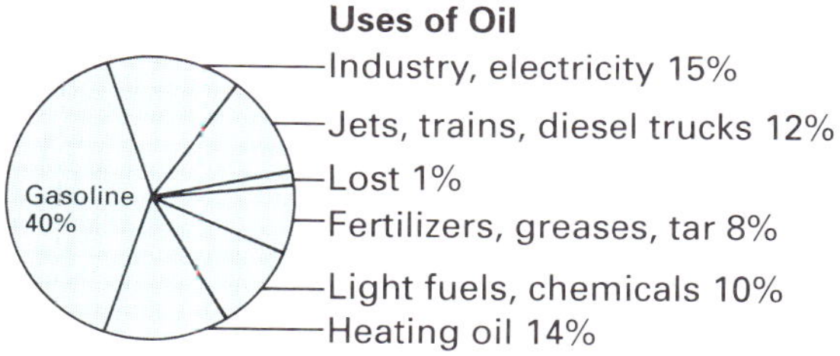

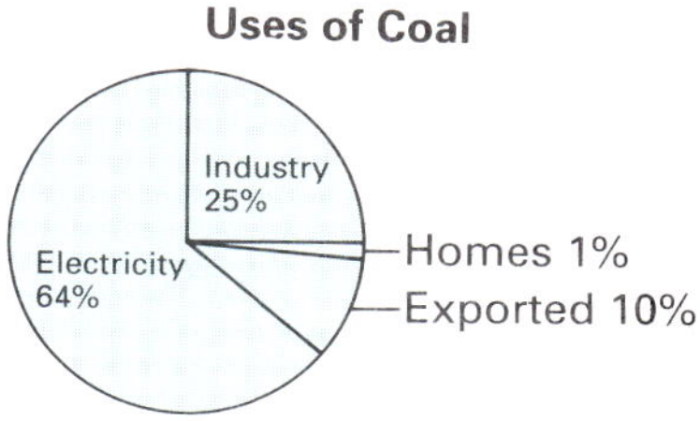

62. The largest use of oil is for
(1) transportation
(2) heating
(3) electricity
(4) making chemicals

63. Note that this question has only three choices.
According to the diagrams, what is the main energy source for all the electricity made in the United States?
(1) oil (2) coal
(3) The question cannot be answered because there is no information on the total amounts of energy obtained from oil and from coal.

64. Electric companies charge customers for the total amount of electrical energy that each customer uses per month. Which unit is a measure of total electrical energy used?
(1) amperes
(2) volts
(3) watts
(4) kilowatt-hours

65–66. Base your answers to questions 65 and 66 on the graph below, which shows the main energy sources that supply world energy needs.

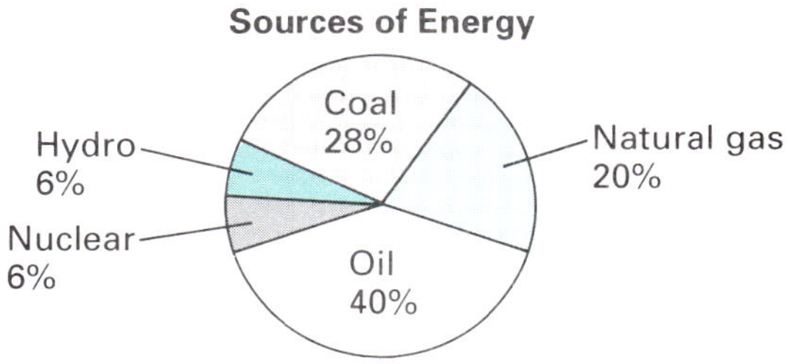

65. What percentage of the world's energy comes from fossil fuels?
(1) 6%
(2) 12%
(3) 48%
(4) 88%

66. What percentage of the world's energy comes from renewable sources?
(1) 6%
(2) 12%
(3) 88%
(4) 100%

67. Base your answer to question 67 on the paragraph below.

Recycling takes effort. People must separate their trash into food, cans, glass, plastic, and paper. These must be collected separately. However, the waste food can be burned as a fuel or buried. Waste vegetable matter can be composted and used later as fertilizer. The cans, bottles, and paper can be reused to reduce pollution and energy consumption.

This paragraph suggests that recycling is a
(1) benefit to people who do it and a burden to society
(2) benefit to people who do it and a benefit to society
(3) burden to people who do it and a benefit to society
(4) burden to people who do it and a burden to society

68. Society has an effect on science. An example of this fact occurs when society
(1) creates a new invention
(2) makes laws about and gives funds for research
(3) makes the laws of physics and chemistry
(4) discovers new medicines to help people

69. Which statement about inventions and technology is most correct?
(1) They can solve every problem of society.
(2) They cannot solve every problem of society.
(3) They make all of the problems.
(4) They have little or no effect on society.

70. Insecticides are chemicals that are sprayed on fruits and vegetables to kill insects. As a result, more fruit and vegetables can be sold by farmers. However, insecticides not washed off the food can cause illness, and they can harm the soil and lakes nearby. Therefore, the use of insecticides to grow better crops provides
(1) a benefit, only
(2) a risk, only
(3) both a benefit and a risk
(4) neither a benefit nor a risk